T0323396

Rethinking the Great Transition

Rethinking the Great Transition

*Community and Economic Growth
in County Durham, 1349–1660*

PETER L. LARSON

OXFORD
UNIVERSITY PRESS

Great Clarendon Street, Oxford, OX2 6DP,
United Kingdom

Oxford University Press is a department of the University of Oxford.
It furthers the University's objective of excellence in research, scholarship,
and education by publishing worldwide. Oxford is a registered trade mark of
Oxford University Press in the UK and in certain other countries

First Edition published in 2022

Impression: 1

Published in the United States of America by Oxford University Press
198 Madison Avenue, New York, NY 10016, United States of America

British Library Cataloguing in Publication Data
Data available

Library of Congress Control Number: 2021947628

ISBN 978–0–19–284987–8

DOI: 10.1093/oso/9780192849878.001.0001

Printed and bound in Great Britain by
Clays Ltd, Elcograf S.p.A.

Contents

List of Maps and Figures	vii
List of Tables	ix
Common References	xi
Notes on Currency, Spelling, and Dates	xiii
Acknowledgements	xv

Introduction	1

1. Development and Capitalism	4
The Agrarian Roots of Industrial Development	4
The Transition Debate	7
The Great and Little Divergences	9
Local and Regional History	11
Reassessing the Transition from 'Medieval' to (Early) 'Modern'	14
A Transition in Durham	21

2. Villages and Parishes	26
Durham and the North	27
The Case Study: Bishop Middleham and Sedgefield Parishes	29

3. Life, Marriage, Death, and the Household	39
Population Estimates	39
The Late Middle Ages	41
Early Modern Period	45
Family and Household	52
Marriage and Widowhood	52
Family and Household Size	58
The Significance of Population Growth	61

4. The Foundation of the Agrarian Economy	64
Tenure and the Tenurial Structure after the Black Death	65
Copyhold and Leasehold	67
The Land Market	72
Widow-Right	76
The Costs of Expansion: Rents and Entry Fines	80

5. Agrarian Development	89
Durham before the Black Death	89
Durham after the Black Death	94
Turning Points in Tenurial Change	98
*c.*1390–1418	99

*c.*1450–*c.*1500	99
*c.*1580–1640	101
A Divergent Agricultural Development	102
6. Standards of Living in an Age of Transition	104
Food and Drink	107
The Costs of Living	109
A Consumption Revolution?	115
The Poor of the Parish	125
The Rise and Fall of Wealth in Durham	128
7. The Expanding and Evolving Economy	136
Arable and Pastoral Agriculture	136
The Dynamics of Agrarian Change	145
Service and Labour	147
Local Industry	151
Credit and Debt	156
8. Individuals and Communities	160
Variety of Community	162
Village, Parish, and Locality	168
Community Leaders	170
Communities in Crises	173
Community and Change	175
Conclusion	178
Transition	180
Divergence	182
Local, National, and Global History	183
Appendix A Landholding Database	185
Appendix B Baptism, Fornication, Marriage, and Funeral Databases	187
Appendix C Probate Inventories	189
Bibliography	191
Archival Sources	191
Printed Primary Sources	192
Secondary Sources	194
Websites	213
Working and Conference Papers	214
Unpublished Theses and Dissertations	215
Index	217

List of Maps and Figures

2.1 Map of north-eastern England with principal locations in the text   33

2.2 Map of settlements in Bishop Middleham and Sedgefield parishes   36

3.1 Tenant mortality, c.1349–1659 (decennial sums)   45

3.2 Crude population change, 1559–1699   46

3.3 Baptisms, 1559–1660 (five year moving average)   47

3.4 Burials, 1559–1660 (five year moving average)   48

3.5 Comparison of mortality trends, 1580–1660   49

3.6 Marriages, 1559–1660 (five year moving average)   55

4.1 Transfers of copyhold land, 1349–1659 (decennial sums)   74

4.2 Bishop Middleham: Transfers and leases of copyhold land, 1349–1659 (decennial sums)   75

4.3 Cornforth: Transfers and leases of copyhold land, 1349–1659 (decennial sums)   76

4.4 Sedgefield: Transfers and leases of copyhold land, 1349–1659 (decennial sums)   77

4.5 Rents per acre, c.1383–1662   81

4.6 Husbandland rents per acre, c.1383–1662   82

4.7 Entry fines, 1349–1659 (decennial means)   85

5.1 Tenurial distribution, late twelfth century   96

5.2 Tenurial distribution, c.1383   97

8.1 Map of major settlements in south-eastern Durham   169

List of Tables

3.1 Village and parish population data, early fourteenth century to 1666   42

3.2 Village population estimates, early fourteenth century   43

3.3 Village population estimates, *c*.1383   44

3.4 Estimates and projections of population, early fourteenth century to 1801   51

6.1 Estimated yields and income from grain sales, *c*.1407   110

6.2 Durham peasant budget model, *c*.1407 (in shillings)   111

6.3 Gross inventory values for Bishop Middleham, Sedgefield, and Whickham parishes in constant prices, 1570–1699   128

6.4 Occupational distribution of probate inventories, 1550–1699   130

6.5 1666 Hearth Tax households and probate inventories   131

6.6 County Durham gross probate inventory values in constant prices, 1550–1699   132

Common References

Boldon Book   *Domesday Book Supplementary, vol. 35: Boldon Book, Northumberland and Durham* ed. by David Austin (Stroud: Phillimore & Co., 1982).

CCB   Church Commission Deposit of Durham Bishopric Estate Records, Durham University Library, Archives & Special Collections.

DHC   Durham Bishopric Halmote Court Records, Durham University Library, Archives & Special Collections.

DPR   Durham Probate Records, Durham University Library, Archives & Special Collections.

Durham Hearth Tax   *County Durham Hearth Tax Assessment, Lady Day 1666*, ed. by Adrian Green, Elizabeth Parkinson, and Margaret Spufford (London: British Record Society, 2006).

Hatfield's Survey   *Bishop Hatfield's Survey*, ed. by William Greenwell, Surtees Society, vol. 32 (Durham: George Andrews,1857; reprinted London: W. Dawson and sons, 1967).

Parliamentary Surveys   *Parliamentary Surveys of the Bishopric of Durham*, vol. II, ed. by David Kirby, Surtees Society, vol. 185 (Gateshead: Northumberland Press, 1929).

TNA: DURH   Records of the Palatinate of Durham: Chancery Court: Cursitor's Records, The National Archives: Public Record Office, Kew, London.

Wills and Inventories   *Wills and Inventories from the Register at Durham*, vol. I, ed. by James Raine, Surtees Society, vol. 2 (London: J.B. Nichols, 1835).

Wills and Inventories   *Wills and Inventories from the Register at Durham*, vol. II, ed. by William Greenwell, Surtees Society, vol. 38 (Durham: Andrews, 1860).

Wills and Inventories   *Wills and Inventories from the Register at Durham*, vol. III, ed. by J. C. Hodgson, Surtees Society, vol. 112 (Durham: Andrews, 1906).

Wills and Inventories   *Wills and Inventories from the Register at Durham*, vol. IV, ed. by Herbert Maxwell Wood, Surtees Society, vol. 142 (Durham: Andrews, 1929).

Notes on Currency, Spelling, and Dates

Note on currency:

The primary units of curreny in England in this period were:

- The pound (£), consisting of 20 shillings;
- The shilling (s.), consisting of 12 pence;
- The penny (d.), divisible into 2 halfpennies (ob.) or 4 farthings (q.).

A crown was worth 5vs. The mark was a unit of account worth 13s. 4d.

Note on spelling:

- Proper names have been standardized within families, but not modernized. Quotations from early modern documents have been left unmodified, including names.
- For the Priory, later the Dean and Chapter, of Durham Cathedral: I have used the relevant term pre- and post-Dissolution; when the reference includes both, Dean and Chapter has been preferred.

Note on dates:

- All dates use the New Style calendar when possible.

Acknowledgements

This book has been a long time in the making. I am grateful to the Huntington Library and British Academy for a Short-Term Fellowship that let me begin this project, and to the University of Central Florida for additional support. Jeffrey Moore, Dean of the College of Arts & Humanities at the University of Central Florida, has been consistently supportive as I finished writing while chairing a department.

The research for this book took place at several archives. The archivists, librarians, assistants, and those who have reproduced documents are invaluable in historical research. The staff of Durham University Archives & Special Collections deserve especial praise for their unstinting support and patience through the years. Durham County Record Office, Lambeth Palace Library, London School of Economics, and The National Archive in Kew have likewise been welcoming and professional; I simply have not had the pleasure of spending more time there. I have been fortunate to have been supported by numerous research assistants at UCF: Danielle Aguirre, Luke Bohmer, Jessica Hoeschen, and Alexis Rodriguez. Ryan Wicklund at Durham University photographed numerous probate documents for me when administrative work limited my travel. Matthew Patsis created the maps in GIS.

I have benefitted from the support, encouragement, and friendly critique of many colleagues. I am especially indebted to James Davis and Ben Dodds, who read the entire manuscript. The support I have received has been invaluable in keeping me going; in this regard, notably from Jim Masschaele, Mark Bailey, Judith Bennett, Chris Briggs, Chris Dyer, Maryanne Kowaleski, and Steve Rigby, but also many others. I have also had productive discussions on Durham with

Alex Brown. Much of this is possible thanks to the triennial Anglo-American Seminar on the Medieval Economy and Society, founded by Bruce M.S. Campbell and convened by Phillipp Schofield for the past several sessions. The seminar has been a delightfully warm and intellectually stimulating space to test out ideas.

The anonymous readers for the proposal and manuscript prodded me to expand the scope of my argument: they saw more potential than I did. Along with the patience of the editors at OUP, who let this project develop at its own pace, they have made the book all the stronger. This book was completed and revised during the COVID-19 pandemic, and I gratefully acknowledge the tireless work of the Interlibrary Loan staff at the University of Central Florida Library and libraries around the country.

My wife likely knows this book better than I do, and my gratitude knows no bounds. The evolution of my writing over the years owes much to her—just ask my undergraduate and graduate advisors what my writing used to be like. She has provided intellectual and emotional support: a sounding board, reader, and answerer of apparently random questions ('how much does a pound of saffron cost today?'). It is good to be married to a librarian with an interest in English history.

Portions of Chapters 3 and 4 are based on or originally appeared in 'Widow-right in Durham, England (1349–1660)', Continuity and Change 33 (2018), © Cambridge University Press 2018, reprinted with permission.

This book is dedicated to the late Richard Britnell, who invited a bewildered young student to come to Durham and write an MA thesis on the Durham bishopric halmote books, and who continued to offer a warm welcome, wise words, and careful critique.

Introduction

When Thomas Shepherd of Sedgefield, County Durham, acquired 30 acres of land by copyhold and then another 35 acres by leasehold, it made him one of the largest, possibly the largest, single landholder in that village (which some called a town).[1] In the nearby village of Norton, Gilbert Spurner held sixteen cottages along with his 90 acres. Later, in Bishop Middleham (the next major village over from Sedgefield), Robert del Gate Sr and Jr acquired 165 acres of copyhold and leasehold there and in neighbouring Cornforth plus additional little parcels jointly with other men in the villages.[2] They are exemplars of rising yeomen in England, men who used hard work, credit, local institutions, and luck to accumulate larger holdings and then farm them for profit rather than subsistence, and whose children or grandchildren might marry into the county gentry. This is the classic story of the development of agrarian capitalism in England in the later fifteenth to seventeenth centuries, which would in turn facilitate the Industrial Revolution of the eighteenth and nineteenth centuries. Except, Thomas acquired his lands in 1350–51, Gilbert before 1383, and the del Gates during 1393–1417—a century or more before the so-called 'rise of the yeoman' in Kent, the Midlands, and East Anglia.

Why then, if Durham was so precocious in its rising yeomen, did it fail to develop as southern England did and instead retained into the eighteenth century a society and agricultural practice that some modern commentaries have described as 'medieval?'[3] That is asking the wrong question, for this was not a failure to develop fully, nor did the agriculture remain medieval. In the seventeenth century, maybe earlier, farmers used the readily available lime and coal by-products to increase their crop yields, and many of the townfields were enclosed before those in much of southern England.[4] Eighteenth-century Durham was famed for certain agricultural developments, including the famous Durham Ox (the first shorthorn breed with a pedigree), Culley sheep, and Mrs

---

[1] TNA: DURH 3/12 ff. 37v, 51r, 57r.

[2] TNA: DURH 3/13 ff. 92r, 216r, 284v; 3/14 ff. 8v, 381v, 428r.

[3] Allen provides a discussion of the generally disparaging attitude towards medieval small farmers as well as studies that disprove them (particularly for other regions of the world): *Enclosure and the Yeoman*, pp. 2–5, 11–13.

[4] Durham County Record Office, 'Subject Guide 1: Records Relating to Inclosure;' *County Durham Hearth Tax*, p. xxv.

Rethinking the Great Transition: Community and Economic Growth in County Durham, 1349–1660. Peter L. Larson, Oxford University Press. © Peter L. Larson 2022. DOI: 10.1093/oso/9780192849878.003.0001

Clements's Durham Mustard (later merged with Colman's).[5] Those developments presuppose an earlier agricultural development resulting from different conditions and a different transition from 'feudalism' to 'capitalism'. As with elsewhere in England, these developments created both human and financial capital and so it would not be surprising if Durham's population and agriculture contributed to the rapid expansion of coal mining in Tyneside. Durham was not a late-developing backwater; parts of the northeast experienced the large farms, rebuilt homes, and new consumer goods at the same time as even southern England. Not all rose, however. Wealth and success coexisted with the penury typically associated with the northeast, which partially explains perceptions of the region as poor.[6]

This development in the northeast helped in part to fuel England's rise to overtake the Low Countries to be the leading economic power in Europe and the world. Economic historians frequently point to the emergence of new draperies in the later sixteenth century to compete with foreign cloth imports. Their importance cannot be understated. These textiles comprised more than a quarter of England's manufacturing by 1700: Allen observed that 'the success of the new draperies in the seventeenth century was of great importance... [and was] responsible for a larger proportion of the growth... in agriculture as farmers successfully responded to the greater demand for food, wool, and labour'.[7] Yet the northeast was already growing economically as the Flemish refugees were settling in England. My argument here is that England's rise in the seventeenth century had earlier roots, but not only in the northeast as variations of this story may be found in other regions. This comes as little surprise; Dyer labelled the period from 1250 to 1550 an 'Age of Transition' and Britnell noted that the century after the Black Death was a period 'in which regional variations mattered', a sentiment echoed by Hare for Wiltshire and the West Country.[8] London and the Midlands were vital for England's economic growth, but they were not England; Hatcher's study of agriculture and mining in Cornwall makes that point clearly.[9] Understanding England's (later Britain's) eventual dominance requires examining the country as a set of interlocking regions that developed at different speeds and on different trajectories. As more people migrated to London and London's

---

[5] Jones, 'London Mustard Bottles', p. 70; Green, 'Durham Ox', pp. 46, 54–58. There is a reference to mustard seed in the village of Wolviston in 1368: Durham Priory Halmote Rolls, Spring 1368. George Shepherdson, yeoman, held the lease of a lime pit as part of his expanding portfolio: Brown, 'Church Leaseholders', p. 36. Sunderland was a major export hub for lime: Cookson, *History of the County of Durham, Vol. V*, p. 234.

[6] Green, 'Houses and Households;' Weatherill, *Consumer Behaviour*. The variations in wealth explain the difference between Durham and some wealthier counties, like Kent: Zell, 'Landholding', pp. 47–9.

[7] Allen, 'Progress and Poverty', p. 431. The reverse could also happen: Hare, *Prospering Society*. For a comprehensive study of England's economic growth, see Broadberry et al., *British Economic Growth*.

[8] Dyer, *Age of Transition*; Britnell, 'English Agricultural Output and Prices;' Hare, *Prospering Society*, pp. 1–2.

[9] Hatcher, *Rural Economy and Society*.

foreign trade increased, its needs and the new opportunities spurred on other regions, for example later development of the textile trade in the northwest. Development in one facilitated development in another in a continuous interplay that drove national growth. That process makes national development uneven and slow until the nineteenth century. The pace or trajectory of development in the different regions could change, however. Agricultural and industrial development in the northeast was only one factor that enabled London to expand. Durham and Newcastle were not backwards in the early modern period. They were developed, with an integrated regional and international market system in place and the potential to scale up production. As mining intensified, the pace of agricultural growth eventually slackened as demand plateaued; meanwhile ever-increasing demand from London led farmers in southern England to experiment with new crops, technology, and approaches and take the lead in grain production. Durham then became synonymous with mining and its agriculture was perceived as antiquated not because it was 'medieval' but because it had been overtaken. The region's earlier contribution to England's rising gross domestic product (GDP) should not be overlooked. The Low Countries provided initial momentum to the region in the sixteenth century, and then London's voracious appetite for coal helped the region realize its full potential.

I have three main goals in this book. Its heart is a case study of two parishes: the story of local communities that endured economic change, political upheaval, war, the Reformation, and the many changes between 1349 and 1660. Sometimes we simply need to see the human face of change. Second, this book offers a fresh take on the Transition Debate, the shift from 'feudalism' to 'capitalism' well known to medieval and early modern historians. An intersection of individuals, institutions, and structures in this peripheral region of England ushered in a more modern agrarian regime before its counterparts elsewhere in England. Finally, this is a local and regional contribution to a debate normally approached at an abstracted, national, macroeconomic level: the Great and Little Divergences in which Europe overtook Asia on the global stage and northwestern Europe overtook the Mediterranean region as Europe's economic powerhouse. Here I argue that subnational regions were significant in the growth of national economies. These regions play an oft overlooked but key role in the stories of nations and empires.

1

Development and Capitalism

The Agrarian Roots of Industrial Development

The trade in coal to London and abroad should not have been able to expand so quickly had the northeast been truly poor and underdeveloped. Newcastle-upon-Tyne is synonymous with coal, much of which originated on the Durham side of the River Tyne, but its late medieval trade involved much more. In her study of the provisioning of Durham priory, Threlfall-Holmes concluded '[w]hat this study illuminates is the extent to which a substantial local consumer, willing and able to source goods from elsewhere in the country when it wished to do so, chose to buy from Newcastle.'[1] Enough records survive to give a sense of the trade, although the years represented could be typical or exceptional. Moreover, these records are concerned with customs and only cover international trade.[2] They do provide the names of ships, masters, merchants, the ship's origin, and dutiable cargo. Antwerp, Danzig (Gdańsk), Elbing (Elbląg), Dieppe, Boulogne, and many other ports are represented in the fifteenth century. Ships entered Newcastle carrying a wide variety of goods: flax, hemp, madder, wine, hops, wainscot, fruit, spices, books, inkhorns, and an array of consumer goods including kettles, felt hats, bonnets, playing cards, and more. Far fewer types of goods left the port: cloth wool, fells, hides, lead, millstones, and of course, coal.[3] In his classic work, Nef found that just under 33,000 tonnes of coal were shipped from Newcastle-upon-Tyne in 1563–64 according to the city's port books, nearly doubling in ten years, and then by 1597–98, over 160,000 tonnes left the port. By the late seventeenth century, the quantity was higher still, over 600,000 tonnes.[4] Using sources not available to Nef, Hatcher raised those estimates: 45,000 tonnes were shipped in the coastal and overseas trade at the beginning of the sixteenth century, over 60,000 tonnes on average in the third quarter of that century, and over 200,000 tonnes at the end of the century, peaking at nearly 800,000 tonnes in the 1680s.

---

[1] Threlfall-Holmes, *Monks and Markets*, p. 229.
[2] *Customs Accounts of Newcastle-upon-Tyne*, p. 5.
[3] *Customs Account of Newcastle-upon-Tyne* provides collectors' and/or controllers' accounts for eleven years in the second half of the fifteenth century. Newcastle's share of wool exports rose in the fifteenth century, though remaining far smaller than London (p. 14). Some sixteenth-century probate records for Newcastle merchants note foreign coins and goods owned in foreign ports: *Wills and Inventories* I, pp. 164–8, 335–42, 359–65, and II, pp. 68–80. See also Davis, *English Overseas Trade*, pp. 16–8, 27–9.
[4] Nef, *Rise of the British Coal Industry*, vol. I, p. 21.

Rethinking the Great Transition: Community and Economic Growth in County Durham, 1349–1660. Peter L. Larson, Oxford University Press. © Peter L. Larson 2022. DOI: 10.1093/oso/9780192849878.003.0002

Perhaps even more impressive, as Hatcher observed, 'there can be no doubt whatsoever that far more coal could have been produced had there been a market for it'.[5] Sunderland began shipping coal in the late sixteenth century, and inferior coal helped expand its salt industry.[6] The rapid expansion of the coal industry transformed Newcastle and the northeast.[7] When Sir William Brereton visited the northeast in 1635, he concluded Newcastle to be 'beyond all compare the fairest and richest town in England, inferior for wealth and building to no city save London and Bristow, and whether it may not deserve to be accounted as wealthy as Bristow, I make some doubt'.[8] The coal trade transformed England as well. London required massive quantities of coal, and coal would liberate England from the limitations of what Wrigley termed its 'organic economy' and lead to the Industrial Revolution.[9] The coal trade is not the subject but the background of this study, and the implications of its expansion inform several key questions here. The expansion of the coal trade out of Newcastle required more than coal and capital. Primarily it required labour; increased output was achieved through more labour and other factors, not technological improvements in mining.[10] More output meant more equipment and ships, as well as more miners, waggoneers, sailors, supplies, and above all, food.

The answer lies in lowland Durham in villages such as those home to Shepherd, Spurner, and the del Gates. Similar in settlement and husbandry to central England, these villages experienced tenurial developments from the fourteenth century onwards, a rapid population rise in the sixteenth century, and rising levels of wealth, all of which fly in the face of the general view of north-eastern England as backward, stagnant, and poor. County Durham is absent from the various national records used to calculate wealth for medieval England on account of its palatinate status, yet the diocese of Durham was one of the wealthiest in England. On the subject of population, Hodgson's study of several post-medieval taxes and censuses found south-eastern settlements declining in population while the coal mining areas outpaced the national average in growth.[11] There is no 'smoking gun' directly connecting this to Newcastle or the coal trade of the sixteenth century, but it follows logically upon the work of others who have tied the county's later agriculture to the coal trade.[12] Brassley deduced that the region must have been capable of producing the food necessary to feed Newcastle

[5] Hatcher further noted 'the rise of the British coal industry depended as much if not more upon established practice, improved by ad hoc pragmatic embellishments, as it did upon thoroughgoing innovation', and that rising use of coal as fuel was halted by the Black Death and its aftermath: *History of the British Coal Industry*, pp. 8–11, 26–31, 44–6.

[6] Nef, *Rise of the British Coal Industry*, p. 29.

[7] See Levine and Wrightson, *Making of an Industrial Society*; Burn, 'Seasonal Work and Welfare'.

[8] Brereton, *Travels*, p. 85.   [9] Wrigley, *Path to Sustained Growth*.

[10] Clark and Jacks, 'Coal and the Industrial Revolution'.

[11] Hodgson, 'Demographic Trends in County Durham'; *County Durham Hearth Tax*, pp. xxxviii–xliii.

[12] *County Durham Hearth Tax*, p. xxxv.

in the late seventeenth and eighteenth centuries, importing Baltic grain only in times of dearth; Hodgson observed that 'enclosure in County Durham was a function of London's demand for coal'.[13] Introducing an edition of the 1666 Hearth Tax for Durham, Green noted that 'farmers were prospering indirectly from the expansion of the coal trade, and often gained larger holdings at the expense of smaller farmers (often copyholders)' but that prosperity actually began earlier and some copyholders were the beneficiaries rather than victims.[14] Durham's seventeenth- and eighteenth-century agriculture had late medieval roots; the agriculture and society of the sixteenth century could have fulfilled the prerequisites for the industry's rapid expansion while developing further to match the needs of the coalfields. Such a hypothesis accords with findings on material culture. Green found that the rebuilding of houses in Durham was in line with the rest of England, in chronology and style.[15] For consumer goods, Weatherill placed the northeast ahead of the rest of the country, London excepted, and Heley's thesis on middling Newcastle merchants revealed material culture consistent with a thriving economy in the early sixteenth century.[16] The money to pay for this had to come from somewhere.

Hatcher identified the 1570s–80s as a turning point in the expansion of the coal trade.[17] Those decades witnessed the *second* major tenurial change in the villages studied herein, resulting in larger farms that could no longer be considered family farms and in enclosure. The studies of later seventeenth- and eighteenth-century Durham show the results of earlier developments. *Circa* 1600, some areas and people of the northeast were thriving, at the same pace or ahead of the rest of the country. Here we find the crux of the apparent paradox of the north as backward yet advanced: some were prosperous, rebuilding houses, and buying consumer goods, but many were not. It was not a simple case of the rich getting richer, as many gentlemen and aspiring yeomen saw their fortunes stagnate or decline. Nor was it the result of outsider entrepreneurs snapping up land to build large farms and creating a new landless class. The villages of the Durham bishopric estate, the key to much of this development, remained under an administration uninterested in maximizing rents and this allowed a slower development of the capitalist farming that kept communities intact.[18]

---

[13] Brassley, *Agricultural Economy of Northumberland and Durham*, pp. 34–44, 172–4; Hodgson, 'Progress of Enclosure', p. 90. Allen concluded that enclosure resulted from urban and industrial demand: 'Progress and Poverty', p. 430.

[14] Green, 'County Durham at the Restoration', p. xxxv.

[15] Green, 'Houses and Households', pp. 47, 117–23.

[16] Weatherill, *Consumer Behaviour*, pp. 25–29, 43–69; Heley, 'Material Culture of the Tradesmen of Newcastle'. See also Scammell, 'Was the North-East Different?'

[17] Hatcher, *History of the British Coal Industry*, p. 78.

[18] Estate administration often was a factor in tenurial development, but not a predictable one: Whittle and Yates found a slow land market in Berkshire: ' "Pays Réel or Pays Légal?" ' pp. 15, 26.

That difference—or rather, indifference—made it easier for some men to flourish but not others. The development is rooted in community as well, as village, parish, and local communities shaped many changes and thus persisted rather than being left behind. Community and change were not mutually exclusive; this was evolution, not revolution. It forces us to reconsider the narrative based on central England. The northeast had its own trajectory of economic and agrarian development, linked to but different from the Midlands and East Anglia so often associated with agrarian capitalism. The overarching economic narrative for England then Britain is a heterogenous interconnection of regional narratives, rather than a single 'transition from feudalism to capitalism'. These narratives did not hinge solely on large capitalist farmers and there is increasing evidence of smaller entrepreneurs who drove agrarian and economic change.[19] Outcomes depended on many local factors, as Overton and his team demonstrated with Cornwall and Kent, and even neighbouring villages developed differently.[20] Too often, talk of economic development obscures the agency of individual men and women that led to these divergent paths, but the context of these decisions is critical.[21] Community values, religious preferences, and political loyalties all influenced economic choices that, aggregated, became social and economic change on a macro scale.

While the present work began as a straightforward local history case study, it has implications for economic debates of global importance. Those two parishes did not change the world, but they were part of a process that was part of a larger process that did. The aggregated choices referred to just above touch on the world of macroeconomics. As readers may be coming to this book from different levels of historical analysis, what follows is a brief (!) discussion of the several important debates relevant to understanding this book.

The Transition Debate

Those changes are among the most momentous historical developments that ushered in modernity. Scholars from a range of disciplines have attempted to explain their emergence from what we conveniently refer to as 'feudalism' and medieval village society, and why this occurred first in England. The 'when' and 'how' are harder to pin down.[22] Economically, this 'transition debate' centres on the key

---

[19] For example, see Allen, *Enclosure and the Yeoman*; Croot, *World of the Small Farmer*; Hare, *Prospering Society*; Yates, *Town and Countryside in Western Berkshire*; Zell, *Industry in the Countryside*.

[20] Overton et al., *Production and Consumption in English Households*.

[21] Ogilvie discussed the tensions between peasant choice and constraints in Europe: 'Choices and Constraints'.

[22] An accessible perspective is Heller, *Birth of Capitalism*. French and Hoyle provide a historiographical analysis relevant to the English countryside: *Character of English Rural Society*, pp. 1–50. For the origins of the modern transition debate see Tawney, *The Agrarian Problem*; Dobb, *Studies in the Development of Capitalism*; Hobsbawm, 'General Crisis of the European Economy', and 'Crisis of the

factors to development, and the various weights assigned to each. Assessing the cultural side is more difficult, as this requires determining what changed in the culture and psyche to create individualism, and what changed moral judgements regarding profit and interest. In any analysis, the transition witnessed a significant reorientation of English rural society during the late medieval and early modern periods. The withering of serfdom following the brutal mortality of the plague unbalanced the traditional rural economy, and a succession of political and religious crises (the Wars of the Roses, the Reformation and its rebellions, and the Civil War and Restoration) added further turmoil. The transformation was not merely economic or social, but cultural, mental, and psychological as well. Ways of life transformed, unevenly, across time and space. Serfs vanished and yeomen appeared. Villages were deserted. New associative networks arose. After more than a century of stagnation and decline, population increased rapidly leaving many landless, with standards of living improving for the lucky few. Communal cultivation of open fields by peasants gave way to individualized cultivation through engrossment, enclosure, and wage labour. Manorial (or 'feudal') and communal means of organizing people and production gave way to more modern capitalistic and individualistic ones.

The study of the agrarian and economic transition, particularly by those interested in development, tends to be teleological if no longer monodeterminist. Although there is still significant discussion regarding the timing and the relative importance of different factors, there is consensus on a standard trajectory for successful development, unfolding like an equation. The heavily quantitative and theoretical nature derives partly from the easiest available sources and partly from a legacy of imperialist and paternalistic discourse of development and tends to be impersonal. Moreover, the model itself was based not on the whole of English experience, but on a generalization drawn from East Anglia and the Midlands, which has then been adapted and applied to the economic development of other places and other times. Valuable as these models are, they come at a price: historical contingency is lost, as is the human element underlying changes in tenure or movement of labour. The search for divergent paths and analysing them not as examples of failed or retarded development but as alternate trajectories is worth the time, especially as the so-called 'first world' moves into a post-industrial age littered with rust belts and 'sustainability' has progressed from buzzword to essential component in planning.

Seventeenth Century, II', and the subsequent debate, particularly *The Transition from Feudalism to Capitalism*. The Brenner Debate of the late 1970s and early 1980s marked a new phase; Robert Brenner's original essay, several responses, and his own response are printed in *The Brenner Debate*; see also Hoyle, 'Tenure and the Land Market'. For a useful periodization of the transition debate see Ormrod, 'Agrarian Capitalism and Merchant Capitalism'. There also are case studies, for example van Bavel, 'Land, Lease and Agriculture', or *Peasants into Farmers?* On British exceptionalism and the Industrial Revolution, I recommend Allen, *British Industrial Revolution in Global Perspective*, and Wrigley, *Path to Sustained Growth*.

The Great and Little Divergences

The Transition Debate is itself part of a grander debate in global economic history on the Great Divergence: how and when western Europe broke out of the 'Malthusian Trap' and overtook Qing China, Mughal India, and other more advanced cultures through economic development and industrial revolution. In the late twentieth century, new findings on the strength of Asian economies called into question the traditional explanation of the rise of European powers to global dominance. The original revisionists of the California School, notably Pomeranz, Frank, and Wong, argued that the East was not stagnant and tottering but instead equal or even superior to Europe until the late eighteenth to nineteenth centuries (although Pomeranz later shifted his timing to focus on 1700).[23] Others have pushed the timeline back. Broadberry argued the divergence 'was already well underway during the sixteenth and seventeenth centuries' with key turning points earlier *c.*1348 (the Black Death) and *c.*1500 (new trade routes to Asia), and Maddison looked to an earlier origin in the late medieval period.[24] Attempts to explain the Great Divergence employ a range of factors including demography, literacy and human capital, form of government, market structures, and technological advances; Frank went so far as to reject any significant internal change within Europe and instead attributes the divergence to long-term global cycles.[25] The increasing research employing GDP suggests that the eighteenth century likely was the point of the Great Divergence, yet this built on earlier developments that aided society to evolve to a point where escape from the Malthusian trap became possible.[26]

This debate spawned another, overlapping debate on the Little Divergence, in which the North Sea region (specifically England and the Low Countries) caught up with and then overtook the earlier European economic powerhouses of Spain and the Italian states. Differences in real wages and GDP, literacy rates, urbanization, and agricultural productivity are all clear after 1600, but untangling cause and correlation is difficult. Epstein argued that centralization of state power supported market integration by undoing the fragmented liberties of the Middle Ages; for Mokyr, the divergences and the Industrial Revolution resulted from a

---

[23] Pomeranz, *The Great Divergence*; Frank, *ReOrient*; Landes, *Wealth and Poverty of Nations*; Wong, *China Transformed*.

[24] Broadberry pointed out that some parts of Europe may have been ahead earlier, but this was regional variation rather than a true divergence: 'Accounting for the Great Divergence', pp. 1, 10; 'Industrial Revolution and the Great Divergence'. See Maddison, *The World Economy*, pp. 29–30, 51, 119; Broadberry et al., 'When Did Britain Industrialise?' pp. 16–27; *British Economic Growth*; 'China, Europe, and the Great Divergence', pp. 955–1000. Clark denies the Black Death affected economic growth: 'Microbes and Markets'.

[25] Frank, *ReOrient*. For a very long-term approach, see Galor, *Unified Growth Theory*.

[26] For a recent statement of this view, see Broadberry, 'Industrial Revolution and the Great Divergence'. Clark disagrees with this view of growth; for example, Clark, 'Long March of History', and Clark et al., 'Malthus, Wages, and Preindustrial Growth'.

'culture of growth' rooted in the Enlightenment; 'just breaking out of the Malthusian "regime"…does not constitute the entire story'.[27] Allen located England's economic success *c.*1600 in 'structural transformation including the remarkable release of labour from English farming' and '[t]he openness of the economy to international trade'.[28] Broadberry saw the Black Death and the new trade routes to Asia *c.*1500 as external shocks affecting 'the type of agriculture, the age of first marriage of females, the flexibility of labour supply and the nature of state institutions' pushing agrarian development that spilled over to industry and service.[29] Several models have been offered to evaluate various factors and disentangle cause from correlation, and the debate is still wide open.[30]

Human capital—a more educated and healthier workforce—has emerged recently as a popular explanation, often rooted in the European Marriage Pattern (EMP) enumerated by Hajnal where later female age at first marriage reduced fertility. EMP has been connected to greater opportunities for women, even a 'girl power' economic expansion.[31] The timing, nature, and significance of EMP have all been challenged: EMP predated the Black Death in England and is associated with poverty more than opportunity.[32] This has not stopped scholars from looking to EMP as a factor; Foreman-Peck and Zhou agreed with the negative aspects yet still conclude '[w]ithout the contribution of late marriage…real wages in England would not have increased strongly' during the Industrial Revolution.[33] Dennison and Ogilvie suggested the answer lies in factor markets and other economic institutions, and Ogilvie has recently stressed a combination of institutions for England.[34] Combining the Durham evidence discussed below with Bennett's observations of the pattern in the thirteenth century, we can see that EMP was a symptom of growing insecurity thanks to declining access to land within a commercialized society, not a factor in stimulating growth.[35] England's developed—if atrophied—market economy and society allowed for the slow and eventually

---

[27] Epstein, *Freedom and Growth*; Mokyr, *Enlightened Economy*, p. 7, *British Industrial Revolution*, and *Culture of Growth*.

[28] Allen, 'Progress and Poverty', p. 434; the article gives an overview of major hypotheses.

[29] Broadberry, 'Accounting for the Great Divergence', pp. 1, 11–12.

[30] Allen, 'Progress and Poverty'; Galor and Moav, 'From Physical to Human Capital Accumulation'; Boucekkine et al., 'Disentangling the Demographic Determinants'; De Pleijt and Van Zanden, 'Accounting for the "Little Divergence"'.

[31] Most recently see Van Zanden et al., *European Marriage Pattern, Female Empowerment, and Economic Development*. Hajnal laid out the pattern in 'European Marriage Patterns'. See also De Moor and Van Zanden, 'Girl Power'; Voightländer and Voth, 'How the West "Invented" Fertility Restriction'. Wrigley provides an evaluation of Hajnal's essay and its influence: 'European Marriage Patterns and their Implications'.

[32] Bennett, 'Wretched Girls'; Dennison and Ogilvie, 'Does the European Marriage Pattern Explain Economic Growth?' Smith, 'Relative prices'.

[33] Foreman-Peck and Zhou, 'Late Marriage', p. 1073. This led to a debate: Edwards and Ogilvie, 'What Can We Learn from a Race with One Runner?' and Foreman-Peck and Zhou, 'Response to Edwards and Ogilvie'.

[34] Dennison and Ogilvie, 'Does the European Marriage Pattern Explain Economic Growth?' p. 687; Ogilvie, 'Institutions and Economic Growth', pp. 9–10; see also her '"Whatever Is, Is Right?"'

[35] Bennett, 'Wretched Girls'. The thirteenth century was a period of increasing commercialization and market integration: Masschaele, *Peasants, Merchants, and Markets*.

successful response to exogenous shocks.[36] The English culture that permitted women to work (despite poor remuneration and a need to govern women) helped reallocate labour; in this way, the misfortune of young men and women rather than their choice supported economic growth that was already underway.[37] The key to England's economic development lay in social and cultural institutions conducive to active factor markets. Outlook helped the English make more of its land, labour, and raw materials than other European countries.

In a recent working paper in favour of human capital and the EMP, de Pleijt and van Zanden offered two important observations: (1) that the North Sea region benefited from a high per capita GDP thanks to a developed market economy, while other parts of Europe fell behind; (2) that 'the North Sea region should be seen as one economic entity, highly integrated by movements of goods and people and capital' although '[t]he economic core of this region...does however change over time'.[38] The concept of a single economic unit with changing core can be adapted for late medieval and early modern England; London was the only metropolis but regions contributed at different times to support national development. The lack of metropolitan competition for London meant that any development in the periphery must support the core. Innovation thus comes from the periphery but may not be easily recognizable as such.[39]

The study of both the Great and the Little Divergences makes use of national-level data: wage rates, GDP, literacy rates, and so forth. This requires abstractions, blurs regional variation into a single national data set, and often renders the division between urban and rural sharper than it is. The scholars involved in this work are well aware of this, and constantly refine publicly available datasets.[40] A study such as this will not solve the grand debates. Instead, it contributes to understanding components of those debates and, I hope, suggests possibilities.

Local and Regional History

Turning from the global to the local, the village, manor, and parish are where we can finally approach ordinary English men and women. There is a strong

---

[36] Campbell discusses the formation of England's factor markets in 'Factor markets in England before the Black Death'. On the integration of town and countryside to the benefit of both, see Masschaele, *Peasants, Merchants, and Markets*.

[37] This view of the EMP fits the conclusion of Broadberry et al. that it helped keep fertility down and did not slow economic growth: *British Economic Growth*, pp. 389–90.

[38] De Pleijt and van Zanden, 'Tale of Two Transitions', pp. 14–16. Contrast with Goldstone, 'Efflorescences and Economic Growth in World History'.

[39] For a possible example of the interplay between region and metropolis, see Zell, 'Credit in the Pre-Industrial English Woolen Industry', pp. 667–91, in which he stated 'both the capital and control of rural manufacturing were firmly in the hands of the manufacturing entrepreneurs' and not the London merchants (quote from p. 686).

[40] Broadberry, 'Accounting for the Great Divergence', pp. 5–9; Kelly and Ó Gráda, 'Numerare Est Errare', pp. 1132–63.

tradition of local studies and Ramsey, Havering, Halesowen, Earls Colne, Morebath, and Terling are common names among generations of scholars and students, while the Cambridge Group for Population and Social Structure and the Birmingham, Leicester, and Toronto Schools produced generations of leading historians.[41] While demonstrating the importance of local histories and structures, this scholarship has done much to outline rural economy and society: how manors were organized and administered, the family life of peasants, the role of women and children, the oppression of lords and then landlords, and so on. Scholars have built on these to explore further the underlying dynamics of specific groups or themes. Beyond such famous village and manor studies one can find studies employing parish, village, and manor data on topics such as customary law, women and gender, religion, and demography. Alongside works on commercialization, we have a good picture of medieval and early modern rural society: individualistic, producing for and responding to the market, in constant tension with lord and neighbours, and, for many, one poor harvest away from starvation.

Studies are shaped by the records used. The manorial court and account rolls used for the later medieval period no longer survive for the early modern period or no longer contain the same information; they are replaced by parish registers, letters, and other sources that did not exist earlier. Few localities have both sets of records. Survival is only part of the puzzle; method and interpretation matter greatly. One example is the utility of manorial records for demography, particularly reconstructing families. Raftis, Razi, Smith, Poos, and others debated how to define kin and the reliability of tracing families over generations.[42] Probate records have their own temptations and weaknesses, seen later in Chapter 6. The great weakness of local studies, however, is typicality: villages, manors, and estates are chosen because their records have survived, not necessarily because they best exemplify a type. This is what we must work with, but is it significant? The study of Terling is a prime example, and Wrightson revisited these debates in a 'Postscript' to a new edition in 1995.[43] The issue is inescapable, resulting in caveats, digressions, and (usually useful) debate. In the end, much comes down to the humours of the historian.

There are numerous ways to approach agrarian development in a local context. To name but a few: Allen took a statistical approach in his analysis of the south

---

[41] The corpus of work in late medieval and early English manors and villages is substantial; the following list of seminal works could be doubled or tripled with ease. A good starting point is the overview by Schofield, *Peasant and Community*, and the essay collection *Medieval Society and the Manor Court*. Key works include Thirsk, *English Peasant Farming*; Raftis, *Tenure and Mobility*; DeWindt, *Land and People*; McIntosh, *Autonomy and Community* and *A Community Transformed*; Razi, *Life, Marriage & Death*; Poos, *Rural Society After the Black Death*; Duffy, *Voices of Morebath*; French and Hoyle, *Character of English Rural Society*; Wrightson and Levine, *Poverty & Piety*. And this does not include works examining towns and their hinterlands.

[42] Poos et al., 'The Population History of Medieval English Villages'.

[43] Wrightson and Levine, *Poverty & Piety*.

Midlands; Whittle employed a manorial analysis of Norfolk; Zell explored the proto-industrialization hypothesis in Kent; Thirsk, Hatcher, Hare, and Yates looked at subregions (or pays) within a county; and French and Hoyle examined turnover and the effects of a new lord in an Essex village.[44] A rural focus is not enough; town and countryside became more integrated in the high and late Middle Ages, but towns did not necessarily command local or regional agricultural activity, even more so when the town in question was a port.[45] With all that in mind, this book examines landholding, production, consumption, and society alongside important administrative structures, with a rising town in the background, and over a longer period than many studies. The central thesis is that some lowland villages in Durham experienced agrarian development in the later Middle Ages more commonly associated with the early modern period, thanks to the administrative and local cultures of the Durham bishopric estate and the local economic and demographic context. This provided a head start to the rise of the yeoman and larger farms relative to southern England *when the conditions were right*, explaining the wealth and material culture seen in the seventeenth century while acknowledging that not all of Durham was so fortunate. The positive and negative aspects of growth supported the rapid expansion of the coal trade and in this, Durham's development prefigured elements of agrarian capitalism in the Midlands and East Anglia, meeting the needs of the emerging industries rather than feeding the masses of London. Consequently, this study offers a different take on the transition debate and helps explain England's rapid economic growth in the seventeenth century.

These parishes and other ones like them in Durham had the potential for even further growth. Based on the quantities of grain imported into Newcastle when the harvest failed in 1728, Brassley concluded that '[c]learly, therefore, the amount of food produced within the region itself must have risen rapidly enough to cater for the increased demands of the growing urban and rural populations'.[46] One of the major implications of examining a north-eastern but non-industrial subject is placing the changing role of a region within a national context, rejecting a single, teleological path to development. This further undermines the artificiality of the traditional periodization of medieval and early modern. It even brings into

---

[44] Campbell, *English Seigniorial Agriculture*, *The Great Transition*, and many other works; Allen, *Enclosure and the Yeoman*; Whittle, *Development of Agrarian Capitalism*; Zell, *Industry in the Countryside*; Thirsk, *English Peasant Farming*; Hatcher, Rural Economy and Society; Hare, Prospering Society; French and Hoyle, *Character of English Rural Society*; Yates, *Town and Countryside in Western Berkshire*. See also the work by Yelling on early modern Worcestershire, for example 'Common Land and Enclosure in East Worcestershire'. Hare and Yates tied their study to the countryside and a particular town.

[45] This is not a study of the trade networks of Newcastle, Darlington, or Bishop Auckland, but such studies have shaped the analysis: Britnell, *Growth and Decline in Colchester*; Kowaleski, Local Markets and Regional Trade in Medieval Exeter; Masschaele, *Peasants, Merchants, and Markets*.

[46] Brassley, 'Northumberland and Durham', p. 43, and *Agricultural Economy of Northumberland and Durham*, pp. 42–7.

question the utility of region as a category of analysis. Contrasting the traditional reputation of north-eastern England as described by Jewell with the entrepreneurial, wealthy, and not-so-ardently Catholic face of Durham demonstrates how 'the northeast' and 'the North' are cultural constructs and not natural divisions.[47]

This is more than an analysis of data-driven narratives of economic change. I seek where possible to tell the stories of how ordinary men and women experienced extraordinary times. To say no more than that people experienced these changes is to sell them short. While they were not kings or theologians (well, one was), the acceptance of change by them and people like them was necessary for that change to occur, and their reception and implementation shaped how those changes occurred locally. The great issues of the period—engrossment and enclosure, population change and polarization, religious and political debate, ideas of the community and the individual—are grounded in the experiences of real individuals and families. Villagers like Annabilla and Brian Headlam, Lancelot and Ralph Mason, William Hall, Roland Hixon, and many others made decisions based on what they knew and felt. Their stories, as well as the transformations of their lives and communities, cannot be told in full. Still, what that can be told is a salutary reminder that chaotic events underlie the tidy theories of historical change. Engrossment and individualism cannot be understood isolated from the stories of individuals and families—their marriages and remarriages, migration, conflicts, joys, and woes—which in turn cannot be removed from local, national, and religious politics. This is the humanity behind the development of agrarian capitalism: the innovation and failures, the cooperation and conflict, the fruits of success and the price paid.

Reassessing the Transition from 'Medieval' to (Early) 'Modern'

These villagers had much to contend with over three centuries, even though they did not know just how much future scholars would obsess over the times they lived in. Leaving aside three dynastic changes, two civil wars, multiple rebellions, and an interregnum, the period covered by this study witnessed four major transformations in England:

- the decline of serfdom;
- the Protestant Reformation;
- an agricultural revolution;
- a consumer/consumption revolution (linked possibly to an industrious revolution).

---

[47] Jewell, *North-South Divide*.

The timing, contours, and revolutionary nature of the latter two are debated but the change is clear.[48] Collectively, these reshaped England and contributed to two major changes left off the above list: individualism and capitalism, altogether resulting in new ways of conceptualizing society and in new economic structures. In theory, the change is easy to describe. Gone were the collective identity and agriculture of the Middle Ages, buttressed by Catholicism and the common field system, replaced by individualism and profit-oriented production in conjunction with a focus on individual salvation, new agricultural methods and technologies, and increasing consumerism. This easy division blurs medieval and modern; for example, 'modern' elements such as individualism and consumerism are found in the fourteenth century if not earlier.

In the literature on capitalism, 'capitalism' is in the eye of the beholder. In *An Introduction to Capitalism*, Swanson defines capitalism as '[a]n economic system in which the owners of the means of production hire wage labourers to produce goods and services in order to sell in the market for a profit'.[49] 'Owner' is a problematic concept in a system in which only the monarch truly owned land. Profit is even more problematic! With little effort, that or any definition could be stretched to include thirteenth-century nobles employing peasants as wage labourers on their demesnes with the profits spent on castles and armour. Few would comfortably call that capitalism. Stricter definitions, such as that used by Robert Albritton, mean that English agriculture is not considered capitalist until the nineteenth century, while Macfarlane even argued that there were no peasants in England.[50] Scale is a factor, and it is easy to see how nineteenth-century agriculture was more commercialized than fourteenth-century agriculture; and Overton observed the cultural difference, as modern farmers expect new technology and improvement rather than the methods used by previous generations.[51] Another significant difference is that modern concepts of capital equipment (such as buildings and machinery) derive from the Industrial Revolution, whereas pre-modern capital goods were items such as ploughs, carts, spinning wheels, and looms; moreover, much pre-modern wealth was found on the hoof or in the fields.[52] Asking if something is agrarian capitalism, particularly using too-modern concepts, is the wrong question.

So, let us turn from definitions to processes, of the Transition Debate on the emergence of 'capitalism' from 'feudalism', and the emergence of individualism

---

[48] To start, see Allen, *Enclosure and the Yeoman*; Broadberry et al., *British Economic Growth*; Clark, 'Long March of History'; Kerridge, *Agricultural Revolution*; Overton, *Agricultural Revolution in England*; Williamson, *Transformation of Rural England*, pp. 1–3. Turner et al. located the revolution in the early nineteenth century: *Farm Production in England*, p. 230. On the consumer revolution, see Chapter 6.

[49] Swanson, *Introduction to Capitalism*, p. 5.

[50] Albritton, 'Did Agrarian Capitalism Exist?'; Macfarlane, *Origins of English Individualism*.

[51] Overton, *Agricultural Revolution in England*, pp. 203–4.

[52] Broadberry and De Pleijt, 'Capital and Economic Growth in Britain', pp. 2–10.

associated with it. The debate on the causes of economic change has grown so large and diverse that there are books on the debate itself alongside conferences and proceedings examining important scholars and ideas. In the last few centuries, three different 'prime movers' emerged as potential drivers of economic development in late medieval England: the market, demography, and class conflict. All hark back to earlier theorists (Smith, Weber, Malthus, Ricardo, and Marx) and later scholars have articulated, modified, and interpreted the models further. These locate England's transition to a modern, capitalist, industrial society in the shift from communal to individualistic patterns of land use, what Kerridge characterized as Tawney's 'relentless and remorseless capitalism'.[53] Allen aptly termed the long-prevailing orthodoxy 'agrarian fundamentalism', as the broad outline is shared even by those whose interpretations differ: inefficient, medieval farming was modernized, increasing agricultural productivity—this supported the Industrial Revolution—and the changes created or exacerbated inequality.[54]

Students of late medieval English economic history have rejected the search for a prime mover, but the interpretative models still exercise influence over historical inquiry. Excellent evaluations are available, so I will give only a bare outline.[55] The commercialization model argues that urbanization, trade opportunities, and above all competition encouraged people to find ways to innovate and increase production while driving institutions such as markets to evolve. In some ways this is the triumphalist Whig narrative of progress: better use of resources, new crops, and new technology transformed England from backwater to world leader.[56] The population-resources or (neo-Malthusian) theory has England's population move economics. Rising population in the thirteenth century led to increased strain on resources and falling standards of living. The Black Death radically changed the balance of land and people, with prices and rents falling as wages and standards of living rose. The cycle would have repeated were it not for an agrarian then an industrial revolution. The Marxist model argues for conflict over the means of production as the driving force of change. The surplus extracted by lords from the peasants, so famously mocked by Monty Python, stifled innovation, while the lords frittered that surplus away on chivalric life and warfare. The increasing oppression of serfs, monetarily and in degrading exactions such as paying for the right to marry or to leave the manor, led to a 'crisis of feudalism' following the Black Death when lords could no longer maintain their power. The crown and old aristocracy later tried to stifle the new landlords and urban bourgeoisie, leading to the English Civil War in which the new, puritan capitalists were

---

[53] Kerridge, *Agricultural Revolution*, p. 15.   [54] Allen, *Enclosure and the Yeoman*, pp. 1–2.

[55] Hatcher and Bailey, *Modelling the Middle Ages*; French and Hoyle, *Character of English Rural Society*, pp. 1–50.

[56] For a nuanced critique, see Langdon and Masschaele, 'Commercial Activity and Population Growth'.

victorious over both the old regime and the radical revolutionaries. The monarchy was restored but the bourgeoisie remained triumphant.[57]

Each approach to economic change offers the power of simplicity, acknowledging but subordinating the factors of the others. Yet all fail to hold up when applied to historical examples. The pre-modern market operated under vastly different rules and cultures; in his study of late medieval commercialization, Britnell stated '[t]he abstract idea of a market order in society is nevertheless a modern one which had no parallel in the Middle Ages'.[58] He and others have emphasized the complexity of economic change and its evolutionary rather than revolutionary aspect. The population-resources model runs into major difficulty in the fifteenth century, as population stagnated despite higher standards of living and England experienced a severe recession. Hatcher has argued convincingly against the idea of a rising real wage and standard of living at all, while Campbell and others looking at the situation before the Black Death are less pessimistic than Postan about diminishing agricultural returns.[59] Finally, the Marxist model faces serious hurdles. There was far more to medieval English society than lords and peasants. Even the experiences of English serfdom varied from manor to manor, and population change at key moments is hard to subordinate to a struggle over means. There is also significant disagreement among Marxist scholars, first regarding the timing of the transition as evinced by the Sweezy-Dobb Debate, and second regarding the divergence between England and other European countries revealed in the Brenner Debate.[60]

A universal point of agreement is the agrarian transformation from small landholdings worked primarily by the peasant family to support their household to large farms worked by wage labour to generate capital or permit greater levels of consumption. The rise of the yeomen is seen as a stage in this process, as successful peasants enlarged their holdings while remaining connected to local society; the progeny of more successful yeomen married into the gentry.[61] Eventually, ambitious landlords and capitalists bought out or forced out smallholders and some yeomen, creating an ever-growing and exploited population of labourers on

---

[57] Best exemplified by the work of Hill, esp. *The English Revolution*.

[58] Britnell, *Commercialisation of English Society*, p. xv.

[59] Hatcher, 'Seven Centuries of Unreal Wages'; Poos, *Rural Society after the Black Death*; Campbell, *English Seigniorial Agriculture*, esp. pp. 18–21, and 'Unit Land Values', p. 48; Clark, 'Long March of History'. Bailey directly challenged the Postan thesis with a study of the East Anglian Brecklands: *Marginal Economy?*

[60] Dobb, *Studies in the Development of Capitalism*; Hobsbawm, 'General Crisis of the European Economy', and 'Crisis of the Seventeenth Century, II'. See also Trevor-Roper, 'The General Crisis of the 17th Century', and Mousnier et al., 'Discussion of H.R. Trevor-Roper'. Brenner's original essay and several responses were printed in Aston and Philpin, *The Brenner Debate*.

[61] The classic work on the yeoman is M. Campbell, *The English Yeoman*. Allen argued that yeomen were responsible for many of the improvements of the early modern agricultural revolution: *Enclosure and the Yeoman*.

top of an already growing population.[62] Although defenders of enclosure argued that the changes increased employment, critics then and since linked enclosure with dispossession and unemployment, such as Sir Thomas More's famous line in *Utopia* about sheep eating men.[63] The difference among scholars is their view on how this all came about. Tawney's *The Agrarian Problem in the Sixteenth Century* is the *locus classicus*; Stone's introduction to the 1967 republication summarizes the thrust of the work, and of the debate more generally: 'small-scale peasant farming on the open-field strip system of the Middle Ages did not die naturally in England, a casualty of inexorable economic forces; rather, it was murdered by the greed, folly and cowardice of landlords, lawyers and governments.'[64] In his famous article, Brenner fastened onto this dispropriation as the outcome of conflict between lord and peasant in which insecurity of peasant tenure led to engrossment by landlords and thence agrarian capitalism. Although refuted by Marxists and non-Marxists alike, his argument continues to influence scholarship.[65]

Historians have moved on from the emphasis of Tawney and Brenner on large farms and a disenfranchised peasantry, questioning the supposed inefficiency of medieval agriculture and the timeline of change. In a brief response to Brenner, Croot and Parker rejected the necessity of large farms as well as landlords for agrarian capitalism, pointing out the contributions of individual peasants and legal protections for copyhold.[66] Croot later argued that '[t]here is nothing intrinsically "backward" or subsistence-oriented about a small farmer'; after all, they had reason to maximize their resources and innovation was a rational response.[67] Allen and Whittle argued for small-scale producers as propelling the emergence of capitalism. Allen proposed that the sixteenth and seventeenth centuries were the 'consolidation—not the collapse—of the English peasantry', with the yeomen's revolution of the seventeenth century as the catalyst in the Midlands. Whittle's position is that the 'significance of the period between 1440 and 1580 does not lie in any major structural change in the nature of rural economy or society' but in 'the freedom, prosperity, and...lack of land-lordly interference without heavy

---

[62] Tawney, *The Agrarian Problem*; Kerridge, *Agricultural Revolution*; Spufford, *Contrasting Communities*; French and Hoyle, *Character of English Rural Society*, pp. 35–8.

[63] More, *Utopia*, p. 18.   [64] Tawney, *The Agrarian Problem*, p. viii.

[65] Rejecting more than three decades of critiques, Dimmock marshalled a Kentish case study to resurrect Brenner's arguments of insecure tenures permitting 'a top-down imposition by lords and their tenant farmers and manorial officials' so that 'the fundamental basis and blurred outline of the classic agrarian capitalist triad of commercial landlord, capitalist tenant farmer and wage labourer had emerged' in the sixteenth century: *Origin of Capitalism in England*, pp. 364–5.

[66] Croot and Parker, 'Agrarian Class Structure and the Development of Capitalism'. See also Hoyle, 'Tenure and the Land Market', pp. 1–20, and French and Hoyle, *Character of English Rural Society*, pp. 4–12. Hatcher and Bailey critiqued Brenner's approach (and that of Marxist historians in general): *Modelling the Middle Ages*, pp. 66–120 *passim*.

[67] Croot, *World of the Small Farmer*, p. 8. Others have shown how small farmers, particularly those working part time, were able to thrive: Hatcher, *Rural Economy and Society*, pp. 10–13; Blanchard, 'The Miner and the Agricultural Community', p. 93–106; Thirsk, 'Industries in the Countryside'; Zell, *Industry in the Countryside*.

taxation that allowed capitalism to flourish in Norfolk.[68] Hare placed agrarian change in Wiltshire alongside the development of the cloth industry, an interdependence that caused suffering during the fifteenth-century recession; Yates's study of Newbury (Berks.) likewise emphasizes the relationship of industry, trade, and the countryside. These offer an interesting 'what if' scenario for Durham and the coal trade through Newcastle.[69]

The change in mentality is another key component of agrarian and then industrial development. The medieval peasantry is often depicted as communal and stagnant, emphasizing the group rather than the individual. This is due in part to the types of medieval record that survive; individuals and individualism appear largely in legal records that seem to punish them and enforce conformity. The decisions necessary for open field farming have long been touted as examples of a traditional communal mentality, as each tenant had to plant the same crops and follow the same general schedule. The Marxist emphasis on conflict assumes that peasants, left to their own devices, would maintain the status quo or shift to an even more communal model. Peasant rhetoric from protest and revolt, namely the 1381 Rising, seems to support such a view, yet a snappy rallying cry does not necessarily represent the general wish of the people. Tenants had choice when it came to garths and closes. The common-field system of intermingled strips offered a measure of risk-avoidance, but we do not know the extent to which tenants chafed at the system of forced cooperation.[70] The activity in land markets and the rise of yeomen indicate that segments of the peasantry had very different ideas about the best way to farm, and the increasing scholarship emphasizing the agency of peasants suggests that capitalism arose out of the peasantry as seigneurial influence declined.[71] The family-land bond, the supposed emotional attachment of peasant families to 'their' land, weakened following the Black Death and most historians have concluded that pragmatic factors influenced peasant decisions to keep or part with land; to Campbell the peasants of fourteenth-century Coltishall (Norf.) were 'a hard-bargaining and resilient lot, emotionally unattached to their

---

[68] Allen, *Enclosure and the Yeoman*; Whittle, *Development of Agrarian Capitalism*, pp. 66, 315. Whittle edited a collection revisiting Tawney's agrarian problem: *Landlords and Tenants*; see also her 'Tenure and Landholding in England'.

[69] Hare, *Prospering Society*; Yates, *Town and Countryside in Western Berkshire*.

[70] On the rationality of the common fields, see McCloskey, 'The Persistence of English Common Fields', 'English Open Fields as Behavior towards Risk', and 'The Prudent Peasant'; Fenoaltea, 'Risk, Transaction Costs, and the Organization of Medieval Agriculture', and 'Fenoaltea on Open Fields'.

[71] Macfarlane ignited a firestorm in 1978 when he argued that English peasants were not peasants because they were so individualistic: *Origins of English Individualism*. While his analysis has been criticized, research shows a surprisingly market-oriented, individual peasant: see Whittle, 'Individualism and the Family-Land Bond' and Smith, 'Some Issues Concerning Families'. French and Hoyle revisited Macfarlane's ideas and found a mixture of family influence and individualism but could not address the broader attitudes asserted by Macfarlane in his 'English Individualism Refuted; French and Hoyle, *Character of English Rural Society*.

land, and inured to crisis'.[72] Dyer named this an 'Age of Transition' for the scope and complexity of change, and the literature reflects this.[73]

Another challenge to agrarian fundamentalism comes from studies of the productivity of medieval agriculture, where the assumption had been that a mix of enclosure, new crops, new ideas, and new technology greatly improved grain yields over what had been possible in the Middle Ages. Some peasants were thriving within manorial institutional structures.[74] Medieval yields could be on par with those in later centuries.[75] In a study of Durham tithes, Dodds demonstrated that while grain production was stagnant in the fifteenth century, peasant producers certainly were market responsive and participated in the speculative purchase of grain tithes.[76] The implication of more complex approaches to farming and higher than believed grain yields is that the use of productivity as a marker of change is increasingly problematic, as is the assumption that large farms equalled greater productivity or commercialization.

Likewise, the timeline for these changes continues to be modified. For medievalists, the Black Death and the decline of serfdom loom large in the explanation of change, with emphasis on flight and migration, class conflict, and the shedding of servile dues in a world turned upside down; but perhaps plague and serfdom loom *too* large in the debate. Early modern historians, unencumbered by dealing with serfdom or rapid population decline, have focused on the engrossment of land and economic polarization of society but come to different conclusions on the timing and key factors of the shift to agrarian capitalism.[77] The divide between the medieval and early modern periods has been increasingly eroded, with medieval commercialization laying the groundwork for future developments.[78] Earlier scholars had offered a longer transitional period, but now the changes seem to have occurred earlier but also unevenly. Hatcher, Yates, and Hare examined counties outside of the traditional Midlands and southern areas of England, and with distinct subregions that affected development; these regions also had extant or

---

[72] Campbell, 'Population Pressure, Inheritance and the Land Market', p. 129.

[73] Dyer, *Age of Transition?*   [74] Raftis, *Peasant Economic Development*.

[75] Campbell, *English Seigniorial Agriculture*; Clark, 'Long March of History', and 'The Price History of English Agriculture'.

[76] Dodds, *Peasants and Production*. Stone went further, arguing that yield was not the main goal of peasant producers, who considered efficiency and profit when deciding how much labour or capital to invest in a crop: *Decision-Making in Medieval Agriculture*. See also Dyer, 'Peasant Farming in Late Medieval England'. For Kilby, field and other names reflect what peasants knew about their lands and how to cultivate them: *Peasant Perspectives*, Chap. 7, 'Scientific Fields', Kindle loc. 4596–820.

[77] For an excellent discussion, see Shaw-Taylor 'The Rise of Agrarian Capitalism', pp. 27–33. Where once Marxist and neo-Malthusian models held sway, commercialization became popular after key publications in the 1980s and 1990s including Kowaleski, *Local Markets and Regional Trade in Medieval Exeter*; Britnell, *Commercialisation of English Society*; and Masschaele, *Peasants, Merchants, and Markets*. Campbell recently suggested shifting the focus of agrarian productivity from labour inputs to other factors, including climatological and botanical ones: 'Grain Yields on English Demesnes'. Hopcroft argues for a contingent origin in a combination of unique factors: 'The Social Origins of Agrarian Change'.

[78] Shaw-Taylor, 'The Rise of Agrarian Capitalism', p. 58.

emerging industries.[79] Bailey's combination of synthesis and structured case studies in *The Decline of Serfdom in Late Medieval England* reveals many significant changes in the later fourteenth century. Elsewhere, he argues that 'there is now conclusive evidence that [changes in customary tenure] had gained their initial and decisive impetus in the 1350s and 1360s'.[80] Yet emergence is not the same as maturity, and this transitional period needs to be aligned with both the medieval and early modern scholarship to determine at what point the changes to the whole amounted to something new. There must be a balance between broader structural changes in population, economy, and society with local conditions and factors, with a wariness of assuming certain developments or outcomes as normal. As Overton et al. rightly pointed out, '[i]t is rather an obvious point perhaps, but capitalist development was not a single process but several different processes'.[81]

A Transition in Durham

Where does that leave us? Demography, control of production, and commercialization are vital in explaining the development of England. The problem is that they do not explain all changes in all locations. Once, there was the hope that a critical mass of case studies would permit accurate generalization, but those hopes foundered on the questions of typicality and the vagaries of record survival. Nor is pure contingency an acceptable explanation. Path dependency as advocated by Brown is a useful analytical framework but still needs an original driving force and room for endogenous or exogenous disruption.[82] Hatcher and Bailey take a very practical approach and suggest the best method is a blend of dialectical and functionalist approaches with a good dash of common sense.[83]

What we observe in Durham is one of those differing processes, without which the common outcome might have been different. It is helpful to explore examples contrary to the assumed norm rather than dismiss them as aberrations, to refine the overall model. In doing so, I draw heavily on the humanistic and dialectical ideas of the historical materialist approaches of Rodney Hilton and E. P. Thompson but without the assumptions of conflict, along with Britnell's approaches to a

---

[79] Hatcher, *Rural Economy and Society*; Yates, *Town and Countryside in Western Berkshire*; Hare, *Prospering Society*, pp. 124–30. Yates's study is a direct challenge to the traditional divide, arguing that key 'medieval' features were gone by 1400; Hare found serfdom disappearing earlier in some Wiltshire manors, not until the mid-fifteenth century in others. These are not the first to bridge the divide: see Howell, *Land, Family and Inheritance in Transition*, and Marjorie McIntosh, *Autonomy and Community* and *A Community Transformed*.

[80] Bailey, *Decline of Serfdom* and 'The Transformation of Customary Tenures', p. 229.

[81] Overton et al., *Production and Consumption in English Households*, p. 177.

[82] Brown, *Rural Society and Economic Change*, esp. pp. 73–106.

[83] Hatcher and Bailey, *Modelling the Middle Ages*, pp. 239–40.

commercializing society. One base premise of historical materialism is that man makes his own history but within the limits imposed by material context, and to that I would add intellectual and cultural contexts such as gender constructs and ideas of community. The approach here is inherently humanistic, privileging the ability of individuals and communities to make choices, and, consequently, acknowledging the potential for different paths and outcomes.

This leads to a deeper reconsideration of the transition. First, timelines should be relative and the discussion moved from 'when' to 'why then'. Second, the impetus for agrarian development arises from the upper strata of the peasantry and the lesser gentry, a bottom-up transition, at least at the start.[84] Production capacity, market structures, and the potential for population growth existed but were not realized in the fourteenth and fifteenth centuries. Had demography been a more important factor on its own, population should have risen in the fifteenth century, but it took more than expanded production to spur population growth or to support growth resulting from other factors. Altogether, while many necessary ingredients for agrarian capitalism had been in place since the fourteenth century, two elements were lacking. One was the opportunity for peasants to acquire and maintain ever-larger holdings with secure tenure, which hinged on available land and credit, but also on local institutional structures. The second factor was demand, from a mix of increasing population, urbanization, specialization, and trade.

To make the significance of these factors clearer, it is worth looking at the idealized results and the necessary factors. The hallmarks of full-fledged agrarian capitalism, not truly realized until the eighteenth or nineteenth century, were increasingly large, enclosed farms worked by hired labour, with farmers employing scientific techniques, new crops, and technologies to maximize output. These farms were essentially rural factories, carefully managed to provide steady or increasing profits. The new farmers sought out new technologies or approaches to minimize labour cost, or more accurately to make the most efficient use of expensive labour.[85]

Concomitant to agrarian capitalism were several transformations in economy and society:

- an increasing number of landless men and women, who worked the new farms or migrated elsewhere in search of work;
- (re)investment of profit to generate more profit;
- production and consumption increasingly reliant on market exchange rather than household production at all levels of society.

---

[84] Masschaele saw the peasantry as a major force in the creation of trade networks: *Peasants, Merchants, and Markets*, esp. pp. 33–54.

[85] Both Allen and Wrigley argued the high cost of labour led to the exploitation of coal and steam power; Allen, *British Industrial Revolution in Global Perspective*; Wrigley, *Path to Sustained Growth*.

This encompasses much of what Allen described as agrarian fundamentalism: that modernization led to agricultural revolution and thus capitalism, increased agricultural production facilitated the Industrial Revolution, and that increased inequality was inherent in the agricultural revolution. Consequently, 'peasant farming was seen as a stumbling block…Agrarian Fundamentalism prompted the collectivization of agriculture in the Soviet Union and other communist countries. Analogous ideas have been applied by non-communist governments in many poor countries of Asia, Africa, and South America'.[86] Simply put, 'medieval' and 'traditional' techniques were a brake on progress, but the cost of progress was people. Allen disagrees with the belief that traditional structures impeded progress, and after studying medieval and early modern Durham, so do I.

Let us strip away as many assumptions as possible and look at the parameters for development. Drawing on the literature of English agrarian development, there were several prerequisites for a transformation of the countryside, first in organization and then cultivation:

- personal freedom;
- secure tenure (copyhold and leasehold);
- capital and credit to acquire and work holdings;
- adequate supply and cost of labour;
- a market structure capable of handling increased output;
- economic and social institutions conducive to engrossment and different agricultural approaches.

The timing of these prerequisites, once seen as early modern, are now located in the late medieval period by Whittle and others; in fact, some were in place earlier. Furthermore, it could be debated that some, including freedom and secure tenure, were not necessary as manorial demesnes could have been worked in such a manner. The above were necessary but not enough, otherwise demesnes would not have been leased in parcels and serfdom may not have ended. To the above we must add the following necessary catalysts and conditions:

- demand for foodstuffs to require and encourage increased production, or to require innovative changes such as new crops;[87]
- sufficiently low cost of acquiring land to encourage expansion of holdings;

---

[86] Allen, *Enclosure and the Yeoman*, p. 2.

[87] Brassley noted that 'the late introduction of turnips as a field crop was not such a serious disadvantage as it would have been in an area where high quality grazing was in short supply', *Agricultural Economy in Northumberland and Durham*, p. 175. Croot argued that '[i]t is surely no coincidence that it was a small farmer who is found growing turnips…rather than the larger farmer with plenty of hay', *World of the Small Farmer*, p. 198.

- sufficiently low transaction costs (tolls, transport) for marketing the produce;
- durable goods such as table linens, pewter dishes, and clocks available cheaply enough on the market to encourage a consumer rather than household economy.

Notably, individualism and stratification are not among those prerequisites; it could be argued that they are neutral regarding open field versus enclosure.[88] Finally, there are two considerations often overlooked because of the modern western mindset: the extent to which someone with the means to increase production chooses to do so, and the lengths to which someone is willing to go to increase production. These are given short shrift because of modern western ideas of labour and consumerism, and a long history of ruthless industrialists, real and fictional. There had to be reason, ability, and desire to improve or transform production. Together these form the benchmark for standard economic development in England, although it should be noted that the increased production often comes at significant human cost, and one wonders if the increased demand could have been met in a different way. The Durham evidence shows the complexity of the situation. In the fourteenth and fifteenth centuries, personal freedom and secure tenure led to larger (40–80 acre) farms, and seigneurial attitudes played a crucial role. Lay lords and the Dean & Chapter of Durham Cathedral tried to maximize rents, making it difficult for peasants to amass and maintain large farms, effectively installing a ceiling on the rise of yeomen from those estates; whereas the consistently low rents and copyhold for life on the bishopric estates made it possible for their tenants to rise higher—and outsiders, too, if they could gain access.[89] This created expanded holdings but was not sufficient for the emergence of truly large farms. Those came later in the fifteenth and into the sixteenth centuries as population began to rise. Throughout these four centuries, these ambitious farmers had options concerning the type and intensity of agriculture practised. Perhaps most surprisingly, these transformations happened within existing communities rather than destroying them. Capitalism, individualism, and community coexisted in early modern Durham.

As larger farms could have appeared earlier in Durham but did not, it is worth asking if agrarian development in southern England could have occurred earlier. This renders the medieval–early modern divide, c.1485–1500 in England, as even more artificial, with industrialization in the eighteenth and nineteenth centuries a truer marker of a new era; certainly that accords with more recent histories of the

---

[88] See Allen, *Enclosure and the Yeoman*, pp. 12–13.

[89] Brown, *Rural Society and Economic Change*, pp. 107–48 and 197–249. Foster noted a similar difference in strategies in Cheshire, with some lords moving to fixed-term leases where rents could be raised, while others allowed copyhold for life to continue at customary rates, with similar outcomes: *Capital and Innovation*, pp. 51–67.

Industrial Revolution and the Great Divergence. Leading up to that point was a longer, slow process, dating back possibly to before the Black Death. Agriculture and economy in Durham evolved in stages from the mid-fourteenth to mid-sixteenth centuries. Then, agrarian development in Durham fed and in turn fed off the expansion of coal mining. The latter offered employment opportunities to the increasing population of Durham and stimulated demand for food and other items; Durham's rising population found employment and its farmers an expanding market. Both spent money on making their lives more comfortable. Just as migration spurred London's growth and agrarian development in the Midlands to feed the capital, population and production went hand-in-hand in the northeast. Newcastle was not London and the northeast not the Midlands, but the historical processes were part of the same system.

Consequently, this book focuses less on measuring Durham against existing benchmarks than using its development to critique those benchmarks and identify the critical elements of the transition. Many elements of 'modernity' emerged here between 1349 and 1660, but not always as expected. Periods of equilibrium were reached at various times, and it is preferable to speak of development and sustainability than of revolution. Southern Durham was neither southern England nor the Tyneside coalmining area.[90] Because of that, the history of Durham shows that agrarian development did not have to be destructive of communities to accommodate population growth; community and local structures shaped the development of individualism and capitalism. This is an important critique to development theory and a rejection of unrestrained capitalism. It also reminds us that history is messy and due as much to individual choice as to impersonal forces.

---

[90] Levine and Wrightson explored the latter in *Making of an Industrial Society*.

2

Villages and Parishes

This study of rural change is built around a case study of three neighbouring villages: Bishop Middleham, Cornforth, and Sedgefield, which lay five to eleven miles south and east of the city of Durham. This was part of Stockton Ward, one of the four wards into which the medieval county was divided. Unlike most other counties, there were no hundreds and wapentakes except the wapentake of Sadberge, purchased from King Richard I in 1189.[1] The three villages formed an administrative unit of the Durham bishopric estate; there was a manor house and demesnes at Bishop Middleham at which tenants of all three villages owed labour services, and the three villages formed one of the stops during the bishopric halmote court tourn.[2] Bishop Middleham and Sedgefield were each the centre of a parish, with Cornforth not becoming an independent parish until the nineteenth century.

These villages were part of the sixty-plus settlements that made up the bishop of Durham's estate in County Durham, one of the two large ecclesiastical estates that dominated the county. The other was the estate of Priory (later the Dean and Chapter) of Durham, most of which was administered by the bursar before the Dissolution. Its compact nature aside, the priory main estate resembled other ecclesiastical estates while the bishopric was run more as a lay lordship. Unlike many, these two were concentrated, although a fair number of small manors and hamlets were interspersed; these were held by laymen, either in chief from the bishop or from one of the two larger estates. The estates originated in the Patrimony of St Cuthbert, a collection of lands and rights slowly accumulated since the seventh century which was divided between the bishop and monks in the twelfth century. Sedgefield (and presumably neighbouring Bishop Middleham and Cornforth) was acquired in the early tenth century when Bishop Cutheard 'bought with the money of St. Cuthbert the vill called Ceddesfeld [Sedgefield] and whatever pertains to it'.[3] By the fourteenth century, the two estates contained more than one hundred villages and other settlements, covering large parts of Durham.[4]

---

[1] There were originally three wards: Emsley and Fraser, *Courts of the County Palatine*, p. 14. The earliest mention of four wards is from 1330, Durham Cathedral Archive, Misc. Ch. 2640.

[2] The halmote court was held in a circuit, three times a year (spring, summer, and autumn) until 1512, when it began to meet twice yearly. The court for these vills usually met at Bishop Middleham.

[3] *Historia de Sancto Cuthberto*, pp. 58–9.

[4] The estate was divided between bishop and monks in 1229: *Feodarium Prioratus Dunelmensis*, pp. 212–17. See Barlow, *Durham Jurisdictional Peculiars*, pp. 1–52, for more information.

Rethinking the Great Transition: Community and Economic Growth in County Durham, 1349–1660. Peter L. Larson, Oxford University Press. © Peter L. Larson 2022. DOI: 10.1093/oso/9780192849878.003.0003

The three villages lay in the part of Durham most similar to southern England, with nucleated villages farming land suitable for the production of wheat. There was more pasture and waste available than found in most southern villages, and the vills have been described as 'islands of cultivated land in a sea of waste' and that could only have become truer following the Black Death.[5] Many smaller settlements were shrinking or disappearing in this period, becoming little more than collections of farms. The experiences of these villages and their inhabitants are comparable to their southern counterparts and readers familiar with those works should find themselves often nodding. Yet there were notable differences, too, in timing and tenurial dynamics.

The contrast with the coalmining village and parish of Whickham, in northern Durham, is significant once coal mining took off in the sixteenth century. Wrightson and Levine chose Whickham in 'an attempt to reconstruct the making of Britain's first industrialised society', focusing on an industry and place that experienced rapid change and growth.[6] In the fourteenth and fifteenth centuries Whickham was much like any other village and parish in Durham focusing on agriculture, with tenure by copyhold and rising yeoman families. From the third quarter of the sixteenth century, however, Whickham took a very different path. Coal pits and waggon ways destroyed its fields, its population swelled, the disparity of wealth greatly increased, and the culture changed; the authors rightly titled the chapter on the shift from agrarian to industrial focus 'A World Turned Inside Out'.[7] Coal mining radically reshaped Whickham. The present study charts the less stunning transformation of other Durham villages, whose agrarian output and growing population powered the mining industry. By tracing the history of these villages back to the fourteenth century, the study does even more, showing the common development of the Durham villages up to that sixteenth-century divergence and how the focus on mining became possible. One development led to the other, and both were deeply connected to the rest of England.

Durham and the North

Questions about typicality are even greater when the study looks at an area outside central England. Northern England had a reputation as poor, backward, stagnant, warlike, remote, and after the Reformation, Catholic—the opposite of London and its surrounding counties.[8] That image was not without truth: the distance from the capital, terrain, soil, and wars with Scotland made the North

---

[5] Dunsford and Harris, 'Colonization of the Wasteland', p. 35.
[6] Levine and Wrightson, *Making of an Industrial Society*, p. vii.
[7] Levine and Wrightson, *Making of an Industrial Society*, pp. 83–151.
[8] Medieval Cornwall also possessed a reputation as poor, distant, and different: Hatcher, *Rural Economy and Society*, pp. 1–2.

poorer and less easily controlled. The kingdom of Northumbria that became the earldom of Northumbria was restless, welcoming challengers to the throne and resisting the Norman conquest, resulting in the Harrying of the North and the creation of Durham as an episcopal bastion of royal power. The readiness to repel Scottish raids led to greater militarization and independent mindedness among its lords, most famously the Percy Earls of Northumberland and Neville Earls of Warwick. The role of northern lords in rebellions, from Henry Bolingbroke's invasion in 1399 to the 1569 Northern Rising, added further to the region's reputation. The Pilgrimage of Grace marked out the northern populace as militantly Catholic. Much of this could be said about the southwest and west of England, and the easy North–South dichotomy obscures differences within the north as well as similarities to the south. The true border area in the North, predominantly Northumberland, Cumberland, and parts of Weardale in Durham, formed a sharp contrast with the lowland areas, including Newcastle, eastern Durham, and the North and East Ridings of Yorkshire.[9] Many villages here resembled their southern cousins.

County Durham straddled the boundaries of the two Norths. Although not on the border with Scotland, it was close enough to be raided and King David of Scotland was captured at the Battle of Neville's Cross in 1346, which could be seen from the cathedral. The city of Durham was all but surrounded by water and the bishop's castle was built high on the central hill; Sir Walter Scot famously described the cathedral as 'Half church of God, half castle 'gainst the Scot'.[10] The bishops held the authority of the old earldom of Northumbria within the county, holding their own courts, minting coins, and possessing such a number of other royal prerogatives that it was not that much of a stretch for Bishop Antony Bek's steward to claim in 1302 that 'there were two kings in England'.[11] The bishops were trusted royal servants, and several were keeper of the Privy Seal or Chancellor; Bishop Thomas Hatfield (1345–81) may have been at Crecy with King Edward III.[12] Their authority reinforced that of the king in the North, but much of their time was spent away from Durham, whether with the king or on diplomatic missions. As part of his attempt to gain greater control over the church, Henry VIII began the dismantling of the bishop's powers, a process finally completed by William IV in the early nineteenth century.[13]

---

[9] Jewell, *North-South Divide*.

[10] Scott, 'Harold the Dauntless' (1816), Canto Third, line 11, in *The Bridal of Triermain*.

[11] Fraser, *History of Antony Bek*, p. 98, quoting TNA: PRO JUST 1/226 (formerly Assize Roll 226) m. 1d. On Durham's palatine status, see Lapsley, *County Palatine of Durham*. Coins were still being minted in 1530: 'Henry VIII: June 1530, 17–30', in *Letters and Papers, Foreign and Domestic, Henry VIII, Volume 4*, pp. 2902–21.

[12] Barker examined the conflicting evidence of Hatfield's whereabouts: '"If the King Had Asked for an Ass"'.

[13] Parliament abolished many palatine rights in 1536, 27 Hen VIII, cap. XXIV: Emsley and Fraser, *Courts of the County Palatine*, p. 32; Lapsley, *County Palatine of Durham*, pp. 196–8; *Statutes of the Realm*, vol. iii., 555–8.

The influence of Durham's political situation on village life is hard to evaluate. Durham sent no men to Parliament and Parliament had no authority in Durham until the seventeenth century. However, Durham knights served in Parliament for Northumberland and Yorkshire.[14] The bishop levied taxes on behalf of the king, and clerical taxation operated normally. Some of the bishop's Weardale tenants and many priory tenants later claimed to hold their lands by tenant-right, owing military service against the Scots, but there is no evidence of this until a legal dispute in the sixteenth century.[15] The bishop issued his own writs, but justice was much like that found throughout England.[16] County Durham was different and those differences are important, but that is true of every county and region.

The medieval city of Durham was small, maybe 2000 inhabitants in the later fourteenth century and 2000–3000 during the Reformation.[17] By 1801, it contained only 7530 persons, and unlike many other places in the county was not a part of the Industrial Revolution, as its narrow streets still testify.[18] The bishop and cathedral gave the city a presence unmatched by any other north-eastern city no matter their greater size or wealth. Newcastle was a more important, developed, and populated town. Besides Durham, there were several boroughs of varying importance in the county: Barnard Castle, Bishop Auckland, Chester-le-Street, Darlington, Gateshead, Hartlepool, Stanhope, Staindrop, Stockton-on-Tees, and Sunderland. Yet the county was very much rural even into the seventeenth century. The south and east were a champion landscape of mixed arable and pastoral farming, while large areas in the west were sparsely populated and used for summer grazing. The increased mining of coal, especially in the nineteenth century, would transform the landscape of the county as the Durham Coalfield was worked intensively and railways expanded.

The Case Study: Bishop Middleham and Sedgefield Parishes

County Durham has been increasingly well-served by medieval and early modern scholars. There are numerous other studies of the county and region that provide an excellent context for the case study, particularly in the early modern period: studies of the lead and tobacco industries, the county gentry, or material culture, for example.[19] Numerous scholars have mined the accounts of Durham

---

[14] Foster, 'Struggle for Parliamentary Representation', pp. 177–8.

[15] Drury, 'More Stout Than Wise', pp. 71–100; Marcombe, 'Dean and Chapter of Durham, 1558-1603', pp. 141, 149–50; and Morrin, 'Transfer to Leasehold'. See Hoyle, 'An Ancient and Laudable Custom', pp. 24–55.

[16] Emsley and Fraser, *Courts of the County Palatine*; Larson, 'Local Law Courts', pp. 97–109.

[17] Russell, *British Medieval Population*, p. 145; Dobson, *Durham Priory*, pp. 36–7.

[18] *Abstract of the Answers and Returns, Enumeration Part I*, p. 100.

[19] Liddy, *Bishopric of Durham*; James, *Family, Lineage, and Civil Society*.

priory, providing a clear understanding of that estate's workings and insights into the marketing activities of the monks and the decision making of its tenants in producing for those markets. Threlfall-Holmes studied the market activities of the monks in supplying their needs, whether from their own estate or from merchants. Dodds used records on the priory's tithes to look at grain production and the decision making of priory tenants, both in their planting and in the buying and selling of tithes. We know much about the economy of the priory estate.[20]

There are fewer bishopric records suitable for the predominantly economic analyses used for the priory estate. Those works that touch on the bishopric do so in combination with the priory estate, as together they provide a good picture of the county. We know how the administrations and tenants approached the challenges following the Black Death, and the effects of the different decisions on administrative attitudes and community cohesion. Brown has studied the reaction by the two estates and their tenants as well as laymen in the county to the severe recession of the fifteenth century and the results of those choices into the seventeenth century. His county-level study focuses on the landed estates, whether lay or ecclesiastical, and reveals the rise of the lesser gentry and of men involved in coal mining. Brown explains the general fate of the tenants from the two estates, using path dependency to explain the various trajectories in Durham. Path dependency provides an accurate model but it leaves little scope for unexpected events or the personal decisions that, in aggregate, created the paths taken.[21] By looking at these three villages we can explore those paths and, sometimes, the people who trod them.

One advantage of looking at those villages is that one of the few studies of a bishopric holding is on 'Middleham Manor' from 1600 to 1850. Clifford's central argument here was that this period saw the transformation from medieval open field to modern agriculture, with enclosure setting the pattern for future farm allotments, although '[n]ew agricultural practices were slow to develop with medieval tenures persisting into the 19th century and new crops and rotations not introduced until a relatively late date'.[22] While the present case study refutes his assumptions and arguments on several points, especially for the later middle ages, Clifford's work on the eighteenth and early nineteenth century meshes well with the present study. The nineteenth-century farms he describes are the direct descendants of holdings that began to emerge following the Black Death. They represent a persisting if increasingly stratified community rooted in the yeomen and gentry of the local area. His discussion of farming patterns, despite assuming a false changelessness before 1600, adds weight to the argument that local factors

---

[20]   R. Lomas, 'Durham Cathedral Priory', 'The Priory of Durham and its Demesnes', and 'A Northern Farm'; Dodds, *Peasants and Production*; Threlfall-Holmes, *Monks and Markets*.

[21]   Brown, *Rural Society and Economic Change*.

[22]   Clifford, 'Settlement and Field Systems', p. i/Abstract.

and needs encouraged the development of agrarian capitalism, with traditional approaches being adapted to support increased demands. In short, his thesis underlines the need to take a long view of rural agrarian development assessed on its own context, rather than applying a model developed for a different place with different circumstances.

The vagaries of record survival due to fire, rats, rebellion, neglect, and the whims of bored clerks shape what the historian can do.[23] The Durham records exemplify this. The records of the bishopric halmote courts survive from 1349 to the abolition of copyhold in 1925 (though with a little business afterwards), and for a good portion of the sixteenth century both the original paper and official parchment versions survive. Fewer priory halmote rolls survive, primarily for the 1360s to early 1400s, all in varying condition. Other records from both estates, mainly financial, survive in varying numbers well into the early modern period. For most of the period covered in this book, the records were in abbreviated Latin, with sentence structure often mirroring that of English, with the occasionally odd or erudite abbreviation or construction.

The halmote was the original 'manorial' court for the bishopric and priory. A major seigniorial purpose was to record land transfers, making it an excellent source for examining agrarian development. Based on the earliest surviving priory halmote records, by the end of the thirteenth century tenants were using the halmotes for interpersonal business (primarily suits of debt and trespass) and this formed a significant portion of the bishopric business to the mid-fifteenth century. At that point, other courts drew away most of the lawsuits, leaving the regulation of agrarian practice—ploughing, stints, maintenance of fences and watercourses— the other main concern of the courts. Taken together, the one constant through the records is control: who controlled the land (the tenants) and who controlled the village (the jurors of the halmote court).

Probate records provide another source for understanding the period, with the first surviving will for these villages dating to 1553. These can reveal much about the testator's life, from family to servants to wealth, particularly if both will and inventory survived. Some wills detail business and agrarian practices, while others are incredibly terse. Many have a formulaic quality, limiting what can be inferred about private belief. Still, social expectations and ties of kinship and friendship do show through. The inventories too can be a mixed bag, ranging from a few lines to a few sheets. The men who conducted the inventories came from a small group of prominent yeomen in the village, adding another layer of interpretation between us and the past while providing a window onto the general tastes of that group.

---

[23] There is a story, source unknown, told in the archives that many Durham bishopric and palatine records were lost to clerks playing football. Raine blamed Bishop Cosin's executors for the loss of many diocesan records: *Scriptores Tres*, pp. xviii–xxii. Lapsley said that 'there are even tales of broken windows stopped with medieval parchment, and of kites made of documents invaluable to the historian', *County Palatine of Durham*, p. 328.

While probate records have failed to be a holy grail for understanding belief or daily living, they still reveal what people valued, and how people were valued.

Parish registers form a third major source. Required in every parish in 1538 to record baptisms, marriages, and burials, and to help ensure conformity with the new reformed religion, they offer useful proxies for demographic analysis of fertility, nuptiality, and mortality. Gaps, evasion by recusants and later non-conformists, and attempts to hide illegitimate births keep them from being as complete a record as one would like. Yet their attempted universality makes the parish register one of the few avenues to approach those less present in other records, especially children and servants.

Taken together, these records reveal much. Who was in the villages, what they did, their wealth, their demographic milestones, can be recovered with confidence but not always linked. Aggregated, these reveal much in turn about the village and parish, including economic development, mobility, and socio-economic stratification. Court records, predominantly the halmotes but also higher courts and church courts, crack open a window onto processes and motivations. Sometimes this is direct. Often it requires inference from patterns, particularly when discussing communalism versus individualism, leadership, or entrepreneurism; the records are not going to name someone as a bully or an innovator. There are holes; families cannot be reconstructed to the extent in other studies; and as time goes on, there is less information about women, servants, and the poor.

The villages in which the people and events documented in the records lay near the northern end of the Magnesian Limestone Plateau (which extended south to Nottingham).[24] The premodern village of Bishop Middleham was located on and between two hills, with the parish church, St Michael's, and the manor hall on the southern hill. The manor was the site of an episcopal palace that was still in use in the fourteenth century although that use was coming to an end. At the time of Bishop Hatfield's survey in the late fourteenth century, the village included approximately nearly 1000 acres of arable land and 100 of pasture and meadow, numerous parcels of unspecified size, and an orchard and park attached to the manor.[25] Of the three, it most resembled the 'typical manor' of medieval England with free and customary tenants, open fields, and a substantial demesne. In contrast, Cornforth was a smaller settlement, so small that it was lumped in with Bishop Middleham in *Boldon Book*, and it became smaller over time. The village had nearly 800 acres of arable, meadow, and pasture, as well as a watermill and a limekiln.[26] Sedgefield was by far the largest in size and population, and by the fourteenth century had one of the largest tenant populations in the county. Some

---

[24] *National Character Area profile 15. Durham Magnesian Limestone Plateau.*
[25] Curtis, 'Bishop Middleham', pp. 180–4.
[26] *Hatfield's Survey*, pp. 184–6.

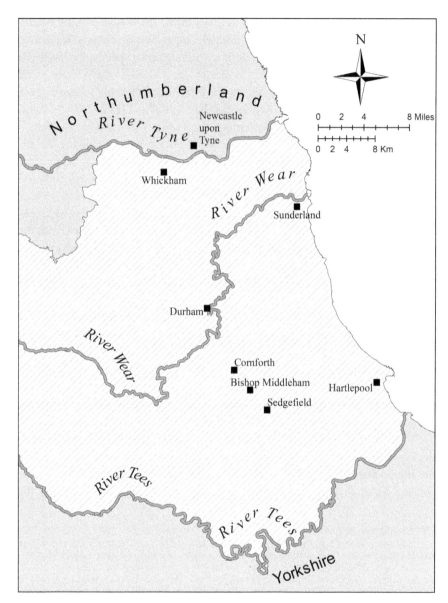

Figure 2.1 Map of north-eastern England with principal locations in the text

Source: Ordnance Survey GIS datasets, Boundary-Line v.2020–05 and OS Open Places v.2020–07.
Contains OS data © Crown copyright and database right 2020.

of its early modern residents referred to it as a town. There were over 1600 acres of arable land plus moor and pasture, multiple forges, two dovecots, a bakehouse, and a kiln or brewhouse. There was both a windmill and a watermill as well as a fulling mill noted as being 'beside Cornforth' (*juxta Corneforth*).[27] There was a weekly market on Fridays and a fair on the feast of St Edmund (16 November), granted in 1312. By 1430 the Friday market had lapsed and trading was happening on Sundays, but later in the century the bishop was renting out stalls.[28] Sedgefield also was home to one of the wealthiest ecclesiastical livings in the county. The two parishes were on the way of the north-south route from Darlington to the city of Durham, and an east-west route from Bishop Auckland to Hartlepool on the coast. Studies of late medieval urban supply networks are consistent in identifying an eight- to twelve-mile radius for foodstuffs (with considerably larger waterborne networks if a port).[29] This put the parishes within the reach of Bishop Auckland, Durham, Darlington, Hartlepool, and Stockton. The latter two, as ports, provided access to Newcastle as well as the coastal and North Sea trade.[30] These were not isolated settlements, but part of a regional and international market network.

Each village had its own trajectory, but a comparison of estate surveys from the late twelfth to mid-seventeenth century proves that many other villages shared similar experiences, some all the way through the period. County Durham is associated with coal mining but in the Middle Ages that was largely limited to south Tyneside and the Durham fells. Coal pits in Cornforth were noted twice in the later fourteenth century, but a mining industry did not develop there until the 1830s and in 1348–49 the bailiff of Middleham manor had coal carted in for the use of the servants there.[31] In this regard, the villages provide a counterpoint to the Tyneside village of Whickham. Part of the bishopric estate, Whickham became the site of major coal mines and underwent significant transformations as the demand for coal increased.[32] The present study shows that the history of the

---

[27] *Hatfield's Survey*, pp. 186–92.

[28] *Register of Thomas Langley*, vol. III, pp. 175–7. Letters, 'Online Gazetteer of Markets and Fairs in England Wales to 1516'. The fair lasted possibly into the nineteenth century: Curtis, 'Sedgefield', p. 321.

[29] Lee provided an excellent summary alongside his own work in 'Feeding the Colleges', pp. 248–51. See also Britnell, *Growth and Decline in Colchester*, pp. 41–47, 141–42, 246–7; Kowaleski, *Local Markets and Regional Trade in Medieval Exeter*, pp. 280–88, and 'The Grain Trade in Fourteenth-century Exeter'.

[30] Masschaele, *Peasants, Merchants, and Markets*, p. 17. The sophistication or maturity of the networks are harder to determine. Dyer saw peasants as connected (if only indirectly) with international trade: 'Did Peasants Need Markets and Towns?' He presents a neat summary of the question of market network maturity in 'Trade, Urban Hinterlands and Market Integration', pp. 103–6.

[31] *Hatfield's Survey* p. 239. Hatcher, *History of the British Coal Industry*, pp. 70–1. Cornforth colliery operated from 1835 to 1851 although other collieries (including the Thrislington/West Cornforth colliery) and an ironworks in Thrislington did spur growth in the town. A pit was not sunk in Bishop Middleham until 1846: 'Local History: Bishop Middleham', 'Local History: Cornforth', 'West Cornforth (Cornforth)'; see also 'Bishop Middleham Colliery' and 'Cornforth Colliery'. On medieval mining by the bishop of Durham, see Britnell, 'The Coal Industry in the Later Middle Ages'.

[32] Levine and Wrightson, *Making of an Industrial Society*.

northeast in the sixteenth through eighteenth centuries is really three intertwined histories of agriculture, urbanization, and industrialization.

Bishop Middleham was the centre of one the bishopric's administrative units (although Sedgefield may have been the original *caput*[33]) and it was the site of a *manerium*, so while much had changed it remained the centre for a bishopric administrative unit. The remaining components of the earlier medieval estate unit are likely to be found among the neighbouring manors and 'little vills' (*villatae*) in the rest of the parishes shown in Figure 2.2 (all in lay hands except for part of Mainsforth):[34]

<u>Bishop Middleham</u>[35]

- Mainsforth, a village partly in lay hands and partly in the bishopric estate, and therefore sometimes included in bishopric records;
- Thrislington (or Thurstanton), a small settlement turned into a farm by the end of the sixteenth century, whose archaeological exploration provides information on life in the area.

<u>Sedgefield</u>[36]

- Bradbury and the Isle and Hardwick, tiny settlements that became farms;
- Butterwick, Embleton (or Elmden), Layton, and Fishburn, small settlements;
- Foxton and Shotton, two associated, disappearing settlements;
- Mordon, another small settlement and manor.

These smaller settlements contained mainly freehold farms held by local families or non-resident tenants, so few records remain beyond charters. Most were small and shrank or disappeared following the Black Death, and the tenants overlapped considerably with those of the three villages, moving back and forth or holding land in more than one village.[37] The three villages, in

---

[33] *Historia de Sancto Cuthberto*, pp. 58–9.

[34] South included Garmondsway, Mainsforth, and Butterwick based on the grouping in *Domesday Book supp. vol 35: Boldon Book* and thinks that Bradbury and Mordon should be included as well: *Historia de Sancto Cuthberto*, pp. 102–3. *Hatfield's Survey* includes Hardwick and Oldacres as *villatae* under Sedgefield; the *Survey* lists Mainsforth as a separate village with its own court (with perquisites valued at 3s. per annum), but land transfers were recorded under Bishop Middleham; Mordon appeared as an independent vill, although there were only five tenants: *Hatfield's Survey*, pp. 161, 178–79, 186. The 1642 Protestation Oath included Fishburn, Embleton, Mordon, Butterwick, Foxton & Shotton, and Bradbury under the parish of Sedgefield: *Durham Protestations*, pp. 179–82.

[35] *Domesday Book supp. vol 35: Boldon Book*, pp. 24–7; *Hatfield's Survey*, pp. 178–9, 180–6; 'Garmondsway', and 'Thrislington', in 'Beresford's Lost Villages'.

[36] *Domesday Book supp. vol 35: Boldon Book*, pp. 24–7; *Hatfield's Survey*, pp. 161, 179–80, 186–92; Curtis, 'Sedgefield', pp. 322–48; 'Butterwick', 'Embleton', 'Foxton', 'Shotton', in 'Beresford's Lost Villages'; Dunsford and Harris, 'Colonization of the Wasteland', p. 52.

[37] 'Beresford's Lost Villages'; Roberts, *Rural Settlement in Britain*, pp. 110–16. The level of dispossession if any of tenants must have been small; compare with Goodacre, *Transformation of a Peasant Economy*, pp. 91–100.

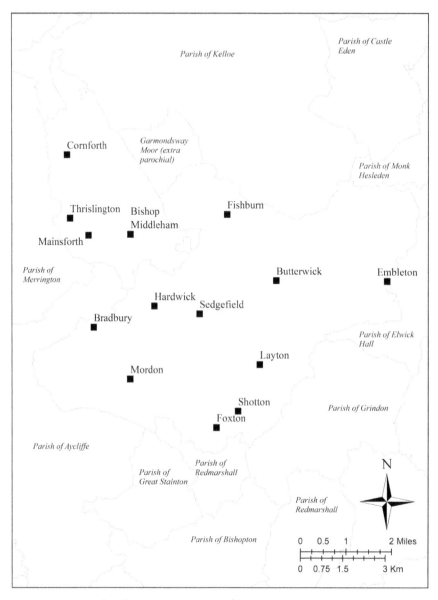

Figure 2.2   Map of settlements in Bishop Middleham and Sedgefield parishes

Source: Ordnance Survey GIS datasets, Boundary-Line v.2020–05 and OS Open Places v.2020–07.
Contains OS data © Crown copyright and database right 2020.

many ways autonomous, need to be considered as a unit in multiple ways and as having multiple layers of identity, in ways that would not necessarily be found in 'typical' southern English manors and parishes. This must be seen in a context of larger communities.[38]

Bishopric villages were overseen by a halmote jury of four to six men who reported to the halmote court held three times (later two) each year on a circuit throughout the estate. These juries were made up of wealthier tenants who served for extended periods.[39] The jury presented offences and information at the halmote court and represented the village in other capacities, such as leasing lands for the entire community. Outside of the jury, the reeve (or greve, in the North) directed agricultural labour and summoned men and women to works. He functioned as a general bailiff as well, seizing lands and goods at the direction of the court. He was also responsible for organizing the village meetings at which agricultural decisions and bylaws were made. Although not necessarily the wealthiest tenant, the reeve tended to be a man of relatively high means and standing in the village, and like the jury tended to serve continuously for long periods. The churchwardens also came from such families. As such, reeves feature prominently in the history of agrarian change in the villages, as both entrepreneurs and enforcers. Their actions provide the material with which to track many of the changes in the villages, as well as the continuities.

The same was not true of estate and county officers, with whom the villagers came into regular contact and often conflict in the fourteenth and early fifteenth centuries. The bishop's steward oversaw the entire bishopric estate and presided over the halmote court. Many decisions were left to his discretion, although more delicate matters would be referred to the bishop's council; the steward leaned heavily on the villagers for information and to make decisions within the villages. The county coroners (one for each of the four wards) were responsible for collecting freehold rents in addition to the usual duties of investigating deaths and hearing abjurations of the realm, while the village collectors made indentures with and delivered customary rents to the bishop's Receiver General in the city of Durham. Despite the importance of these men in the villagers' lives, they did little to shape the communities other than by their relative inaction.

The attitude of the bishopric administration gave considerable agency to the tenants and leaders of each village. This surrendered considerable power to the villagers to shape their own futures; but there were opportunities for the administration to intervene if desired. Wrightson and Levine stated that 'if the industrialization of Whickham was the harbinger of a new economy and society, it was also

---

[38] Contrast with Highley, which had a strong identity centered on the parish: *Highley*, p. 3.
[39] Larson, 'Village Voice or Village Oligarchy?'

the nemesis of an older social formation'.[40] That 'older social formation' persisted in other parts of the county and followed its own evolutionary path. The economic and social developments in villages such as Bishop Middleham, Cornforth, and Sedgefield—while not nearly so revolutionary as in places like Whickham—were critical in their own right to the overall development of England.

---

[40]   Levine and Wrightson, *Making of an Industrial Society*, pp. 83–4.

3

Life, Marriage, Death, and the Household

It is impossible to escape the power of population when examining economic development; plague, urbanization, and the later expansion of London affected the whole of England. The general trend for England is clear. The first outbreak of the Black Death in 1348–49 reduced England's population anywhere from 30 to 50 per cent and subsequent outbreaks of the plague, in conjunction with other factors, caused the population level to stagnate or even decline until the end of the fifteenth century, at which point the population began to recover, although it would not reach or surpass its pre-plague peak until the seventeenth century. Population change played a role in the northeast as well, but it was only one factor. Low population following the plague allowed for development of large, family-plus farms within the tenurial scheme of the great ecclesiastical estates. The low population and higher standard of living eventually encouraged the recovery of the county's population, earlier than England as a whole, aiding further development and the quick expansion of the coal trade. The latter's growth required both food and labour, spurring migration and agricultural development in the seventeenth century. As with England, the outlines are clear and reveal a dynamic society.

Pre-modern demographic analysis is complex. The following pages deal closely with questions of methods and sources, calculating appropriate modifiers, projecting estimates, and so on, and the approaches taken lean heavily on even more technical demography. The overall results and significance are straightforward. The populations of Bishop Middleham, Cornforth, and Sedgefield, and many other Durham villages, began recovering from the Black Death earlier than southern England. Towns such as Darlington eventually saw even greater growth, but the greatest gains in population were in Tyneside. The population was growing quickly enough to satisfy the labour requirements of larger farms and then the needs of the expanding coal industry.

Population Estimates

Estimating the size of the population and smaller population trends is devilishly difficult for the late medieval period, as conjuring an estimate of the population requires analysis and extrapolation from sources not intended to count the population, notably tax and court rolls. The Crown was not interested in the

Rethinking the Great Transition: Community and Economic Growth in County Durham, 1349–1660. Peter L. Larson, Oxford University Press. © Peter L. Larson 2022. DOI: 10.1093/oso/9780192849878.003.0004

population at large but in who could pay taxes, while lords were concerned with their tenants. Even though historians can develop reasonable multipliers to account for family members and servants, many people were omitted from these lists because they were poor and/or landless. The estimates by Russell and Postan are the most common. Russell estimated a national population of 3.7 million people before the plague, dropping to 2.2 million by 1377, then to 2.1 million by 1430, before rising to about 3.2 million in 1545. Postan's estimates were considerably higher.[1] Recently, Broadberry et al. returned to this question and arrived at post-plague numbers close to Russell's, with 2.5 million in 1377 and 2.02 million in 1430, rising to 2.83 million in 1541 and to 4.1 million in 1600.[2]

We are on firmer ground for the early modern period, as the Reformation made the religious identity of every individual a matter of national concern. The Reformation of Henry VIII brought with it the parish register, designed to record every baptism, marriage, and burial in a parish beginning in 1538. Registers have been lost or damaged, and religious dissent and nonconformity kept some persons out of the register, but there is still far more information than for the preceding centuries. Wrigley and Schofield, with a small army of volunteers, used a portion of these registers to approximate the overall population of England from 1541 to 1871. Their reconstruction estimated a population of 2.77 million in 1541, rising to 4.11 million in 1601 and 5.06 million in 1666. While taken as general orthodoxy, this has not been accepted uncritically. The revised late medieval numbers should change little barring significant revisions to our understanding of medieval agricultural productivity that would raise upwards the ceiling of population that could be supported.[3]

Estimating the population of County Durham presents a greater challenge than for many other localities. Durham's palatinate status means that it was exempt from parliamentary taxation until the seventeenth century, so while its inhabitants still paid taxes there are no taxpayer lists for the lay subsidies or poll taxes so often used to estimate population for the rest of England.[4] This led Russell to rely on neighbouring counties and the relation of lay to clerical population in estimating Durham's population in 1377 at 20,618 persons, after accounting for children and the untaxed but not mendicant friars.[5] Broadberry et al. estimated Durham's population in 1377 as significantly higher, at 24,587, with the population tripling over the next two centuries to 76,483 based on Durham's share of the national population.[6] Applying Arkell's suggested Hearth Tax-derived population

[1] Russell, *British Medieval Population*, pp. 235–81; Postan, *Cambridge Economic History of Europe*, vol. i, p. 562.
[2] Broadberry et al. *British Economic Growth*, p. 22.
[3] Wrigley and Schofield, *Population History of England*, pp. 208–9, 528; Broadberry et al., *British Economic Growth*, p. 33.
[4] *Poll Taxes of 1377, 1379 and 1381*, p. xxi.
[5] Russell, *British Medieval Population*, pp. 144–6.
[6] Broadberry et al., *British Economic Growth*, p. 25.

multiplier of 4.3 to the 13,281 households listed in Durham's Lady Day 1666 Hearth Tax, the approximate population of Durham at the Restoration was considerably lower, at 57,100 persons.[7] This underscores the difficulty in devising reliable estimates of population using national multipliers, which become even more unreliable when shifting down to the parish or village level.

The Late Middle Ages

Several sources can be used as 'snapshots' of the three villages in certain years from which a rough understanding of population change can be theorized, as shown in Table 3.1. *Bishop Hatfield's Survey* provides two measures *c.*1383 as it lists both tenants and dwellings, while the Hearth Tax lists provide the basis for an estimate at the end of the period, in 1666. The 1563 Diocesan Returns, the Protestation Returns from 1641–42, and Parliamentary Survey of 1647 provide additional points for estimation. The 1588 bishopric rental has been omitted here as it did not include all tenants. From 1559 onwards, the parish registers can be used to explore the population change although they do not of themselves provide a count of population at any given time. These sources measure different units (tenants, households, holdings, adult males), use different scales (village, parish), and may contain persons from the smaller settlements of the parish alongside the three main villages. This introduces a level of uncertainty even before attempting to apply multipliers to account for non-recorded persons, but it can provide a working demographic model. The question, then, is how can these different units of measurement be converted to provide a more consistent measurement of population size?

Russell, Postan, and others used the 1377 Poll Tax as the basis to estimate England's population before and after the plague. This tax was not levied or recorded as such in Durham, and so the comprehensive list of tenures and tenants contained in *Hatfield's Survey, c.*1383, must be employed as a proxy. The *Survey* yields two important sets of information that can be used as a baseline for the population: the names of individual tenants and the number of dwellings (messuages, cottages, and tenements). The tenants roughly reflect the number of households at the time, while the dwellings could be used to estimate population before the plague struck although that is very speculative even for medieval population estimates. The first population estimate in Table 3.2 assumes that there were 3.51 persons (adults and children) per household, based on Russell's estimates for neighbouring Northumberland; the second estimate uses the multiplier of 3.7 persons per household that Howell found in Kibworth Harcourt; and

---

[7] *County Durham Hearth Tax*, pp. xcix, cxvii; Arkell, 'Multiplying Factors', p. 57.

Table 3.1 Village and parish population data, early fourteenth century to 1666

Date	Population Type	Bishop Middleham		Sedgefield	
		Villages	Parish	Villages	Parish
Pre-1348	Dwellings	77	89[b]	92	95[c]
c.1383	Tenants[a]	55	91	86	238
1563	Households	91	120	195	335
1641	Adult Males	120	-	322	-
1647	Tenants	41	-	55	-
1666	Households	105	116	163	290

[a] This presumes based on analysis of the fifteenth century that tenants in different villages with the same name are the same men.
[b] Includes Mainsforth.
[c] Includes Hardwick and Moreton.

Source: Hatfield's Survey, pp. 161, 178–92; Diocesan Returns pp. 136–7; Durham Protestations, pp. 157–58, 179–80; Parliamentary Surveys, pp. 189–219; County Durham Hearth Tax, pp. xcix, cxvii.

the third uses a multiplier of 4.15 derived from the 'best estimate' of Broadberry et al. The estimates have been rounded.[8] Assuming that each dwelling recorded in 1383 represented a household when population was at its highest in the early fourteenth century, the estimates are show in Table 3.2.

Approached in this way, the models suggest a pre-plague population of around 600 to 700 for the three main villages combined, with another 100 and more in the various smaller settlements. By way of comparison, the population of Whickham would have been between 235 and 280, approximately.[9] One drawback with this model is that a landless population could have contributed more to the overall totals—if there was a landless population. In the immediate aftermath of the Black Death in the spring of 1349, at least half of the tenants on the great bishopric and priory estates were dead and more had fled. Tenant mortality on the Durham priory estate ranged from 21 to 78 per cent based on lists compiled shortly after the plague, and of the monks themselves, not quite two-thirds perished. There are no comparable sources for the bishopric in those years, but anecdotal evidence and entry fines between the spring of 1349 and the summer of 1350 indicate substantial death and flight throughout the estate. Mortality of this level was common, but many parts of England had others able to take up the empty lands. Instead, Durham plunged into a tenurial crisis and early 'feudal

---

[8] The multiplier of 3.51 is based on Russell's number of persons per household in Northumberland modified by his adjustments for children and indigent and non-paying adults (2.23x1.5x1.05); 3.7 is based on Howell's findings in Kibworth Harcourt for 1379; and 4.15 (2.23x1.69x1.10) is a modification of Russell's numbers based on the 'best estimate' of Broadberry et al.: Russell, British Medieval Population, pp. 27–29, 146; Howell, Land, Family and Inheritance, pp. 232–5; Broadberry et al., British Economic Growth, pp. 8–10. Arkell warned against appearing too precise: 'Multiplying Factors', p. 56.

[9] Hatfield's Survey, pp. 93–7.

Table 3.2 Village population estimates, early fourteenth century

	Bishop Middleham & Cornforth	Sedgefield	Fishburn, Mainsforth, & Moreton
Total dwellings	77	92	29
Russell model (3.51)	270	325	100
Howell model (3.7)	285	340	110
Broadberry et al. model (41.5)	320	380	120

Source: Hatfield's Survey, pp. 161, 178–92.

reaction' described by Britnell. As incredible as it may sound, men were forced to take lands.[10]

We are on firmer ground when assessing the population *c*.1383, although still at the mercy of models designed on the poll tax. The following estimates are made with the assumption that each tenant represents a household with the multipliers accounting for servants, and that there are no non-tenant household (such as sub-lessees); the Russell-based estimate includes his adjustment for non-taxpaying persons and the indigent. With a tenant population of 141, the models estimate a total population of 495–585 in the three main villages, with another 40–50 in the rest of the parish. The subletting in Durham suggests that these numbers could be low, but the subtenants may have been tenants of that or other villages as the names were not recorded.[11] The bishopric estate had an average tenant population only 20 per cent higher than in the late twelfth century, based on the number of tenants and empty or decayed dwellings. Bishop Middleham, Cornforth, and Sedgefield had 56 per cent more tenants in the late fourteenth century.[12] That only 18 per cent of dwellings lay vacant at the end of the century demonstrates some population recovery in the decades following the plague, although lack of records prevents knowing how much was from immigration. Dunsford and Harris concluded that 'in Durham the medieval expansion of settlement remained well within the margins of what was available, and that in *c*.1300 there was land available to be reclaimed using essentially medieval techniques.'[13] Durham had not reached its population limit before the disasters of the first half of the fourteenth century. With the different population models shown in Table 3.3, a comfortable

---

[10] R. Lomas, 'Black Death in County Durham'. p, 129 and pp. 112–16 and 'Durham Cathedral Priory', pp. 39–36; Piper, 'Size and Shape of Durham's Monastic Community', pp. 157, 159–60; Britnell, 'Feudal Reaction after the Black Death', esp. p. 31; Larson, *Conflict and Compromise*, pp. 74–5. Contrast this with other areas that experienced a quicker recovery: Hatcher, *Rural Economy and Society*, pp. 102–47; Levett, *Studies in Manorial History*, pp. 253–4; Harvey, *Medieval Oxfordshire Village*, p. 44.

[11] Subtenancy was not always present; see Whittle and Yates, '"Pays Réel or Pays Légal?"' pp. 18–19, 26, and Yates, 'Change and Continuities'.

[12] *Domesday Book supp. vol 35: Boldon Book*, pp. 24–7; *Hatfield's Survey*, pp. 180–92.

[13] Dunsford and Harris, 'Colonization of the Wasteland', p. 40.

Table 3.3 Village population estimates, *c.*1383

	Bishop Middleham & Cornforth	Sedgefield	Fishburn, Mainsforth, & Moreton
Occupied dwellings	55	86	12
Russell model (3.51)	195	300	40
Howell model (3.7)	205	320	45
Broadberry et al. model (41.5)	230	355	50

Source: Hatfield's Survey, pp. 161, 178–92.

population estimate of around 550 to 650 persons seems tenable, although the villages could support more. Broadberry et al. found that the highest rates of population growth 1377–1600 were in Cumberland, Westmoreland, and Durham, all just over 50 per cent.[14] It is possible that rate is too conservative. The population estimates for these two parishes in the early modern period indicate that population doubled soon after the mortality of 1556–59. These may be well above average, balanced out by slower rates in other parts of Durham, but the county was underpopulated just as standards of living were rising; subsequent demographic growth could have been earlier and higher than thought.

Information on fertility rates is lacking until the series of surviving parish registers begins in the late sixteenth century. The bishop's administration simply was not interested in recording births or other milestones, such as joining a tithing, which Poos used to examine population trends in Essex.[15] The one instance in which mortality did concern them was on the death of a tenant. To ensure the correct inheritance of land, proclamations were made at the next three halmotes calling for the heirs to come forward and claim the lands. Although these proclamations were not always recorded in the halmote books, additional information about tenant deaths can be extracted from the conveyances. Together, these provide a long series of mortality data. There is an important limit: this is data only for tenants, who were predominantly male. Still, it provides a barometer as to whether mortality was 'normal' or 'crisis'. These trends for the three villages combined can be seen in Figure 3.1. The early fifteenth century was a period of higher mortality, with sharp spikes in 1399–1400 and 1416, which are reflected throughout the bishopric estate and resonated in more than just the land market. Mortality rates also rose in 1423, and it is possible that the beginning of the record series gap coincided with another year or two of high mortality. There is a gap in the halmote books from 1424 to 1438, when a relatively stable pattern emerges until a peak in the 1540s followed by a decline in tenant mortality in the middle

[14] Broadberry et al., *British Economic Growth,* pp. 36–7.
[15] Poos, *Rural Society after the Black Death.*

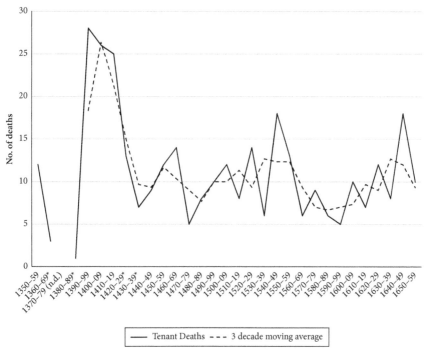

Figure 3.1 Tenant mortality, *c*.1349–1659 (decennial sums)
Source: Appendix A: Landholding Database.
= partial data.

to late sixteenth century, before peaking in the 1640s. That lower mortality rate in the second half of the fifteenth century could have enabled some population growth possible; the decline a century later coincided with such growth. This would go against what other scholars have found, but then, the county was under-populated relative to central and southern England.[16]

Early Modern Period

The parish registers for Bishop Middleham survive from 1559 and for Sedgefield from 1580 (with a gap from 1647–52). The baptisms and burials recorded in the registers may serve as a proxy for births and deaths, making it possible to recon-struct population change by working either forwards or backwards from a certain record. A crude rate of population change can be derived by subtracting the

---

[16] For example, see Poos, *Rural Society after the Black Death*, p. 109; Yates, *Town and Countryside in Western Berkshire*, pp. 41–44, 235–6; and Blanchard, 'Population Change', pp. 434–5.

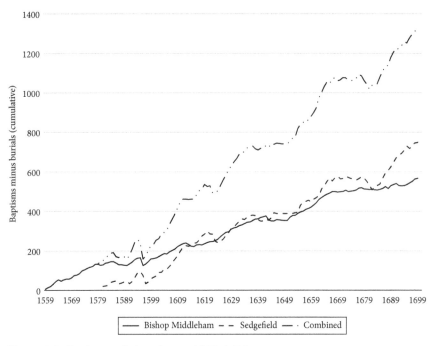

Figure 3.2 Crude population change, 1559–1699

Source: Appendix B: Baptism, Marriage, and Funeral Databases.

number of burials from baptisms each year for the three villages combined as shown in Figure 3.2, albeit with a significant caveat: the unknown variable is migration.[17]

The cumulative increase of population suggested in Figure 3.2 was not sustainable, and the population estimates discussed below underscore how many people left the parishes. Movement of people and families in and out of villages was a common part of life. In the fourteenth and fifteenth centuries such movement may have been small but did provide labour and marriages. In the sixteenth and seventeenth centuries, there was more migration in both directions. Many more men and women entered the parishes looking for love and work, while many others left for similar reasons. Surname evidence provides additional evidence of mobility. Surnames in the fourteenth and early fifteenth century were still fluid, so some men and women had only locative surnames (e.g. William de Heighington), while some with a surname were tagged in the records with a locative identifier, and sometimes to indicate origin rather than to distinguish them from others of the same name. Some had occupational identifiers that sometimes were and

---

[17] In her analysis, Issa found a downward trend, with burials outnumbering baptisms: 'Obligation and Choice', pp. 71–2.

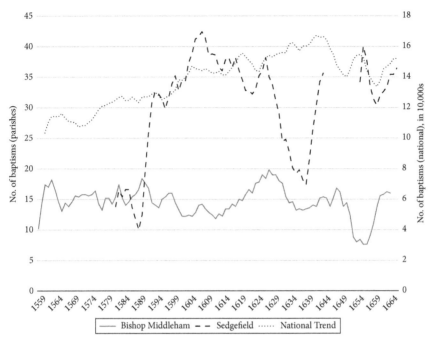

Figure 3.3 Baptisms, 1559–1660 (five year moving average)

Source: Appendix B: Baptism Database; 'National Trend' derived from Wrigley and Schofield, eds, *Population History of England*, pp. 537–83.

sometimes were not treated as surnames, such as John Forster Piper or William Johnson Souter. Variations in translation practice and orthography add additional uncertainty: were John Addy, John Adamson, and John Atkinson the same man? However, the importance to the bishopric administration of identifying tenants permits us a fair amount of certainty in using surnames to study the villages, although linguistic evolution and scribal practice alongside common surnames such as Smith and Johnson put limits on any conclusions on relationships without additional evidence, even after surnames stabilized around the middle of the fifteenth century. *Hatfield's Survey* contains 104 recorded surnames in the villages, nearly all of which represented resident families.[18] From the 1430s to 1660, the halmote records contain around 250 surnames representing resident landholding families, plus about two dozen surnames representing non-resident outsiders and special transactions. In the *Parliamentary Survey*, only 65 surnames were recorded

---

[18] *Hatfield's Survey*, pp. 161, 178–92. I have made no attempt to calculate migration or mobility based on surnames in different records. For one, the absence of a surname might mean the family was in a neighbouring village only to return later. Second, tracing families in that manner has a patriarchal bias; did not the family remain when a daughter married? From early modern wills, sons-in-law often were considered as family, and bequests to grandchildren did not necessarily differentiate those by a son versus those by a daughter. For a similar situation, see Nair, *Highley*, p. 157.

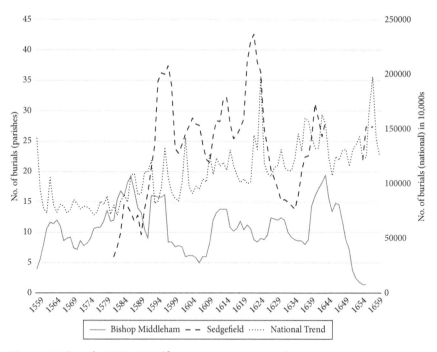

Figure 3.4 Burials, 1559–1660 (five year moving average)

Source: Appendix B: Funeral Database. 'National Trend' is derived from Wrigley & Schofield, eds, *Population History of England*, pp. 545–48.

but the parish registers reveal over 500 surnames from the late sixteenth to the mid-seventeenth centuries, and thus far more families. Some of these families held land in the other settlements, and others would have been subtenants, but others were landless, serving as household or agricultural labour. Stratification and landlessness had increased with the population.

The baptismal rate (Figure 3.3), our proxy for birth rate, was steady in Bishop Middleham parish, around fifteen baptisms per annum until the 1650s, necessitating that the major growth in population in that parish occurred earlier, especially in comparison with the national trend. For Sedgefield, the rate appears to rise sharply at the end of the sixteenth century, indicating either underreporting before then or a significant population influx that could generate such a rise in the number of births. The baptism rate in Sedgefield then declined slowly for the 1610s and early 1620s, and the resurgence in the later 1620s was followed by a sharp drop in the 1630s, returning to the earlier high level in the 1640s and remaining there until rising to new highs late in the century.

While the burial/mortality rates (Figure 3.4) of the two parishes frequently mirrored each other, the parish of Sedgefield demonstrated far more variability in both the number and severity of spikes in mortality. Again, the rate for Sedgefield

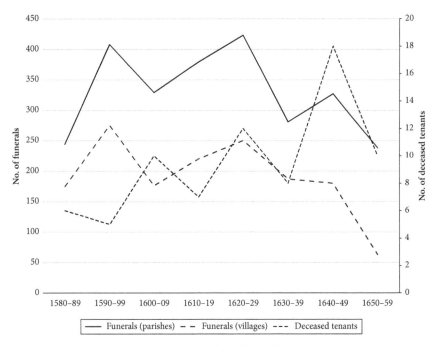

Figure 3.5 Comparison of mortality trends, 1580–1660

Source: Appendix A: Landholding Database; Appendix B: Funeral Database.

indicates either undercounting before 1600 or a sudden and prolonged mortality crisis.[19] This returns us to the question of mortality among tenants. Figure 3.5 displays the number of burials in the three villages and in the parish against the number of tenant deaths. The mortality of tenants roughly follows that of the broader population, but not always, particularly in the 1590s and 1640s.

In terms of demographic expansion, the combined average rate of growth for these two parishes from 1580 to 1600 was +4.4 per year, enough to raise the population by 92 despite crisis mortality in 1597 (120 recorded burials). From 1600 to 1660 the net growth was even more impressive, an average of +11.1 per annum despite the missing Sedgefield records. That should have raised the population by more than 650 souls, but if the diocesan population and Protestation Oath return estimates are accurate, the actual population was shrinking. Errors and omissions in the registers account for some of this difference, but emigration must have been high before the Civil War and higher still in the following decades. Wrightson and Levine found that many of those employed in the mining at Whickham came from throughout Durham, and in that context, they noted

[19] Slack concluded that the 'crises of 1557–59 and 1597–98 were more serious on a national scale': 'Mortality Crises and Epidemic Disease in England', p. 21.

Sedgefield's relatively low population growth from 1563 to 1666.[20] Such a demographic situation is not unheard of; Zell found a similar pattern in the sixteenth-century Weald, with the population 'constantly changing, both through emigration and immigration'.[21]

For the sixteenth and seventeenth centuries, three 'snapshots' allow estimation of the population of the villages and parishes: the diocesan return of 1563, the Protestation Oath of 1641–42, and the Hearth Tax of 1666. Arkell devised a population multiplier of 4.3 using Hearth Tax records for the county, and Moore reached a multiplier of 4.75 using the 1563 and 1603 diocesan returns; Arkell's multiplier is used below to provide a more conservative estimation.[22] The first national census in 1801 provides a relatively accurate endpoint. The estimates from these sources and multipliers, shown in Table 3.4, show clear but complex population growth in villages and parishes.

The estimate for 1563 shows the population of Sedgefield more than doubled since 1383, which seems extreme except that the county's population more than tripled between 1377 and 1600, from 24,587 to 76,483, and parish register evidence indicates a similar story in Bishop Middleham and Sedgefield parishes.[23] The population was higher before the influenza epidemic of 1556–59, where Moore estimates a decline of 12 to 27 per cent depending on the county.[24] Bishop Middleham was the same size as the more well-known Earls Colne (Essex) and a third larger than Terling (Essex), although Earls Colne more than doubled in size between the early sixteenth and seventeenth centuries and Terling saw greater growth than Bishop Middleham.[25] Moving into the seventeenth century, the estimate from the Protestation Oaths of 1900 persons is reasonable compared to the Hearth Tax estimate of 1745 for the entire parish. Such a decline during the Civil War and Commonwealth periods is not implausible. The three snapshots imply substantial emigration during the seventeenth century when put beside data from the parish registers, which yield a crude net gain of population (total baptisms minus total burials). Going solely by parish register baptisms and funerals from 1563 onwards, the population of Bishop Middleham parish in 1666 would have been 870 persons and Sedgefield 1720 persons, if there had been no migration; but migration there was. Also of note is the earlier start to population growth in

[20] Levine and Wrightson, *Making of an Industrial Society*, pp. 186–7. Issa also noted 'modest' population growth: 'Obligation and Choice', pp. 68–73.

[21] Zell, *Industry in the Countryside*, p. 85. Hare found substantial migration in the late medieval period, often among local villages or for industrial expansion: *Prospering Society*, pp. 122–3.

[22] Moore, 'Population Trends in North-East England'.

[23] Broadberry et al., *British Economic Growth*, p. 25.

[24] Fisher, 'Influenza and Inflation'; Moore, '"Jack Fisher's Flu"'. and 'Demographic Dimensions of the Mid-Tudor Crisis'; Zell, 'Fisher's 'Flu and Moore's Probates'. This is significantly higher than the mortality proposed by Wrigley and Schofield, *Population History of England*, pp. 208–9.

[25] French and Hoyle, *Character of English Rural Society*, p. 51; Wrightson and Levine, *Poverty and Piety*, p. 45.

Table 3.4 Estimates and projections of population, early fourteenth century to 1801

	Bishop Middleham & Cornforth	Sedgefield	Other Settlements	Bishop Middleham Parish	Sedgefield Parish	Bishop Middleham Parish (projection)[a]	Sedgefield Parish (projection)[a]
Pre-1349	320	380	120	-	-	-	-
1383	230	355	50	-	-	-	-
1540s[b]	485	1045	230	485	1280	n/a	n/a
1563	430	925	205	430	1130	300	750
1641[c]	-	-	-	515	1385	505	1260
1666	450	700	595	500	1245	500	1245
1801	655	1184	1310	738	1756	855	2130

[a] Projected estimate if the parishes followed the national population trend identified by Wrigley and Schofield (backwards from 1666 to 1563 and forwards from 1666 to 1801).

[b] Estimate based on Moore's comparison of chancery certificates to the 1563 diocesan returns.

[c] Using Arkell's modifier of 4.3.

Source: *Hatfield's Survey*, pp. 161, 178–92; Moore, 'Demographic Dimensions of the Mid-Tudor Crisis', p. 1058; *Diocesan Returns* pp. 136–37; *Durham Protestations*, pp. 157–58, 179–80; *County Durham Hearth Tax*, pp. xcix, cxvii; Wrigley & Schofield, eds, *Population History of England*, pp. 531–33.

these villages, compared with the national trends calculated by Wrigley and Schofield as well as the estimates for Terling by Wrightson and Levine, implying that the earlier emergence of larger farms or new attitudes toward farming led to earlier growth.[26] However, that growth slowed significantly, reflecting the greater pull of mining. Kirby's estimate of population densities in mid-seventeenth century Durham puts these two parishes in the middle range of both density and land value per capita, with Bishop Middleham having a higher value and density than the geographically larger parish of Sedgefield.[27]

Family and Household

The history of population is, naturally, intertwined with that of the family and household, and all are significant in the economic development of the two parishes. Where family ended and household began was not as sharp as it might seem, as parents could treat children or other relatives as servants and employers look out for their servants as kin. The marriage patterns present, along with the increasing population and consequent number of servants, reveals another part of the economic potential of the county. The marriage patterns in the parishes contribute to a significant debate on women's employment and economic growth; the patterns also, by the seventeenth century, resemble those found elsewhere in England. Supposedly, much of the northeast retained an older, almost clannish notion of kinship, where extended family was of great importance. Issa tested that assumption using three Durham parishes and instead found all to resemble the nuclear households of southern England.[28] This study of Bishop Middleham and Sedgefield parishes confirms many of her conclusions, while offering some nuances, most importantly that a single parish alone is insufficient for studying kinship.

Marriage and Widowhood

Marriage is a crucial topic, and not solely for demography. Age of marriage, choice of partner, and other factors were determined by social, cultural, and economic contexts. While marriage was considered the norm in pre-modern England, some men and women never married while others married multiple

---

[26] Wrigley and Schofield, *Population History of England*, pp. 531–3; Wrightson and Levine, *Poverty & Piety*, pp. 45–6.

[27] Kirby, 'Population Density and Land Values', pp. 85–9.

[28] Issa, 'Obligation and Choice', esp. p. 120. James claimed the nuclear households of the south and east had 'no awareness of the extended family of uncles, aunts, and cousins, both of father's and mother's kin': *Family, Lineage, and Civil Society*, p. 21.

times.[29] Bennett chose a single peasant woman, Cecilia Penifader, as the subject of a biography and Froide has refocused attention on the importance of marital status for women in the early modern period.[30] Clear information on single-women in Durham is uncommon, however, and Müller has argued convincingly that married women are not always identified as such so there is a strong possibility that the number of married women in medieval villages has been underestimated.[31] Presentments for leyrwite (fornication by a woman) reveal some never-married women but most of those amerced were wives or widows.[32]

In late medieval and early modern England, most non-aristocratic marriages tended to be both companionate and relatively late, with both men and women waiting until their twenties to marry. Hajnal named this the European Marriage Pattern (EMP), although it is most associated with north-western Europe.[33] In this model, delaying marriage allowed men and women to work and save before starting a new household. This has led scholars to see it as a factor in economic growth and the Little Divergence, on its own and for its potential in developing human capital. For De Moor and Van Zanden, the 'co-evolution of the demographic regime and the emerging labour market helps to explain the strong commercialization of society economy that occurred' before the sixteenth century.[34] The pattern's positive role in economic development has come under fire from several directions. Bennett has found the pattern in England as early as the thirteenth century, and believes it could be older; more pointedly, she makes the case that it was a reaction to poverty. Dennison and Ogilvie demonstrated that the countries with the most extreme version did not have growing economies, whereas England and the Netherlands had a moderate regime.[35] Nonetheless, a moderate EMP must connect to economic development in some way.

Late medieval Durham provides an interesting viewpoint on this debate. Marriage to a widow was common from 1349 to the 1450s. The greater proportion of widows in the marriage pool does not preclude an EMP regime; marriage to a widow (or widower) could be analogous to delayed marriage. Durham's under-population and the tenurial distribution following the Black Death, on the other hand, implies fewer potential barriers to marriage. With no data on age at marriage, other evidence must come into play. The bishopric halmote books provide

---

[29] Wrigley and Schofield estimated 13–27% of those born between 1575 and 1700 remained single: *Population History of England*, pp. 257–65.

[30] Bennett, *A Medieval Life*; Froide, *Never Married*. See also Bennet and Froide, *Singlewomen in the European Past*, and Erickson, *Women and Property*.

[31] Müller, 'Peasant Women, Agency and Status'.

[32] On leyrwite, see Bennett, 'Writing Fornication'.

[33] Hajnal, 'European Marriage Patterns'.

[34] De Moor and Van Zanden, 'Girl Power', pp. 27–8; see also De Pleijt and Van Zanden, 'Accounting for the "Little Divergence"'.

[35] Bennett, 'Wretched Girls'; Dennison and Ogilvie, 'Does the European Marriage Pattern Explain Economic Growth?'; Humphries and Weisdorf, 'Wages of Women'.

information on tenant marriage for a little over a century following the Black Death: the merchet fines levied when the daughter of a customary tenant married and the *licensia vidualis*, permission to marry the widow of a customary tenant. The books recorded fines for fifty-seven maidens and fifty-two widows in the three combined villages from 1349 to 1464. Of those, nine likely involved someone marrying into or out of the village and seven were to servants who may or may not have come from the village, and the rest were between families already in the village. Looking at the two periods with best record survival, the average marriage rate works out to 2.7 marriages per annum for 1349–62, and from 1394–1424 the average was 2.1 per annum. Almost half the marriages involved a widow.

From 1569 onwards, marriages were recorded in the parish registers, in theory capturing more marriages, as shown in Figure 3.6. The trends in marriages are consistent with other demographic indicators. Bishop Middleham's registers reveal a steady rate for most of the period, with a sharp decline in the 1650s. The registers for Sedgefield show the increase to c.1600 although not as sharply as for baptisms and funerals, with a likely return to the earlier level in the 1640s and 1650s. Considering that the population of the villages was more than three times that of the fourteenth century and with far more emigration, the low marriage rates of the fourteenth and early fifteenth century based on merchet fines may in fact be very close to the actual marriage rate if non-tenant marriages were recorded. If that is the case, then the likely period of sharp population growth is sometime between 1450 and 1550, for Bishop Middleham parish and possibly for Sedgefield as well, with the latter experiencing another spurt of growth starting late in the sixteenth century.

For those individuals whose baptism and marriages are traceable in the parish registers, most married in their mid-twenties, with 26.4 the mean and 26.5 the median age of marriage for men and a mean of 23.9 and a median of 24 for women. This puts the marriage pattern at the same level as Terling.[36] However, far fewer men and women in these parishes married before the age of twenty. Only 10 per cent of men and 15 per cent of women were married in their teens, and at least one of those cases was due to a pregnancy. Many marriages were companionate, with an average of 3.8 years separating man and wife. In this way, these parishes eventually fit the EMP model for early modern England.

The dramatic shift in marriage patterns necessitates an even greater focus on widows. In turn, this reveals that widows played an important role in local landholding: the widely exercised right of a customary tenant's widow to his holdings for her life, a right not invalidated by remarriage.[37] Widow-right made these women very visible in the bishopric records and the contours of this practice are

---

[36] Wrightson and Levine, *Poverty & Piety*, pp. 47–50.
[37] Some husbands willed that the widow would lose goods or lands if she remarried.

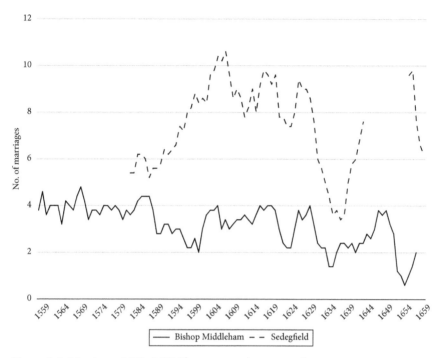

Figure 3.6 Marriages, 1559–1660 (five year moving average)
Source: Appendix B: Marriage Database.

further explored in Chapter 4. Until the advent of the parish registers, widow-right provides evidence of the length of widowhood. For some widows this was very short, because of remarriage or their own death. Cecilia del West remarried immediately, while Christiana Stevynson died fewer than two years after her husband.[38] Other widows lived quite long after their first husband's death. Alice Bentley died twenty-nine years after her husband Thomas, while Agnes Sander lived fifty-three years more according to the descent of her husband Robert's tenure.[39] The latter is far more than the average widowhood of twelve years, but it demonstrates what was possible.

Identifying widows who remarried is even easier before 1456 through the marriage fines. Although many English manors lumped all marriage fines under the term *merchet*, the halmote books differentiated between merchet and a licence to marry a widow. Because these were fines, marriages for both types of women are under-represented throughout the period due to evasion and after 1448 because

---

[38] TNA: DURH 3/13 ff. 309r, 329r, 421v; 3/14 f. 21r.
[39] TNA: DURH 3/23 ff. 228v, 302v; 3/24 p. 737; 3/26, f. 114r. Whittle also found instances of widows as long-term landholders, of nineteen and twenty years, although the average was just under six years: 'Inheritance, Marriage, Widowhood and Remarriage', pp. 59–60.

of the decline in enforcement. Of the seventy-one recorded fines, thirty-eight involved a widow (of whom twenty-three held land in widow-right), while another fifty widows holding land did not remarry (or were not fined). These numbers are comparable to the bishopric as a whole and at the higher end of what has been found for high and late medieval villages elsewhere in England after the Black Death. In post-plague Halesowen (Worcs.) Razi found that 26 per cent of widows remarried; there was a greater range on the Winchester bishopric estates, between 9 and 38 per cent in 1350–1415, but in Ramsey Abbey from 1397 to 1458 only about 10 per cent of merchet payments were by widows.[40] In some years, all the marriages recorded in the Durham halmote books were to a widow. Marrying a widow frequently cost more than marrying an unmarried woman. The merchet fine charged for a maiden was normally twelve pence although it could be halved or forgiven entirely; to marry a widow often cost twelve pence but could be substantially higher.[41] William Erby paid forty pence to marry Annabilla Headlam and John Py paid twice that to marry Juetta del Gate.[42]

Between 1464 and 1559 there is no data for marriages; evidence from conveyances in the halmote books indicates that four widows remarried.[43] With the parish registers, information on marriages becomes plentiful but not necessarily useful for finding widows; the priests (or their clerks) did not record whether a bride was a widow. In the funeral section of the registers, the clerks provided the husband's name when his wife died; when a man died, the clerk did not indicate his widow's name. When a widow died, sometimes the clerk simply entered her surname, as with Widow Noble (*vidua* Noble) in 1581. Even when the clerk provided a first and last name for a widow, he did not provide the name of her pre-deceased husband, which is surprising as community constructed the widow's identity as the relict of her deceased husband.[44] Acknowledging these difficulties, analysis of the registers indicates approximately 13 per cent of marriages between 1559 and 1662 involved a widow. Widows who held land are more readily traceable, and only five of forty-seven such widows remarried. Remarriage (for

---

[40] Smith, 'Some Thoughts on the "Hereditary" and "Proprietary" Rights'; Bennett, 'Medieval Peasant Marriage', p. 205; Mullan and Britnell, *Land and Family*, p. 105. Mate observed an increase in widows remarrying in fifteenth-century Suffolk: *Daughters, Wives and Widows*, pp. 126–7; see also Spufford, *Contrasting Communities*, pp. 116–18. The numbers before the plague varied from 6% in Brigstock (Hunts.) to as high as 63% in Halesowen (Worcs.): Bennett, *Women in the Medieval English Countryside*, p. 146; Razi, *Life, Marriage and Death*, p. 138; Titow, 'Some Differences between Manors', p. 8; Franklin, 'Peasant Widows' "Liberation" and Remarriage', p. 193.

[41] Larson, *Conflict and Compromise*, pp. 41, 94–7. The difference between these fines was less pronounced than in Cottenham before the plague, where Smith found that one man paid five marks to marry a widow, but a father paid only two shillings for the marriage of his daughter: Smith, 'Some Thoughts on the "Hereditary" and "Proprietary" Rights', pp. 124–5.

[42] TNA: DURH 3/14 ff. 143r, 417r. There is insufficient evidence to speculate confidently about sex ratios in Durham before the seventeenth century. Bardsley estimated that the sex ratio was around 110–15 men for every 100 women: 'Missing Women'.

[43] TNA: DURH 3/18 f. 21r.

[44] Durham County Record Office, Sedgefield Parish Registers, EP/Se 1/1, 2.2.

women) had become less common as population rose, and this is now in line with findings for other English communities, where widows comprised 11 to 17 per cent of brides.[45]

The extent of women's agency when it came to (re)marriage is a major point of debate. Hanawalt saw greater choice and agency for rural widows and Fleming has described the late medieval period as a 'golden age' for those widows who had property, while Franklin talked about widows' 'liberation', linking remarriage with economic necessity.[46] Landless widows may have remarried out of necessity. Widows *with land* certainly had more options but over two-thirds did not remarry. One who did remarry was Annabilla Headlam. She waited over a year to remarry, her holdings in widow-right were substantial and she could have sublet them or let her son work them. Her second husband, William Erby, was a smith. His own agricultural skills seem wanting, as the holding was run-down when Annabilla's son by her first marriage returned to take it up.[47] Agnes Pollard's husband William held a messuage and 15 acres by lease, which she took up when he died in 1399 and then surrendered to a new tenant later that year. In her own right she held a cottage and 4 acres, and she continued to brew ale for sale regularly until her death in 1408.[48] In 1409, Juetta widow of John Tose recused his 48 acres in favour of her son John, who sublet part back to her for her life. The next year she sued him in court for breach of contract, although her suit was dismissed, and later that year John's brother William successfully claimed that as elder brother he had the right to the holdings. One wonders whether Juetta may have been behind William's suit, or at least benefitted from it.[49] Joan Durand took up a messuage and two bovates of malland when her husband Hugh died in 1392; the lands went to her son Thomas two years later and then to his widow Alice in 1400, who promptly married William de Heighington a scant few months later.[50] Alice Stowe retained a cottage and 4 acres when she was widowed in 1407, passing the main holding of 30 acres on to her son.[51] Widow-right was not a homogenous experience.

[45] Erickson, in her study: *Women and Property*, p. 197, found only 17% of widows remarried. Holderness reported an aggregate rate of about 11% in the late seventeenth and eighteenth centuries: 'Widows in Pre-Industrial Society', p. 430. In Nair's small sample, no widows remarried: *Highley*, p. 49. Wrigley and Schofield estimated that as many as 30% of marriages in the period involved a previously married bride or groom: *Population History of England*, pp. 258–9.

[46] Hanawalt, *The Ties That Bound*, p. 220 ff.; Fleming, *Family and Household in Medieval England*, p. 91. Franklin, 'Peasant Widows' "Liberation" and Remarriage'; Bennett, 'Widows in the Medieval English Countryside', p. 103. Gates consciously moved away from considerations of the land market, looking at other economic, demographic, and social factors affecting widows and remarriage: 'Widows, Property, and Remarriage', pp. 19–22.

[47] TNA: DURH 3/15 f. 207v.

[48] TNA: DURH 3/13 ff. 309r; 333r; 3/14 ff. 664, 74v117r.

[49] TNA: DURH 3/14 ff. 123r; 166r; 174v.   [50] TNA: DURH 3/13 ff. 47r, 128v, 325v, 329r.

[51] TNA: DURH 3/14 ff. 56v, 66r.

In Durham and other parts of England, there was a decline in widows remarrying from the fifteenth century onwards.[52] Why did fewer widows remarry? The answer is the rapidly rising population. While some men in their wills stipulated that their widow might lose goods or non-customary lands if they remarried, many others charged a son with ploughing and manuring the widow's land and ensuring she had food, drink, clothing, and coal. Widows with lands had greater freedom of action, if not pressured to relinquish their holdings. The rising population may have limited opportunities to find land or employment elsewhere, encouraging sons to remain rather than leave. The general absence of remarriage by landless widows is readily explained by the rising population as well; men had more potential mates. Wills leaving money to 'poor widows' attests to the increasing poverty of widows in the seventeenth century.[53]

The combined evidence from fines and conveyances yields a picture different from that usually theorized for late medieval England. Marriage to a widow was frequent and remained so well after the initial shocks of the plague. Durham was underpopulated following the Black Death: labour was scarce, lands were vacant, and the proportion of widows in marriages was high. Widows likely could allow someone to work their land in exchange for support, which could be agreed upon outside the halmote court. Consequently migration, particularly local mobility, was for marriage or experience as much as to find work; several female servants married into the household where they worked while some sons left the village to return later for their inheritance. In this scenario, there was little need to delay marriage. The tenurial situation had settled c.1380–1420 and population began to recover in the later fifteenth and early sixteenth centuries, demonstrated by the increased population alongside larger farms, increased demand for land, and fewer widows remarrying. The EMP only emerged here in the later sixteenth century. The Durham evidence supports the arguments that the EMP was not a positive development for women, or a factor in encouraging economic growth. It was a result of growth, indicative of rising fortunes for some and declining opportunities for others, reflecting the commercialization of labour.

Family and Household Size

We have mainly anecdotal data for family and household size until the mid-sixteenth century. Across the board, the records depict families much the same as

---

[52] Mate observed a decline in widows remarrying in Sussex: *Daughters, Wives and Widows* pp. 126–7, 132. For London, Hanawalt found a remarriage rate following the Black Death of 50% falling to 38% in the fifteenth century and then to 25–30% in the sixteenth: *Wealth of Wives*, pp. 106–7. On the other hand, Todd found higher remarriage rates for widows in sixteenth century Abingdon (Berks.): 'The Remarrying Widow', p. 61.

[53] Robert Wilkinson left 20d. each to twenty poor widows: DPRI/1/1622/W8.

throughout England: nuclear families, some with servants, a few with a widow or widower or some other kin. Parish families kept in touch with and thought of their kin outside the household; wills mention siblings, cousins, nieces and nephews, with in-laws often treated the same as blood relatives.[54] Evidence from the halmotes suggests that two or three children were common in the later Middle Ages, and while the records of land transfers name only the nearest heir, in some cases additional children can be traced. Some households had servants, both local women and immigrants. The overall impression is that a tenant with a husbandland would be married with two children and perhaps employ a servant. Those with two husbandlands or more would have had one or two servants, if available. The increasing population at the end of the Middle Ages implies that the average number of children was creeping up to an average of three, as found using early modern sources.

Unlike in Terling, the age of a woman at marriage made little difference in the number of baptized children, although couples who migrated and baptized children in other parishes may be skewing the results here.[55] Children were traced for 345 out of 837 married couples in the baptism recorded for the parishes. The overall mean number of children was 2.98, which aligns with the mean of 2.92 in those marriages where the age of the wife at marriage is known. The median number for both sets was 2. This compares well with the more limited data from wills. Based on the dates of marriage and baptism, sixty-two brides were pregnant when they married, and about one third of these gave birth within three months. Another eighty-six couples had their first child baptized in one of the parishes nine months to a year following the wedding, and seventy-seven in the second year following marriage. After that, the number of couples with their first baptized child drops off quickly: thirty-eight in the third year, and twenty-four in the fourth year. Even at that point, this is speculative, as children, especially those of landless couples, may well have been baptized in another parish.

The data on family size, while limited and incomplete, shows that many families preferred two to three children; only a third of families had more than three children and 13 per cent had six or more children. This shows a pattern of family size and childbearing like that of Terling.[56] Some families were very large.

---

[54] Wrightson, *Earthly Necessities*, pp. 30–4; Laslett, 'Introduction: The History of the Family', pp. 26–34, 39–40, and 'Mean Household Size in England'. The nature of the Durham household has been debated. James claimed the north and west of the county had lineage-style households with the more populated south and east of the county containing nuclear households: *Family, Lineage, and Civil Society*, p.21. Chaytor argued that a complex household was common: 'Household and Kinship'. Wrightson concluded that 'there was a general cultural preference for the nuclear family household as the usual residential arrangement': 'Household and Kinship in Sixteenth-Century England', p. 154. Issa found nuclear households to predominate although more than two-thirds of testators acknowledged kin outside their household: 'Obligation and Choice', p. 120.

[55] Wrightson and Levine, *Poverty & Piety*, pp. 47–50.

[56] Wrightson and Levine, *Poverty & Piety*, p. 51.

Marmaduke Blakiston, rector of Sedgefield 1599–1631, had eleven children in one marriage: eight sons and three daughters. He could afford it, as he was a scion of the Blakiston family and his maternal grandparents were Sir William Bowes of Streatlam and Muriel daughter of Sir William Eure of Witton, three major armigerous families of the county. He was well-connected in ecclesiastical circles, as well: three sons followed him into the church including his son Robert, who married a daughter of Bishop John Howson and succeeded his father as rector of Sedgefield, while his daughter Frances married John Cosin, future bishop of Durham. Marmaduke's second son, John, would be one of the Regicides, and another son, George, after a rough time as sheriff, emigrated to Maryland.[57] Having many children could concern even those with sufficient wealth, however. Francis Barker (d.1628), a yeoman, stipulated in his will 'whereas yt hath pleased almightie god to blesse me with many children vidt. six by my first wife and other six by this wife' each would receive a legacy so that they would not 'molest her for any further part or portion of my goodes'. Others did not worry; Robert Hixon (d.1630) managed to see all six daughters married and could concentrate on his son.[58] Not all families possessed the wealth, connections, and good fortune, however.

The wills also reveal households without children. Testators left goods to their spouse, siblings, nieces, and nephews but there is no indication of children alive or deceased. Robert Maddison left bequests for his brother, his sister's three children, and a cousin. Ann Gadge left bequests of varying worth to her sister, cousin, nieces, and nephews, and named one nephew an executor.[59] William Richardson of Sedgefield mentioned five siblings, one of whom had six children. Local mobility prevents drawing conclusions on childlessness from the marriage and baptism records, but as baptisms are traceable for less than half of recorded marriages, this supports the impression drawn from probate records.

Servants were common in the wealthier households but could be found lower down the social scale, too.[60] Two to four domestic servants, mainly women from local families, were not uncommon for yeoman households. James Hall had at least one servant, Elizabeth Litster, and possibly two more, Anne Widdifield and Christiana Hutcheson.[61] Samuel Walker had five servants, three men and two women (one a widow).[62] The line between child and servant could blur, for instance when the halmote clerk identified Joan Proudlok as 'daughter and servant' of her father John.[63] Some masters paid for their servant's merchet, whether marrying outside the household or to a son, as when William Ketill paid a shilling

---

[57] He had eight sons and three daughters; six were baptized at Sedgefield: J. Overton, 'Cosin, John', p. 264.

[58] DPRI/1/1628/B2/1, 1630/H5/1–2.   [59] DPRI/1/1621/G1/1, 1627/M1/2.

[60] For example, Foster used some unusually surviving sources to illuminate households in early modern Cheshire and Lancashire: *Seven Households*, esp. pp. 14–18, 77, 126–7. For information on servants in Yorkshire, see Goldberg, *Women, Work and Life Cycle*, pp. 158–202.

[61] DPRI/1/1613/H3/2.   [62] DPRI/1/1665/W4/1.   [63] TNA: DURH 3/14 ff. 211r.

for his servant Alice de Bedlington to marry his son in 1408.[64] English culture expected masters to control their servants just like their children; they were a part of the household too.

The Significance of Population Growth

The medieval population of Durham was stagnant or steady, while the early modern population of the villages was booming, both through birth and immigration. The implications for individual men and women are explored in later chapters. In a wider county context, the changing population levels in villages such as Bishop Middleham demonstrate the precocity of agrarian development alongside the different paths taken between 1349 and 1660. It also indicates the pressures put upon traditional society that transformed villages in different ways. Settlements on the bishopric, such as Bishop Middleham and Cornforth that retained their 'traditional' 'manorial' orientation, doubled in size over those three centuries, with remarkably stable baptism, marriage, and burial rates. Sedgefield, with its market, followed a similar path but was more dynamic, experiencing sharper peaks and troughs. Villages such as East and West Boldon, Killerby, and Middridge saw similar growth; other agricultural villages, such as nearby Heighington, had grown even larger; and some had shrunk. Strangely enough, several nearby Dean and Chapter villages experienced very little growth over the period: Billingham appears to have grown only 13 per cent between 1396 and 1666, Middlestone only 4 per cent, and Westerton declined 34 per cent. However, several of those parishes, including Billingham parish, had far larger populations based on the 1563 returns than in either 1396 or 1666. The differences are substantial enough; Billingham had an estimated population around 420 in 1396 and around 580 in 1666, but 965 in 1563. There must have been a larger poor and landless population than the proposed multipliers can account for. While there may have been little polarization among tenants, as Brown concluded, there must have been a significant gap between tenants and non-tenants just as in the bishopric.[65]

While many villages grew modestly, the more important towns, such as Darlington and Stockton, saw substantial growth as might be expected. The largest growth came in Tyneside and Sunderland. Whickham's population was five times higher in 1666 than c.1383, and Bishopwearmouth and Tunstall, near Sunderland, were nine times larger. Dean and Chapter villages such as Nether Heworth near Gateshead (nearly sixteen times larger) and Monkwearmouth (nearly seven times larger) shared in that industrial growth.[66] Urbanization

---

[64] TNA: DURH 3/14 f. 87v.   [65] Brown, *Rural Society and Economic Change*, p. 204.
[66] *Domesday Book supp. vol. 35: Boldon Book* and *Hatfield's Survey*, passim; *Durham Cathedral Priory Rentals Bursars Rentals*, pp. 31–67, 73–128.

had its pull, and coal and salt were drawing the growing population away from agricultural villages. The rapid population growth in agricultural villages provided the labour pool not only necessary for increased agricultural output in the villages and neighbouring farms such as Hardwick and Butterwick but also to support the growth of the coal and salt industries and trade.

This returns us to one of the tenets of 'agrarian fundamentalism': that enclosure and development led to the dispossession of much of the peasantry. Roberts and Hodgson noted depopulation due to enclosure in Durham, but some of these settlements had ceased to be true villages earlier.[67] As will be seen, the number of tenants shrank as husbandmen lifted themselves up into the yeomanry during a period of low population. The fertility and mortality among tenants suggest that these were a greater factor than dispossession. The number of tenants, or at least the number of men able to acquire and work larger holdings, was shrinking. At the same time, the overall population was rising rapidly. The result was increasing imbalance and stratification, not between tenants but between tenants and the landless. Consider the multipliers used to convert payers of the 1377 poll tax into a population estimate, ranging from 3.51 to 4.15, while the multipliers used to convert households to population estimates for the sixteenth and seventeenth centuries were 4.3 and 4.75. If the population estimates for the seventeenth century were used with the number of tenants listed in the Parliamentary survey to derive a multiplier of tenants to population, they would be 12.1 for Bishop Middleham and Cornforth, and an incredible 25.1 for Sedgefield.[68] It was not greedy yeomen and capitalist farmers who created a large landless population in the bishopric villages through dispossession, but the population itself.

Many people were leaving the villages but not always permanently. The tenant families in the parishes of Bishop Middleham and Sedgefield were stable even though they moved from village to village within the subregion and diversified their interests among the settlements. Some families were resident in the parishes for centuries, including the Bentlay, Grenell, Elstob, Reay, Hall, Headlam, Lambert, Mowbray, Mason, and Rawlyn families, and some were still resident in the twentieth century. Some newcomers established a connection through marriage, such as the Hardgills from Billingham who married into the Croud family, or John Colling who married a daughter of Thomas Bentlay.[69] It was unusual for a newcomer to simply take up land without a family connection. In the fourteenth

---

[67] Roberts, *Green Villages of County Durham*, p. 21; Hodgson, 'Demographic Trends in County Durham'.

[68] The nearby Dean and Chapter village of Cowpen Bewley had more than twenty-six persons per resident tenant: Brown, *Rural Society and Economic Change*, pp. 216–17; *County Durham Hearth Tax*, pp. xcviii, 43. The gross number of persons per total number of tenants was six, but many tenants were not resident.

[69] The precise dynamics are unclear. William Hardgill took land in Bishop Middleham in 1442; a George Hardgill in the following generation was the grandson of Robert Croud, while George's daughter married a Lambert: TNA: DURH 3/12 f. 60v; 3/15 ff. 105r-v; 3/18 f. 108r; 3/24 p. 737.

and early fifteenth centuries, most daughters and widows married men already within the parishes. Many men married within the parishes, sometimes to servants who may have come from outside looking for work.[70] Marriage to a woman in the village was no guarantee of gaining land. From 1600–60, a quarter at most of the new men marrying to the village became tenants (thirteen of fifty-two). Most women marrying into the villages (thirty of forty-five), on the other, hand, married into established tenant families.[71] These were not closed communities, but there were clear distinctions and little movement between those families with land and those without.

These long-established families did not always remain resident or hold land in the same village; they did not remain tenants of the same holdings; and sometimes members of the family were absent for years before returning. Yet there was a clear attachment to the locality, made possible by the bishopric administration and community culture. That attachment fostered a sense of community but also is indicative of individualism. As with so many other aspects of the parishes, they were not mutually exclusive.

---

[70] TNA: DURH 3/14 ff. 417r, 582v. Some masters took advantages of their servants. Raphe Davison of Bewley Grange, who was married, fathered a child on his servant Margaret Moreland, from Sedgefield, in 1540: Dolan, *Nurture and Neglect*, p. 199.

[71] See Appendix A: Landholding Database and Appendix B: Baptism, Fornication, Marriage, and Funeral Databases.

4

The Foundation of the Agrarian Economy

Land and tenure shaped and were shaped by local and national conditions. Landholding thus functions as a metric for broader changes in society, such as the progression from serfdom to freedom, or from medieval to early modern agricultural practice.[1] Land and society were inextricably intertwined, but neither determinative of the other. Furthermore, landholding epitomizes the mixture of tradition and innovation that is the hallmark of this period in England's history. The impersonal discussions of market velocity, the relationship of intra- and extra-familial transfers, and legal formulae all reflect (and in turn influence) very personal choices; attention to the human element truly reveals the dynamism of landholding. In these parishes, the mixture of administrative interests, community culture, and individual desire saw the rise of larger and larger farms that set these and other bishopric villages apart.

The keys to agrarian development, on which nearly all scholars agree, were personal freedom and secure tenure of land (whether by copyhold or leasehold). For most of England, historians see these as arising in the fifteenth and sixteenth centuries, as the demographic then economic shifts following the Black Death led to the de facto end of serfdom. Ambitious peasants acquired more lands to profit from the rising demand for grain, becoming yeomen, and eventually large, enclosed farms worked by wage labour would become the norm. The model is simple: freedom plus security led to engrossment and profit, which led to a greater disparity between rich and poor. The agrarian fundamentalism narrative privileges the development of agrarian capitalism in the South and East as a one-size-fits-all-eventually model and ignores the possible variations throughout England. Copyhold is a major example. Hoyle commented in 1990 that 'it is shocking that so little attention has been paid to the matter' of the emergence of copyhold, and despite subsequent work the process is still not well mapped for the late medieval period.[2] Another example comes from Kent, which shared in many of the general agrarian transformations but was shaped by a free peasantry and gavelkind

---

[1] French and Hoyle observed the variation in tenurial practices, reflecting local structures, often led to different histories of development: *Character of English Rural Society*, pp. 8, 30–2. Bailey saw fourteenth-century practices setting the pattern for variations in fixed-term tenures of the sixteenth century: 'The Transformation of Customary Tenures', p. 226.

[2] Hoyle, 'Tenure and the Land Market', p. 8. Also see Whittle, *Development of Agrarian Capitalism*; Bailey, *Decline of Serfdom*.

Rethinking the Great Transition: Community and Economic Growth in County Durham, 1349–1660. Peter L. Larson, Oxford University Press. © Peter L. Larson 2022. DOI: 10.1093/oso/9780192849878.003.0005

tenure.[3] The experience in many Durham villages confirms part of the accepted model, but not all of it, and even then, the experiences of bishopric and priory villages diverged. The different timeline of development and the different experiences between estates underline the great importance of freedom and tenure but also of community.

Tenure and the Tenurial Structure after the Black Death

Undeniably, the unusual situation of the Durham bishopric estate when the Black Death struck in 1349—the probable existence of copyhold tenure—made possible the different trajectory from southern England discussed above. Brown argued that the Durham estates were an example of path dependency, with patterns set during and in response to the fifteenth-century recession 'affect[ing] the distribution of profits between different types of lords and tenants in the sixteenth and early seventeenth centuries', and for these bishopric villages, at least, the roots went back even further, such that it might be better to talk about an agrarian evolution rather than a revolution.[4] On the Durham bishopric estate, copyhold likely had developed *before* the Black Death, and a new structure of landholding had emerged by the 1380s as the bishopric tenantry and administration hammered out a new modus vivendi in the wake of the plague.[5] Engrossment on the bishopric estate had begun by the late fourteenth century and several families emerged to join existing village elites. Along with low rents and entry fines this should have laid a foundation for swift accumulation of lands and greater polarization of society, but the land market was not driven by straightforward supply-and-demand.[6] Greater engrossment did not happen until much later and with different consequences from southern England.[7] On the priory estate, the prevalence of short-term leasing alongside greater fragmentation of holdings did not result in a more

---

[3] Easy alienation of the land offset the partible inheritance; Zell, 'Landholding', pp. 39–49.

[4] Brown, *Rural Society and Economic Change*, pp. 1–2, pp. 7–10. Brown focused on estate structure and the choices of each estate's administration, though naturally their relation to their tenants was a key factor; the bishopric's extensive approach to customary land granted bishopric tenants scope to chart their own destinies: *Rural Society and Economic Change*, pp. 9–10, 69–70, and Larson, *Conflict and Compromise*, pp. 225–40. This approach separates the bishopric villages from their priory neighbours as well as many villages throughout England, such as Earls Colne, where a new lord attempted to change relations: French and Hoyle, *Character of English Rural Society*, p. 81 ff. Dimmock saw class conflict as the root of agrarian capitalism: *Origin of Capitalism in England*. However, although class conflict could contribute to the development of agrarian capitalism, it was not a prerequisite.

[5] Bailey, Whittle, and Allen among others saw copyhold as developing out of customary tenure: Whittle, *Development of Agrarian Capitalism*, p. 64; Allen, *Enclosure and the Yeoman*; Bailey, 'Transformation of Customary Tenures', pp. 210–30.

[6] T. Lomas, 'Land and People in South-East Durham', pp. 131–8. Again, contrast with Cornwall's more active market and rising rents in the fourteenth century: Hatcher, *Rural Economy and Society*, pp. 122–47.

[7] Clifford, 'Settlement and Field Systems'.

active market. While a similar pattern of engrossment leading to yeomen took place, the formation of syndicates was itself another divergence from southern England. In this way, the Durham evidence challenges the traditional timeline and recipe for change, more so as each of the three villages of this case study took variants of a similar path. The history of the lands and tenures of Bishop Middleham parish parallels the dynamics of continuity and change seen in other aspects of life.

One of the distinguishing features of development on the bishopric was the early emergence of a tenure that was or would become tenure for life by copy of the court roll—copyhold. For Bailey, there were four significant parts in the development of copyhold: the decline of servile dues and labour services; tenants receiving a copy of the conveyance; removal of servile language in the conveyances; and fixed-term tenures.[8] Applying this paradigm to Durham is not straightforward. Suit of mill and merchet were levied on free men holding customary land as well as tenants of exchequerland and even some drengage tenants, although at lighter rates. The copy of the court roll (on the Durham bishopric, a court book) existed in 1349 and probably earlier. The customary tenures were not servile so there was no servile language to disappear.[9] Except for the emergence of tenures for fixed terms, the bishopric customary lands fit the rest of Bailey's criteria in 1349 or earlier. That does not mean that they did not change between then and the early modern period, rather it is better to speak of progression rather than a transformation from one type of tenure to another. The inapplicability of the model is yet more evidence of regional variations.[10] These villages in Durham are not representative of the English experience but are significant for two reasons: to articulate an alternative model of economic and social development, and as a foil for models and concepts based on central and southern England.

Despite superficial similarities, the general assumptions about land and tenure in the rest of England simply did not hold true for much of Durham, and did not hold true before the Black Death as confirmed by *Boldon Book* and the handful of pre-plague records of the Durham priory halmotes.[11] There was no simple division of lands into free and servile, but between works and money rent, which complicates one of the key processes in the end of medieval landholding in England: the transition from serfs holding lands for life for labour services, in-kind renders, and servile dues to free men holding land for monetary rents either by copyhold (with hereditary right provable by a copy of the court record) or for a fixed term (leasehold).[12] Historians had come to a consensus that the transition began late in

---

[8]   Bailey, 'Transformation of Customary Tenures', pp. 213–215, and *Decline of Serfdom*, pp. 87–95.
[9]   Larson, *Conflict and Compromise*, pp. 62–67, 91–94, 102–3.
[10]   Bailey, 'Transformation of Customary Tenures', p. 229. An exploratory study found similar developments in other north-eastern manors: Larson, 'Tenure and the Land Market'.
[11]   Larson, *Conflict and Compromise*, pp. 62–7.
[12]   For a summary of the scholarship see Bailey, *Decline of Serfdom*, pp. 21–2.

the fourteenth century after failed 'feudal reactions' (and the 1381 Rising) and lasted through much of the fifteenth, but Bailey's argument for a quicker transition that started soon after the Black Death is persuasive.[13] As it holds true for much of England, Bailey linked the tenurial change with the decline of serfdom more generally, demonstrating a correlation between changes in tenure and changes in personal servility.[14] In Durham, at least, many lands were held for money rents and light services even in the twelfth century, and for the remainder the shift from in-kind renders and services to money rent was connected to population change and lord–tenant relations, rather than to a decline in serfdom. The Durham evidence demonstrates that an absence of serfdom (and the association of unfree personal status and unfree tenure) may be necessary for changes in tenure, which would confirm the general link between the decline in serfdom and tenurial change. And yet some of the personal aspects of serfdom, the decline of which Bailey sees as part and parcel of tenurial change, continued to be exacted from free men and women in these villages because the dues were linked to tenures and not persons.[15] Copyhold was in place *before* serfs and servile dues disappeared in Durham. The relationship between the decline of serfdom and tenurial changes is more complex than anticipated and varies considerably by location. It is very possible that both resulted from the economic changes brought about by declining population and the subsequent renegotiation of rents and services.

Copyhold and Leasehold

Customary lands on the bishopric and priory estates were transferred by a process of surrender and admittance: at death or if the tenant decided to give or sell his holding to another, the land was taken into the lord's hand in the halmote court (or before an official outside of court) and then the new tenant took the land from the lord along with a copy (*copia* or *recordum*) of their admission. On the bishopric estate, tenants were using copies of the court record to prove their rights in the halmote as early as 1349.[16] Although the process of surrender and admittance maintained the lord's rights, customary lands were held for life with

---

[13] Bailey, *Decline of Serfdom*, pp. 16–36, and 'Transformation of Customary Tenures'. In western Berkshire, serfdom had all but disappeared with works commuted to rents by 1400: Yates, *Town and Countryside in Western Berkshire*, pp. 212–13, 244–6.

[14] See Whittle, 'Tenure and Landholding in England', p. 240.

[15] Bailey, *Decline of Serfdom*, pp. 37–41, 92–3; Larson, *Conflict and Compromise*, pp. 92–7.

[16] TNA: DURH 3/12 f. 4v; Larson, 'Tenure and the Land Market'. The earliest explicit reference to a copy of the admission is from 1358, when the steward demanded tenants exhibit them in court, with those who failed having their rent restored to the 'ancient rent': TNA: DURH 3/12 f. 195r; Larson, *Conflict and Compromise*, p. 147. Brown saw the development into copyhold and leasehold coming between *Hatfield's Survey* and an Elizabethan survey in the 1580s: *Rural Society and Economic Change*, pp. 97–100.

heritable right enforced in the halmote.[17] The earliest halmote books record tenants holding 'in right' (*in jure*) or, if deceased, as 'in right while they lived' (*in jure dum vixit*). The entries can be maddeningly abbreviated. Take, for example, 'Cecilia Rauf for one cottage with garden adjacent, which was in the tenure of Alice Rauf in right whence Dionisia sister of the aforesaid Cecilia renounces (or renounced) her right in court in favour of the said Cecilia, to have in right, to render the old rent, to perform to the lord etc.', or 'John Hewetson for one whole husbandland and five acres of exchequerland upon the moor, which were in the tenure of Alice del Gate in right while she lived, to have and render etc. to perform etc.'.[18] The search for a single, clear statement is not necessary, as we can accept the sheer number of conveyances containing the various pieces as evidence of an established usage (as well as a certain looseness about legal phrasing that is strikingly unusual). The phrase 'and to their sequels' did not appear until 1523, making the standard language 'in right while they live, having to them and to their sequels in right according to the custom of the court'.[19]

Despite the absence of clear language, Cecilia Rauf's was a hereditary tenure in practice and in the unwritten customary law of the Durham halmotes.[20] The halmote records reveal a clearly defined descent pattern for customary land. On the death of a tenant, a proclamation was made at three succeeding halmotes for the heirs to come forward and lay claim to the land. A widow had first right of refusal of all lands; widowers did not receive the same right, although they could acquire the land if the deceased woman's heirs refused the land. After the widow, the right went to sons individually by seniority; then to all daughters jointly, although in practice one would take the land and the others would decline the holding; then to grandsons individually by seniority; and after that there are too few instances to draw conclusions about priority. If no-one came forward, the land was taken into the lord's hand and could then be taken by someone from outside the family. Although the new tenant received the land in right, sometimes they were warned of the possibility that a relative could return and claim the land.[21] While the ten-

---

[17]   As it emerged elsewhere, copyhold was protected in both Common Law and Equity courts in the sixteenth century: Garrett-Goodyear, 'Common Law and Manor Courts'; Baker, *Oxford History of the Laws of England*, vol. 6, p. 648; Gray, *Copyhold, Equity and the Common Law*; French and Hoyle, *Character of English Rural Society*, pp. 8–10; Whittle, *Development of Agrarian Capitalism*, pp. 74–81.

[18]   TNA: DURH 3/13 f. 4v. *Cecilia Rauf pro uno cottagio cum gardino adjacente que fuerunt in tenura Alicie Rauf in jure unde Dionisia soror predicte Cecilie renunciavit jus suum in curia ad opus dicte Cecilie habendum in jure, reddendo antiquam firmam faciendo domino etc.*

[19]   *in jure dum vixit habendum eidem* [name] *et sequelis suis in jure secundum consuetudinem curiae.* TNA: DURH 3/22 p. 10.

[20]   A conflict over lands in Sedgefield came before Chancery in 1655, where it was decided that the phrase *sequelis in jure* was as good as *heres in jure* and thus the lands were heritable: TNA: C 5/25/58, Middleton v. Middleton.

[21]   Lands could also be demised 'at their own risk' (*suo periculo*). The halmote books do not explain this but imply two causes. The first is that the steward would admit a relative after the lands were forfeited into the lord's hand; the other is that the steward reserved the right to admit a 'better' tenant who would pay a higher rent or was more likely to work the land properly.

ant did not own the land in a modern sense, some surrender-and-admittances concealed sales of land from one person to another (as evidenced by pleas of debt or broken contract) and later, mortgaging of land.

One of the most significant changes in tenure and thus society across England was the widescale shift to monetary as opposed to labour rents. Heritable life tenures with rent primarily in money existed in the twelfth century, although the *firmarii, malmanni*, and other such tenants also owed light labour services. True commutation came later. The occurrence in 1349 of a term in the bishopric to describe this transformation into tenure for monetary rent, *pennyfarm*, coupled with the absence of any explanation in the halmote books as to how the rent was determined, implies that commutation for set rates existed before the plague.[22] The lack of bishopric halmote records before 1349 precludes any attempt to establish how widespread the practice was, but clearly it was not yet standard. This changed after the Black Death devastated the population of Durham. In his article on Bishop Hatfield's feudal reaction, Britnell explored how the difficulty in finding tenants to accept vacant lands led both to the feudal reaction and to a willingness to compromise.[23] One such compromise was the expansion of *pennyfarm* into an estate-wide phenomenon, beginning with the tenants of Sedgefield. In the spring of 1351, Thomas Shepherd agreed to take half the husbandland of Robert Yong (which earlier had been imposed on the entire village) for three years at *pennyfarm*, the commutation of the works owed at the manor into an unstated monetary sum. The steward struck this deal only 'if it pleased the lord bishop', but at the same court this was granted to the other tenants of Sedgefield and to the husbandmen of Cornforth for three years. The solution must have been acceptable as Thomas took the other half of the husbandland on the same condition in the next court. The practice spread to other villages; on an ad hoc basis, with the tenants of Cornforth gaining a year's extension for 1354 and the tenants of Sedgefield a six-year extension in 1355, although in 1356 they were required to come to the Exchequer at Durham on the Wednesday following the feast of the great Durham saint Cuthbert 'for measuring their works in cash'.[24]

In *Hatfield's Survey*, even though the old labour services were enumerated just as in *Boldon Book*, it is abundantly clear that money rent had become the conceptual norm, even if rents were paid in kind rather than in cash.[25] *Hatfield's*

---

[22] Earlier I interpreted *pennyfarm* as a lease akin to the *firmarii* of Sedgefield in *Domesday Book supp. vol 35: Boldon Book*, but it appears to relate more to the type of payment than to the tenure: Larson, *Conflict and Compromise*, p. 89; *Domesday Book supp. vol. 35: Boldon Book*, pp. 24–5.

[23] Britnell, 'Feudal Reaction'; Larson, *Conflict and Compromise*, pp. 77–141. Bailey expressed serious doubts about whether there were seigneurial reactions: 'Myth of the "Seigniorial Reaction"'.

[24] TNA: DURH 3/12 ff. 51r, 57r; 112v, 121r, 141r; Larson, *Conflict and Compromise*, p. 90. In 1360, the malmen of Sedgefield demanded an inquest into the value of their work services; 3/12 f. 265v. Other villages sought to hold their lands at 12d. per acre but the steward would not agree: TNA: DURH 3/12 ff. 53r, 73r; Britnell, 'Feudal Reaction', p. 43.

[25] Bolton, *Money in the Medieval English Economy*, pp. 21–3.

Survey provides a snapshot of the estate that remains relevant for the remainder of the Middle Ages, so much so that a new survey commissioned by Bishop Langley was never completed and the bishopric administration continued to refer back to *Hatfield's Survey* throughout the fifteenth century.[26] Holding land for monetary rent was so common by the late fourteenth century that there no longer was any reference to *pennyfarm*. Certain boon works, in particular mowing and transportation, were retained and occasionally employed. The collector of Sedgefield noted for 1397–98 that henceforth commutation would be at the lord's will. But little changed. The old 'manorial' system of regularly expecting rent in labour was now in the past.[27] Fourteenth-century records from the priory estate paint a similar picture of consistent commutation of earlier work services. These rentals did not enumerate services as *Hatfield Survey* did, but the commutation of works from the holdings with the heaviest services were listed under a separate heading and dues such as *wodladpenis* were broken out separately from the rent. The survival of many of the bursars' account rolls reveal some of the contours of the shift to regular commutation. Prior to the 1353–54 accounting year commutation was in the hands of the manorial bailiffs, but that year commutations were handled centrally and entered under a new section added to the account. The following year, commutations were listed by village rather than by individual tenant.[28] The administration of each estate left open the possibility of reversing the commutation, but for both a cash rent was the new normal.[29]

These estate records and particularly *Hatfield's Survey* present a deceptively static picture in which tenure in right was near universal. This can blind us to the dynamism of the villages. A prime example is the development of leasehold, seen by Brenner and Tawney as gateways to agrarian capitalism.[30] Originally applied to mills and demesnes, by 1410 leasehold could be applied to any type of land. Normally the steward required the 'ancient rent' and levied an entry fine of sixpence or occasionally one shilling.[31] The low entry fine and the length of term were significant differences between leasehold and copyhold at this point, but perhaps not the greatest difference, for leasehold was not secure, initially. Tenants

---

[26] Britnell, 'The Langley Survey'.

[27] CCB B/65/1, Collectors' Accounts, Stockton Ward. Customary works initially were included with the lease of certain demesne land as late as 1486: TNA: DURH 3/14 ff. 482v-483r, 499r; 3/17 f. 34v; and 3/18 f. 21r.

[28] *Durham Cathedral Priory Rentals: Bursar's Rentals*, pp. 71–128; Larson, *Conflict and Compromise*, p. 259 n.7.

[29] This is not to say that the rent could not be paid in kind, as the 1495–96 Rent Book for the bursar reveals: *Durham Cathedral Priory Rentals: Bursar's Rentals*, pp. 129–97. The rents were calculated in monetary terms, however.

[30] Tawney, *Agrarian Problem*, esp. pp. 200–14; for Brenner's and his critics' responses, see Aston and Philpin, *The Brenner Debate*. Allen rejects that argument: *Enclosure and the Yeoman*, pp. 21, 59, 70. Van Bavel and Schofield provide a highly useful overview of leasehold and its variations: 'The Emergence of Lease and Leasehold', pp. 11–30.

[31] The Priory ceased charging entry fines on leasehold by the 1420s: T. Lomas, 'Land and People', pp. 142–4; Brown, *Rural Society and Economic Change*, p. 53.

would be admitted to lands for a term of years, but with the warning that they would be ejected if someone came forward to take the land as normal, even if the holding were theirs by hereditary right. For example, John, the son of Thomas and Annabilla Headlam took up his father's land for twelve years 'unless in the meantime someone shall come who is willing to make fine for the said tenure'.[32] While leasehold carried no official hereditary right, it was not uncommon for sons to lease land held by their recently deceased father, and in four instances, the widow took the lands at lease.[33] Unlike priory leases, the terms of the bishopric leases became longer, from multiples of three years in the fifteenth century, to twenty-one year terms in the sixteenth century, and to three lives in the seventeenth century (which Bishop Cosin lamented).[34] As the length of the term increased, so did the security of the tenure, and the leases ceased to be recorded in the halmote books after 1505, although some had been absent for decades at that point.

Leasehold quickly replaced copyhold for nearly all husbandlands in Cornforth and for a substantial number in Bishop Middleham and Sedgefield as well, although copyhold predominated. Leases comprised only 26 per cent of conveyances in Bishop Middleham and 35 per cent in Sedgefield, and in both renewals were rare, fewer than 15 per cent of all leases. Leasing became dominant in Cornforth, but in 1509–10 the administration ceased recording of leasehold for the village in the halmote books, after which only sporadic conveyances would be recorded. The different experiences but similar chronologies demonstrate just how dangerous it is to generalize about landholding even within a small unit such as a parish.[35]

Those differences mean that we should explore the bishop's motivations as potentially dynamic as well, even though the overall trajectory of estate administration largely was a hands-off affair, and that we must consider the relative strength of landlord and tenants.[36] It is not clear whether lord or tenants initiated the practice of leasing, but the terms suggest that the lord was not the main beneficiary. Instead, the tenantry was the driving force for leasehold and the trends in that tenure's popularity become windows onto the changes in the parish, as will be seen in later chapters.[37] Men in all three villages experimented with holding land for a term of years but the outcomes were different. In Bishop Middleham and Sedgefield, the flexibility of leases was attractive, at least for a time, while in Cornforth it all but displaced copyhold. Leases offered the tenant the ability to

---

[32] TNA: DURH 3/15 f. 111v.   [33] TNA: DURH 3/15 ff. 76v, 386v; 3/16 f. 277v; 3/20 f. 97r.

[34] Brown, *Rural Society and Economic Change*, p. 96; *Correspondence of John Cosin*, vol. 1, p. 27.

[35] The same is true for neighbouring bishopric villages. In Stockton Ward, Brown found that 59% of rents in 1588 came from copyhold: Brown, *Rural Society and Economic Change*, p. 94.

[36] Larson, *Conflict and Compromise*, pp. 225–40; Brown, *Rural Society and Economic Change*, pp. 48–56.

[37] On local dynamics and the emergence of leasehold, see Bailey, 'Transformation of Customary Tenures', pp. 222–7; Whittle, 'Individualism and the Family-Land Bond', pp. 53, 58 and *Development of Agrarian Capitalism*, pp. 70–2 ; Faith, 'Peasant Families and Inheritance Customs', pp. 88–92.

change lands, perhaps even to try out a new holding. This was important for men who had yet to hold a full husbandland, but it offered an opportunity to experienced tenants as well. The tenant had the flexibility to renew the lease or walk away, and generally paid a smaller entry fine than for copyhold. The average leaseholder in the 1410s paid sixpence for a three- or six-year lease, while the average copyholder of a husbandland paid just over 3s. 8d.

For the bishop, leasehold was a way to make something of a difficult situation. The holding had a tenant who could be replaced by a copyhold tenant when the lease ran out. Even if the lease were renewed, the steward could collect another small entry fine no matter how small the holding. But many of the men who took leaseholds could have afforded the entry fine anyway.[38] In some cases the steward may have offered or been asked for the shorter-term lease as a sweetener to take up a dilapidated tenement, and sometimes reductions in rent were included as well, as when the steward gave the first eight lessees in Sedgefield an allocation towards their rent in 1399.[39] That further indicates that the lord was not the only beneficiary of leasing. Leasehold allowed the steward to compete with Durham priory for much-needed tenants, while the bishop usually retained the right to oust the lessee if someone was willing to pay the full rent or take it for life. Finally, the inability or unwillingness to take advantage of the market by charging higher rents and entry fines for leasehold lands coupled with the continuing vitality of copyhold demonstrates that the bishopric administrators were not in control of leasehold. Even if leasing had begun as a seigneurial initiative, the power was in the hands of tenants.

Copyhold tenure in the bishopric villages remained little changed from the fifteenth century. Leasehold on the bishopric experienced two changes, one the lease for lives, the other the fixing of the fine for leasehold at a year's rent. In the sixteenth century, a prolonged fight on the Dean and Chapter estate led to the establishment of 'beneficial leasehold' in 1626, in which tenants enjoyed fixed rents for twenty-one year leases in exchange for fines to renew that were based on the value of the land rather than the rent. On both estates, the tenants enjoyed security of tenure, but Dean and Chapter tenants relied on leases and faced higher fines, differences that would affect the fortunes of lands and tenants.[40]

The Land Market

The weakness or indifference of the bishops turns the land market into an important barometer for understanding the transition from medieval to early

---

[38] Larson, *Conflict and Compromise*, pp. 201–2.   [39] TNA: DURH 3/13 f. 285r.
[40] For the development of beneficial leasehold, see Morrin, 'Merrington: Land, Landlord and Tenants'.

modern in these villages. It functions as the backbone for much of this book, using a database containing all of the land transactions and land- or tenure-related entries for these villages found in the bishopric halmote books.[41] A broad definition of the land market is employed here; although technically the land market should exclude inheritance, post mortem conveyances are included because these still record a holding changing hands and the new tenant still had to choose whether or not to take the holding.[42] Transfers of holdings such as the mills, the common ovens, and occasionally even the vills themselves are discussed elsewhere and not contained in the following analysis of the land market, rents, and entry fines. Demesne lands are included, however, as they frequently were a regular part of the land market and peasant holdings, but intact and separated into parcels.

Figure 4.1 shows the number of *inter vivos* transfers, leases, vacant tenures taken from the lord's hand, post-mortem transfers (including widow-right and inheritance), and other transfers of copyhold and demesne land, meadows, and pasture. Lomas was pessimistic in his characterization of the land market of south-eastern Durham as 'slack', but for some years in the early sixteenth century 'non-existent' would seem a more accurate description of the land market in these villages, certainly in comparison with Whittle's analysis of Hevingham Bishops in Norfolk.[43] A closer look at the market for these villages suggests a more complex situation as the market experienced several significant trends and developments. The land market in the 1380s to 1420s reflects continuing adjustments following the Black Death alongside the dynamism of the experimentation with leasehold. The effects of the fifteenth-century recession can be seen from the 1440s to 1480s, with one reaction being an increase in leasing.[44] Leasehold's initial impact on the land market is evident, and the decision to omit the records of leasing husband-lands in stages during the fifteenth century gives the illusion of a more stagnant market in the sixteenth century. The land market does not reach its earlier heights of *inter vivos* transfers until the seventeenth century. There are deeper currents to

[41] See Appendix A: Landholding Database. The nature of the records made this a different database from the one constructed by French and Hoyle for *Character of English Rural Society* (discussed there on pp. 181–209), and their analysis of the turnover of individual holdings rather than of the aggregate is not possible. T. Lomas wrote a 'tenure and mobility' style doctoral thesis comparing villages held by the bishopric (although not Bishop Middleham, Cornforth, or Sedgefield), Priory, and other lords. He made his calculations for the period c.1350 to c.1500 rather than by year or decade, missing some nuances such as the prevalence of subletting: 'Land and People', pp. 112–14.

[42] Historians have offered different definitions of the land market; see Harvey, *Peasant Land Market*, p. 4; Hyams, 'Origins of a Peasant Land Market', p. 19. Whittle critiqued these and other definitions and fashioned her own around the choice of the holder of the new tenant: *Development of Agrarian Capitalism*, pp. 94–5.

[43] T. Lomas, 'Land and People', pp. 131–8. Whittle, *Development of Agrarian Capitalism*, pp. 102–4. Whittle and Yates found a slow land market in Berkshire: '"Pays Réel or Pays Légal?"' p. 16.

[44] On the fifteenth-century recession, see Hatcher, 'The Great Slump of the Mid-Fifteenth Century'. Pollard believed that the North came out of the recession later, although Brown disputes that: Pollard, *North-Eastern England*, pp. 78–80; Brown, *Rural Society and Economic Change*, pp. 29–72.

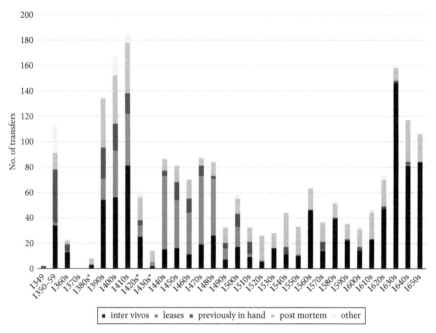

Figure 4.1 Transfers of copyhold land, 1349–1659 (decennial sums)
* = *partial data.*
Source: Appendix A: Landholding Database.

those patterns. For example, for most of the fifteenth century *inter vivos* transfers were predominantly extrafamilial, that is, men and women surrendered lands to tenants outside of their immediate family, and in most decades less than 10 per cent of all such transfers went to another family member. Lands were more likely to stay in a family after a tenant's death with anywhere from 15 to 55 per cent of post-mortem transfers in any decade going to the widow or a relative, in contrast to what was observed for Wiltshire and the Midlands.[45] Starting in the 1490s (although signs can be seen earlier) those patterns shifted, in line with the increasing population. There was a stronger preference to retain lands within a

---

[45] Appendix A: Landholding Database. T. Lomas found similar rates of *inter vivos* and post-mortem transfers within the family: 'South-East Durham', p. 298. Hare found 'a quarter or a third' of post-mortem transfers going to a widow or relative, varying based on local conditions: *Prospering Society*, pp. 132–4. Razi noted a decline from 71% to 26% after 1430: 'Myth of the Immutable English Family', pp. 28–9. Including *inter vivos* transfers is a different matter; the villages' land market exhibited a weaker family-land bond compared to what has been found elsewhere: Faith, 'Berkshire: Fourteenth and Fifteenth Centuries', pp. 14–15; Whittle, 'Individualism and the Family-Land Bond', pp. 33, 45 and *Development of Agrarian Capitalism*, pp. 119–25; Harvey, *Westminster Abbey and Its Estates*, p. 324; Mullan and Britnell, *Land and Family*, p. 89. Razi rejected the idea of a weakened bond, arguing that it was harder to see: 'The Erosion of the Family-Land Bond', pp. 295–304. Alan Macfarlane argued that peasants had a deep connection with their land that was destroyed by increasing individualism: *Origins of English Individualism*, esp. pp. 18–21.

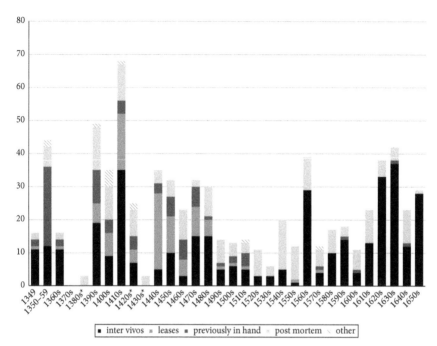

Figure 4.2 Bishop Middleham: Transfers and leases of copyhold land, 1349–1659
(decennial sums)

*= partial data

Source: Appendix A: Landholding Database.

family and on average 30 per cent of *inter vivos* transfers were to family members,
although in some decades nearly 70 per cent of such transfers went to a relative,
while on average holdings stayed in the family post mortem 75 per cent of the
time.[46] Although the halmote books no longer recorded leasehold on a regular
basis, the surviving sixteenth- and seventeenth-century rentals suggest similar
trends were operating for these tenures as well. The land market was more complex
than assumed.

The complexity of the market is especially true when examining the market for
each village, as shown in Figures 4.2–4.4. As would be expected, the broad contours of land market activity are the same for each village. Yet the types of transfers experienced significant variation, most pronounced in leasehold. In each
village, leasehold debuted around the same time, but for Cornforth very quickly it
became standard and thus evidence of the Cornforth land market was virtually
non-existent after 1510 when leasehold disappeared from the halmote books. The
tenants of Bishop Middleham quickly resumed their preference for copyhold.

---

[46] Dyer suggested *inter vivos* transfers increased in the sixteenth century because available holdings
elsewhere had dried up: *Lords and Peasants*, p. 304 ff.

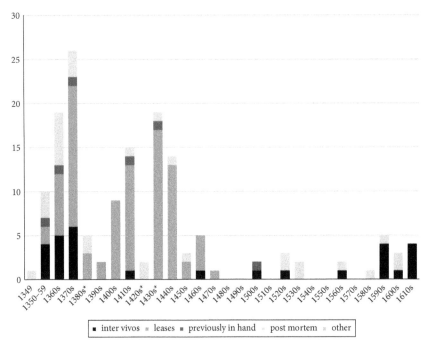

Figure 4.3 Cornforth: Transfers and leases of copyhold land, 1349–1659 (decennial sums)

* = partial data

Source: Appendix A: Landholding Database.

Looking beyond tenure, the land market in Sedgefield was much more stable, generally around forty per decade in the latter part of the fifteenth century, falling to around twenty transfers for most of the sixteenth and into the seventeenth century before rising sharply in the 1630s. There were far more peaks in Bishop Middleham in the sixteenth and seventeenth century with a peak in the 1620s and 1630s and then falling back. There are broad similarities between all three villages, but each responded to its own dynamic.

Widow-Right

Landholding by widows was a small but regular feature of Durham society.[47] On the Durham bishopric estate, the widow had first right of refusal to her deceased husband's holdings of customary land. Most widows took at least one holding and even as other aspects of society and economy were transformed in this

---

[47] For an extended discussion of widows and landholding in Durham, see Larson, 'Widow-Right in Durham'.

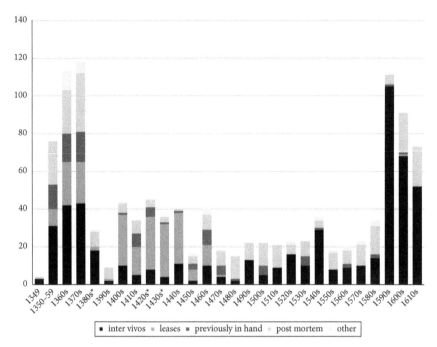

Figure 4.4 Sedgefield: Transfers and leases of copyhold land, 1349–1659 (decennial sums)

* = partial data

Source: Appendix A: Landholding Database. Excludes transfers connected to the enclosure process.

period, widow-right persisted.[48] The institution of widow-right in Durham was an extension of the relationship of man and wife; the widow maintained the link between tenant and tenure. Unlike a jointure, she had no independent right and the lands remained linked to her husband. Interestingly, this interpretation of widow-as-relict generated no restrictions on her right to remarry.[49] The wording of some conveyances reflects this by referring to both her current and past

[48] Larson, 'Widow-Right in Durham'. Hare found a different pattern: *Prospering Society*, pp. 134–6. Common Law governed goods and freehold lands. The right of a widow to some or all her deceased husband's customary land is normally referred to as free bench or dower; the amount of land involved, process, and conditions varied: *Select Cases in Manorial Courts 1250–1550*, pp. cxxi–cxxvii. In some areas, widows had no right to the lands: Whittle, 'Inheritance, Marriage, Widowhood, and Remarriage', pp. 40, 48–49, 56–9.

[49] Compare with Ravensdale's findings for Cambridgeshire: 'The Transfer of Customary Land', pp. 209, 216–17. There, because of the high fine to marry a widow with land (and because fornication or marriage could cost a widow her lands), marriages to widows declined sharply after the Black Death, and widows ceased taking on lands that they could not work. His case study shows some similarities (intact holdings, *inter vivos* transfers, widow-right in the whole holding, higher fines to marry widows) but different outcomes.

husbands, such as 'Agnes widow of John Webster now wife of Richard Brewster' or 'Alice Yong now wife of Robert Yong recently widow of Brian Lamb'.[50]

The halmote books contain 410 land transfers following the deaths of 326 different male tenants in the parishes between 1388 and 1660.[51] Of those male tenants, 169 left an identifiable widow of whom 139 chose to take possession of some or all of their husband's holdings.[52] The adoption of leasehold greatly reduced the opportunities for widow-right, with exceptions such as Juetta del Gate who received a 'license to occupy [Robert's] tenure' in Cornforth for the remainder of the year and then married John Py, who took del Gate's lands at lease.[53] Looking solely at the period after 1438 for which nearly continuous records survive, 230 male tenants left 103 widows of whom 92 took their right. That high percentage is even more remarkable considering how little fragmentation there had been of traditional tenures and that the widow retained her life interest even if she remarried. *Inter vivos* transfers offered husbands ways to circumvent widow-right but few men took advantage of that option, and frequently an *inter vivos* transfer to a son was followed by a demise back to the father and his wife for both their lives, little different from widow-right. The tenurial structure and land market sustained widow-right in an era of reduced or declining population, yet the patterns of widow-right persisted even as population grew.

Widow-right could delay the transmission of land from father to son, and because widows were not penalized for remarrying, a new husband could enjoy the lands for her lifetime without an entry fine. Some remarrying widows lived quite some time after starting their widowhood.[54] The women themselves served to connect and transmit land through multiple families; the increasing size of holdings stands out and transmission could be complex. By the seventeenth century the median size of a holding in widow-right rose to over 50 acres, and many widows had similarly sized holdings prior to that.[55] In 1510 Katherine Turnour held 60 acres as widow while another 45 acres had just left the family, reflecting the increasing engrossment of lands.[56] The widow-right lands Helena Hall received reflect the apogee of that engrossment and the intermarrying of yeomen and gentry. She came from the Hebburns of Hardwick and their marriage attested to the growing wealth of her husband, William Hall. Widowed in 1549, within a year she had married Henry Eure, Esq, son of the first Lord Eure of Witton. In 1562 they surrendered the lands to William Hall's nephew Ralph Firbank; in 1568, Ralph's widow Katherine (who herself remarried) surrendered the lands to

---

[50] TNA: DURH 3/13 f. 233v; 3/27 p. 270.

[51] This excludes lands taken in-hand when no one came forward.

[52] In Thornbury, two-thirds of male tenants left a widow: Franklin, 'Peasant Widows' "Liberation" and Remarriage', p. 189.

[53] TNA: DURH 3/14 ff. 404v, 417r. For Agnes Pollard, TNA: DURH 3/13 f. 309r.

[54] TNA: DURH 3/20 f. 31r, 3/23 ff. 9v, 134v; 3/25 f.100v; *Registers of Bishop Middleham*, p. 142.

[55] Excluding lands for which the size was not given or could not be otherwise calculated.

[56] TNA: PRO DURH 3/21 f. 98r.

his sister, who then returned them to Henry and Helena. Eventually the lands passed to their son.[57] Helena's second marriage to Henry Eure, from an old family of the county, and the eventual transfer of the Hebburn freehold and Hall customary lands to George Freville, a Staffordshire gentleman (knighted by James I) involved in quelling the 1569 rebellion, reflected further gentry involvement in the parish and the touch of national politics.[58]

Widow-right endured because it was useful to the communities. Sons inherited directly from their father only 22 per cent of the time, but 57 per cent of lands held in widow-right eventually descended to a son or grandson.[59] The widow extended the family line, providing stability in possession of land against a changing household. Several times—at least fifty, in fact—the halmote clerks even omitted the widow when identifying the next tenant of a holding, even though it had been in widow-right. Most of these were written as if the husband had died, with no indication of either the widow's death or surrender of the holding.[60] The clerks almost never omitted prior male tenants, indicating a view of the widow as an extension of her deceased husband.[61] The absence of restrictions on remarriage permitted access to an important asset while maintaining the deceased man's right and thus preserving the rights of his heirs. Resources thus continued to circulate while channelling conflict or competition, providing stability for the community, akin to Hanawalt's observations about the self-limiting patriarchy in late medieval London.[62] Rural Durham was a far cry from London, but similar principles operated in both. This system worked sufficiently that even with the many economic and demographic changes the men of Durham did not alter or ignore the custom.[63] That the preservation of widow-right gave those widows more

[57] TNA: DURH 3/23 ff. 288v, 316v; 3/24 pp. 360–366, 556, 988; 3/25 f. 77r. Surtees, *History and Antiquities*, vol. 3, pp. 1–24. Helena was the daughter of John Hebburn (or Hebborne) of nearby Hardwick: 'Cracroft's Peerage'. William Eure later surrendered the lands to George Freville, who had acquired Hardwick after Anthony Hebburn was attainted for his role in the 1569 rebellion: TNA: DURH 3/25 f. 77r; *Memorials of the Rebellion of 1569*, p. 268.

[58] Mackenzie and Ross, *Historical, Topographical, and Descriptive View of the County Palatine of Durham*, p. 48.

[59] Larson, 'Widow-Right in Durham'.

[60] The clerk erased Isabella Jopling's two-year tenure as a widow in recording her grandson taking the land in 1618: Larson, 'Widow-Right in Durham', pp. 178–9; TNA: DURH 3/27 pp. 37, 118, 220; 3/28 f. 21v.

[61] There is one known exception: TNA: DURH 3/23 ff. 273v, 503r.

[62] Hanawalt, *Wealth of Wives*, p. 12. Erickson identified a similar contrast between ideology and practices, writing 'limiting a wife's bequest to her widowhood was considered the natural result of a man's desire to protect his own and his children's property from the grasp of any future husband of his widow's, or of her children by another man' but then notes that 'more than half of all men—and in some places up to three quarters of all men—imposed no limitation on their wives' bequests': *Women and Property*, p. 166; see also pp. 162–9.

[63] An example of changing custom comes from Smith, 'Some Thoughts on the "Hereditary" and "Proprietary" Rights', pp. 125–7. Bardsley concluded that the lord and local leaders changed inheritance custom because they preferred male tenants: 'Peasant Women and Inheritance', p. 317. Whittle linked landholding by women to the land market: 'Inheritance, Marriage, Widowhood and Remarriage', p. 66.

personal agency and a better chance of economic security was an unintentional consequence.

The Costs of Expansion: Rents and Entry Fines

The land market in the parish reflected broader changes in economy and population and as relevant to each specific village. Were we to take a simplistic approach, the land market should be reducible to supply and demand. The best expression of the latter would be found in rents and fines relative to the value of land. If the market were the determinant, rents and fines should correlate positively with demand. High demand should have led to high fines and low demand to low fines. Low fines should have encouraged higher demand when the value of the land was higher than the rent, while high fines should have discouraged demand. Above all, there should be economies of scale, with wealthier individuals willing and able to pay higher rents. This approach to rent leaves out too many social and cultural factors. Custom was strong in limiting rents.[64] Lower rents could be used to reward bishopric servants or good tenants. The power of tenants, built on a foundation of low population, successful resistance, and custom, is discernible in the land market, particularly in the rents for the core husbandlands and mallands.

In common with estates throughout England, the bishopric tenants originally rendered goods and services for their lands, although even in the twelfth century some of these were reckoned in cash. For example, according to the twelfth-century *Boldon Book*, husbandmen in all three villages owed 3s. 10d. in cash payments, half a scot-chalder of oats (equivalent to six bushels), five wagonloads of wood, two hens and ten eggs, three days of week-work, four autumn boonworks, reaping three rods of oats and ploughing and harrowing three rods of oat stubble, plus some cooperative works reckoned by the plough, a pair of tenants, or the whole village.[65] There is no indication that bishopric tenants were liable to *heriot* (the payment of a beast to the lord on a tenant's death) or any other death duty. In the aftermath of the Black Death, the shift to pennyfarm and a money rent became standard. The cash payments listed in *Boldon Book* did not change, but for labour services and other renders a monetary value is given in *Hatfields's Survey* following itemization of the works. The mallands of Sedgefield still carried a 5s. rent; husbandland rents in the villages were around 14–15s. Rents for cotlands were

---

[64] Hoyle, 'Introduction: Custom, Improvement and Anti-Improvement', p. 4.
[65] *Domesday Book supp. vol 35: Boldon Book*, pp. 12–18, 22–5. I have found no evidence that tenants in these villages ever held by 'tenant right' through service on the Scottish border; on that practice see Drury, 'More Stout than Wise'; Morrin, 'The Transfer to Leasehold', pp. 117–20.; Hoyle, 'An Auncient and Laudable Custom'.

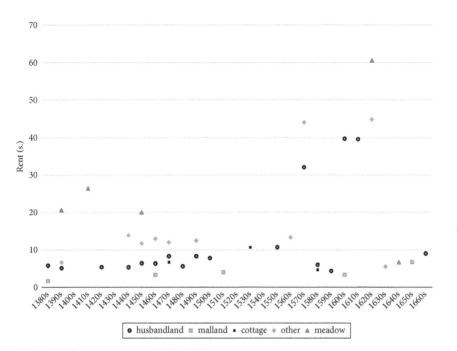

Figure 4.5 Rents per acre, *c*.1383–1662

Source: Appendix A: Landholding Database; *Hatfield's Survey*, pp. 182–92; DHC 1 M64; *Parliamentary Surveys*, pp. 212–13; Add.MS. 1930 Photostat copy of Durham Cathedral Library, MS Sharpe 167.

1-2s. but could be higher, depending on size and perhaps as the result of individual negotiations.[66]

As seen in Figures 4.5 and 4.6, after the labour services were commuted into money rents, the level of rent remained remarkably stable over the three centuries, and this was particularly true for husbandlands (and mallands) whether held as copyhold or leasehold. This is a very different story from other estates across England, where lord turned copyhold into leasehold to realize the greatest profit from rents.[67] The surviving rolls of the village collectors show little change in rents through the fifteenth century, with no change at all in Cornforth. The rolls for the coroner of Stockton Ward, who collected the free rents, are little more than copies from year to year with the occasional update when a holding changed hands.[68] Halmote and the survey evidence shown in Figure 4.6 show that the

[66] *Hatfield's Survey*, pp. 182–92.

[67] Whittle noted leasehold rents were lower on many estates in the fifteenth century but rose in the sixteenth: 'Leasehold Tenure in England', p. 143. See also Whittle, *Development of Agrarian Capitalism*, pp. 69, 112. Although not necessarily new, seven-year leases were common on the Duchy of Cornwall's manors and while rents remained stable, the entry fines were variable: Hatcher, *Rural Economy and Society*, pp. 52–57, 71–9.

[68] CCB, Collectors' Accounts, Stockton Ward, B/65/1–16, 18–25, 27, 34, 40 (covering 1397/98 to 1525/26); Coroners' rolls B/50/1, 3, 6, 11, 18, 20, 23, 28, 35–8 (covering 1397/98 to 1540/41).

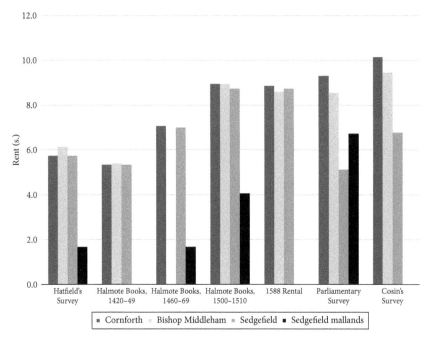

Figure 4.6 Husbandland rents per acre, c.1383–1662

Source: Appendix A: Landholding Database; *Hatfield's Survey*, pp. 182–92; DHC 1 M64; *Parliamentary Surveys*, pp. 212–13; 'Cosin's Survey', pp. 71–9, 132–3.

collectors and coroners rolls accurately reflect the situation. There was a small increase in Sedgefield between 1440 and 1460, with the main increase coming early in the sixteenth century. In the three hundred plus years between Bishop Hatfield and Bishop Cosin's survey, the average rent for an entire husbandland rose 55 per cent from 174d. to 270d.; the increase was lowest for Sedgefield (18 per cent) and highest for Cornforth (77 per cent), the latter made easier by the widespread leases in the village.[69] The rent increase for Sedgefield mallands was significantly higher, bringing that rent into line with the husbandlands. The change cannot be located with precision as nine times out of ten—literally—the halmote clerks did not specify the amount of rent, and even when rent was specified the acreage rarely was. Yet later rents often were lower than in *Hatfield's Survey*; in some cases this was in exchange for repairs, but often it was the steward making the best of the situation.[70] In 1422, the steward accepted nearly 2s. less for a tenement and 30 acres in Bishop Middleham, while in 1447, a messuage and

---

[69] *Hatfield's Survey*, pp. pp. 182–92; Durham University Library Archives and Special Collections Add.MS 1930 (hereafter 'Cosin's Survey') pp. 71–79, 132–3. These changes fall in the range of those Whittle found in Norfolk although the overall average price per acre had risen substantially higher: *Development of Agrarian Capitalism*, pp. 73, 106–7.

[70] Frequently these were for meadows and closes.

bovate in Sedgefield were leased for 6s. 8d., 4d. below the old rent.[71] Although few
in number, those rents listed in the halmote books rose in the 1460s. A number of
new leases in Sedgefield saw rents rise to 8s. 9d. for a bovate of husbandland and
17s. 8d. for a husbandland, with the explanation added that it was a 'rent beyond
the works (*opera*)'. At the turn of the century, husbandland rents were near 23s.
and a malland, 12s. 2d.[72] The consistency and timing suggest that the bishop successfully raised rents for this category of land twice, consciously and by small
amounts. Such success was not attempted, or at least not repeated, as a 1588 survey shows that rents for husbandlands had dipped slightly to 21s. 2d. in Sedgefield,
21s. 6d. in Bishop Middleham, and 22s. 4d. in Cornforth.[73] Surviving rentals
from the seventeenth century show that rent levels could fluctuate slightly based
on variations in rents for the same holding, but as these usually were only a few
pence higher or lower the change must be due to negotiation (or even scribal
error) rather than true responsiveness to the market.[74] Rents remained stable
when the lands were surveyed by parliament during the English Civil War, with a
husbandland averaging 23s. 1d. in Cornforth and 21s. 4d. in Bishop Middleham.[75]
The enclosure of Sedgefield lands renders precise comparison more difficult, but
for an example, John Harrison Sr exchanged two holdings each containing one
messuage and two bovates malland, and the rent for the two post-enclosure holdings in the Parliamentary Survey was 40s. 4d. or 20s. 2d. per original malland.[76]
The 1662 survey of the bishopric by Bishop Cosin included only leasehold lands,
and it continued to reflect stable rents, with 21s. 2d. to 34s. for a standard holding
and 42s. to 55s. 10d. for a double holding.[77]

The rents were well below the market value of the lands. Robert Swift of
Lincoln's Inn, son of the rector of Sedgefield, held the lease of Sedgefield mill and
three bovates of land when he made up his will in 1599/1600, a total value of
£40.[78] Some tenants recorded sublet agreements in the seventeenth-century halmote books, while some surrender-and-admissions included the terms of mortgages and conditional sales of customary land. Some probate inventories note
rents due and owed that reflect subtenancy. Copyhold and leasehold rents were
around 10s. 10d. to 11s. 9d. per bovate. In 1615, John Harrison leased 75 acres to
John Young for six years for £16, or 64s. per bovate. In 1636, a husbandland was let

[71] TNA: DURH 3/14 f. 598r; TNA: DURH 3/15 f. 199r; Larson, 'Tenure and the Land Market'.
[72] TNA: DURH 3/16 ff. 150v-151r; 3/18 f. 128v; 3/21 f. 131v.
[73] DHC1 M64. Copyhold rents could not be calculated due to lack of information.
[74] DHC 4/194253–194263, Box 13 Bundle 1. On rents and market levels, see Kerridge, 'Movement
of Rent', pp. 16–34.
[75] *Parliamentary Surveys*, pp. 189–201. The practice of leasing out entire vills kept rents down:
Brown, *Rural Society and Economic Change*, p. 95.
[76] *Parliamentary Surveys*, pp. 212–13.
[77] 'Cosin's Survey', pp. 71–79, 132–3. Compare with Kent, where rents quadrupled in the sixteenth
century alone: Zell, *Industry in the Countryside*, pp. 44–6.
[78] *Wills and Inventories* III, p. 175.

at £12 for the first five years. In 1660, a small 6-acre close was let for £52.[79] Both the *Parliamentary Survey* and 'Cosin's Survey' included an estimate of the value of each holding well beyond the rent. In the 1640s, the surveyors indicated that many husbandlands were worth £5–7 more.[80] When he compounded with the Parliamentary Commissioners, William Frizell paid 10s. rent for a 20-acre copyhold and 39s. 4d. for a leasehold (presumably 30 acres) in Cornforth; the values of the two holdings were £3 16s. 6d. and £16 4s. respectively. Nicholas Woodhouse, also of Cornforth, leased a farm called Fifty Acres for a rent of 10s.; it was valued at £10.[81] Despite lower rents, 'Cosin's Survey' put the value of lands significantly higher, from £13 to £40 for a standard holding and £40 to £48 for a double holding. The surveyors' speculations may have been optimistically high but were not unreasonable; a pair of sublets recorded in 1636 included the rent paid by the sublessee: £12 per annum for a husbandland and for a malland, £15 per annum.[82]

The rents for other holdings varied greatly, even for holdings of equal size. There were few cottagers recorded in *Boldon Book* but many more in *Hatfield's Survey*, with rents ranging from 8d. to 3s. 6d. Assarts and demesne also had been taken up by the villagers, with rents from 6d. to just over 1s. 1d. per acre.[83] In the 1440s, exchequerland rents ranged from 12 to 16d. per acre. The lack of rent data makes tracking other identifiable lands difficult. Those that can be studied in this way show that despite the overall trend, the value of these lands did not correlate with the value of husbandlands. A close in Sedgefield called Les Lesours was taken for 33s. 4d. in 1443; two decades later the rent had risen to 54s. 4d., but by 1565 the rent had fallen to only 10s.[84] Three demesne meadows totalling over 50 acres, Edmondsmedowe, Newmedowe, and Grangemedowe, often were leased together; in the late fourteenth century these commanded a rent of nearly £5 but were let for only £2 a century later.[85] The rent for the meadows is not recorded again; however, in 1627 Elizabeth, Lady Freville, sublet Newmedowe alone for £18 per annum.[86] The rent charged for demesne lands, other than meadows, was fairly steady, with a core rate of £6 per annum, although with other lands and meadows the total often rose to £10 or slightly higher.[87]

---

[79] TNA: DURH 3/27 f. 180; DHC1/I/78 f. 67v,/82 f. 1011r.

[80] *Parliamentary Surveys*, pp. 189–201.

[81] *Records of the Committees for Compounding*, pp. 211, 385. Frizell was fined £40, Woodhouse £20.

[82] Christopher Fawdon sublet to Nicholas Chipchase his right to two bovates which he had on demise from John Chipchase for £12 per annum and then no rent. Fawdon also sublet to Jacob Wilkinson his right to one messuage, two bovates malland, and four acres in the Ryalfield demised to him by Roland Hixon, for £15 for the first five years and then no rent: DHC1/I/78 f.67r-v.

[83] *Domesday Book supp. vol 35: Boldon Book*, pp. 12–15, 22–5; *Hatfield's Survey*, pp. 182–92. Meadowland commanded higher rents.

[84] TNA: DURH 3/15 f. 111v; 3/16 f. 107r; 3/24 p. 231.

[85] *Hatfield's Survey*, p. 183; TNA: DURH 3/18 f. 50v; CCB B/73/9 (188815) Bailiff of the Bailiwicks; Larson, 'Tenure and the Land Market'.

[86] DHC1/I/75 f. 1324r.

[87] The demesne contained 270 acres of arable and 102 acres of meadow plus a park, pasture, orchard, and manor house and buildings: *Hatfield's Survey*, pp. 183–4. As these were leased both whole

Some lords offset low customary rents by charging higher entry fines, but bish-opric entry fines remained low.[88] Unlike rents, the entry fine—the payment made by the new tenant on taking up a holding—was recorded regularly in the halmote books, so despite the occasional blank we can trace the pattern with far more detail, as shown in Figure 4.7. Entry fines peaked in the 1390s for husbandlands and in the first decade of the fifteenth century for cottages, showing a recovery after the Black Death on a variety of fronts. By the 1410s, however, fines were declining rapidly, perhaps reflecting the deepening recession of the fifteenth cen-tury or a consistently low population. Entry fines did not return to their 1390s

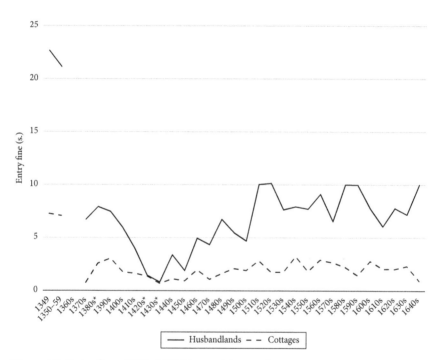

Figure 4.7 Entry fines, 1349–1659 (decennial means)

N= 688 (husbandlands) and 602 (cottages).

Source: Appendix A: Landholding Database. Excludes transfers with no or zero entry fine.

and in part over the years, gauging the precise rent is difficult. For demises of the entire demesne: TNA: DURH 3/14 ff. 43r, 294v; 3/17 f. 34v; 3/18 f. 21r. The manor was leased to John Hall in 1509 for 21 years at £6 per annum, and later in the century it came into the Eure family: Surtees, *History and Antiquities*, pp. 3–4.

[88] Mullan and Britnell found that on the Winchester bishopric estate '[r]egional economic differ-ences affected the outcome' of entry fines trends on different manors: *Land and Family*, p. 83. In West Berkshire, entry fines varied from a year's rent to the equivalent of ten years' rent: Yates, 'Change and Continuities'.

levels until the 1520s and 1530s, a trend seen on other manors and estates.[89] Afterward, the level of entry fines for husbandlands fluctuated between that higher level and the earlier level of the 1390s. The entry fines for cottages followed the same general pattern as for husbandlands until the middle of the sixteenth century after which they display a series of peaks and troughs. Entry fines for leaseholds were essentially minimal (by bishopric standards). Of the ninety-one leaseholds recorded in the halmote books between 1388 and 1660, fifty-two were for 6d., a further nine were less than 6d., and another twelve were between 6d. and 1s.[90]

There is strong positive correlation between entry fines for husbandlands and market velocity up to 1450 (at 0.96), but little correlation thereafter (at 0.11). For cottages, the correlation is positive but weaker up to 1450 (at 0.78), although for the remainder of the period the correlation is stronger than for husbandlands though still very weak (at 0.24). Some of the change can be ascribed to greater use of leasehold which may have dampened entry fines of copyhold land, but alongside the rent data from the latter half of the fifteenth century (and sporadic later information) it provides quantitative support for the broader changes in land-holding discussed in Chapter 7. On their own, the entry fines sometimes functioned as a useful indicator of broader economic or population trends as well as for the strength of social and cultural institutions.

The evidence, scattered and patchy though it sometimes is, indicates clearly that rents and fines in Durham were not market or rack rates. Custom determined many rents, while favouritism had a role for meadow and various other parcels. While this is not surprising for copyhold lands, the same pattern held true for lands taken as leasehold, no matter the length of the lease. Entry fines also remained low (lower still for leasehold) and for some husbandlands the fines underwent little inflation.[91] Fines and rents elsewhere in England began to recover and rise from the mid- to late fifteenth century, leading to greater pressure on land even as large farms were being formed.[92]

For these reasons we must look at social and cultural factors to understand the land market, and thus the economy, in this transitional period. Yes, changes in population were at work, but administrative and cultural factors also were in play. Like that of Westminster Abbey, the bishopric estate did not experience the fragmentation of holdings common on many estates in England, and even when some

[89] Dyer, 'The Agrarian Problem', pp. 24–25, and *Lords and Peasants*, pp. 287–91; Bean, *Estates of the Percy Family*, pp. 51–67, 138–40. In the Norfolk manors studied by Whittle, there was a rising trend from 1444–68 to 1556–74: *Development of Agrarian Capitalism*, pp. 79–80.

[90] James observed a much greater range of entry fines: *Family, Lineage, and Civil Society*, pp. 81–2.

[91] Müller linked entry fines with servility: 'Peasants, Lords, and Developments in Leasing', pp. 172–3.

[92] For example, see Yates, *Town and Countryside in Western Berkshire*, pp. 143–46, 235, 243; Blanchard, 'Population Change', pp. 433–4. Clark found that real rents (deflated to account for inflation) remained flat from the Black Death to the end of the fifteenth century, although he focused on demesnes of large ecclesiastical estates: 'Microbes and Markets', pp. 150–1.

husbandlands and mallands were split into logical units such as halves or quarters, they were reckoned as thus and not in terms of acres, and often the link to the original holding was maintained. Many Dean and Chapter villages likewise preserved many of the old customary holdings even if freeholds fragmented.[93] For this reason, Durham did not have the multiplicity of parcels of customary land of varying size found in central and eastern England, although this was balanced somewhat by assarts and demesne lands.[94] While this could be chalked up to the conservatism of the administration, the role of the tenants is significant, as it was in subletting and leasehold.[95] Once they acquired a holding, men seemed to prefer to retain their lands rather than try new lands or acquire additional holdings. Certainly, the ease of subletting reduced the need to acquire or shed holdings based on position in the life cycle as suggested by Chayanov.[96] Subletting could also offset the lack of small parcels for those looking to establish a foothold in the village.[97] But since rents and entry fines were low, tenants either could not or chose not to be active in the land market.

The main elements necessary for agrarian capitalism were in place at the beginning of the fifteenth century if not earlier, even if it took longer for the language of the halmote books to fully reflect the practices: a free tenantry, copyhold and leasehold with secure title and tenure, low entry fines, and stable and below-market rents. The timing supports the chronology put forward by Bailey even though it also complicates the connection between tenurial change and the decline of serfdom.[98] Clearly, the absence or profound weakness of serfdom was linked to these changes, but was it a prerequisite or a correlation deriving from some common factor? Despite the early start, other segments of the Durham trajectory more closely follow what is expected with the agrarian capitalism of early modern England: in particular, the appearance of yeomen and capitalist farmers largely follows the timing found in other parts of England.

---

[93] Harvey, *Westminster Abbey and Its Estates*, pp. 264–6. In some ways this is surprising as there had been more fragmentation of holdings on the priory estate: R. Lomas, 'Developments in Land Tenure', pp. 28–33. On the fragmentation elsewhere in England, see Homans, *English Villagers of the Thirteenth Century*, p. 204; Hyams, 'Origins of a Peasant Land Market', pp. 19, 27–8; Miller, *Abbey and Bishopric of Ely*, pp. 142–51; Williamson, 'Norfolk: Thirteenth Century'; Campbell, 'Population Pressure, Inheritance and the Land Market'; Smith, 'Families and Their Land'; Bailey, *Medieval Suffolk*, pp. 54–5; Mullan and Britnell, *Land and Family*, pp. 44–8; Zell, *Industry in the Countryside*, pp. 12–13, 230.

[94] Dunsford and Harris, 'Colonization of the Wasteland'. Fragmentation of holdings was common but not universal; see Yates, 'Change and Continuities', p. 629; Hare, *Prospering Society*, pp. 118–20, 131.

[95] If the holdings had broken up as was common in much of England, it is possible that transactions and rents might have increased.

[96] Chayanov, *Theory of Peasant Economy*, pp. 107–13. See also Dyer, *Standards of Living*, p. 123; Müller, 'Peasants, Lords and Developments in Leasing', pp. 160–1. On subletting see Kerridge, *Agrarian Problems*, pp. 50–1.

[97] French and Hoyle referred to these as 'small change' which could be used to enter the tenantry: *Character of Rural Society*, p. 211.

[98] Bailey, *Decline of Serfdom*, pp. 285–337.

Copyhold and the like were prerequisites of agrarian change but not the catalyst, and the same is true of yeomen and capitalist farmers. With low rents and security of tenure, the possibility existed for assembling larger farms while widow-right helped keep those farms intact from generation to generation. The Durham evidence demonstrates that the answers lie in the aggregated choices of individuals, families, and communities; history is made by people, not by models. Tenure and the land market do not explain the *whys* of landholding. Those answers must be sought through examining the individuals and groups involved, not only to reveal what men and women were doing but to show how these individual decisions contributed to the broader patterns. Demography and the broader economy are only part of the story, alongside the changing relations between lords and various types of tenants. This even more strongly demonstrates the need to move away from one-size-fits-all models of economic modernity and give greater weight to markets, population, and sociocultural factors in different regions. Although developments in East Anglia and elsewhere were critical in England's economic evolution, the broader regional differences in England require us to consider different paths or models rather than condemning constructed regions as backward or romanticizing them.[99]

---

[99] For example, 'to the gentle southerner…the whole province was a wild savage country, its inhabitants primitive in their passions and morals, and entirely without understanding of the rules of a law-abiding society': Thirsk, 'Farming Regions of England: The Northern Province', p. 16.

5

Agrarian Development

The different timeline of development and the different experiences between estates underlines the great importance of freedom and tenure but also of community. The yeoman stage, rather than being the result of a few enterprising peasants, could have been part of a broader movement from 15–30-acre farms to those in the 60–80-acre range, not as part of ever-spiralling farm size and profit, but as a move to a new, sustainable equilibrium. That is, instead of grasping engrossment with no end, this was a phase of general promotion to a desired farm size. The bishopric estate's tenurial history and demography made this possible, whereas elsewhere the land market and different timeline of population and tenurial change restricted such opportunities. Those who were able to move to this new level of a double holding were set to promote themselves further as market demand increased. As many of that new stratum of farmers used hired labour, adjusted to the market, and enclosed land where possible, agrarian capitalism is even more clearly an evolution rather than a revolution. Additionally, the dispossession of husbandmen and smallholders was not necessary.

What all this comes down to is that the agrarian change in many Durham villages followed a different, lower-pressure trajectory that resulted in less impact on local society compared both to southern England and coal-mining villages. The origins of the difference are rooted partially in the tenurial and communal histories of these Durham villages, but the effects of London on central and southern England cannot be understated. In the latter, in what has been seen as 'classic' development, the intense demand of London necessitated quicker transitions, and in a society that already prized individualism and competition, there was a heavy price. With serfdom holding on longer and secure tenure taking longer to develop, there was less time for the evolution of the 45–60-acre tenant as a regular part of village society. Instead, when the floodgates opened, the active land market in small parcels allowed those with means to snatch up holdings, accelerating the division of have and have-nots. That open land market also allowed outsiders to move in and acquire lands more easily. One trajectory was evolutionary. The other was much more revolutionary.

Durham before the Black Death

Setting aside the distinction between lands held in chief of the bishop *qua rex* and lands held of him *qua episcopus*, there were three types of lands found in Durham

Rethinking the Great Transition: Community and Economic Growth in County Durham, 1349–1660. Peter L. Larson, Oxford University Press. © Peter L. Larson 2022. DOI: 10.1093/oso/9780192849878.003.0006

villages—free, customary, and demesne land.[1] The free lands were held of the bishop or priory in a multitude of ways, from military service to riding to symbolic rents; on the bishopric estate, the bishop's coroners collected the free rents and these tenants owed suit of court to the bishop's free court at Durham. However, most lands discussed here were customary lands: standard peasant holdings with an admixture of odd parcels and assarts. Most of these tenants owed suit at the halmote courts, performed labour services, and paid traditional renders in kind to the village collector. While suit of court and the means of rent collection show the general nature of the divide, the line was not always clear.[2] The demesne lands were originally worked by peasants from neighbouring villages, and when leased out this normally followed the practice used for customary land.

The customary lands fall into four general categories. Two of these, the husbandlands (yardlands) and cotlands, originally owed labour services and renders in kind; the third may have once owed labour services or the services of a dreng but paid a money rent by the time of *Boldon Book*; and the fourth category is a miscellany of other lands, including assarts and often without a messuage or tenement, held for money rents.[3] In contrast with much of England, these customary lands were not considered servile or villein lands, although they were understood to be different from *terra libera*. Tenants held them for life and only very rarely 'at the will of the lord' (*ad voluntatem domini*), and nearly all such tenants were personally free.[4] Husbandlands contained two bovates (oxgangs) although the Durham bovate could vary in size. Fifteen acres was common, but as few as 12 or as many as 20 acres are recorded. Cotlands originally tended to be in multiples of 3 acres, up to 15 acres.

Few records for Durham villages from before the Black Death survive. For the Durham bishopric estate, the late twelfth-century survey known as *Boldon Book* provides a snapshot of many villages following any restructuring by the Anglo-Norman bishops. The villages detailed in the survey consisted of a mix of husbandmen, half-yardlanders, cottagers, and holdings attached to the offices of smith, pinder, and so on, and some villages had additional larger holdings attached, whether the carryover of older drengage tenure or lands held by leaseholders or *firmarii* primarily for a money rent. Frequently the villages had

---

[1] The former are free lands, generally associated with lords and knights holding of the bishop in chief; these do not appear in most bishopric records but can be tracked through charters and Inquisitions Post Mortem.

[2] See Larson, *Conflict and Compromise*, pp. 32, 51–53, 101–3.

[3] *Domesday Book supp. vol 35: Boldon Book*, pp. 12–15, 22–5; *Hatfield's Survey*, pp. 182–92.

[4] See Larson, *Conflict and Compromise*, pp. 62–7. For a more typical English manor with servile tenants, see Whittle, *Development of Agrarian Capitalism*, pp. 28–84. There are numerous estate studies; classic examples include Miller, *Abbey and Bishopric of Ely*; Harvey, *Westminster Abbey and Its Estates*; and Dyer, *Lords and Peasants*. Bailey provides a synthesis with his study focusing on customary lands in *Decline of Serfdom*; see also Schofield, *Peasant and Community*.

freeholds of varying size, from a few acres to a carucate, held for a variety of rents and services. According to a fifteenth-century priory record enumerating grain renders from the thirteenth century (the 'Gilly-Corn' rental), most Durham priory villages consisted of a core of husbandlands or single-bovate holdings with few to no cottages, some owing works at nearby demesne farms and others paying rents like the bishopric *firmarii*, plus a variety of freeholds. Just under half the tenants held between 20 and 40 acres. The priory however was more assiduous in buying out freeholders, assigning some of these lands to other obedientiaries or cells or otherwise letting them out for money rents.[5]

Those settlements on the East Durham Limestone Plateau, such as Carlton and Easington, tended to be almost exclusively husbandlands. Easington, for example, had thirty-one husbandlands, a half-carucate (likely a former drengage holding), and smallholdings for the pinder, carpenter, and smith. Settlements on the edge of the plateau and in the Wear valley tended to be more mixed. For example, in Boldon, the first village and namesake of the survey, twenty-two tenants each held two bovates of 15 acres; alongside them were twelve cottagers holding 12 acres each; a pinder with twelve acres; and one tenant with 36 acres who paid half a mark in rent.[6] A few villages consisted solely of cottagers, such as Coundon (holding 6 acres each) and Newbottle (12 acres each). Upland settlements tended to be much smaller, comprised largely of freeholds and assarts held for money rents. As the villages of the priory main estate were more uniform in organization, there is less variety in terms of distribution. Those settlements consisting primarily of cotlands or single-bovate holdings tended to be part of a cluster of settlements, such as Nether Heworth and Westerton. Altogether, the variety and location of the different village plans, alongside the location of demesne farms that tended to draw on the labour of several settlements, hark back to a pre-Conquest multiple or dispersed estate structure with a central *caput* and dependent settlements.[7]

The villages of Bishop Middleham, Cornforth, and Sedgefield, which form the case study of this book, exemplify the general pattern in *Boldon Book*, and resemble many priory villages, at least prior to the Black Death. The first two (recorded together in that survey) had twenty-six husbandlands of 30 acres yielding

---

[5] See the Gazetteer in *Bursars Rentals*, pp. 199–228; see also R. Lomas, 'Developments in Land Tenure', pp. 30–1.

[6] *Domesday Book supp. vol 35: Boldon Book*, pp. 12–15, 20–21, 54–7.

[7] The piecemeal granting out of villages and commutation of labour services severed most links between vills and *caput*, but many villages owed labour and renders to a lordship farm that often hosted the halmote court. Late medieval records refer to several *scirs* including Aucklandshire, Billinghamshire, Heighingtonshire, Quarringtonshire, and Staindropshire: Roberts, *Rural Settlement in Britain*, pp. 60–4; G. Jones, 'Basic Patterns of Settlement Distribution', pp. 192–200; Liddy, *Bishopric of Durham*, p. 34. Kapelle, *Norman Conquest of the North*, pp. 50–85; Jolliffe, 'Northumbrian Institutions'; Faith, *English Peasantry and the Growth of Lordship*, pp. 8–14, 201, 218–19; Kilby, *Peasant Perspectives*, Chap. 2, 'From Inclusive to Exclusive', Kindle loc. 725.

services, and another two paying monetary rents, one a freehold and one attached to the office of reeve; seven cotlands holding 6 acres and another four holding only a toft and croft; a punderland of 12 acres; and one tenant holding 60 acres for a money rent. In Sedgefield there were twenty husbandlands rendering services, twenty other husbandlands paying money rents and light services, a husbandland for the reeve, 12 acres apiece for the smith and the pinder, 2 acres for the carpenter, and five tofts and crofts. The tenants owed services at the demesne attached to Bishop Middleham. Husbandmen owed three days of work per week on the demesne, in addition to boon works and other agricultural services, plus renders in kind such as a hundred eggs at Easter or helping to build booths at the Fair of St. Cuthbert. Mallands (whose tenants were called malmen, or *malmanni*) were found in Sedgefield, and consisted of two bovates of 18 acres each. Malmen were obliged to plough and harrow half an acre, find men for reaping, mowing, and haying, and participate in the autumn boon works with their household. Cottagers held lands varying in size and obligation; a 'standard' cotland of 6 acres required autumn boon works and haying.[8]

The thirteenth century saw England's population grow and agriculture expand. New villages appeared and existing ones grew. More land was taken into arable cultivation, whether from waste, marsh, or moor, or by converting pasture. With labour plentiful, the old services and dues were commuted into monetary rents. That expansion can be seen in Durham as well. The core husbandlands and cotlands were supplemented by an assortment of parcels and closes, both arable and pasture, and both estates saw an explosion of cottages with varying amounts of land. These were all held for a money rent, not services. Some of the newly cultivated lands were added to existing common fields or became new ones, while others were enclosed. Only the echoes of this expansion of population and cultivation can be seen, and after considerable contraction, by counting the number of dwellings in *Bishop Hatfield's Survey*. On both estates, the growth in (estimated) tenant population was approximately 53 per cent (bishopric) and 57 per cent (priory). The amount of land under cultivation increased as well, 35 per cent on the bishopric and 17 per cent on the priory, although there is a greater level of uncertainty to these figures as by looking only at established settlements, the true expansion may be undercounted.[9]

[8] *Domesday Book supp. vol 35: Boldon Book*, pp. 12–15, 22–27, and *Hatfield's Survey*, pp. 161, 182–92.

[9] The priory estimate is based on twenty-one villages administered by the bursar: Aycliffe, Billingham, Cowpen & Newton Bewley, Dalton, Ferryhill, Fulwell, Over & Nether Heworth, Jarrow, Middle & West Merrington, Monk Hesleden, Monkton, Monkwearmouth, Moresley, Pittington, East & West Rainton, Southwick, Westoe. For the bishopric, forty-one settlements for which direct comparison was possible were employed: Bishop and North Auckland, Bishop Middleham, Bishopwearmouth, Blackwell, Bondgate-in-Darlington, Burdon, Carlton, Cassop, Cockerton, Cornforth, Coundon, Easington, Escomb, Hartburn, Haughton-le-Skerne, Heighington, Houghton-le-Spring, Killerby, Lanchester & Newbigging, Middridge, Moreton, Newbottle, Newton & Boldon,

In Bishop Middleham parish, where there had been ninety dwellings in the twelfth century, Hatfield's surveyors recorded 169, a growth of 85 per cent, and that likely undercounts the number of dwellings.[10] Many of these new dwellings had a few acres or a garth, while many were no more than a cottage. Much of the newly added land was in parcels of a few rods or a few acres. *Hatfield's Survey* cannot tell us who originally held these parcels, whether it was the cotmen and husbandmen or the new smallholders. However, some of the assarting was tied to existing holdings in an organized fashion, as the husbandlands in Bishop Middleham now had another 4 acres each in the Ryalfield.

The most significant divergence between Durham and the general pattern in England lies in the general preservation of the bovates and husbandlands, and even many cotlands, as integral holdings. While some fragmented, in most villages these persisted intact into the sixteenth century and sometimes beyond.[11] The bishops' administration originally must have been behind the preservation of the holdings, as the stewards would have needed to acquiesce to any official division. In many instances in which husbandlands, bovates, and cotlands were divided they were enumerated as parts of the original holding, sometimes linked explicitly to an original holding. The numerous cottages with little to no land imply a growing population working as labourers or artisans. The persistence of the husbandlands and bovates alongside the sharp increase in smallholders, some with no arable land at all, implies potentially substantial polarization within the villages.[12] Against this, however, Dunsford and Harris argued that Durham never reached the limits of cultivation in the thirteenth or fourteenth century; there was still waste land to colonize.[13] The scarcity of records for the pre-plague period leaves us mostly in the dark with only a broad outline of how growth occurred.

Newton Capp, Norton, Quarrington, Redworth, Ryhope, Sedgefield, Sherburn, Shaldforth, Stanhope, Tunstall, Warden Law, West Thickley, Whickham, Whitburn cum Cleadon, and Wolsingham. Six bishopric settlements (Cockerton, Haughton, Moreton, Quarrington, Ryhope, Burdon) had fewer dwellings or tenants at their height compared to *Boldon Book*; on the priory, where acquisition of freehold was a priority, only East Rainton appears to have shrunk with no ready explanation. Dunsford and Harris used the 1340 rental to analyse change on the priory and found a decrease in cultivated land of 37% between the earlier data and 1340, part of which they attribute to direct exploitation of newly enclosed waste: Dunsford and Harris, 'Colonization of the Wasteland', pp. 49–51. However, the 1340 rental did not include all customary lands.

[10] The surveyors recorded numerous 'places' which sometimes were areas for dwellings and sometimes not; likewise, pieces of arable, meadow, and pasture were not always enumerated.

[11] Yates found a similar practice in West Berkshire and Hare in the chalklands of Wiltshire (but without the extensive subleasing): Yates, 'Change and Continuities', p. 629; Hare, *Prospering Society*, pp. 118–20, 131. Some 'ancient tenures' in England survived into the nineteenth century: Beckett and Turner, 'Freehold from Copyhold and Leasehold'.

[12] Compare with some Chester villages that worked to exclude the poor: C. Foster, *Capital and Innovation*, pp. 80–81, 143–4.

[13] Dunsford and Harris, 'Colonization of the Wasteland', p. 54.

Durham after the Black Death

Beginning in 1349, there is a near-continuous series of records for the bishopric villages into the early twentieth century: the records of the bishopric halmote court. There was enough change then stability by the 1380s to warrant compilation of a new and thorough estate survey, *Hatfield's Survey*. This became the standard reference for the bishopric into the sixteenth century. For the priory main estate, numerous rentals and later rent books survive from 1326 to 1539–40, as well as an incomplete survey from 1411, a survey of freeholders from 1430, and a 1424 survey of lands owing Gilly-Corn dues with contents from 1235. Priory halmote rolls survive in good series from 1364 to 1400.

The bishopric halmote books suggest that stability was returning as early as the late 1350s as a new steward began to investigate tenancies and sublets, but a gap from 1362 to 1388 robs us of the chance to see when and how that stability was established. With so few halmote records before 1364 we can only speculate on the situation on the priory main estate, but financially, the priory had begun to recover in the 1350s and Dobson saw signs of increased confidence on the part of the monks in the latter part of the century.[14] In terms of population and tenure, if not society, both estates seem to have found a new normal by the fourth quarter of the fourteenth century.

The records from the two estates reveal the contraction of population and cultivation that likely began before the plague. The demesne lands were let out to individual or corporate lessees, or to villagers in either random or regular parcels.[15] Many villages had lands that were vacant or decayed. Soon after the Black Death, the bishopric steward had resorted to imposing vacant lands on those able to work them, as part of the 'feudal reaction' analysed by Britnell.[16] Such drastic measures did not last long on the bishopric estate and may not have occurred on the Priory estate. By the end of the century vacant holdings were decaying and the steward was letting arable lands for pasture on an annual basis. Overall there was contraction, but it varied, with some villages showing little change. The bigger problem for the bishopric, according to Harris, was getting tenants (especially free tenants) to pay their rents.[17]

The relative proportion of smallholders remained stable in the bishopric, rising from 53 to 55 per cent. However, this group includes an uncertain number of men and women who certainly were not smallholders, from residents of other

---

[14]   R. Lomas, 'Durham Cathedral Priory', pp. 284–5; Dobson, *Durham Priory*, pp. 54–56, 293–6.

[15]   See Hare, *Prospering Society*, pp. 101–13 for an interesting analysis of demesnes lessees and their backgrounds. The lessees of those Wiltshire demesnes resemble those of the bishopric: many came from the established customary tenants and manorial or estate officers, but the records permit Hare to provide far more detail.

[16]   Britnell, 'Feudal Reaction'.

[17]   S. Harris, 'Wastes, the Margins and the Abandonment of Land', pp. 218–19.

villages to local gentry and knights such as William Featherstone, John Hardwick, Sir Roger Fulthorp, and Sir Richard Scrope, as well as Hugh de Westwick, chaplain, and Sir Ralph Eure, two key bishopric administrators. In Bishop Middleham, this group accounted for 5 per cent to 10 per cent of the 'smallholders' recorded in the *Survey* although the percentage is likely somewhat higher, given the difficulty of identifying the status of individuals. Overall, twenty-one bishopric settlements had the same or fewer smallholders than in the twelfth century; the only ones with substantial growth were Bishop Auckland, Lanchester, Sedgefield, and Wolsingham.[18] On the priory main estate, the proportion of smallholders had risen from 42 per cent to 49 per cent, with the largest growth at Billingham, from 46 per cent to 66 per cent. Unlike the bishopric estate, few of these smallholders were gentry, and instead men with substantial holdings in other villages inflated the overall percentage of smallholders, accounting for about 11 per cent of this category: men such as Thomas Rois, who held 48 acres in West Rainton and 4 acres in East Rainton, or the interestingly named John Uncouth, with 36 acres in Moorsley and 4 acres in North Pittington. The greater size of the bishopric, both in settlements and population, makes finding such men much more difficult.

A much more significant change was the emergence of a new pattern in land-holding: the shift to three to four bovates (45–60 acres) as a regular holding alongside the piecemeal acquisition of parcels and cottages, as shown in Figures 5.1 and 5.2.[19] In the thirteenth century, just under 2 per cent of bishopric tenants and 10 per cent of priory tenants held between 40 and 80 acres, with those holding more consisting of freeholders boosted by a few men holding carucates or leasing demesnes. *Hatfield's Survey* records 17 per cent of tenants as holding between 40 and 80 acres, while just under 24 per cent of priory tenants in 1396 fell into this category. It was common in many villages on both estates for a tenant who earlier would have held a husbandland of two bovates to now hold two such lands, or a husbandland and a half. These men and women became a new standard stratum of tenants throughout both estates, while in villages such as Cornforth (as well as Ryhope, Easington, Cowpen Bewley, and Newton Bewley) the double husband-land supplanted the husbandland as the standard larger holding. Brown noted that in priory villages such as Harton these larger holdings were not 'subsumed into larger farms'. The latter happened in some bishopric villages, but the new conglom-erations remained a collection of holdings rather than a new holding.[20]

Their emergence and continued existence of this group of larger holdings imply a desired level of landholding. Hare found a similar pattern in the Wiltshire chalklands, and the size is very close to the ideal family farm discussed by Allen,

---

[18] Stockton would be included if burgesses without other holdings were counted as smallholders.

[19] This had begun earlier: R. Lomas, 'Developments in Land Tenure', p. 33. There was a similar pattern in Wiltshire where virgates had remained intact: Hare, *Prospering Society*, pp. 137–9.

[20] Brown, *Rural Society and Economic Change*, pp. 45, 197–223.

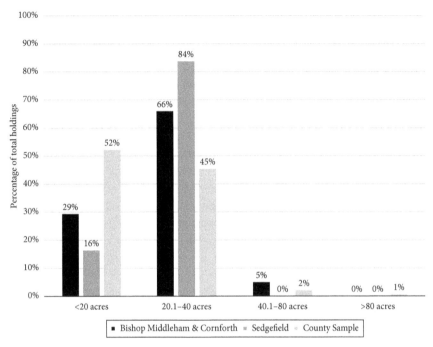

Figure 5.1 Tenurial distribution, late twelfth century

[a] Using forty-one villages (including Bishop Middleham, Cornforth, and Sedgefield) for which direct comparison was possible between the two sources.

Source: Domesday Book supp. vol 35: Boldon Book.

which would require no hired labour.[21] The collection of multiple cottages by men such as Gilbert Spurner of Norton indicates labour may have been scarce. Some of the men with three and four bovates seem to have been content. Some split the additional husbandland with another tenant of the village. But others were acquiring more, moving to 80 or more acres either with additional bovates or husbandlands or by acquiring exchequerland. The latter tenants were more prominent in individual or collective leasing of village and manorial holdings. In the late fourteenth century, the differences can be seen but it is too early to draw sharp divisions. Thomas Headlam of Sedgefield is a good example of a tenant with twice the land of the ordinary husbandman: he held four mallands and 4 acres of exchequerland for a total of 76 acres, along with the village kiln and one of the dovecots. He had the most land in the village, but seven others held over 50 acres. Gilbert Spurner of Norton would be on the upper end of this new class

---

[21] Hare, *Prospering Society*, pp. 114–16; Allen, *Enclosure and the Yeoman*, pp. 56–64. Allen took a somewhat essentialist or nostalgic view of the family farm, however, as even family farms employed servants and seasonal labour while subletting complicates ideas of ownership; for another example, see French and Hoyle, *Character of English Rural Society*, pp. 20, 71–5. 251–92. The medieval farm was more commercialized than Allen gave it credit.

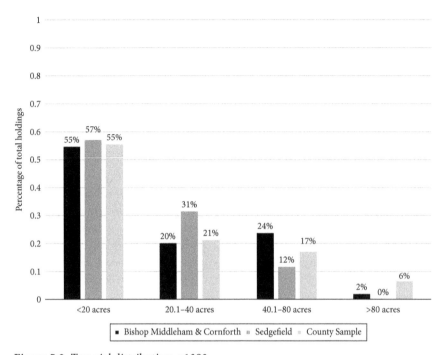

Figure 5.2 Tenurial distribution, *c.*1383

ᵃ Using forty-one villages (including Bishop Middleham, Cornforth, and Sedgefield) for which direct comparison was possible between the two *sources*.

Source: Hatfield's Survey.

of tenant, with 90 acres and sixteen cottages. Spurner was the second largest tenant in the village after Sir Roger Fulthorp and held more than half of the cottages.[22]

These were the emerging yeomen, rather than men from the existing sub-manorial and gentry groups. Few men held above 100 acres, and those tended to be knights and gentry with older freehold or drengage tenures. Some, like Sir Ralph Eure, were acquisitive opportunists: a few acres here, a few acres there, most likely let to local subtenants. They were not building up farms, or even the foundation for farms. Men in the emerging yeomanry, however, were focusing their efforts. They may have been opportunists, but they also had a sense of what they wanted, how large a farm they desired. After all, there was limited need or motivation to aspire to more. Furthermore, the larger holdings became increasingly stable in the following decades and were passed down or surrendered and taken up intact by the new tenant, whether widow, son, brother, or someone outside the immediate family.[23] This further emphasizes the perceived stability of

[22] TNA: DURH 3/14 f. 578v; *Hatfield's Survey*, pp. 174–77, 187–92.
[23] R. Lomas, 'Developments in Land Tenure', p. 35.

these larger holdings, and that both administration and tenants were loath to break them up.

Some tenants took advantage of the withdrawal of the bishops and bursars from direct management of their demesne lands. Some manorial demesne lands were parcelled out in uniform units to tenants while others were leased in their entirety to individuals, small groups, or even the village itself. Attempts by individuals and small groups to exploit the demesne had little lasting success, however, judged by the short terms (often one or three years) and the tendency for the demesne to change hands before a slightly longer term of three to six years had ended. Some villages leased themselves from the bishop, but this never became common. On the priory main estate, this evolved into the practice of syndicates leasing the entire village from the bursar, with each man holding a share of the entire village, a piecemeal practice beginning in 1371 with the final village converted in 1524. According to Lomas, these syndicates were the tenantry as a corporation, as the number of syndics mirrored the number of tenants before syndication, but perhaps these men bought out poorer or less capable neighbours to create landless residents.[24]

Turning Points in Tenurial Change

The tenurial history of the bishopric estate had four critical periods of tenurial development. The first was 1349–c.1383, which saw the tenants and administration adjust to the new situation following the Black Death; that period has already been covered in depth. The second period, to either side of 1400, witnessed the establishment of leasehold alongside copyhold for customary land. The latter half of the fifteenth century witnessed an intensification of earlier trends, with more farms formed from two husbandlands and more over 100 acres. This also was the period when the three villages diverged tenurially. Finally, the half-century before the Civil War saw the true emergence of the yeoman, with larger farms and enclosure in Sedgefield and Cornforth.[25] In any of these major periods, or at various other points, these villages may have taken a different path, such as becoming more like the Dean and Chapter villages, or something altogether different. Following the Civil War, as Bishop Cosin re-established the administration of the bishopric, he could have chosen to raise rents or make other changes. What might have been, we do not know.

---

[24] R. Lomas, 'Developments in Land Tenure', pp. 35–8; Brown, *Rural Society and Economic Change*, pp. 44–5.

[25] Yates identified five key periods of development in her work, 1380s–1420, the mid-fifteenth century, the end of the fifteenth century to 1520, the mid-sixteenth century, and 1570 and after. While some of the time periods are similar to those offered here, the characteristics differed: *Town and Countryside in Western Berkshire*, pp. 232–3.

c.1390–1418

Leasehold practices crystallized on the bishopric and subsequently a significant divergence emerged between it and the and priory estate. Lomas concluded that up until 1390 leases made up only about 10 per cent of tenant tenures, but then they increased and life tenure '[declined] steadily until, during the fourteen-thirties, only seven of these [life tenures] were awarded' and the last occurred in 1464.[26] On the bishopric estate, the loss of nearly all halmote records between 1363 and 1388 means fixing a timeline for the emergence of leasehold is not possible. However, the paucity of leases combined with the terms of the conveyance by which Thomas Smyth of Bishop Middleham took 7 acres that had belonged to the late John del Gate for the term of one year show that leasehold of customary lands remained a stopgap measure while waiting for a new tenant. The terms make it clear that the bishopric administration preferred tenants in right.[27] From there, the practice evolved. By 1399 tenants were leasing bovates and husbandlands and six and twelve years were becoming standard terms. In 1410 men were leasing whole husbandlands that previously had been under lease and with the previous tenant still alive and active (as opposed to in the lord's hand); by 1418 tenants were renewing leases.

Leasehold spread rapidly on the bishopric but unlike on the priory, it did not dominate and eventually a mixture of tenurial patterns emerged: some villages a mix of copyhold and leasehold, with others mainly one or the other. In Cornforth, leasehold quickly replaced copyhold for nearly all husbandlands. Although Bishop Middleham was the first village with leasehold, leasing peaked in the 1410s and renewals were uncommon, with copyhold emerging as dominant. Leasing became more popular in Sedgefield, although renewals were uncommon. In Cornforth, leasing became the standard form of tenure. The varied tenurial patterns depended on the situation in each village, and likely on the attitudes of the tenants therein. As in many things, the bishop's stewards allowed a fair amount of self-determination and continued to do so.

c.1450–c.1500

The latter part of the century saw the difference in tenurial preference between Bishop Middleham and Sedgefield on the one hand and Cornforth on the other

---

[26] R. Lomas, 'Developments in Land and Tenure', pp. 37–9; Larson, *Conflict and Compromise*, p. 167; Brown, *Rural Society and Economic Change*, p. 45. On the conflict between the priory and its tenants, see Morrin, 'Transfer to Leasehold', pp. 117–32. The development of leasehold was contingent on power relations between lord and tenants, no matter which side wished the change: Miller, *Abbey and Bishopric of Ely*, pp. 104–5; Harvey, *Westminster Abbey and Its Estates*, esp. pp. 246–56 and 273–4; Müller, 'Peasants, Lords and Development in Leasing'.

[27] TNA: DURH 3/13 f. 99v.

become permanent. The popularity of leasehold had waned in Bishop Middleham and Sedgefield. Leases in Bishop Middleham had all but disappeared and those in Sedgefield had peaked and would decline sharply after 1489. Renewals continued to be uncommon in both villages. In Cornforth, leasing became the norm with 74 per cent of transactions involving a lease and 37 per cent of leases representing a renewal; many tenants renewed their leases together in the late fifteenth century.[28] Leasing remained dominant in Cornforth, but in 1509–10 the administration ceased including leasehold for the village in the halmote books, after which only sporadic conveyances would be recorded. The different experiences but similar chronologies demonstrate just how dangerous it is to generalize about landholding, even within a small unit such as a parish.

More men rose from holding 45–60 acres to larger holdings in Bishop Middleham parish and in many bishopric villages. The same occurred on the priory estate. Lomas cites Southwick as his example, where the twelve tenants holding 6–106 acres in 1396 became six tenants holding 24–205 acres by 1500.[29] Overall, the number of tenants on the priory shrank to about one-third of what they had been a century earlier as syndicates replaced individual tenants. On both estates these larger holdings remained likely to be passed on intact. At least a dozen bishopric villages were leased out during this period, often to small syndicates of tenants and frequently including demesne lands and manorial buildings. The motivation for doing so is not clear. The rent for the lease resembled the collective rent for the individual holdings, simply lumping the rents into a single sum.[30] Unlike the priory syndicates, these rarely lasted beyond the lease, with a return to individual holdings as before. While the bishopric syndicates disappeared, this period did see lasting success in exploiting demesnes, judging by longer terms and the frequency of renewal. The tenants found ways to make the demesnes more profitable, whether by different use of the lands, greater demand for grain and animal products, or likely some combination of the two. An example of this success is the Hall family of Bishop Middleham. The Hall family, notably Thomas the vicar of St. Michael's in Bishop Middleham and William the bishop's instaurer, became increasingly active in the parish land market in the 1470s and 1480s. Thomas leased the demesne of Bishop Middleham manor in 1478 for 13 years, with William taking the demesne from his brother along with three meadows in 1486 for 11 years. These went to his son John, who became bailiff of the manor, and remained in the extended family until being transferred to George Freville, Esq, in 1592.[31] The coming of the Frevilles signalled a shift in

---

[28] Appendix A: Landholding Database; TNA: DURH 3/16 3ff. 10v-311r; 3/18 f. 51r-v. Sedgefield was on this path in the 1460s, but by the 1470s the men were switching lands again.

[29] R. Lomas, 'Developments in Land Tenure', p. 42; *Bursars Rentals*, pp. 83, 145.

[30] Larson, 'Peasant Opportunities in Rural Durham', pp. 158–9.

[31] TNA: DURH 3/17 f. 34v; 3/18 ff. 21r, 50v, 64v, 80v, 94v, 147r, 154r; 3/19 ff. 27v, 56r, 160v,184v; 3/20 ff. 46r, 73r, 82r; 4/21 ff. 39v, 79v, 132r 160r, 195r, 201v, 211r, 224v, 247r; 3/22 p. 63; 3/23 ff. 117r-v,

the local gentry, replacing the older families of Eure, Hardwick, Hebburn, and others in the locality.

*c.*1580–1640

The seventeenth century would see enclosure of the open fields in many Durham villages, although partial enclosures were already underway. The contraction in the number of priory tenants in the previous period had important ramifications for the sixteenth and seventeenth centuries. Brown has shown how little social stratification *among tenants* existed in the priory villages in the sixteenth century, as most tenants in a village paid a similar rent.[32] Yet the priory halmote records reveal a large group of servants and labourers, with substantial tensions within the villages. In bishopric villages such as Bishop Middleham and Sedgefield, a more mixed tenurial structure persisted. This did not eliminate friction, but it did provide opportunities for the acquisition of land and social mobility, and some voice within village affairs.

While priory tenants saw little social or economic promotion, on the bishopric estate, the last decades of the sixteenth century saw the improvement of yeoman families to the point where fathers could set up younger sons with large holdings, and some created truly large, non-family farms. Ralph Mason, whose family first took land in Sedgefield in the 1540s, held 69 acres by copyhold and sublease in the 1550s and he (or a son also named Ralph) held nearly 200 acres by 1580.[33] His grandsons Ralph, Lancelot, and Dennis held a combined total of twenty messuages and cottages with nearly 300 acres of arable plus other parcels. Ralph's widow Jane took four messuages, eleven and a half cottages, several gardens, and over 100 acres of arable after his death. Lancelot's lands were seized for his recusancy and went to Simon Conyers; he regained some lands and acquired new ones, so that his son Humphrey held 136 acres following the enclosure of Sedgefield in 1637. Humphrey's neighbours John Harrison, Roland Hixon, and Leonard Middleton each held around 100 acres.[34] This stage of development was not unusual in England; Thirsk and Zell found similar increasing farm sizes and stratification in Kent.[35] But it was not nearly so disruptive.

This mixture of a few cottagers alongside men with 30, 60, 100 and more acres existed on many bishopric villages (about half of the sample that can still be

---

288v; 3/24 pp. 85, 704; 3/25 ff. 77r-77v, 100r-100v. Freville was granted Hardwick as a reward for his service against the 1569 rebellion, and the Hall customary lands were among others he acquired: Fordyce, *History and Antiquities of the County Palatine*, vol. 2, p. 342.

[32] Brown, *Rural Society and Economic Change*, pp. 197–223.

[33] Baker Baker Papers, BAK.72/249, f. 3v. This scale of accumulation pales in comparison to some of the men studied by Hoskins: 'Leicestershire Farmer in the Sixteenth Century', pp. 61–5.

[34] Brown, 'Church Leaseholders', pp. 33–43; TNA: DURH 3/26 f. 247v; DHC1/I/76 ff. 2764-227r.

[35] Thirsk, 'Agriculture in Kent', pp. 78–9; Zell, 'Landholding', pp. 22–28, 49.

compared) at least to the middle of the seventeenth century, in varying degrees.[36] Throughout these three-plus centuries, continuity balanced change, and agrarian change was more evolutionary than revolutionary. On the bishopric estate, yeomen emerged and gentry acquired lands in the villages, but a solid core of husbandmen and more substantial cottagers continued to thrive. Lands were enclosed in various periods and many medieval patterns and practices persisted and modernized. French and Hoyle described the 'society of independent freeholders, copyholders and large tenants, which emerged in the sixteenth century' as 'inherently unstable', as yeomen and others across England sold out for economic and non-economic reasons.[37] Clifford found large estates created or enlarged in later seventeenth- and eighteenth-century Bishop Middleham and Sedgefield through consolidation of enclosure allotments, but this seems a continuation of earlier processes that began in the fourteenth century and while the number of yeomen and smallholders shrank, they did not disappear.[38]

Major change originated in non-agrarian vectors: urbanization and industrialization. Of those bishopric villages where the old tenures broke down, some are to be expected: Bishop Auckland, Darlington, and Sunderland, which were growing as towns, and the roots for some of these can be seen even in *Hatfield's Survey*. The truly revolutionary change came with mining. Whickham is the classic example: in the middle of the sixteenth century, it was an agricultural settlement, mainly pastoral, with a mix of husbandmen and cottagers but only one tenant with more than 50 acres. It had changed little since *Hatfield's Survey*. Coal mining transformed the village quickly.[39] Where mining came later, for example in Bishop Middleham, Cornforth, and Sedgefield, the pattern persisted into the nineteenth century, with many of the medieval underpinnings and organization persisting even if in different form and substance.[40]

A Divergent Agricultural Development

Was this agrarian capitalism? It is better to say that elements of capitalist agrarian practice developed and coexisted with older forms, and the question of revolution

---

[36] Of the thirty villages from the sample for which comparison is possible, twelve (Easington, Haughton, Heighington, Middridge, Newbottle, Newton & Boldon, Sherburn, Shaldforth, Cassop, Whitburn, Cleadon) retained a strong system of bovates and husbandlands, thirteen (Bishop and North Auckland, Bishopwearmouth, Coundon, Houghton (maybe), Newton Capp, Redworth, Ryhope, Burdon, Stanhope, Tunstall, Wolsingham, Whickham) saw considerable or complete breakdown of the order, and three (Blackwell, Cockerton, Darlington) fell in between.

[37] French and Hoyle, *Character of English Rural Society*, pp. 35–8. They also found a larger proportion of smallholders in Earls Colne: pp. 210–11.

[38] Clifford, 'Settlement and Field Systems', vol. I, pp. 55–75.

[39] Levine and Wrightson, *Making of An Industrial Society*, pp. 84–92; *Hatfield's Survey*, pp. 93–7.

[40] Clifford, 'Settlement and Field Systems', pp. 49–75.

or evolution assumes too sharp of a developmental dichotomy.[41] Farm size varied greatly, and while some men clearly farmed large holdings in a capitalist way, others may have had a similar outlook despite fewer acres.[42] Instead, the middle of the seventeenth century marks a second period of equilibrium following the Black Death.[43] It would be wrong to assume that this different outcome implied stagnation or retarded development, as Tawney suggested for Northumberland when he dismissed the uniformity of holdings in his sample there by saying that 'Northumbrian agriculture is always several generations behind the South and East'.[44] Perhaps that was true of agriculture in the county of Northumberland, immediately to the north of County Durham, but parts of Durham were generations ahead of the south and east. The assumption that Durham was a backward region until the industrial revolution is false, or perhaps it is clearer to state that not all of Durham was poor and backward. The later and more radical transformation of Durham has obscured the interesting and unusual features of villages and regions before industrialization. Durham's pattern of development did not conform to the classic pattern, yet there was much in common.

The different outcomes of these three villages specifically and of Durham more broadly underscores the importance of a social, cultural, and institutional approach, and studying those outcomes opens further questions about individual and community, land and land use, locality, and nation. The beliefs and actions of Cecilia Rauf, John Hall, Annabilla Headlam, their neighbours and their descendants shaped and were shaped by the broader patterns of transition that we seek to understand. They may have understood local change, innovation, and moving up and down the ladder of rural society far better than we can today, and the challenge is to reconcile the quantitative with the anecdotal. Local society and conditions produced an alternative model of agrarian capitalism in which community pressures permitted greater production for the market while preserving elements of the older agrarian and village structures.

---

[41] For a concise critique of complex definitions, see Shaw-Taylor 'Rise of Agrarian Capitalism', p. 31. The difficulty of measuring the development of agrarian capitalism is made clear by Langdon in his review of Whittle's *Development of Agrarian Capitalism*: 'she opens her last paragraph with the question "How capitalist was rural society in sixteenth-century England?" (p. 314) but leaves it totally unanswered': Review of *The Development of Agrarian Capitalism*, p. 1438.

[42] Allen provides a useful division between family farms and farms run through hired labour, with family farms maxing out at sixty acres and truly capitalist farms starting at one hundred acres: *Enclosure and the Yeoman*, p. 57; see also pp. 56–64 on peasants and family labour.

[43] Many changes would not come until the nineteenth century: Clifford, 'Settlement and Field Systems'.

[44] Tawney, *Agrarian Problem*, p. 64. Shaw-Taylor likewise saw the North as developing later: 'Rise of Agrarian Capitalism', pp. 27–33.

6

Standards of Living in an Age of Transition

Our knowledge of everyday life of rural English society is both feast and famine. Many details are known: what people ate, how they worshipped, what they did for fun, what they wore, what they lived in. Information for the gentry and for monks can be gleaned from numerous sources, which informs us of those of lower rank as well. For the peasantry and gentry, a surprising amount of information has been collected from manorial and other written records, while archaeological evidence adds even more. Manorial accounts and other records of agrarian activity detail the components of peasant diet. While we know many details, crucially we often do not know the quantities and the overall quality. For Durham, the quality of life of the monks of Durham Priory has been well studied, but that of the lay population is less well known. This chapter's goal is to explore what it was like to have lived in these parishes throughout centuries of changes. Unlike previous chapters, much of this will be anecdotal; there are insufficient numbers of sources for the statistical analyses commonly employed. What does survive, however, is rich and detailed and allows the two parishes to be measured against other parts of England.

Diet, housing, and furnishings were three major elements of rural life that reflected changing tastes, life, and economy. Diet has been used as a measure of real economy, representing the buying power of income and thus ascertaining who was above or below the poverty line. Material goods are markers of status and consumption. Housing is an indicator more of the overall wealth of an area and its connection to mainstream society. In all three, Durham was not so different from the rest of England, except perhaps in timing.

The standard of living of the English people is a central concern of economic historians. One of the major differences in explaining England's economic growth is the use of output of the economic sectors versus prices and wages. Broadberry et al., calculating GDP from the agricultural, industrial, and service sectors, saw England's economic growth as slow and erratic but building on its gains instead of declining; Clark, focusing on income and real wages, saw instead stagnation agriculturally and in the broader economy.[1] The weakness of wages comes from the

[1] Broadberry et al., *British Economic Growth*, pp. 187–9, 247–50 ff.; Broadberry and de Pleijt, 'Capital and Economic Growth in Britain'; Clark, 'Microbes and Markets', 'Long March of History' and 'The Macroeconomic Aggregates for England', among others; Clark et al., 'Malthus, Wages, and Preindustrial Growth'; Kelly and Ó Gráda, 'Numerare Est Errare'; Humphries and Weisdorf, 'Unreal Wages?' De Vries critiqued wage and price indices: 'Between Purchasing Power', pp. 210–2. Woodward noted that wage rates needed to be tested for other regions of England: *Men at Work*, p. 3. The debate

nature of the data: we know daily and sometimes weekly rates for various trades, but we do not know how many days of the year a wage earner worked, or whether there was income from other sources; it also excludes those such as farmers or artisans who did not earn wages. However, declining real wages still need to be reconciled with growing GDP; Hatcher's modelling of peasant incomes may be one approach, as it shows the greater income stability of those with land.[2] Probate inventories and other sources indicate that the worth of some groups was growing rapidly, but at different rates in different places. Perhaps part of the solution lies in macroeconomic analysis of regains within a country, to evaluate how they contributed to national growth.[3]

Others are interested in the details of the foods, goods, and homes of the period, and just as with the broader debate on 'medieval' to 'modern' the origins of modern consumer society keep being pushed further into the past. McKendrick posited an eighteenth-century consumer revolution. Weatherill looked to the later seventeenth century, although she believed consumption was more limited; Shammas too argued for this period in her comparison of England with the North American colonies, but thought many of the new items were accessible to a broader range of individuals. To the idea of a consumer revolution, De Vries proposed an 'industrious revolution' where people worked more and harder to afford the new goods.[4] As with so many topics for rural England, Thirsk was an early contributor, examining the explosion of domestic production starting in the Tudor period. The most recent works place the origin of consumer culture even earlier. K. French sees the rising standards of living following the plague as reshaping domestic life and gender roles in London, connecting consumption to other cultural changes. Sear and Sneath also see the late medieval period as significant, arguing for a long evolution beginning in 1350 that involved different sectors of society in different places at different times, 'fueled by a complex interaction of factors which affected both the supply and demand of consumption goods'.[5] Like tenure and population, the centuries following the Black Death are key in the emergence of a consumer culture in Durham, fitting the model of Sear

---

on the fifteenth-century economy had a similar scholarly dichotomy, with Postan (using gross national product) seeing stagnation and decline while Bridbury saw rising wealth per capita: Postan, 'Fifteenth Century', p. 42; Bridbury, *Economic Growth*, pp. 36, 52–3.

[2] Hatcher, 'Unreal Wages'.

[3] The proposed approach would require creation of regional data series, all the more difficult because some regions may not have the necessary sources.

[4] McKendrick, 'Home Demand and Economic Growth'; Thirsk, *Economic Policy and Projects*, esp. pp. 169–75; De Vries, *Industrious Revolution*; Shammas, *The Pre-Industrial Consumer*; Weatherill, *Consumer Behaviour*; Overton et al., *Production and Consumption in English Households*. On food as consumption, see Lloyd, *Food and Identity in England*. Allen and Weisdorf rejected the idea of an industrious revolution: 'Was There an "Industrious Revolution"?'.

[5] Sear and Sneath, *Origins of the Consumer Revolution*, pp. 5, 10–11, 19, 201–29. McKendrick, *Home Demand and Economic Growth*; Overton et al., *Production and Consumption in English Households*; Weatherill, *Consumer Behaviour*; French, *Household Goods and Good Households*.

and Sneath. The Durham peasantry saw an improvement following the Black Death, while the elites may have enjoyed a greater quantity of what they were used to. Later in the sixteenth century, the gentry and middling sort started to have greater access to a range of consumer goods, and in the seventeenth century, these goods became more common lower down the social scale while the middling sort and elites had access to more and more items of higher quality. This was not revolutionary. Nonetheless, comparing 1660 to 1349 or even 1449, the transformation of Durham is clear.

How well off were the people in these Durham parishes, really? The Durham evidence for diet and household living matches the findings of other scholars for England as a whole.[6] Some contemporary accounts lamented the poverty and religious backwardness of Durham, but that rhetoric is at odds with other contemporary perceptions. In his study on rebuilding and architectural change in County Durham and Newcastle, Green pointed out others who saw Durham in a different light. Thomas Fuller, a scholar and preacher who knew Izaak Walton and satirized Oliver Cromwell, concluded that Durham 'may be ranked amongst the middling shires of England' in his *History of the Worthies of England*.[7] That is not the highest praise but clearly Durham was not a poor county. As argued earlier, the tenurial organization of the bishopric villages may be responsible for an earlier recovery of population, promoting further agricultural and economic development as population rose, leading to rising prosperity at the end of the sixteenth century and more wealth in the seventeenth—at least for some. While revealing increasing prosperity, these parishes support Hatcher's critique of positive opinions on late medieval England, particularly the contrast of rural tenants with those working for wages.[8] Late medieval and early modern Durham was a mix of wealth and poverty, and the differences became more marked. In rebuilding houses and consumer goods, Durham was not backward, while Newcastle-upon-Tyne became the fourth or fifth largest city in England in the seventeenth and eighteenth centuries.[9] But, as population increased, more and more had to rely on trades or wage labour rather than farming, and while their standard of living might have risen, they remained poor. Bishop Middleham and Sedgefield, and likely many other parts of Durham, embody the contradictory economic trends of the period. Real wages in England peaked in the middle of the fifteenth century and then declined into the seventeenth century; yet national GDP per capita in the 1620s was 40 per cent higher than in the 1340s and rising, 'an economy on the

---

[6] Primarily see Sear and Sneath, *Origins of the Consumer Revolution*; Dyer, *Standards of Living*; Overton et al., *Production and Consumption in English Households*; Aston and Gerrard, *Shapwick Project*, and *Interpreting the English Village*.
[7] Green, 'Houses and Households', vol. 1, p. 31; Fuller, *History of the Worthies of England*, vol. 1, p. 477.
[8] Hatcher, 'Seven Centuries of Unreal Wages' and 'Unreal Wages'.
[9] Wrigley, 'Urban Growth and Agricultural Change', p. 686.

move'.[10] The economy was growing, and England was challenging the Low Countries as economic leader of Europe, but in Durham as in many parts of England, not everyone shared in this growing prosperity.

Food and Drink

The late medieval diet in Durham can be inferred partially from agricultural practices. The staples were bread (increasingly wheaten the further up the social scale), pottage, and ale. The continued enforcement of suit of mill, alongside the rights of the holders of the common oven and malt kiln to collect payment for use of the buildings, underlines the centrality of grain in the late medieval diet.[11] The greater pastoral focus in the northeast means that this diet could be supplemented with beef, mutton, bacon, and cheese. Poultry was important, too; geese are prominent in the halmote courts for wandering unchecked through the fields. The manor complex at Bishop Middleham included a dovecot and orchard. Archaeological finds from the deserted village of Thrislington indicate that the peasantry included deer, hare, and pigeon in their diet. Besides quantities of certain foods, one apparent difference between a peasant and a more aristocratic diet in this area was fish. The manor house in Thrislington had deposits of eel, herring, and haddock while the peasant dwellings there did not. However, there was a fishpond associated with Bishop Middleham and some tenants and outsiders were hauled before the court for fishing, so the peasants were not denying themselves a readily available source of protein, despite the lack of material evidence at one site.[12] Historians have assumed that medieval folk supplemented their diets further with fruits, vegetables, and herbs grown in their gardens and those were plentiful after the Black Death.[13] All told, the demographic and economic changes following the Black Death resulted in more wheaten bread and stronger ale; better taste and more calories, rather than a significant change in foods.[14]

---

[10] Broadberry et al., *British Economic Growth*, pp. 208–10, 330–2; Clark offers several series at 'Data on the English Economy, 1150–1914', and Allen also offers several series at 'Global Price and Income History Group'.

[11] Sear and Sneath, *Origins of the Consumer Revolution*, p. 65; Aston and Gerrard, *Interpreting the English Village*, pp. 214–16. For a different region, see Dyer, 'Peasant Farming in Late Medieval England'.

[12] John Libras was brought before the halmote in 1356 for fishing in the bishop's waters 'many times' (*pluries*). TNA: DURH 3/12 f. 135v. Austin, *Deserted Medieval Village*, pp. 187–9. Kilby discussed peasant fishing as part of the 'hidden economy': *Peasant Perspectives*, Chap. 7, 'Hidden Peasant Economies: Fishing', Kindle loc. 4011–132.

[13] Aston and Gerrard, *Interpreting the English Village*, pp. 202–3. Some garths in the parishes were given over to hay.

[14] There are several excellent discussions on diet and food consumption: Dyer, *Standards of Living*, pp. 151–60; Sear and Sneath, *Origins of the Consumer Revolution*; Lloyd, *Food and Identity in England*, pp. 37–74; Weatherill, *Consumer Behaviour*, pp. 64–71; Allen and Wesidorf, 'Was There an "Industrious Revolution"?'.

For those with money, spices and more unusual foods were available and becoming more affordable in the northeast. The work of Lord Beveridge and more recently Threlfall-Homes on the provisioning of Durham priory reveal a range of foodstuffs in the fourteenth and fifteenth centuries, including 'aniseed, liquorice, ginger, nutmeg, cloves, mace, pepper, figs, raisins', and other dried fruits. The latter's comparisons with other monastic and aristocratic households show that the priory was a big consumer, spending an average of £23 per annum on spices compared to £14 by Westminster Abbey (for more monks) and £4 12s. by the Duke of Buckingham in 1452/53. She found that the Earl of Northumberland also spent highly on spices, £25 19s. 7d. excluding fruit.[15] There is no evidence to determine their availability further down the social scale, unfortunately. Spices other than pepper would have been out of the question for most of the peasantry, but dried fruits and nuts were cheap enough for many to purchase, if not on a regular basis. A pound of almonds, currants, or liquorice each cost 3–5d. Salt was 3–4s. per quarter while sugar varied from 8–12s. per pound in the fifteenth century.[16]

Probate inventories reveal some changes in diet in the sixteenth and seventeenth centuries, although these generally listed goods that could be sold and omitted food for consumption; sugar, spices, and fruits were not recorded even for the wealthy.[17] The poor made do with peas, oaten porridge, and perhaps some rye bread, with a little cheese and butter, washed down with ale or small beer; as wealth increased, so did consumption of mutton, beef, and wheaten bread, with hopped beer and French wines replacing much of the ale that had been consumed. Cheese and butter were plentiful, and the introduction of turkeys added more variety to domestic poultry.[18] Rabbit, venison, fish, and wildfowl also would have been on the menu depending on one's station.[19] This supports Allen's 'respectability basket' of consumables, which was heavy on meat and dairy, yielding 2,500 calories.[20] Newcastle merchants imported an increasing variety of wine, fruit, sugar, and spices and eventually tobacco. These made their way into Durham; John Bayles (d.1568) was a North Auckland shopkeeper who traded mainly in cloth, but his stock included white sugar, green ginger, aniseed, saffron, pepper, turmeric, cloves, mace, raisins, prunes, liquorice, and other spices plus soap and hops.[21] John Johnson (d.1592) of Darlington was similar, focusing on

---

[15] Threlfall-Holmes, *Monks and Markets*, pp. 60–4.

[16] London School of Economics, Archives and Special Collections, Beveridge/Price History/C/8 Box 1; Threlfall-Holmes, *Monks and Markets*, pp. 93–101.

[17] Inventories frequently listed salts and occasionally a pepper or spice box, so the tendency for generic description surely hides more of these items.

[18] There were turkeys in Durham at least as early as 1568: *Wills and Inventories* I, p. 283.

[19] Lloyd discusses the diet by social status in *Food and Identity*, pp. 37–102.

[20] Allen, 'Great Divergence in European Wages and Prices', pp. 420–24, and *British Industrial Revolution* pp. 33–37, 45–48.

[21] *Wills and Inventories* I, pp. 293–4. A tobacco pipe industry emerged in Newcastle in the 1630s: Edwards, 'Tobacco Pipes, Pipemakers, and Tobacconists'.

cloth but also carrying spices, including Barbary sugar and brown sugar candy each at 1s./lb., liquorice at 3d./lb., and seeing glasses.[22] Anthony Dennis (d.1611) was another Darlington shopkeeper; his goods included ginger, prunes, raisins, sugar, hops, and aqua vite.[23] It is not clear whether supply or demand was more pronounced, but as Newcastle's trade increased, so did the options available to those in Durham with money to spend.

The Costs of Living

The diet of middling and poor peasants and, later, of labourers has attracted the focus of scholars attempting to understand the economic history of medieval and early modern England. The cost of living would have affected the health of the lower classes and how much they worked (or how hard they were worked), feeding into debates on economic change.[24] Besides comparison of wages and prices, the other major approach has been the cost of a basket of consumables (and later, Allen's respectable basket) and modelling of a peasant budget.[25] The budget model particularly is useful for exploring issues of wealth and status in the stratifying villages of Durham.

Titow, Howell, and others argued for 10–12 acres as a holding able to sustain a peasant family, but Hilton and Dyer used a half-virgate (15 acres) and concluded that this holding would have been viable, barely, assuming an austere lifestyle and depending on outside employment.[26] The elaborate model crafted by Kitsikopoulos supports the findings of Dyer and Hilton. His budget model used a family of five (husband, wife, and three children) on an 18-acre holding cultivated on a traditional three-field rotation, with 2 acres of meadow;` and this model peasant would have owned a horse, three cattle, ten sheep, a pig, and some poultry. After accounting for household consumption and tithes, the peasant would have had grain as well as some wool and skins to sell, generating 37s. 6d. in total while other activities would have generated an additional 20s. Against this 57s. 7d., Kitsikopoulos estimates nearly 20s. for rents and taxes, 12s. 10d. for consumption, and 17s. 8d. for maintenance of farming equipment. His model farmer was left with a surplus of 7s. 7d.[27] But that would not necessarily go far because a murrain or poor harvest would leave the family in a bad situation, and those with fewer acres would be in even more dire straits. The model uses a mix of actual and

---

[22] *Wills and Inventories* II, pp. 211–12.   [23] *Darlington Wills*, pp. 111–14.

[24] For a summary of the debate, see Bailey, 'Peasant Welfare in England'; Broadberry et al. *British Economic Growth*, pp. 279–306.

[25] For the 'respectability basket' see Allen, *British Industrial Revolution*, p. 36.

[26] Titow, *English Rural Society*, p.90; Howell, *Land, Family and Inheritance*, pp. 162–3; Dyer, *Standards of Living*, pp. 117, 184–5; Hilton, 'Rent and Capital Formation in Feudal Society', pp. 199–200.

[27] Kitsikopoulos, 'Standards of Living and Capital Formation in Pre-Plague England'.

estimated values and relies heavily on data from seigneurial demesnes, and so it may not be wholly accurate for a peasant farmer.

How well does his model fit a late medieval Sedgefield tenant, such as John Joly from 1407? Joly's tenure is not enumerated in the surviving records, but we know he had 17.5 acres seeded with wheat plus garden, meadow, and pasture.[28] If he held a husbandland (30–34 acres) or malland (36 acres), then he may have planned to seed some of his remaining land with barley and oats, a common scheme, so the for the sake of argument and as a closer fit to Kitsikopoulos's model, I assume he seeded another 2.5 acres with oats and the same with barley, with the remainder left fallow.[29] Employing the same yield estimates as Kitsikopoulos, the estimated gross and net yields are shown in Table 6.1; if he held a malland, Joly's harvest may have been higher if he sowed the additional land at the same proportion. The net sale price of the entire crop represents what Joly could have brought in if he had sold all his grain; he would not have done so, but it makes the comparison possible. The Durham grain price series by Schofield and Dodds has the prices for 1407; and since it was a year of low grain prices, income from the average price for 1400–09 has been calculated to give a better sense of possible outcomes. Aside from grain, Kitsikopoulos included additional income in his model: 10d. for sales of wool and skins, 9s. 9d. for renting out the cart (Joly's neighbour John de Utley had an iron-bound cart with four horses so he may have had a similar one), and 10s. 4d. for outside employment, for a total of nearly 21s. of extra income.[30]

From the harvest and additional income, Joly had to pay his rent and other expenses. His rent would have been either 14s. 4d. (for a husbandland) or 6s. (for a malland), the same or lower than Kitsikopoulos used for a smaller holding

Table 6.1 Estimated yields and income from grain sales, c.1407

	Acres sown	Estimated yield (qr./ acre)	Gross Yield (qr.)	Net of tithe and seed (qr.)	Price – 1407 (s./qr)	Net sale Price – 1407 (s.)	Mean Price –1400–09 (s./qr)	Net sale – 1400– 09 (s.)
Wheat	17.5	1.4	24.1	13.0	3.73	48.6	7.8	102.0
Barley	2.5	2.1	5.2	2.1	3.32	6.9	5.1	10.6
Oats	2.5	1.6	4.0	0.9	1.5	1.3	2.2	1.9

Source: Kitsikopoulos, 'Peasant Budget Model', pp. 238–48; TNA: DURH 3/14 f. 65v.

[28] The men who temporarily held the land paid 11s. 8d. in total for their rent, about a third of the normal rent.

[29] Alternatively, he may have been using more land for pasture, similar to what Hoskins observed in early modern Leicestershire: 'Leicestershire Farmer in the Seventeenth Century', pp. 16–17.

[30] TNA: DURH 3/13 f. 446r.

(14s. 4d. ob. for 18 acres). Kitsikopoulos estimated the following expenses beyond rent (rounded up):

12s. 10d.	home maintenance and household consumption
5s. 6d.	hay and oats for the horse
9s.	upkeep of animals
17s. 8d.	maintenance of farm gear
3s.	tax & tallage
1s. 10d.	other obligations
18d.	court amercements (as opposed to Kitsikopoulos's 4d.)
3s. 4d.	baking (2d. per bushel in these villages, and assuming half the grain is baked into bread)
55s 7d.	total, excluding rent.

The potential bottom line of Joly's budget, depending on his holding, is shown in Table 6.2. If he were a husbandman, he would have had a small surplus with the low prices of 1407; assuming a similar yield he may have done very well in years of high prices. With malland he would have been comfortable with some money to spare. To turn this into a daily wage rate using Hatcher's approach, Joly would have had an income, after tithes, rent, and the 4s. Hatcher added for additional costs, of 2–4.8d. per day. Using average rates for 1450–79, the equivalent wage for that crop would have been 2–2.5d. (again after deducting tithes, rent, and 4s. in expenses).[31] In Kitsikopoulos's model with average prices for 1450–79, Joly's descendant with a husbandland would have little to no surplus, needing either more income or cutting costs somewhere. If he were prudent, Joly would have saved up in good years or worked occasionally to earn more. It is easy to see why larger holdings were more attractive, up to a point; they provided flexibility.

Table 6.2 Durham peasant budget model, c.1407 (in shillings)

	Husbandland (30 acres)		Malland (36 acres)	
	1407	1400–09	1407	1400–09
Income (grain)	56.8	114.5	56.8	114.5
Income (other)	21.0	21.0	21.0	21.0
Rent	−14.3	−14.3	−6.0	−6.0
Other expenses	−56.6	−56.6	−56.6	−56.6
Net income	6.9	64.6	15.2	72.9

Source: Kitsikopoulos, 'Peasant Budget Model', pp. 238–48; TNA: DURH 3/14 f. 65v.

---

[31] Hatcher, 'Unreal Wages', pp. 12–13. Kitsikopoulos's estimate for costs is ten times higher.

Living within easy reach of several markets and a member of a commercialized culture, Joly still would have kept some grain for his own household rather than sell it all. The market provided him with options: he could keep the wheat for himself and make less at the market, or he could sell the wheat and purchase cheaper grains for his own consumption. If Joly could provide more hay or used some oats for fodder, he could have reduced his costs. Likewise, with the greater pastoral emphasis in Durham, he may have had more income from his animals in meat, wool, butter, and cheese. If his wife brewed and sold ale, that would have provided a little more income. Even in a bad year, it would not have taken much belt-tightening to get by: eating more barley and oats or baking bread at home. Through it all, he could have afforded Allen's 'bare-bones basket' and often the respectability basket for a household of five, and in some years upgraded his farm implements or purchased a brass pot or some linens while still saving a little for bad years.[32]

What about those with smaller holdings? In an average year above, a tenant holding half a husbandland would have had a surplus of 5–10s. depending on rent and dietary choices. In some years they might have done very well. They would have been in trouble in 1407, coming up 14–18s. in the red. Such a Durham tenant would have been in a very similar situation as a half-yardlander in the Midlands, perhaps a little better from greater access to pasture. A cottager with 6 acres would have been unable to grow enough food for their family, even if selling wheat as a cash crop and buying cheaper grain for the household, and so would have relied heavily on wages. They still would be better off than a labourer, especially in years of high grain prices. Schofield saw indications of 'some pressure on food resources in the North-East' in the later fourteenth and early fifteenth centuries that would have exacerbated differences in standard of living within the county.[33] Hatcher warned of 'how acutely sensitive household budgets through-out the landholding spectrum' were to wages.[34] The budgets modelled above demonstrate the fluctuations possible from year to year.

Those models also demonstrate the importance of peasant decision making in farming, buying, and selling. Both Dodds and Dyer concluded that changes in tithe receipts after the Black Death indicate higher per capita grain output and greater emphasis on pastoral production via increased production of fodder crops, with Dyer noting the peasant response depended on the region and type of soil. Wheat production dropped and the falling price would have discouraged intensive cultivation, but it still was prized for high quality bread. Dodds noted

[32] Broadberry et al., *British Economic Growth*, pp. 311, 334–37, as derived from Allen, *British Industrial Revolution*, pp. 36–7 and 'The Great Divergence in European Wages'. On peasant posses-sions, see Aston and Gerrard, *Interpreting the English Village*, pp. 210–14; Jervis at al., 'Exploring Text and Objects', and Briggs et al., 'People, Possessions and Domestic Space'.
[33] Schofield, 'Regional Price Differentials'.   [34] Hatcher, 'Unreal Wages', p. 18.

that from the 1370s, due to falling prices for grain, '[t]hose continuing to produce grain would have had to adopt ruthlessly efficient, and independent, agricultural practices but would have come into conflict with those switching to pastoral husbandry'.[35] Such a conflict is visible in the villages, but some men were in a good place to combine both approaches. Dyer suggested that the lack of evidence about pastoral farming meant that arable production 'could be viewed in some locations as an adjunct to livestock husbandry, where good profits were to be made'.[36]

Could that have applied in Durham in the fourteenth and fifteenth centuries? While larger holdings offered the possibility to expand output, it does not hold that there was sufficient demand to do so.[37] Joly and others like him might have been better off making their lives easier by moderating output and spending more time in other pursuits. He could add more wheat, ale, and meat to his own diet, or invest in his farm.[38] A man with two husbandlands could run the holding like a single husbandland, leaving more land fallow or turning parts over to grass; Tuck described a shift to pastoral agriculture in the northeast, and Dodds found that arable output in Durham declined 53 per cent following the Black Death.[39] There were limits to expansion; as noted earlier, a double holding seemed to be a preferred size, and for good reason. Up to a certain point, the size of the holding made it easier to ride out the bumpier years, but eventually the cost of labour would become a hindrance. Sixty acres might be manageable as a family farm, especially with a greater proportion of fallow; larger or more intensively worked farms required hired labour.[40]

Joly's standard of living was altogether not far removed from that over the previous centuries.[41] Durham, and England as a whole, possessed advanced market structures but a weaker consumer culture. The halmote books mention few items, even in the case of fugitives such as John de Utley. Among the goods he left behind in 1404 were an iron-bound cart and four horses worth 20s., some sieves, and a lead.[42] The tenurial developments up to this point sufficed to support initial

[35] Dodds, *Peasants and Production*, pp. 71–85, 94. Dyer, 'Peasant Farming in Late Medieval England', pp. 92–5.

[36] Dyer, 'Peasant Farming in Late Medieval England', p. 102.

[37] Britnell is cautious about the scale of urban demand before the Black Death: 'Urban Demand', pp. 7–9; see also his *Growth and Decline in Colchester*, pp. 41–7.

[38] Dyer suggested that late medieval workers did not work to earn as much as possible, but to meet what they considered a comfortable living standard: *Standards of Living*, p. 224; Allen and Weisdorf demonstrated this in their analysis of days worked by farm and urban labourers: 'Was There an "Industrious Revolution"'.

[39] Tuck, 'The Occupation of the Land', pp. 40–1; Dodds, 'Estimating Arable Output Using Durham Priory Tithe Receipts', p. 261. See also Pollard, 'The North-Eastern Economy and the Agrarian Crises', pp. 103–4.

[40] See Hatcher, 'Unreal Wages', pp. 12–14.

[41] Some late medieval peasant houses in nearby Thrislington were made of stone: Austin, *Deserted Medieval Village*, pp. 65–80. Kilby discusses peasant space in *Peasant Perspectives*, Chap. 3, 'Encountering the Built Environment', Kindle loc. 1341–548.

[42] TNA: DURH 3/13 f. 446r.

population growth, but exogenous demand was needed to increase production. Also absent was incentive, particularly consumer goods cheap and plentiful enough for those beneath the nobility to purchase regularly.[43] There were items for purchase, and in a good year some of the imports through Newcastle may have been tempting, but this sort of consumption had not yet become part of the culture beneath the well-to-do. It is worth noting here that most major enclosure in Durham came after the expansion of the coal trade, in line with Allen's argument regarding the unimportance of enclosure in economic development.[44] Agriculturally, the region was primed and ready in the fifteenth century. Rapid population growth, more imports through Newcastle thanks to expanded coal mining, and local industry eventually provided demand and incentive to take advantage of those late medieval developments.

Two centuries later, we can see the results. To provide a sense of the scope of change, let us look at Richard Gibson who died in 1597 holding two messuages and three bovates of copyhold land in Sedgefield; these lands can be traced back through his family to the mid-fifteenth century and so we know that two of the bovates were malland, for a total of 51 acres of arable land. For that, he paid just over 33s. in rent. His family had acquired and relinquished other lands over the years, so this is an example of a family willing to adjust to change.[45] He had the lease of another 40 acres of land, although the rent is unknown. When his inventory was made in June 1597, he left 20 acres sown with wheat, rye, barley, oats, and peas; he had seventy-five sheep and lambs, thirteen cows and calves, eight oxen, two pigs, and poultry. In the house the appraisers listed wheat, maslin, oats, cheese, butter, and fleeces.[46] Using the average of prices in Durham from the 1590s and assuming equal amounts of each grain sown on those 20 acres, Gibson could sell close to £60 of grain each year, net of seed, tithe, and fodder from those holdings. If he were still following a three-course rotation, then that sum would be higher when his other land is added in (assuming more was not fallowed).[47] If he only sheared adult sheep and lost no other animals besides the one cow slaughtered for beef, his animals would have provided meat, dairy products, and wool worth over £40. His plough gear and dairy implements indicate he was producing

---

[43] See Hatcher, 'Unreal Wages', pp. 20–2. This is not to say there was nothing to purchase. A team led by Chris Briggs has been exploring peasant living standards using Escheator's records among other sources for 1300–1600. See Jervis et al., 'Exploring Text and Objects', and Briggs et al., 'People, Possessions and Domestic Space'.

[44] Allen, 'Progress and Poverty', p. 430.

[45] TNA: DURH 3/13 f. 285r, 388r; 3/14 f. 382r, 404v; 3/15 f. 27r, 76v, 84r, 134r, 154v, 177v, 191r, 199r, 275r; 3/16 ff. 92v, 311v; 3/17 ff. 26r, 34r, 51v, 106v; 3/18 ff. 50v, 79v, 160r; 3/19 ff. 128r, 168r, 174v;/21 f. 224v; 3/22 pp. 15, 133; 3/23 ff. 154r, 248r, 320v; 3/24 pp. 481, 583, 919; 3/25 f. 214r.

[46] DPRI/1/1597/G4/1–5. His good were valued at £93 17s. 6d., plus the lease of other lands worth £8 and debts owing to him of £8 4s. 8d. He forgave several debts in his will, which did not appear in his inventory.

[47] He might have used more land for grass; see Hoskins, 'Leicestershire Farmer in the Seventeenth Century', pp. 16–17.

for the market: 91 acres was not a family farm. Allen's respectability basket (including 5 per cent for housing upkeep but substituting beef for pork) cost about £8 per person in the 1590s, based on a combination of local and national prices.[48] After deducting known rent and the cost of eight respectability baskets (he had five beds, so there was Gibson and his wife Elizabeth, his two illegitimate daughters, a maidservant Isabella, and perhaps three more servants assuming they shared beds), Gibson would have had over £35 plus the income from the rest of his land to pay rent on the leasehold, taxes, court fines, and servants' wages while maintaining home, flocks, and capital equipment. Servants in Durham earned 10–40s. per year, so around £6 for the four assumed above was readily affordable by a farmer like Gibson.[49] Some of his wealth went to his daughters; he entrusted a friend with £80 to go to them when they reached marriageable age. If necessary, he could sell or slaughter more of his livestock. Like Joly, he could expand his flocks and invest in more equipment, or he could spend his money on an increasing number of consumer goods available in the northeast; his inventory included 10s. of pewter, 16s. of brass, a variety of kitchen goods, and a featherbed worth 40s.[50] He may have expanded or rebuilt his house; room-by-room inventories were not yet common, so we do not know. The budgets of these households had grown less sensitive to prices and wages; the same was not true of those with only a few acres, or none at all.

A Consumption Revolution?

The ways in which Gibson and men like or wealthier than him spent their money, in comparison with the increasing poverty of smallholders and the landless, is visible in the greater number of sources for the early modern period. The number of surviving wills increases dramatically in the latter half of the sixteenth century and probate inventories yield evidence of changing standards of living. The tenants with 30 or more acres who emerged in the later Middle Ages were well-placed to take advantage of the changing times while even smallholders may have been able to hold on, both thanks to low rents.

One path was greater specialization in agriculture, originating in the late medieval period. Cattle could be sold to a butcher for meat and hides, with milk used to produce butter and cheese; sheep likewise provided meat and wool. Some

---

[48] Allen, *British Industrial Revolution*, p. 36; price data from Clark, 'National Income, Prices, Wages, Land Rents, Population, England, 1209–1869' series, 'England NNI - Clark - 2015.xlsx'.

[49] The £6 assumes £2 each for two adult men and £1 each for Isabella and a teenager. Foster calculated one adult and two teenage servants as common for men with around 90 acres of land in sixteenth-century Cheshire; a second adult male was added because no sons are mentioned in the will and Elizabeth could not attend court because of her age. Foster, *Capital and Innovation*, p.128, and *Cheshire Cheese*, pp. 71–6.

[50] DPRI/1/1597/G4/1–5. Gibson also had a coat of plate and weapons.

farmers looked to wheat and rye to sell on the market for bread, while others put more land to barley (for malt) or oats (for malt or fodder). The quantities of equipment recorded in some inventories indicate malt and beer production in large quantities. The low rents led some tenants to sublet their lands, letting others do the farming while charging higher rents. Those who acquired the rights to tithes let those out as well, and for substantial sums: a Northamptonshire knight farmed the tithes for Bishop Middleham parish for £23 15s. 4d. by the time of Civil War, while the Parliamentary commissioners valued the tithes of Sedgefield (township only, not the not parish) at more than £102 6s. 8d., and let them to Ralph Mason, John Johnson, Robert Johnson, and Thomas Middleton for £50. The tithes for the entire parish were let for £197 16s. 8d. combined, suggesting a tithable grain crop around £2,000. The lessees would have expected to make some profit; Dodds found that profits on fifteenth-century tithes ranged from 7–81 per cent and so the tithable output of Sedgefield parish may have been upwards of £4,000.[51]

Another approach to understanding wealth and comfort uses the documents created to settle the affairs of the deceased. Probate inventories survive for 253 Bishop Middleham and Sedgefield residents before 1700 and reveal the increasing standard of living of many parishioners alongside the desperate poverty of others; the poorest of the parishes are largely absent from those records. With an average of fewer than two inventories per year, some very wealthy and many not, no attempt has been made to account for the missing inventories or those without inventories.[52] The inventories are invaluable but must be used with care, as numerous scholars have warned; they provide values not price, the ways items were recorded was inconsistent, and the wealthy tend to be over-represented.[53]

Wealth and status often went hand in hand in probate records but this was not a given, as status depended on individual claim and social acceptance and not just on wealth. The wealthiest man noted as a yeoman, Robert Fawdon (d.1667), was worth as much as the poorest twenty-four yeomen who died between 1573 and 1697 combined. He also was worth more than all the gentlemen except Edward Hutton (d.1629) and Fawdon's contemporary Robert Shaw. Another Robert, Robert Smith (d.1681) claimed in his will to be a yeoman. The men who inventoried his goods identified him as a labourer instead. Smith had precious few goods,

---

[51] *Records of the Committees for Compounding*, pp. 4–8, 21. The glebe of Sedgefield was let for £114 3s. 6d.: Dodds, *Peasants and Production*, p. 168. Letting the tithes at half of their earlier value may reflect the devastation of the county.

[52] Overton et al., *Production and Consumption in English Households*, pp. 22–6. Overton proposed a method to account for those too poor to leave inventories: 'Household Wealth', p. 5.

[53] For example, see Arkell, 'Interpreting Probate Inventories'; Overton, 'Prices from Probate Inventories', p. 240; Overton et al., *Production and Consumption in English Households*; Spufford, 'The Limitations of the Probate Inventory'; Yelling, 'Probate Inventories and the Geography of Livestock Farming'; Zell, 'The Social Parameters of Probate Records'. Shammas also addressed these concerns: *The Pre-industrial Consumer*, pp. 18–20; De Vries, 'Between Purchasing Power', pp. 212–24. One of the earliest works using probate inventories is Hoskins, 'Leicestershire Farmer in the Sixteenth Century'.

and only a little grain in the field and three cows, hardly the set-up for a prosperous farmer, yet he owned five horses. Yet John Laing (d.1681) was identified as a yeoman even though the appraisers for his inventory simply valued them at 30s., his 'household stuff being very ordinary and mean'.[54] Labels can be misleading. Perhaps Laing was retired. Many whose wealth and goods suggested yeomen or even gentlemanly status were not identified as such, while some who were instead could have been identified as tradesmen based on their goods. We might categorize others as artisans and tradesmen based on their inventories. The probate inventories reflect the values of the time in more ways than one.[55]

Gentlemen and above were defined by their social standing. A poor gentleman was superior to a wealthy yeoman or tradesman even though such families intermarried and younger sons were apprenticed to a trade. Gentlemanly status rested on having one's claim accepted by others. Even then, the division was unclear and had been for some time. In the Middle Ages there was a broad, liminal group between the husbandmen and cottagers who worked and the gentlemen who held manors. Sometimes this can be traced back to the pre-Conquest period: the dreng who held land by customary rather than free tenure but whose services were more noble, such as accompanying the lord on the hunt. Some of these tenures included the role of overseer or bailiff; two men in *Boldon Book* paid 2s. in rent for their 40 acres and 'ought to be in charge of the obligatory days and go on missions'.[56] These men ranked above the husbandmen, but it is not clear whether they worked in the fields. Alongside these drengs were the sub-manorial families. Liddy pointed out how gentility for some late medieval Durham families owed more to service than to landed wealth. Families such as the Pollards and the Featherstones were 'gentry landholders of very modest rank', with their claim to be esquires founded upon their service. Given the early existence of copyhold, the practical differences between a wealthy customary tenant, a free tenant, and a holder of a 'manor' could be negligible. Liddy concluded that '[a] more fluid concept of gentility allowed men, who in other areas of England would have been quintessential yeoman, to stake a claim to gentle status'.[57]

This liminal group broadened in the early modern period alongside increasing stratification in landholding. In Bishop Middleham and Sedgefield parishes, yeomen outnumbered husbandmen nearly twenty to one in surviving probate inventories. Robert Smith, whose claims to yeoman status were countered by the appraisers, had an inventory worth more than four times as much as two

[54] DPRI/1/1681/L2, 1682/S21/1–3.

[55] Zell observed that in Wealden Kent, the distinction between farmer and artisan rested on whether the decedent did or did not have a farm; Zell, *Industry in the Countryside*, pp. 108–9, 137. Such rural industries are not reflected in the parishes' inventories; whether that is true for all rural Durham remains to be seen. See Arkell, 'Interpreting Probate Inventories', pp. 79–82 for a discussion of different findings on inventories and occupation.

[56] *Domesday Book supp. vol 35: Boldon Book*, p. 63.

[57] Liddy, *Bishopric of Durham*, pp. 71–5.

contemporaries who were considered yeomen. At the other end of the scale, families such as the Masons were rising into the gentry. Shepard and Spicksley, using depositions in church courts, concluded that the worth of yeomen 'out-stripped inflation by a factor of 10', leading to increased polarization, and that yeomen also achieved greater security over their lifetimes.[58] We can see many such examples in Durham.

Many men invested their increasing income by acquiring more land and stock or through purchasing more or better capital goods. The median real value of plough and wain gear nearly doubled between 1600 and 1699 while that of dairy production nearly tripled according to probate inventories from the two parishes. There were other options besides ploughing their money back into their farm. The jurors, churchwardens, and substantial tenants who provided most appraisers were exactly the group attuned to increasing commercialism and wealth trickling down into village society. Several scholars have posited a consumer revolution and De Vries an 'industrious revolution' starting *c*.1600, although this has been challenged.[59] There certainly were an increasing number and variety of household goods in the probate inventories of the seventeenth century and Spaeth sees the appraisers who created the inventories as 'witnesses to economic and social change'.[60] How early and how far down the social scale of the parishes is indeterminable due to limited records and the whims of appraisers, but the probate inventories reveal the spread of increasing numbers, types, and qualities of consumer goods in the parishes, even among the poor.[61] The first inventory that survives is for one of the wealthiest men in the whole period, Robert Hyndmer (d.1558), rector of Sedgefield. He was also dean of the collegiate churches at Bishop Auckland and Lanchester, rector of Stanhope and other benefices, and more importantly the temporal chancellor of Durham, spiritual principal official, and vicar general for Bishop Tunstall. His inventory is unrepresentative of his parishioners but reveals what it meant to be a wealthy gentleman in the mid-sixteenth century. His estate was valued at £891 5s. 4d. Hyndmer owned more than one hundred head of cattle and four hundred sheep, and the tithe corn from Sedgefield and Stanhope was valued at £56 11s. 8d. He had a gold and ruby ring, and several fine gowns. He owned more than ten pounds of silver plate, worth £45, in addition to pots, utensils, and candlesticks made of tin, latten, brass, and lesser materials. Hyndmer lived quite comfortably in Sedgefield; there was an iron chimney, turned and

---

[58] Shepard and Spicksley, 'Worth, Age, and Social Status in Early Modern England', pp. 493–5.

[59] Allen and Weisdorf found no revolution among farm labourers, who had to work harder just to make ends meet, although urban labourers were a different story: 'Was There an "Industrious Revolution?"'.

[60] De Vries, *Industrious Revolution*; Spaeth, '"Orderly Made"', p. 418. Buxton provides a recent discussion of the furniture and goods in the market town of Thame (Oxfords.) in *Domestic Culture in Early Modern England*, pp. 95–207.

[61] On the use and interpretation of probate inventories, see especially Spaeth, '"Orderly made"'; Overton et al., *Production and Consumption in English Households*, pp. 14–19, 87–120.

joined furniture (including chairs and a bed), tapestries and carpets (some Kentish), and a dozen feather beds.[62] Joined furniture did not appear in Terling until 1600.[63] The household of Thomas Hutcheson (d.1587), yeoman, offers an example of a 'middling sort' household. Thomas's goods and chattels were valued at £92 13s. 8d., after Hyndmer's the highest in any surviving probate record for the parishes in the sixteenth century. In his will, he left his leases, plough, and gear to his eldest son, along with his feather bed. His daughter, Katherine, received a (presumably chaff) mattress and bed, kitchen utensils, livestock, and £4 6s. 8d. in money, as well as an acre of wheat and an acre of oats. He left his other three children £8 to be split among them. The inventory of his goods is thorough and shows his wealth, but not much about comfort or luxury: a bolster and three pillows, some finer linen sheets but most of coarser cloth. He owned six brass pots and ten pieces of pewter, as well as other items made of wood or ceramic. He also had forty-four yards of cloth, three stone of wool, nine pounds of linen yard, and two spinning wheels. Livestock comprised over half the value of the inventory, including eight oxen and twenty sheep and lambs. His household was a prosperous one, producing for the market and at a different scale from two centuries before; his plough gear was plentiful, some described as new.[64] The spinning wheels hint at involvement in the cloth industry, whether working with wool, linen, or both.

Imports and import substitution, whether from new industries or pre-existing ones like the aforementioned cloth trade, offered villagers a range of prices and options.[65] Looking at the middling tradesmen in Newcastle, Heley concluded that 'there is a marked increase in consumption of items that had already been around in the 16th century, objects that were becoming widely available at prices the middling sort could afford'.[66] Wealth and status was reflected in the quantity and quality of goods, not just the type.[67] That is true in the two parishes as well. It was not unusual to find different levels of good in the same inventory, such as wood, brass, pewter, and silver utensils. For some villagers, one set was for everyday use and the other for special occasions; for the wealthier, the cheaper goods would be

---

[62] *Correspondence of Reginald Pole: Vol. 4*, p. 295; *Wills and Inventories* I, pp. 160–4; *Registers of Cuthbert Tunstall*, et al., pp. 3–6, 17, 27, 77, 86. Nair noted that featherbeds and brass pots appeared in Highley in the mid-sixteenth century, earlier than other places: *Highley*, p. 37.

[63] Wrightson and Levine, *Poverty & Piety*, p. 38.   [64] DPRI/1/1587/H13/1–7.

[65] See Shammas, *The Pre-Industrial Consumer*, pp. 94–96, on how the average proportions of wealth taken up by consumer goods did not change in her sample for these reasons. It would be interesting to know how much of that local production was import substitution or part of an older local cloth industry. Thirsk argued for spreading industry for consumer products in the sixteenth and seventeenth centuries, providing 'extra cash' to those involved, while expensive imports spurred on domestic industries: *Economic Policy and Projects*, pp. 15–17, 174.

[66] Heley found that many items did not change price significantly in the century before the Civil War: 'Material Culture', pp. 283–85, 331.

[67] Levine and Wrightson make this point about Whickham: *Making of an Industrial Society*, pp. 91, 103.

for the servants. There is also the question of taste and outlook, whether someone was an early adopter or old-fashioned, a spendthrift or frugal.

Harden, straken, coarse and fine linen, 'Holland cloth', diapered cloth, damask, and silk featured on the tables and beds of villagers in the early seventeenth century.[68] Brass pots proliferated; pewter was also a popular choice. The number, type, and quality of kitchen implements increased as well as the quantity. In 1584, the rector of Sedgefield had 10s. of brass and 6s. 8d. of pewter, but husbandman John Cloase had 16s. of brass and 10s. of pewter in 1609. James Hall, yeoman (d.1613) owned more than 66s. 11d. of pewter objects and a brass looking glass. In 1662 Ralph Mason, not described as a yeoman or gentleman but whose wife hailed from a local gentry family, owned £5 of pewter dishes (for both special occasions and everyday use), flowerpots, candlesticks, 33s. 4d. of brass, some iron pots, and other utensils of brass and wood. He also owned a brass clock valued at £2. Silver was a mark of higher status, with yeomen owning a spoon or two and gentlemen more, sometimes gilt.[69] China and glass were rare before the Civil War. Several men had Bibles; the parish clerk and schoolmaster John Farales had three, one in Latin and both an octavo and a quarto in English, as well as several other books valued in total at £1 13s. 4d.[70] Edward Hutton, B.C.L. and bailiff of Durham, had an impressive collection of volumes on Common, Civil, and Canon law befitting his education and station.[71] Furniture improved in number and quality. Ralph Mason had a table with eight stools and four green chairs. Featherbeds likewise proliferated, along with linen sheets (often of imported Holland cloth) and more pillows. The vicar Thomas Middleton had two feather beds in 1584 while wealthy yeoman Thomas Hutcheson and Ralph Elstob, gent. (possibly the grandfather of Ralph Mason's wife) had only a single feather bed; Ralph Mason had four; while George Scurfield, Esq, owned three plus three chaff beds.[72] As Overton et al. found in Kent, the number and variety of items shows improved comfort, standards of living, and consumption, in contrast to the greater impoverishment in Cornwall.[73]

By the mid- seventeenth century the changes are clear in the wills and probate inventories of the parishes, in line with the findings of Sear and Sneath.[74] Furniture such as cupboards were no longer unusual, while the increasingly large

[68] This supports the arguments of Dyer and Sear and Sneath over Weatherill: Dyer, *Making a Living*, pp. 311–22, and *Age of Transition*, p. 137; Weatherill, *Consumer Behaviour*, p. 28; Sear and Sneath, *Origins of the Consumer Revolution*, pp. 71–172.

[69] Margaret Claxton, widow of Sir William Claxton, had four silver spoons stolen in 1437 by William Clerk, parish clerk of Fishburn: *Register of Thomas Langley*, vol. V, pp. 39–40, 45–7.

[70] DPRI/1/1558/H3/3–7, 1609/C11/2, 1613/H3/3–7, 1639/F2/1–2, 1662/M6/1.

[71] DPRI/1/1629/H16/1–23. He described himself as being of Mainsforth: Green, 'Law and Architecture in Early Modern Durham', p. 267.

[72] DPRI/1/1587/H13/2–5, 1603/E1/2–3, 1640/S1/1–2, 1662/M6/1; Overton et al., *Production and Consumption in English Households*, pp. 87–120.

[73] Overton et al., *Production and Consumption in English Households*, pp. 170–1.

[74] Sear and Sneath, *Origins of the Consumer Revolution*, pp. 204–25.

landless population had little use for animals. While the itemization of linens and utensils became longer and more detailed in inventories, those for apparel became less so, being lumped in with the contents of the deceased's purse.[75] In the sixteenth century, bequests were normally of furniture, clothes, and animals. Cash had replaced these for male testators by the mid seventeenth century, apart from small bequests to less-close relations, as when John Gage (d.1614) bequeathed a lamb to each of his godchildren. Thomas Conyers (d.1625) left his relations cash legacies, even though his inventory included gold rings, silver spoons, feather-beds, armour, and various other items of worth.[76] Women continued to bequeath items but also coin. De Vries observed that '[r]ural households in the maritime regions of the Netherlands achieved substantial market dependence via special-isation by the mid-seventeenth century, and many parts of England followed suit in the century after 1650'.[77] The increasing market-oriented agriculture necessary to support the expanding industry in Tyneside, Weardale, and Sunderland encouraged market dependence even in the rural parishes.

The inventories depict the increasingly commercial and materialistic nature of society. The most detailed evidence comes from the middling sort but there is also evidence among the poorer inventories. Looking glasses, glasses, wainscotting, and other formerly scarce items became more common in the houses of the mid-dling sort, furniture was more likely to be joined, and common goods were more likely to be made of iron or brass, or even silver for the very wealthy. Clocks such as that owned by Ralph Mason were still 'a sign of affluence [rather] than a social necessity', according to Whitrow; Mason lived comfortably, with featherbeds, cur-tains on the windows, and an abundance of cooking and dining ware.[78] His was a level of living not far removed from that of gentleman Robert Shaw of nearby Thrislington. Shaw possessed a clock and a looking glass, four featherbeds, rugs, and curtains; he also had pewter for everyday and special occasions, and £7 10s. of table linens.[79] Shaw had more and finer furniture, however, including six leather chairs and six chairs covered with green cloth. His wealth was valued at more than four times that of Mason's, and his goods were finer, reflecting the dif-ference in social status.[80] The inventory for Nicholas Freville, Esq., of Hardwick (d.1673) demonstrates the difference between armigerous and non-armigerous families. His inventory included £23 of silver plate (including various salt cellars, a pepper box, and sixteen spoons) and £13 9s. 6d. of pewter, plus iron and brass items in the kitchen. The chambers in his house had curtains with rods, hangings,

---

[75] Wills do document something about clothing, however; for example, widow Joan Jopling left numerous items to relatives and other women: DPRI/1/1633/J10/1–2.

[76] *Wills and Inventories*, IV pp. 80–81, 190–2. To Nair, the shift from bequests of goods to money marked the end of the 'peasant economy': *Highley*, pp. 39–40.

[77] De Vries, 'Between Purchasing Power', p. 216.

[78] Whitrow, *Time in History*, p. 112; see Sear and Sneath, *Origins of the Consumer Revolution*, pp. 155–8 for a discussion of clocks, their value, and significance.

[79] DPRI/1/1662/M6/1.   [80] DPRI/1/1676/S7/5–7.

and carpets, and plenty of bedding; three chambers had looking glasses and hearths (and in 1666 he was assessed for fourteen hearths total in Sedgefield). His garret was crammed with additional serving dishes, many of wood. He also owned twelve pair of pistols with holsters, three guns, and two suits of armour. The careful itemization stands in contrast to the lack of detail. Luxury must have been assumed, given his rank and wealth. Except for chests (those that were oak, or cypress) and linens (whether harden, linen, damask, or diapered), the appraisers did not describe the items, so for example we do not know how many of his sixteen beds had feather mattresses. His study held a cupboard, two chests, cabinet, bedstand, two desks, two different types of trunks, a standing clock, and books, all to the value of £13 10s.[81] In contrast to these men, Samuel Walker of Swainston, yeoman, (d.1665) lived a different lifestyle. His goods and debts were valued at £415 1s. 4d., one of the highest values for a yeoman. His goods reflect little luxury: a feather bed, and some curtains in the parlour. The value of his goods lay in livestock and farm gear, and in money lent to others: £40 13s. 4d. lent in cash and £169 10s. by bond. He himself had no debts beyond 33s. for servants' wages and £62 3s. 4f. in rents for lands he farmed in Swainston, and in his will he made only monetary bequests beyond his lands in Trimdon.[82]

In addition to more and better household goods, the houses became larger and more complex.[83] Overton et al. cautioned against simple divisions of rooms into 'public' or 'private' based on the goods found therein, in particular during periods of change.[84] Leaving such questions aside, the inventories illustrate Durham houses becoming more complex. Green has shown that Durham participated in the 'Great Rebuilding' of the sixteenth and seventeenth centuries. Wills and the organization of some probate inventories room by room bear out Green's conclusions from surviving structures starting in the third quarter of the sixteenth century. Several gentlemen in other Durham parishes, including Thomas Tempest of Stanely (d.1569), William Kirkhouse of Kirk Merrington (d.1573?), William Lee of Brandon (d.1582), and Ralph Willey of Houghton-le-Side (d.1584), lived in large, two-storey houses.[85] The only similar room by room inventory in the parishes was for Robert Hyndmer, the rector of Sedgefield. His parsonage of Sedgefield was substantial in the 1550s: two stories with a hall, two parlours, chamber, kitchen, and buttery on the ground floor and five chambers including a study and guest room above. In 1666, the rector was assessed for nine hearths.[86] Thrislington Hall contained a hall, two parlours, a second floor, garret, and

[81] DPRI/1/1673/F10/1–6; County Durham Hearth Tax, p. 47.   [82] DPRI/1/1655/W4/3.

[83] The excavation at Thrislington found padlocks, bolts, keys from both manor and peasant houses: Austin, Deserted Medieval Village, pp. 196–7. Buxton provides a discussion of the naming and use of rooms, albeit focused on towns: in Domestic Culture in Early Modern England, pp. 208–36.

[84] Overton et al., Production and Consumption in English Households, pp. 155–6.

[85] Wills and Inventories II, pp. 43–45, 98, 168–70, 193–95, 240–42, 306–10, 337; Wills and Inventories III, p. 48.

[86] Wills and Inventories I, pp. 160–4; DPRI/1/1634/B7/5–6; County Durham Hearth Tax, p. 46.

kitchen, with a total of four hearths in 1666; it was built early in the seventeenth century. The Shaws were acquiring land in Thrislington and Cornforth in the sixteenth century and purchased the manor in 1613, so it may have been constructed soon after.[87] One of Green's examples for the middling sort is Tudhoe Hall, about four miles west of Cornforth. It was rebuilt by a husbandman *c.*1600–09 from a single storey stone house to a two and a half storey structure, later expanded by a yeoman in the 1620s. He concluded '[t]he houses of the region indicate that changes in the way of living were in step with the national picture from the end of the sixteenth century, for the prosperous', and I would add that this included many of the yeomanry and other middling sort in Durham.[88] Inventories for Bishop Middleham and Sedgefield do not show such houses for this group until the 1620s but that may be a function of how the inventories were drawn up. Robert Farrow lived in a house with hall, parlour, two chambers, two lofts, kitchen, and milk house as well as two barns.[89] Ralph Mason's house consisted of a hall, parlour, and low parlour on the ground floor with two chambers above, plus a milk house and likely a separate kitchen as well. His son was assessed for three hearths in 1666.[90]

Green et al. observed that while five hearths generally served as an important dividing line for status, many of the wealthier middling sort in Durham had three and four hearths, like the Masons.[91] With two exceptions, only those in the parish noted as gentlemen or with the honorific 'Mr.' were assessed at five or more hearths.[92] Further up the social scale, the differences were dramatic. Nicholas Freville's house at Hardwick contained seven chambers (one for the maid(s)), a nursery, and a study in addition to the hall, old and new parlours, the 'low rooms', kitchen, buttery, larder, and brewhouse.[93] These houses resembled those elsewhere in England, and beyond. Green posited a 'trans-national housing culture' that connected the North, London, the Netherlands, and the American colonies.[94] Besides rebuilding their country seats, Durham gentry acquired townhouses in the city of Durham, just as gentry from other counties did in London.[95]

It is tempting to read different attitudes into these wills and inventories: Ralph Mason living a lifestyle of a gentleman in hopes of becoming one, Nicholas

---

[87] *County Durham Hearth Tax*, p. 46. Thrislington was excavated in 1973–74, although much had been destroyed by quarrying and later building. One of the farmhouses was rebuilt as a two-storey stone house in the fifteenth century: Austin, *Deserted Medieval Village*, pp. 13, 30–64, 71, 86–7.

[88] Green, 'Houses and Households', pp. 47, 117–20.

[89] DPRI/1/1622/F3/3. Similar houses are described in other published Durham wills: *Wills and Inventories* I–IV, and *Darlington Wills*. See also Overton et al., *Production and Consumption in English Households*, pp. 121–36.

[90] DPRI/1/1662/M6/1; *County Durham Hearth Tax*, p. 46.

[91] *County Durham Hearth Tax*, pp. liii–lv.   [92] *County Durham Hearth Tax*, pp. 42–7.

[93] DPRI/1/1673/F10/1–6.

[94] Middling tradesmen in Newcastle were expanding their houses, too: Heley, 'Material Culture', pp. 296–302.

[95] Green, 'Houses and Households', pp. 279, 315.

Freville with a traditional approach of entertaining and living on a large scale, Samuel Walker embodying puritanism and capitalism. Perhaps these are accurate, perhaps not; for all we know, Samuel Walker may have indulged his stomach instead of furnishing his home. But all three reflect the results of successful farming and some of the opportunities for spending or investing those rewards. The inventories also reveal the attitudes of the appraisers, according to Spaeth, and the changing contents recorded c.1580–1660 would reflect the opinions and discretion of the appraisers as much or more than the deceased's tastes. The minimal amount of detail provided later in the seventeenth century hides both from our view.[96]

Some families chose to invest in education for their sons. There were schools in the city of Durham (founded in 1414), Darlington (1415), Houghton-le-Spring (1574), Heighington (1601), Bishop Auckland (before 1603), and Wolsingham (1614); other than Durham, all these locations were associated with the bishopric estate.[97] Four were within an eleven mile radius of Sedgefield, and in 1615 men representing the town took up a cottage and associated pasture to support the parish clerk for teaching religion and grammar.[98] In 1611, a shopkeeper in Darlington possessed 'two dozen of little bookes for children' as well as paper.[99] Several local sons went to university. Two of Marmaduke Blakiston's sons attended Queens College, Oxford, like their father, while two others attended Cambridge. Thomas Tempest and Nicholas Freville also matriculated into Queens College, Oxford, in the early seventeenth century. Marmaduke Myers matriculated into Trinity College in 1581. More than a century later Thomas Lambton of Hardwick matriculated into the same and later went to the Inner Temple. Charles Elstob (d.1666) left an annuity to a younger son to go to Peterhouse College, Cambridge 'or of some other colledege'.[100] Some, including Thomas Tempest and George Freville, attended one of the Inns of Court.[101] One of the most famous sons was the puritan theologian Samuel Ward, master of Sidney Sussex College at Cambridge and one of the men who worked on the *King James Bible*.[102]

---

[96] Spaeth discusses the 'summary' format used in Thame and its changes in popularity, noting it was rare: '"Orderly Made"', pp. 424–7. Many late seventeenth century Bishop Middleham and Sedgefield inventories are similar, with the household goods lumped together in one or a few categories, with crops and livestock given slightly more detail.

[97] Dolan, *Nurture and Neglect*, p. 119; Carlisle, *Concise Description of Endowed Grammar Schools*, vol. 1, pp. 389–406; Foster, *Alumni Oxonienses*, vol. 2, p. 569. Jones described a surge in school foundations between 1480 and 1660, estimating that by 1660 there was one school for every 6,000 persons and 'in only two counties [out of ten sampled] could a boy have lived at a distance of more than twelve miles from an available grammar school': *Philanthropy in England*, pp. 279–97. Stone provides a useful critique of Jones's work alongside his own analysis of the swift expansion of education in England, 'The Educational Revolution in England'.

[98] TNA: DURH 3/27, p. 220.   [99] *Darlington Wills*, p. 112.

[100] DPRI/1666/E2/1–2.

[101] Foster, *Alumni Oxonienses*, vol. 1, p. 137; vol. 2, p. 536; vol. 3, pp. 871, 1048; vol. 4, p. 1465; 'ACAD, A Cambridge Alumni Database'.

[102] It is not clear whether he was from Bishop Middleham or Sedgefield; the ACAD Cambridge Alumni Database lists him as from Bishop Middleham, but Hutchinson has him from Sedgefield: *History & Antiquities,* vol. III, p. 94. On his puritanism, see Todd, 'Puritan Self-Fashioning', and Milton,

The inventories of those few identified as tradesmen mirrored those of farmers. Christopher Readshaw (d.1669), a Sedgefield butcher, had a two-storey house with two hearths, featherbeds with linen and harden sheets, brass and pewter vessels and utensils, rugs, curtains, a seeing glass, fifteen head of cattle, horses, and two bonds worth £50 each. On the other hand, William Wood (d.1666), mason, owned three kine and five sheep, with 3 acres sown plus a lease for another acre and three-quarters; he had £1 of pewter dishes, a bed, cupboard, table, and some iron cooking implements, with his goods and chattels worth £17 1s. 8d. all told. Thatcher Christopher Dodds (d.1670) owned 5s. of pewter (including seven spoons), some brass and iron vessels, a little furniture, and an old spinning wheel, which with his other goods was worth a paltry 31s. 10d.; but he did pay tax on his one hearth.[103]

Brown noted that men from the bishopric estates were more successful than Dean and Chapter leaseholders. Some of the probate inventories for Dean and Chapter tenants showed a standard of comfort not much different c.1600 than that of Yorkshire folk c.1500 or earlier; more items, but not finer items.[104] Still, Durham's yeomen and elite were on a par with or even ahead of their peers elsewhere in consumption. In a national study of British consumer culture from 1660 to 1760, Weatherill ranked the northeast as the most advanced overall bar London and ahead of Kent and Cambridgeshire, although the instance of different goods varied. She based her conclusions on the goods appearing in probate inventories and whether they were common/traditional (such as tables and cooking pots), uncommon (pewter dishes, looking glasses, table linen), or new and rare (clocks, window curtains, china). The Newcastle coal trade played a significant role in this, spurring trade and commercialization beyond Tyneside and Sunderland; but analysis of the inventories in the parishes implies that this level of consumption likely existed several decades prior to 1660, warranting further study of the timeline.[105] This is only part of the story, however.

The Poor of the Parish

While some thrived and others managed to get by, many were less fortunate. Poorer yeomen had less pewter and simpler furniture, and quality was increasingly lower. The furniture and goods of servants and labourers tended to be described as old and small, and limited in quantity. The goods of labourer John Watson (d.1664) were valued at £36 13s. in 1664. He owned four cattle, two sheep,

---

'Licensing, Censorship, and Religious Orthodoxy in Early Stuart England'. Some of Ward's working papers were discovered: Schuessler, 'Earliest Known Draft of King James Bible Is Found, Scholars Say'.
    [103] DPRI/1/1669/R6/1–3, 1666/W25/3, 1671/D5/1–2; *County Durham Hearth Tax*, p. 46.
    [104] Brown, 'Church Leaseholders', p. 41.
    [105] De Vries, *Industrious Revolution*; Weatherill, *Consumer Behaviour*, pp. 25–29, 43–69.

and a horse; six pecks of oats; a bench and chair; and a small amount of basic cooking vessels and implements. The goods of Steven Watson of Foxton (d.1666) included four 'old little chests', two old cupboards, iron pots and pans, 4s. worth of pewter (several pieces described as little), a table and one stool, and old churns and tubs, with his goods valued at £2 7s. 8d. No animals are mentioned, but he did have a spinning wheel for wool.[106] Old items also featured in the possession of John Gregson: an old glass case, two old chests, and an old pewter flagon. He also owned a spinning wheel for linen, a churn, and a beehive. Thomas Sewell the younger, 'being a poor servant', only had clothing worth a mark and a debt owed to him of 20s., with the appraisers noting 'he having noo goodes at all'.[107]

Many of the 'poor of the parish' are hidden from us because of their poverty. One exception was Robert de Bradbery of Sedgefield parish, 'a pauper inflicted with paralysis…so that he cannot support his wife and family', to whom Bishop Langley in 1425 granted an indulgence of one year.[108] Bequests to the poor were common in wills, reflecting the status and generosity of the deceased and the choice of parish(es) their local attachments. Robert Hilton of Butterwick, gent. (d.1581) left £7 to the poor, with £3 going to Sedgefield and the remainder split between Washington (where he was born) and Monkwearmouth.[109] John Gage, gent. (d.1614) left £3 to the poor of Sedgefield town.[110] Several parishioners set up charities to further relieve the poor. In her will, Dame Elizabeth Freville (d.1630) set up a charity in the two parishes, providing for three poor children to be apprenticed and for 2s. each to sixty of the poor in Sedgefield and twenty in Bishop Middleham. She also left money to the poor of Brancepeth and Heighington. Brian Harrison (d.1663) donated £100 to the poor, with £80 used to purchase a house and a field, the interest going to the poor of Sedgefield. Others bequeathed smaller sums, either charged on holdings or to generate interest or rent as determined by the wardens or trustees. Jane Mason (d.1662) bequeathed 20s. annually from a field called Shotton Nook and in 1696 William Mason left 34s. annually from his land in Fishburn and 6d. to each poor widow at Christmas, Easter, and Pentecost.

How many people in the parish were 'poor?' The term is relative. The eighty people receiving funds courtesy of Dame Freville represented approximately 4 per cent of the estimated population. In the Hearth Tax returns for 1666, 50 per cent of households were deemed too poor to pay, slightly higher than the county average of 47 per cent.[111] A Poor Rate book c.1650 put the rate value of Sedgefield Parish at £43 4s. 2d. and Bishop Middleham at £10, with the total rate for Stockton

---

[106] DPRI/1/1666/W13/1.   [107] DPRI/1/1679/G9/1, 1666/S5/1.
[108] Register of Thomas *Langley*, vol. III, p. 33.   [109] *Wills and Inventories* II, p. 39.
[110] *Wills and Inventories* IV, p. 80.
[111] *County Durham Hearth Tax*, pp. xcvii–cxxiii. The percentage for the county excludes the city of Durham and townships for which there is no data on non-paying residents.

Ward at £262 14s. 4d.[112] On the other side of the coin, many were doing very well. Statements such as that by Dr William James, Dean of Durham, who reported to Secretary William Cecil in 1597 on the 'poor country', should be taken with more than a few grains of salt:

> The decay of tillage and dispeopling of villages offends God by spoiling the Church, dishonours the prince, weakens the commonwealth, etc., etc., but it is nowhere so dangerous as in the northern parts…want and waste have crept into Northumberland, Westmoreland, and Cumberland; many have to come 60 miles from Carlisle to Durham to buy bread, and sometimes for 20 miles there will be no inhabitant. In the bishopric of Durham, 500 ploughs have decayed in a few years, and corn has to be fetched from Newcastle…thus the money goes, and the people can neither pay their landlords nor store their ground…Of 8,000 acres lately in tillage, now not eight score are tilled.[113]

James and Cecil were concerned about religion; the number of recusants in Durham coloured their view even beyond general concerns about enclosure and depopulation. Which side of Durham you saw depended on what you were looking for.

This was also a time of population growth, expanding the number of poor and landless but also the supply of labour. As Brown has shown, the lesser gentry and coal merchants were coming into their own in this period, even as the old guard declined.[114] Bishopric farmers could increase their outputs by hiring more servants, something they could afford to do as they paid such low rents. Industrial employment was rising, with numerous industries including leather and coarse woollen cloth trades.[115] Newcastle had been exporting salted meat and fish, wool, iron, lead, hides, and small quantities of coal early in the sixteenth century, and there are indications of local trade in coarser cloth and leather. As the coal trade expanded, other industries followed, notably salt and glassmaking.[116] In his thesis on the New Poor Law in Durham, Dunkley noted in discussing the late eighteenth and early nineteenth century that 'the growing industrial character of the region endowed it with a means of alleviating the increased pressure of population. Here the rates never assumed the enormous burden they did in the South'.[117] Wealth was increasing, yet more and more struggled to make ends meet. Dr James was telling only one side of the story.

---

[112] Mickleton and Spearman Manuscripts 8, ff. 8v, 22r, 94r.

[113] *Calendar of State Papers, Domestic Series, Elizabeth, 1595–97*, cclxii, no. 11, pp. 347–8; see Bradshaw, 'Social and Economic History', in Victoria History of the County of Durham vol. II, p. 231.

[114] Brown, *Rural Society and Economic Change*, esp. pp. 250–3.

[115] This is a similar situation to sixteenth-century Kent: Zell, *Industry in the Countryside*, esp. p. 74.

[116] Thirsk, *Economic Policy and Projects*, p. 56. For pipes, glassmaking, and other industries, see Edwards, 'Tobacco Pipes, Pipemakers, and Tobacconists'; Welford, 'Functional Goods and Fancies'.

[117] Dunkley, 'The New Poor Law and County Durham', p. 6.

The Rise and Fall of Wealth in Durham

Probate records demonstrate some of this contrast. Table 6.3 shows the gross mean and median inventory values for Bishop Middleham and Sedgefield inventories combined compared with the coal mining parish of Whickham, adjusted to reflect real rather than nominal values.[118] The average gross values were nearly the same in the 1570s but quickly diverged with Bishop Middleham and Sedgefield consistently higher than Whickham. The exceptions, the 1600s and 1620s, are skewed by three very wealthy Whickham men valued at £1116, £929, and £898. Removing them drops the average for those decades to £90 and £43, respectively. Factoring in debts, the difference between the rural south and a Tyneside mining parish were even greater, although very few net inventories were in the red for either. The growth in average wealth in Bishop Middleham and Sedgefield echoes the expansion of the coal trade. The 1580s and 1590s show nearly a 50 per cent

Table 6.3 Gross inventory values for Bishop Middleham, Sedgefield, and Whickham parishes in constant prices, 1570–1699

| | Bishop Middleham & Sedgefield parishes | | Whickham parish | | |
	n	mean	median	*n*	mean	median
1570s	5	£145.99	£45.10	2	£47.05	-
1580s	3	£62.49	£79.82	7	£29.50	£31.88
1590s	10	£62.56	£38.45	4	£26.11	£27.59
1600s	20	£116.35	£93.31	11	£190.25	£66.86
1610s	13	£132.01	£99.44	8	£54.64	£38.07
1620s	15	£124.55	£88.21	6	£329.76	£61.83
1630s	11	£107.39	£100.24	4	£55.55	£48.74
1640s	4	£192.23	£270.90	8	£82.19	£53.92
1650s	0	n.d.	n.d.	0	n.d.	n.d.
1660s	23	£93.67	£61.02	15	£40.91	£36.98
1670s	28	£127.17	£80.87	25	£44.09	£27.94
1680s	30	£102.00	£37.95	19	£29.24	£19.03
1690s	11	£90.00	£71.60	14	£34.41	£10.83

Source: North-east Inheritance Database, http://familyrecords.dur.ac.uk/nei/data/intro.php (accessed 18/9/2019). See Appendix C: Probate Inventories.

---

[118] Overton employed two sets of inventory values: the 'material' value comprised goods but not debts owed to the decedent or leases, and the 'net' included both debts owed to and owed by but excluding leases: Overton et al., *Production and Consumption in English Households*, p. 138, and Overton, 'Prices from Probate Inventories'. The entries in the North East Inheritance database provide the gross value (goods as well as leases and debts owing to if they were in the records) along with debts owed by the deceased plus legacies and funeral expenses when known. Consequently, the gross Durham values represent more types of wealth than Overton's material values, while the net values for Durham represent more deductions. Analysis of a sample of inventories showed the material value to be on average 15% lower.

increase, then nearly doubling from 1600–29. Following the Civil War, the averages did not continue rising with the coal trade, but some individual wealth certainly did; the averages are brought down by a greater proportion of poorer inventories in the second half of the seventeenth century. Regional differences in the county further polarized the county.

That comparison is straightforward. The number of inventories is small and while there are differences in occupational distribution, that is to be expected. There were more yeomen in Bishop Middleham and Sedgefield (42–21 per cent), and more unidentified persons in Whickham (55 per cent in Whickham as opposed to 39 per cent). The proportions of identified clergy, artisans, and labourers were close given the very small numbers involved. The surprise difference in the number of gentlemen (8 per cent in the parishes versus 14 per cent in Whickham) demonstrates that any correlation of status and wealth is not necessarily reliable.

Morrin's work on nearby Merrington allows for comparison with another Durham village. She found an average nominal value for tenant inventories of £69.7 prior to 1600, and £189.27 for 1600–50. The average nominal values for all decedents in Merrington were £102.2 and £139.1, respectively, compared to £59.2 and £159.1 for all decedents in the parishes of Bishop Middleham and Sedgefield. Morrin classified the tenants of Merrington as being of the middling sort, which seems borne out by the difference in Merrington tenant and overall inventories for 1600–50. As Brown noted, other Dean and Chapter estate residents had considerably lower inventories, and his argument that the truly rising yeomanry could be found among bishopric tenants is borne out by the evidence from these parishes.[119]

Comparing the inventories of Bishop Middleham and Sedgefield with the county is more problematic. The different occupational distribution is one potential objection, shown in Table 6.4. The small sample size for the parishes causes certain groups to be over-represented, such as gentlemen in the parishes for 1600–49. By the second half of the seventeenth century, however, the proportions of many groups in the parish resemble those of the county. The significant difference is in the larger proportion of yeomen in the parishes. This comes as no surprise, but it does demonstrate that the county was more than rural parishes like these, with merchants, mariners, and a whole host of trades found within the county. Separating the county inventories into 'rural' and 'urban' does not account for the difference; many urban parishes included rural areas, some areas were urbanizing, and many trades were in rural parishes. Removing those three occupational groups from both the parishes and county samples does not work either. Both attempts reinforce the conclusion of Overton et al. that the 'crude rural-urban

---

[119] Morrin, 'Merrington: Land, Landlord and Tenants', pp. 37–9; Brown, 'Church Leaseholders', pp. 33–43.

Table 6.4 Occupational distribution of probate inventories, 1550–1699

	Bishop Middleham & Sedgefield parishes			County Durham		
	1550–99	1600–49	1650–99	1550–99	1600–49	1650–99
Clergy	6%	2%	1%	3%	2%	1%
Armigerous	0%	2%	1%	1%	2%	1%
Gentlemen	3%	12%	5%	4%	6%	6%
Yeomen	41%	43%	36%	13%	27%	25%
Husbandmen	6%	5%	0%	6%	2%	0%
Labourers & servants	0%	2%	1%	1%	2%	1%
Women[a]	34%	24%	28%	51%	35%	30%
Unstated (men)	9%	8%	20%	11%	12%	15%

[a] Women identified as gentlewomen, dame, or lady were included with armigerous or gentlemen.

Source: North-east Inheritance Database, http://familyrecords.dur.ac.uk/nei/data/intro.php (accessed 18/9/2019). See Appendix C: Probate Inventories.

dichotomy has been overplayed' in examining inventories and commodities.[120] It renders accurate comparison more difficult.[121]

A second objection is that the items and values found in the two parishes might be different enough from the county. This is addressed more easily through the assembly of an 'estate value' basket akin to the 'basket of consumables' and 'respectability basket' used above, containing items commonly found in Durham inventories. The same items generally are found in the parishes as the rest of the county. The values of those items in the two parishes are consistent with values elsewhere, and applying an index based on the changing value of the basket has similar effects on both the parish and county averages. The quality and quantity of goods naturally varied according to taste and wealth, and it would be worth exploring potential regional variations and the effect of distance from markets, but the consistent item values indicate comparison is feasible.

One final issue is how representative the surviving inventories are of the parishes and the county. Overton et al. compared the inventory sample with Kent to the Hearth Tax, finding that households with more than the average number of hearths were over-represented in the sample, and fewer than 3 per cent of inventories could be matched to those exempt from the tax.[122] As seen in Table 6.5, comparing the inventories for Bishop Middleham and Sedgefield to the 1666 Hearth Tax, the exempted are under-represented but less so than in the Kent

---

[120] Overton et al., *Production and Consumption in English Households*, pp. 137, 167–9; see also Arkell, 'Interpreting Probate Inventories', pp. 79–82, and Sear and Sneath, *Origins of the Consumer Revolution*, pp. 256–63.

[121] The very low number of labourers and servants is intriguing; presumably many did not have goods worth inventorying or they are in the group with no stated occupation.

[122] Overton et al., *Production and Consumption in English Households*, pp. 24–6.

Table 6.5 1666 Hearth Tax households and probate inventories

	No. of hearths	No. of households	Percentage of all hearths	No. with inventories	Percentage of all inventories
Bishop	exempt	201	49.51%	10	15.2%
Middleham	1	124	30.54%	37	56.1%
& Sedgefield	2–4	73	17.98%	15	22.7%
parishes	5–9	6	1.48%	3	4.5%
	10+	2	0.49%	1	1.5%
County	exempt	346	42.04%	1	1.7%
Sample	1	295	35.84%	28	48.3%
(8 parishes)	2–4	163	19.81%	25	43.1%
	5–9	15	1.82%	2	3.5%
	10+	4	0.49%	2	3.5%

Source: North-east Inheritance Database, http://familyrecords.dur.ac.uk/nei/data/intro.php (accessed 18/9/2019). See Appendix C: Probate Inventories.

sample; those with two or more hearths are over-represented though again not to the same extent. Surprisingly, those with a single hearth are over-represented. The parish of Whickham has few inventories that can be matched to taxpayers, all of whom had two or more hearths, so for the sake of comparison eight parishes were selected from across the county (Billingham, Boldon, Coniscliffe, Dalton, Hamsterley, Merrington, Pittington, and Washington), representing different sizes of parish and different regions. In this sample, households with a single hearth are also over-represented, and the exempted are even more under-represented than in Kent; those with ten or more hearths are more over-represented than in Kent. Although skewed towards the wealthy, the inventories from County Durham are more inclusive of those with wealth linked to a single hearth, and in the two parishes studied here, the poorest make a greater appearance in the inventories. Compared with other counties, the averages for Durham may underestimate the county's wealth.

Thus, two of the three potential objections can be addressed. A straightforward comparison of the mean and median decennial averages for the parishes and the county from 1570 to 1699 returns a weak correlation (Pearson coefficients of 0.32 and 0.19). For the period from 1570 to 1639—before the war and excluding the very high average for the parishes in the 1640s—the correlation is stronger (0.68 for the mean and 0.65 for the median). For the final three decades, the decennial means correlate very strongly for the final three decades at 0.88, but the median is slightly lower (0.63). The average wealth of the parishes and county fell following the Civil War, then started to recover at the end of the century. Moreover, the wealth ceiling certainly was climbing, pushing up the Gini coefficient (a measure of wealth distribution). The comparison suggests that these parishes contributed to but do not fully represent the prosperity to be found in the county, although they come close. The question left unanswered is whether agriculture or something else was lifting the county average. Growing trade and industry are likely; coal is a possibility, but it is also possible that those reaping the benefit lived in Newcastle rather than Durham.

A comparison between the parishes and the counties may not be authoritative, but the extensive work done on probate inventories by Overton, alone and with others, allows for some comparison of Durham as shown in Table 6.6 with samples from Cornwall, Hertfordshire, Kent, Lincolnshire, and Worcestershire. Comparison of the gross totals for Durham with the inventory totals from the aggregate samples from the five counties studied by Overton show Durham having a consistently higher mean and median average until the 1670s.[123] After smoothing out some of the peaks and troughs in the Durham series, there is rapid growth in value at the end of the sixteenth century and then relative stability through the 1660s, in contrast to the slower but steady rise of Overton's larger sample. Applying a generous adjustment to the gross inventory so they better approximate material values, the trend is still similar although Kent catches up with Durham around the time of the Civil War and Lincolnshire even earlier in the seventeenth century.[124] The differences reflect earlier economic development in

Table 6.6 County Durham gross probate inventory values in constant prices, 1550–1699

	n	mean	median	stdv	Gini
1550s	42	£93.03	£53.10	£172.88	0.62
1560s	15	£145.91	£54.89	£179.59	0.59
1570s	224	£81.45	£49.79	£125.27	0.55
1580s	450	£115.61	£57.79	£200.29	0.57
1590s	313	£143.23	£64.42	£360.54	0.59
1600s	463	£164.10	£72.78	£284.55	0.63
1610s	738	£122.88	£57.12	£299.74	0.62
1620s	474	£167.34	£76.70	£493.34	0.64
1630s	550	£144.21	£77.90	£293.13	0.60
1640s	323	£145.03	£79.62	£220.56	0.56
1650s	29	£155.33	£132.75	£131.90	0.46
1660s	1005	£149.84	£128.05	£127.23	0.62
1670s	1408	£134.27	£62.73	£232.85	0.60
1680s	1382	£93.17	£37.00	£164.96	0.64
1690s	816	£116.59	£41.80	£378.53	0.68

stdv = standard deviation
Gini = Gini coefficient of inequality (scale of 0–1)

Source: North-east Inheritance Database, http://familyrecords.dur.ac.uk/nei/data/intro.php (accessed 18/9/2019). See Appendix C: Probate Inventories.

[123] Overton, 'Household Wealth', Table 2. Zell argues that many of the middling sort were unable to keep up with inflation in late sixteenth century Kent: *Industry in the Countryside*, pp. 110–11, 150–2.
[124] Results of an analysis of sample of inventories where material, gross, and net values could be calculated showed that material inventory values in Durham averaged 85% of gross values before the

the northeast, propelling England's nation growth in the late sixteenth and early seventeenth centuries to eventually surpass the Low Countries as Europe's economic leader.

Besides from probate inventories, there are few other ways to assess the county's overall wealth. Durham's palatinate status combined with the paucity of county records leaves us largely in the dark regarding wealth and taxation until the sixteenth century, with very few exceptions. The *Taxatio Ecclesiastica* ordered by Pope Nicholas IV in 1291–92 for England, Wales, and Ireland valued the archdeaconry of Durham at £2,588 13s. 4d., with the total for the diocese at £6,724 19s. 3d. q. By way of comparison, the diocese of London was valued at £6,283 8s. 3d., Hereford at £3,933 13s. 6d. q., and Winchester at £9,568 10s. 7.5d. The rectory of Sedgefield was valued at £1,13 6s. 8d., with only the churches at Easington (£120) and Chester-le-Street (£146 13s. 4d.) valued higher, excluding all chantries. Bishop Middleham parish fell lower on the scale at £42 13s. 4d., while Whickham was only worth £20.[125] The war with Scotland had a deleterious effect, shown in the *Nova Taxatio* levied c.1318: Sedgefield's value fell to £51 and Bishop Middleham's to £19 6s. 8d., while Whickham, just south of the Tyne, was valued at £1. This tax followed several truces with the Scots costing more than 1,600 marks from 1312–15.[126] By the sixteenth century, Bishop Middleham fell further to £4 19s., while Sedgefield was valued at £73 18s., third highest parish church behind Houghton-le-Spring at £124 and Bishopwearmouth at £89 18s. By the middle of the seventeenth century, the churches had increased in value: Bishop Middleham to £60, while Whickham had risen from £20 9s. to £160. The rectory at Sedgefield was the wealthiest in the county at £650. This explains Bishop Cosin's displeasure at his son-in-law, Denis Grenville, rector of Sedgefield and archdeacon of Durham, for resisting Cosin's wishes in 1670: '[t]he next time I give him such a Parsonage as Segfield is…hee shall not serve me so'.[127]

The increasing subordination of the palatinate to king and Parliament resulted in more and more comparable data on the wealth of Durham in the sixteenth and seventeenth centuries, supplemented by greater records survival. Sedgefield was one of the highest-valued parishes in County Durham when it came to taxation. In the three subsidies for 1624, Sedgefield paid £9 12s. while Bishop Middleham paid £4 8s., which together was a quarter of the subsidy paid by Stockton Ward (£52 13s. 4d.). In the assessment for ship money in 1636, Sedgefield had the highest assessment in the county at £9; the weight of the assessment in Durham fell on

---

Civil War, and just over 80% over the entire period. To be cautious, gross values for Durham were reduced by 30%.

[125] 'Taxatio Ecclesiastica'.

[126] The date is uncertain, as Foss suggested it was in Bury's episcopate instead of Kellawe's: 'Episcopate of Richard de Kellawe', pp. 42–3, 107–8, xxxix.

[127] *Injunctions and Other Ecclesiastical Proceedings*, pp. 4–6. *Correspondence of John Cosin*, pp. 236–7; 'Grenville, Denis', p. 112.

the collieries, with the assessment for the 'Grand Lease' at Whickham at £75. Kirby used a Book of Rates c.1642 to study Durham's land values, and Sedgefield had the third-highest rate of the parishes although with the seventeenth-largest population.[128] In the assessment towards the 1677 ship money tax, Sedgefield was assessed at £37 12s. 11d. and Bishop Middleham at £8 5s. 8d. q., out of a total for Stockton Ward of £317 10s. 3.5d.[129] Pre-modern taxes do not necessarily reflect the wealth of the assessed village or county, so these numbers must be used with caution; yet their agreement with the trend in inventory values with the parishes cannot be discounted either. Wealth had risen and to an extent contracted.

Whether looking at housing or consumer goods, mean values of inventories, or other indicators, Durham was on par with or even ahead of the rest of England going into the middle of the seventeenth century. It is not possible to turn a blind eye to the correlation between the expansion of coal mining and the rising wealth in Durham in the early seventeenth century or even earlier, since Hatcher located the turning point in the coal trade in the 1570s to 1580s.[130] The late sixteenth and early seventeenth centuries had been the turning point in the parishes as well, with growing farm sizes, enclosure, expanding capital outlay on the farms, and more wealth in inventories. This cannot be a coincidence. Agricultural development drove a population increase that provided labour for local industry and then the expansion of the coal and salt trades, made possible by increased application of labour more than labour-saving machines.[131] The more human input was directed to industry, the more agricultural production had to expand.[132] Those like Richard Gibson and Ralph Mason could upgrade their homes and acquire an increasing variety of consumer goods, promoting their social aspirations. Newcastle became to Durham as London to its surrounding counties albeit on a much smaller scale, drawing both people and food from the countryside, encouraging specialization and new industries, and providing an outlet for wealth. Rebellions and economic change saw the end of the old aristocracy, but as Brown has shown, coal provided the means for new men to rise.[133] The

---

[128]   Kirby, 'Population Density and Land Values', pp. 86–7.

[129]   Mickleton and Spearman Manuscripts 7, ff. 35r-v, 47v; the total for Durham was £287 14s. q.; Mickleton and Spearman Manuscripts 9, pp. 193–8; Mickleton and Spearman Manuscripts 25, f. 8r. County Durham's overall assessment was £2,000, one of the lowest in England: Cannon, *Parliamentary Reform*, p. 265; Nef, *Rise of the British Coal Industry*, p. 278. Sedgefield's assessment was less than that of Earls Colne: MacKinnon, *Earls Colne's Early Modern Landscapes*, p. 115.

[130]   Overton speculated that some famine mortality in the early seventeenth century was due to 'premature specialisation' and a reliance on purchasing grain: *Agricultural Revolution in England*, p. 141. Hatcher, *History of the British Coal Industry*, p. 78; Nef, *Rise of the British Coal Industry*; Levine and Wrightson, *Making of an Industrial Society*; Brassley, *Agricultural Economy of Northumberland and Durham*, pp. 34–44, 142–3; and Brown, *Rural Society and Economic Change*, pp. 29–106.

[131]   Clark and Jacks, 'Coal and the Industrial Revolution',

[132]   Clark et al. found a low share of non-agricultural occupations in the north; this could indicate either high specialization, or many individuals mixing farming and other activities: Clark et al., 'Malthus, Wages, and Preindustrial Growth', pp. 376–9.

[133]   Brown, *Rural Society and Economic Change*, pp. 172–96.

consequences of the Durham bishopric's tenurial system allowed copyholders there to profit from grain, cattle, and sheep. Even those with relatively small holdings had a chance to benefit from low rents and high prices. Those without land suffered. There was some demand for apprentices and farm labour, otherwise migration for industrial employment was the only option. Comparison of the Gini coefficients (used to measure wealth distribution, with zero representing equal distribution and one representing that one individual held all the wealth) for Durham inventories in 1600–09 and 1690–99 confirms this, with the coefficient rising from 0.6 to 0.7. Penury existed side by side with comfort.

7

The Expanding and Evolving Economy

Agriculture in Durham may not have been the most revolutionary, but neither was it static or stagnant. There were four notable developments: larger farm sizes; a stronger emphasis on pastoral agriculture; enclosure; and specialization for market. All had their origins in the fourteenth century, even if full development came later. Customary rents and renders on the Durham priory and bishopric estates were fixed by custom and commuted soon after the Black Death; tenure was for life and de facto hereditary, as copyhold tenure. The tenants on these estates possessed a greater sense of certainty than their counterparts elsewhere. This made it easier for these peasants and yeomen to consider what they and their families desired when determining whether to pursue the market or reduce their workload, to indulge in luxuries or to store up capital and credit. The continuity of practice is evident, but so are the changes, and we can see the strength and adaptability of 'medieval' farming practices.

There was more to pre-modern Durham than farming and mining: wool, cloth, hides, and leather were produced in much of the county, and salt, lime, and pottery industries developed as well. The effects of these many changes, in Durham and the world, is visible in other ways. Wealth in the fourteenth century was measured in rents, grain, stock, and plough gear; by the seventeenth century, in napkins, mirrors, clocks, and feather beds. Men lent money to others and developed their own credit networks. The monks of Durham had been purchasing all manner of delicacies through Newcastle before the Reformation, and the expanding economy trade enabled further imports.

Arable and Pastoral Agriculture

Earlier works were pessimistic about Durham. Recent work has been more positive. Brown stated that 'the century between the dissolution of the monasteries and the English Civil War was a period of opportunity for agricultural producers in England, especially in the north-east, where the precocious development of various industries provided not only a market for agricultural goods but also a potential area of investment for the emerging yeomanry', while Green argued that '[e]arly modern north-east England was precocious in its experience of industrialization

Rethinking the Great Transition: Community and Economic Growth in County Durham, 1349–1660. Peter L. Larson, Oxford University Press. © Peter L. Larson 2022. DOI: 10.1093/oso/9780192849878.003.0008

and commercial agriculture.[1] The villages of Durham had larger farms earlier than Midlands, with the dynamics of tenure preservation and the land market making this possible in the northeast. Those developments, however, were not matched by 'revolutionary' agricultural practices—because those were not necessary. Common-field agriculture persisted into the late seventeenth century. There is no evidence of 'scientific' approaches to farming (although there is no evidence to the contrary, either). There were changes, but absent the intense demand from London and the sharp competition that generated, Durham farmers looked to tried-and-true methods to increase income. Enclosure, greater emphasis on stock raising, and a preference for wheat marked the Durham farmer's adjustment to market conditions. On the surface this reliance on traditional practices might seem to be stagnation or resistance to change, yet that presupposed that the later innovations were 'natural' when instead they were adaptations to specific conditions.

The villages in southern and eastern Durham centred on arable farming, but even these 'champion' villages had a strong pastoral element to their farming, as the moor and waste in eastern Durham provided ample grazing. The twelfth and thirteenth centuries saw more land taken into cultivation, and this process reversed in the later fourteenth and fifteenth centuries. Tuck observed a shift from arable to pasture throughout the northeast in the fifteenth century and Pollard argued that the shift to pasture led to considerable contraction of grain production. In his study on Durham tithes, Dodds estimated a 47 per cent reduction in arable output following the Black Death.[2] While the bishopric administration commuted nearly all labour services, they made occasional use of works for haying and transporting hay, with tenants amerced several times between 1392 and 1401 for failing to appear when summoned to work. The men leasing the demesne meadows in the fifteenth century received the right to collect those works as part of the terms of the lease, and in at least two instances the lessees were considered the bailiff of the manor.[3] Change is clear in the increase in animal numbers, the use of garths for hay or pasture, and the conversion of arable to pasture. Those villages not affected by mining still produced grain in the mid-seventeenth century, but some farmers had substantial herds of sheep and cattle, and the Enclosure Awards legitimized and encouraged this flexibility of production. New crops were not adopted until the nineteenth century, although Brassley

[1] Brown, 'Church Leaseholders', p. 42; Green, 'Houses and Households', p. 47.
[2] Tuck, 'The Occupation of the Land', pp. 40–1; Pollard, *North-Eastern England*, pp. 48–52, and 'The North-Eastern Economy and the Agrarian Crisis', pp. 103–4; Dodds, *Peasants and Production*, p. 71; Dyer in 'Peasant Farming in Late Medieval England' found Worcester priory tenants responded differently based on local conditions.
[3] TNA: DURH 3/13 ff. 74v, 105r–106r, 139v, 223v, 288v–289r, 348v, 365r–366r; 3/14 ff. 43r, 175r, 294v, 366v, 372v, 482v, 483r, 499r, 586v; 3/17 f. 9v, 34v; 18 ff. 21r, 50v; CCB B/65/14, Collector's Account, Stockton Ward for 1469/70; Bailiffs of the Bailiwicks Accounts, B/73/2 m. 3 (1443–4), B/73/8 m.2 (1472–73), B/73/10 (1475–76), among others; Durham Cathedral Archive, Misc. Ch. 6305 (account of the Bailiff of Middleham Manor, 1428–9).

found evidence of clover and trefoil in the northeast in the 1720s.[4] He also argued that the availability of pasture in the northeast meant that adopting turnips and other fodder crops was not as critical as for crowded central England and concluded that the adoption of new crops and approaches to farming in the eighteenth century was a response to population growth in the northeast. Clearly, some Durham tenants were challenging traditional agrarian approaches from the early fifteenth century and in the seventeenth century we can see tenants, especially the more substantial ones, made different choices about their farms. The earlier changes allowed them to produce the food needed to support the growing rural, industrial, and urban populations in the wider region, demonstrating that existing practices could be adapted and expanded before needing radical changes.[5]

In comparing grain prices from Durham priory estates with national series for the later medieval period, Schofield concluded that the Durham prices were generally consistent with national trends although certain years suggested stress if not crisis with the food supply.[6] The stagnant or declining population in Durham in the century following the Black Death and the greater emphasis on pastoral agriculture, and indeed a preference for wheat, supports his observations. It also suggests why many tenants tended to cease acquiring lands once they held 50–60 acres. A holding that size provided a cushion in poor years, but if they farmed less intensively it would lessen the overall food supply. From 50–60 acres provided flexibility and safety, permitting a little experimentation without too much risk. As prices for grain rose, larger farms became more viable and allowed tenants to specialize.

The gross yields of grain in mid-seventeenth-century Durham compare favourably to Overton's work on Norfolk and Suffolk, although the sample is considerably smaller. The acres sown with wheat recorded in inventories between 1603 and 1676 would, using Overton's revised calculation, have yielded seven to fifteen bushels of wheat per acre. Seven bushels is low, but the upper end of these estimated yields fits comfortably with Overton's results of 14.5 bushels per acre in 1628–40 and 1660–79. Both barley and oats yields were higher than in Norfolk and Suffolk; barley yields were between eighteen and twenty-five bushels per acre, and oats around twenty-five bushels per acre. Overton's yields reflect only the cost of reaping and carting the grain, not seeding rates; the prices used to calculate the Durham yields are from a national price series, so there is greater margin for

---

[4] Clifford, 'Settlement and Field Systems', pp. 97, 113, 119–125, 137–8; Brassley, *Agricultural Economy of Northumberland*, p. 159.

[5] Brassley, *Agricultural Economy of Northumberland*, pp. 167–79, 184. He concluded that the success of agricultural gave farmers a cushion for experimentation in the eighteenth and nineteenth centuries: they could afford to fail. In a study of West Midlands, Dyer concluded that the two-field system in use there 'was resilient and adaptable…enabling villagers to avoid wholesale enclosure for centuries after the Middle Ages': 'Open Fields in Their Social and Economic Context', p. 45. Croot likewise argued for the adaptability of 'traditional' agriculture and small farmers: *World of the Small Farmer*.

[6] Schofield, 'Regional Price Differentials', p. 50.

error. Schofield's work on late medieval Durham prices suggests similarity of early modern prices and yields, as does the evidence from inventories.[7]

The villages of Bishop Middleham, Cornforth, Sedgefield, and some of the smaller settlements contained open fields, closes, meadow, and pasture. A demesne still existed intact at Bishop Middleham, leased out to ambitious men. The number of open fields in a village was irregular. Fishburn had four fields, but Sedgefield had seven fields: West Field, North Field, Ryall Field, Hauxley Field, South Field, Dolliop, and Cramyre. Most of the open fields, at least the older ones, were divided into strips so that a tenant's holdings were scattered across the fields: a half-acre here, a rood there, and so on. Some, like the Ryalfield, were large-scale assarts, held as exchequerland. Four-acre parcels in this field became standard additions to the husbandlands of the village. Based on the regularity of the parcels, newer fields such as this were likely held in severalty, with plots fenced or hedged. Open or not, the number of fields permitted greater flexibility and complexity in cultivation. Presumably, the tenants followed a three-crop rotation like that recorded in eighteenth-century Durham records; but with that many fields, rotations could be more complex.[8] The fields of southern and eastern Durham were planted with wheat, barley (particularly six-row barley), rye, oats, and peas. The need to continue the cultivation of the lands of a fugitive or deceased tenant until a replacement was found resulted in some detailed descriptions of how a holding was cultivated and reveals the awareness of the different qualities of land. After he fled Sedgefield in 1406, John Utle's 45 acres were split among seven men: 4 acres had been seeded with wheat, valued at 7s., and other lands had been seeded with barley and oats to the value of 18s. 6d. He also owned a plough valued at 6d and seed worth 6s. 8d. The following year, the lands of John Joly were enumerated in more detail: 17.5 acres of wheat in seven parcels with values ranging from 6.5d. to 10.6d. per acre, plus half an acre of meadow, 4 acres of pasture, and a garden, for a total land value of 16s. 6d.[9] These, along with plaints of trespass and debt, demonstrate a preference for wheaten bread in the villages, while barley was important for malt and oats for fodder. In the early modern period, wheat and rye were frequently mixed, although some fields were seeded solely with wheat; oats and barley continued to be grown in quantity, for feeding stock and making malt. Robert Shaw of Thrislington at the time of his death had sown wheat, oats, and barley on his Pittington lands and wheat, rye, oats, and barley on his lands in Thrislington; nothing was said of his lands in Ferryhill, Fulwell, and Westerton. Other probate records and halmote records refer to similar crops. Some men had large quantities of beans and peas in their barns, for fodder.

---

[7] Overton, 'Re-Estimating Crop Yields from Probate Inventories', pp. 931–5; Schofield, 'Regional Price Differentials'; DPRI/1/1584/M4, 1588/W11, 1615/E1, 1622/F3, 1639/M3, 1639/F2, 1663/M7, 1664/D6, 1665/J5, 1669/W19, 1670/M7, 1673/F10, 1673/H27, 1677/W22.

[8] Clifford, 'Settlement and Field Systems', p. 97.

[9] TNA: DURH 3/13 f. 309r; 3/14 ff.26r, 65v.

Leonard Middleton (d.1639) possessed nearly as much by value in beans and peas as he did in wheat, £40 and £48, respectively. Robert Smith had £23 6s. 8d. worth of oats in his barn in 1658 and had sown 14 acres of oats and 9 acres of barley, while widow Jane Mason had £22 worth of barley.[10] They were specializing, in their planting and/or purchasing.

Sheep and cattle were the primary livestock raised for market although most tenants of at least moderate means had a horse, some pigs, and poultry. There is little data for the number of animals owned before the sixteenth century, but some tenants had sizable numbers. In 1406, Dionisia Shephird exceeded her grazing allowance by twenty sheep; in 1465, William Watkin had more than 260 sheep. Brian Garry had six oxen above his stint in 1472, and it was common for tenants to be amerced for several oxen or horses beyond stint or not placed with the village herder. Given the size of some holdings, it should come as little surprise that some tenants fielded an entire plough team on their own. In 1479, John Robinson had eight (scabby) horses, and two years later William Jackson was recorded as having at least ten oxen in a field that had been seeded.[11] These are not the numbers of peasants on the edge of subsistence or who had to pool their resources, but they may not be typical, either. From the mid-sixteenth century, probate inventories provide information on stock, and it was a poor person indeed who had none.[12] The size and distribution of these yeomen's herds echo those of the Harlakenden lords of Earls Colne and their chief subtenants, though not those of the greatest Kentish yeomen.[13] John Jenkin Hutcheson had ninety-seven sheep and twenty-one cattle listed in his inventory in 1573. A century later, George Ord had more than 270 sheep and more than 80 cattle, while Nicholas Freville, Esq, had 203 sheep, 13 horses, and 41 cattle. These represent the larger flocks, but there was more to wealth than stock; Robert Carter, yeoman, who died in 1634, owned only six sheep and five cattle.[14] The types of cattle listed reflect large-scale dairying, and fattened cattle were common. Butter and cheese were important products. Many well-to-do men possessed the equipment necessary to produce these in quantity, while those with fewer resources often owned tubs in lesser quantities. By 1684 (and likely earlier), butter and cheese were exported in quantity to London.[15] Horses appeared in over half of the inventories, with men styled as

---

[10] DPRI/1/1675/S7/5, 1639/M3/3–4.

[11] TNA: DURH 3/14 f. 21v; 3/16 ff. 146r, 263r; 3/17 ff. 40r, 64v.

[12] Contrast this with early modern Cornwall, where lack of pasture prevented some smallholders from owning a cow: Overton et al., *Production and Consumption in English Households*, p. 82.

[13] French and Hoyle, *Character of English Rural Society*, pp. 53–5; Zell, 'Landholding', p. 72. It is possible that other parishes in Durham had yeomen as wealthy as those in Kent.

[14] DPRI/1/1573/H5/2, 1672/O1/1, 1673/F10/5–6, 1634/C2/3. Compare with Hoskins's findings for Leicestershire where there was far more emphasis on sheep: 'Leicestershire Farmer in the Seventeenth Century', pp. 16–18.

[15] Brassley, *Agricultural Economy in Northumberland and Durham*, p. 148. See French and Hoyle, *Character of English Rural Society*, p. 54.

gentlemen and esquires owning the most, but on average even a yeoman owned four horses.

Together, the different records for these parishes and for rural Durham more broadly show a land and people in flux. Individualism clashed with the communal tradition that encouraged it. Village by-laws provide most of our information on agricultural practices until the sixteenth century. These were set annually or seasonally in plebiscites that all tenants were expected to attend. These by-laws governed what was seeded where and when, the timing of ploughing and harvest, the number of animals a holding could place on the common pasture, when livestock could be released to graze on the stubble, and so on. The reeve, jurors, and other officers of the village policed these infractions, and the halmote court amerced those presented for such infractions, usually at sixpence except for particularly egregious violations. Up through the fourteenth century, most villages had a pinder charged with impounding strays, and for many villages this man served as hayward. Initially the pinder occupied a holding connected to the office (the punderland), but by the late fourteenth century that connection was being severed, the office being held either by the entire village or by someone elected at the court.[16] Because of this, many villages paid a common herdsman or took turns watching over the commixed flocks and herds, a collective approach referred to as keeping *hirsell*. The practice was not always popular; Cecilia de Cornforth was amerced for infractions of her sheep and her failure to pay the common herdsman in the early fifteenth century, and her offence was far from exceptional.[17] The many small enclosures, and use of arable for pasture, made animal trespass common.

More evidence for the greater emphasis on stock farming comes from references to existing and new enclosures. The colonization of waste in the twelfth through the early fourteenth century resulted in many piecemeal assarts, which might have been enclosed.[18] The description of freeholds suggests enclosure or at least separation from the open fields. The first reference to field closes in the three villages comes in 1442, but *Bishop Hatfield's Survey* contains many 'places' (*placea*), some named and some not, that could imply severalty. Most were meadow or pasture. John Hardwick was listed as holding Grangecroke, described as 'one place of meadow', and 'one place of land by the tenure of William Calvehird'. The term *placea* was used to refer to housing plots, such as 'one place built upon, called Le Swynesty' as well as other types of land, as when the village of Bishop Middleham collectively leased 'one place of meadow called Le Newmedow' in

---

[16] Punderlands were found in twenty-three bishopric villages, ranging in size from 1–20 acres: *Domesday Book supp. vol 35: Boldon Book*. They were less common on the priory estate.

[17] TNA: DURH 3/14 ff. 66r, 156r, 204v.

[18] Dunsford and Harris, 'Colonization of the Wasteland', pp. 41–3. Goodacre observed the Tudor enclosures were the end of a late medieval process: *Transformation of a Peasant Economy*, pp. 94–5.

1391.[19] These were meadows or small assarts likely enclosed from the beginning. In 1420 the term 'several' (*seperalis*) was applied to certain pastures when describing trespass by animals, and in 1449 it was applied to fields indicating that by the middle of the fifteenth century, some tenants were consolidating their holdings.[20] In 1443, Richard Fysshburn, Esq., took Le Lesours and was permitted to enclose it 'at his peril'.[21] As early as 1470 a distinct parcel of land—and 'parcel' and 'close' were used interchangeably—was described as containing twenty selions, implying that it had been part of the common field.[22] Some closes may have been created earlier. In 1421, John Tose was amerced for trespassing in the grass of John Matthewson because the latter had not maintained his close, but this could refer to his croft or garden.[23]

By 1500, there were more than a dozen closes recorded in the halmote books.[24] Many of these were intended for use as pasture or meadow, with 'meadow' appearing in the name of some closes (such as Grangemedowe and Newmedowe) or as part of the description in the halmote books. Horsecarr was described as marsh; it and other meadows were noted as requiring draining.[25] Some tenants did use them for arable. In 1486 William Hall secured the bishop's licence to plough the close in Bishop Middleham called Le Eland for six years.[26] Eight more closes were named in the sixteenth century, and twenty-three more in the first half of the seventeenth century; this excludes the many small parcels measured in feet. In the first decades of the seventeenth century, men were prosecuted at the quarter sessions for illegally enclosing their land for pasture. John Shaw Jr was charged twice, in 1607 and 1610, of converting arable to pasture with ditch and hedge, the first time for half of a 40-acre holding and the second time presumably for the remainder. He would later accuse two other men, in Thorpe Thewles and Norton, of the same.[27] Incidents like these occurred elsewhere in the vicinity, although only freeholds were reported at the quarter sessions, and then only if someone informed (who could also claim a share of the fine).

Most of the early closes were between 6 and 12 acres, although some were higher, such as Watkinstiles at 20 acres and Horsecarr at 36 acres.[28] The new surge of enclosures in the early seventeenth century were larger. More closes had appeared in the common fields, labelled as parcels of larger holdings. In 1610, Samuel Johnson sublet 'one close called Shalleyfurres abutting Watkinstiles containing

---

[19] *Hatfield's Survey*, p. 181; TNA: DURH 3/13 f. 35v.

[20] TNA: DURH 3/14 f.523r; 3/15 f. 245r. There is a reference to a field in severalty in Sedgefield in 1408: 3/14 f. 87v.

[21] TNA: DURH 3/15 f. 111v.   [22] TNA: DURH 3/16 f. 201v.

[23] TNA: DURH 3/14 f. 577v.

[24] Thirteen are named, but there are additional unnamed closes and parcels.

[25] *Hatfield's Survey*, pp. 183–4.   [26] TNA: DURH 3/18 f. 21r.

[27] *Durham Quarter Session Rolls*, pp. 160, 196, 316. Shaw enclosed land at Quarrington; *Durham Quarter Session Rolls*, p. 325.

[28] Appendix A: Land Market Database.

16 acres, parcel of one messuage and three bovates of malland', and in 1616 John Leede sublet 'one close called Comonclose containing seven and a half acres 3 roods of arable in three fields, parcel of one messuage and one bovate of malland', both in Sedgefield.[29] Had these men and others consolidated their entire holdings into closes, or just portions of their holdings which they then let out to subtenants? At the same time, others still held their land in selions. The enclosure of the common fields may have been a formality for some and a major change for others. For Nair, formal enclosure in Highley was the end of a slow process that had begun in the Middle Ages, and that rings true for the parishes.[30] Some of Sedgefield's fields were enclosed in 1579–80. This was not full enclosure, however. Tenants were permitted to enclose 3 acres per bovate that they held, and a total of 239 acres of arable was enclosed by 33 tenants holding 81 bovates. Among them was Ralph Mason with twelve bovates of land.[31] The deserted settlement of nearby Layton was enclosed by 1608, when a map was drawn up; the list of tenancies contains closes and garths from 5 acres to over 100 acres, some named after local families, such as Wheatley Close, Jopling Close, and Chipchase Farm.[32] It is likely many of the other small settlements had similar arrangements. Cornforth was the first of the three villages to generally enclose its fields, in 1620–21, followed by Sedgefield in 1637. Bishop Middleham was not enclosed until 1693, although a set of amercements from 1661 for the failure of six tenants to repair their hedges in the common field suggests informal enclosures had taken place.[33] Clifford found that two-thirds of the open fields of Bishop Middleham had already been enclosed prior to the Enclosure Award in 1693.[34] Rather than a simple open field system of scattered strips of land, these villages were a mixture of traditional communal and individual cultivation much earlier than anticipated, including, possibly, convertible husbandry. Even as many were complaining of recent enclosures of arable for pasture, John Gage complained in 1610 of the tenants of Sedgefield regarding 'medows inclosed and laid out...of longe tyme' in the townfields were now being ploughed up.[35]

The general shift in preference for stock raising can be seen in seventeenth-century probate inventories. Brown found a stronger preference for arable production among Dean and Chapter tenants than with bishopric tenants, and in these and other bishopric villages the value of livestock often, though not always,

---

[29] TNA: DURH 3/26 f. 308v; 3/27 pp. 181, 270.   [30] Nair, *Highley*, pp. 12, 246.
[31] This memorandum is from a seventeenth-century copy: Baker Baker Papers, BAK.72/249 ff. 3v-4r.
[32] Rents were 4–20s. per acre: Baker Baker Papers, BAK.72/249 ff. 11v-12v; Beresford, 'East Layton, Co. Durham, in 1608', pp. 257–60.
[33] DHC1/I/72 f. 367r/18r;/80 f. 1439v/636v (note two foliation systems in these two books); /81 ff. 29v, 162r. Durham Bishopric Halmote Court Copies of Durham Chancery Decree, Inclosure Awards and Related Material, DHC 6/IV/10 (187614). Durham Bishopric Halmote Court miscellaneous books, DHC1/M.76.
[34] Clifford, 'Settlement and Field Systems', p. 62.   [35] DHC1/I/63 f. 35r.

eclipsed that of grain.[36] Ralph Mason, who died in 1662, held more than 250 acres by copyhold. At the time of his death, he had seeded 5 acres with wheat and rye and 2 acres of barley in the Southfield and 8 acres of barley in the Westfield, valued at £55, and for stock he owned twenty-one cattle, sixty-five sheep, and four horses, plus some pigs, valued at £127 18s. 4d. He had rented out some of his lands to two other men, for rents worth £22 10s. (assuming the amount noted was for a half year's rent, as was common). The balance of grain to livestock varied among the tenants, and the increasing number of enclosures provided flexibility in farming method. Robert Johnson, who died in 1665, held 225 acres and several closes plus another 47 acres jointly with Leonard Middleton. At the time of his death, he had sown 41.5 acres and had £16 of various grain in stacks or threshed for a total of £73 3s. in grain, and he owned thirty-three sheep and twenty-four cattle and other animals totalling £70 18s. His co-tenant's grandfather, also Leonard Middleton, had held 105 acres of copyhold. His inventory included grain worth £46, but hay worth £42 and thirty-one cattle valued at £80 5s. Abraham Wright held 30 acres of copyhold in his own right but must have leased more as on his death he had 40 acres seeded; his grain was valued at £75 and he owned three ploughs, two long wains, and three other wains. His stock was clearly geared towards arable cultivation and a little dairying, as he owned four yoke of oxen, six horses, eleven milch cows and a bull, and a pig but only six sheep, although that still was worth £87.[37] There are clear similarities between yeomen and their agriculture in lowland Durham with those in southern England, although the latter had options for cash crops such as hops.[38]

The court and probate records reveal a rising yeomanry approaching agriculture in different ways. Some focused on stock while others on grain, although all made some use of both. Enclosed fields and meadows, followed by formal enclosure of town fields, provided additional flexibility. All this was possible through the lax attitude of the bishopric administration; as Brown has shown, Dean and Chapter leaseholders did not share in these opportunities. Had the bishops raised rents and switched to short leases, this would not have been possible. The result was rising wealth, seen in consumption and housing, and laying a foundation for future improvement.

---

[36] Brown, 'Church Leaseholders', pp. 33–4.
[37] DPRI/1/1662/M6/1, 1639/M3/3–4,/1696/M6/3, 1677/W22/1.
[38] Compare these inventories with farmers elsewhere. In Earls Colne, Richard Harlakenden (d.1631) had corn valued at £105 and stock worth £151, like wealthy yeomen in Durham, but he also possessed hops worth £400: French and Hoyle, *Character of English Rural Society*, pp. 54–5. Hoskins's work yields interesting comparisons as well, although the graziers focused on sheep rather than cattle; one such is Samuel Bickerston of Beeby, who was worth £857 10s. and owned 14 cattle and 520 sheep: 'Leicestershire Farmer in the Seventeenth Century', p. 18. Durham farmers had more arable sown than those in Leicestershire, indicating a more mixed approach. Humphrey Hall of Brownslane in Cheshire (d.1578) held more than 90 acres, and his inventory included twenty-eight cattle, five horses, thirty sheep, and over £37 of grain: Foster, *Capital and Innovation*, p. 125.

The Dynamics of Agrarian Change

The shifts in farming were not without conflict as shown by amercements for breaking bylaws. Tenants trampled each other's grain, attacked or impounded livestock, put scabby horses into the common pasture, pasture animals in the stubble too early, and rescued animals that the pinder impounded. They ploughed and harvested at the wrong time, broke fences and hedges, and more. Moreover, these infractions offer glimpses of agriculture in transition. Tenants were keeping more animals, and access to designated pasture was a point of conflict. Some tenants ignored the common herdsman, preferring to look after their own flocks, and the number of tenants and animals increased over time. Refusal to pay or feed the common herdsmen continued to be a problem into the seventeenth century. On the arable side, there are fewer indications of change, but as the fifteenth century progressed there are glimpses of a lessening emphasis on grain production. Vacant lands were leased out for a year for grass, and these were enclosed with temporary hedges; it could be that some of the animals caught in the fields had escaped from these temporary closes.[39] These and other infractions increased in frequency and some 'traditional' offences dwindled. There were fewer and fewer incidents of illegal purprestures or ploughing additional land, replaced by charges of ploughing independently or refusing to plough the exterior parts of the field. Garths were being used for grass or hay, and their proper fencing became a point of conflict in the villages. After Sedgefield was enclosed, the infractions for overloading commons disappeared, although wandering animals were still a problem.

Some of these infractions resulted from men and women being unpleasant neighbours or from village feuds rather than innovating agriculturalists, while other cases more clearly represent change. Often, it was the leading tenants, particularly the jurors, who were overloading the pastures. Of the ten men amerced in one session in 1445 for infractions with their animals in Cornforth, six were or would be jurors. When six men and one woman were accused in Bishop Middleham of putting calves into a sown field in 1458, four of the accused men were or would soon be jurors. These are not isolated examples, and jurors (former, current, or future) figured prominently in trespasses and overloading pasture with beasts. While not true for all, in the fifteenth century the men frequently breaking by-laws about animals tended to be jurors or related to a juror, and they also tended to hold 50–60 acres or more. Others who frequently or flagrantly committed infractions often were linked to a leading landholder.

Some of these individuals worked together. John Garry held 30 acres and a tenement called Blackhall in Cornforth by copyhold and later leased a malland in

---

[39] For a non-Durham example, see Goodacre, *Transformation of a Peasant Economy*, p. 133. Hoskins believed convertible husbandry was practised in open fields before the sixteenth century, with some strips used as pasture: 'Leicestershire Farmer in the Seventeenth Century', p. 16.

Sedgefield, but he was more than an aspiring farmer. He leased the mill at Cornforth in 1439 for ten marks, and then with Robert Croud, John Hutcheson, and Richard Findlaw (two of whom were amerced with him in 1445), he leased the vill of Cornforth from the bishop for six years at £22 6s. 8d. John Cornforth at one point or the other held two husbandlands, a cotland of 3 acres, and another 25.5 acres spread over the three villages, plus the brewhouse and right to brew ale in Cornforth. However, he did not work all these himself; he sublet a messuage and 45 acres in 1450. Ralph Brounsmyth appeared ten times between 1442 and 1457 for various infractions and often in the company of other men like Robert Croud, Thomas Fery, William Hardgill, Thomas Raynald, and Richard Rawlyn, taking lands together or standing pledge for others. William Hardgill leased 42.5 acres plus the Bishop Middleham demesne park, dovecote, orchard, and a close in 1442 with Brounsmyth and Fery as his pledges. Croud and Raynald were pledges when Brian Garry leased the mill in 1454, and when Croud leased the watermill of Cornforth in 1458, John Garry and Thomas Raynald were his pledges.[40] Some associations were smaller but perhaps more powerful. Thomas Watkin, who over-loaded the pasture and got into several affrays in Sedgefield during the 1470s and 1480s, had few regular associates other than William and Richard Gibson and William and Robert Tele. Robert Tele was reeve for twenty-four straight years and the others were regular jurors, while Watkin was more of an outsider, only leasing land, and not participating in any joint ventures.[41]

That village leaders such as these were clashing with village by-laws is not unexpected. They are exactly the sort of men one would expect to be taking a more individualized path. What is unexpected is that they were being amerced, as they often were the officers and jurors of the village (or connected to them). This raises interesting questions about the decision making of the village; even if they could not set the by-laws to their liking, it is likely that they concealed many more transgressions than appeared in the court. It is also likely that there were limits to what could be done. Men like these worked with and through the community as well as against it.

With some men, the conflict passed beyond a basic difference in agricultural opinion. The perhaps aptly named William Newcomer first appeared in Sedgefield co-leasing a bovate with William Watkin in 1445, and he acquired 51 acres of copyhold in 1451. Newcomer was brought before the halmote court to answer for offences and infractions more than twenty-six times between 1445 and 1471. Many of his offences were common: animals where they should not be, improper fencing of his garth, and so on. But he tended to be amerced multiple times in a session. In October 1454 he was amerced for eleven infractions with his animals,

---

[40] TNA: DURH 3/15 ff. 44r, 53v, 92r, 154v, 167r, 267v, 334r, 356r; 3/16 ff. 26v, 50r, 298v.
[41] TNA: DURH 3/15 f. 84r; 3/16 f. 196r; 3/18 ff. 8v, 42v; 3/19 ff. 118v, 160v, 168r; 3/20 f. 82r; 3/21 ff. 60v, 111r; 3/21 ff. 131v, 181r, 186v, 211r, 412r.

and in November 1456 he was amerced for six infractions and fined 12d. for arguing with the jurors. Moreover, he was litigious and violent: Newcomer was involved in several suits and affrays, with some incidents incurring high fines: 3s. 4d. for an affray against Robert Tele and 12s. for one against John Watson. His wife was fined 8d. for an affray with the wife of Richard Lynn.[42] Whereas many men worked mostly within the community even if they crossed the line, Newcomer was a rebel. But, eventually, even he conformed. Were it not for community pressure, or at least the pressure of leading tenants, the price of agrarian change could have been higher.

Service and Labour

Service and labour were an important sector of the rural economy but there is little information on them, sadly a common complaint of historians.[43] Labourers paid by the day or for piecework were common in the fields and barns at key times of the year, working alongside the tenant's family and any contracted servants. Some tradesmen and artisans would also be paid a wage, but some of them and labourers held lands and animals and it is rarely possible to distinguish between casual, frequent, and full-time labourers. What they were paid is difficult to find. Woodward's research on labourers and craftsmen in northern England provides a general sense of wages in Durham: 3–4d. for labourers and 5–6d. for craftsmen in the later fifteenth century, 5–6d. for labourers and 7–9d. c.1560, then to 8d. and 16–18d. c.1660. This was lower than wages in London and the south, and the real wage fell. Woodward was pessimistic about the lifestyle of the labourers, and rightly so.[44]

Service was common for young men and women in England. Kussmaul estimated that nearly two-thirds of folk from age fifteen to twenty-four did so in the early modern period.[45] Whittle argued that the demand for servants was stable or increased in the century before the Civil War, driven by growth in the rural economy. Farms in the 40–60-acre range might have had one or two servants, preferably women, while large farms needed more, preferably men. Mansell's studies have shown that service often continued through an early modern woman's life, offering flexibility.[46] One of the supposed elements of the European Marriage

---

[42] TNA: DURH 3/15 ff. 154v, 167v, 199r, 205v, 225r, 231v, 253r, 260r, 279v, 285v, 305v, 334v, 349r-v, 356r, 371v, 386v, 402r-v; 3/16 ff. 19r, 77v, 86r, 118v, 115v, 233r.

[43] Poos argues that wage labour was normal for many people: *Rural Society after the Black Death*, pp. 183–229.

[44] Woodward, *Men at Work*, pp. 176–8, 213–5, 247–9, 259–61.

[45] Kussmaul, *Servants in Husbandry*, p. 3.

[46] Whittle, 'A Different Pattern of Employment', pp. 59–60; Mansell, 'Female Service and the Village Community', and 'The Variety of Women's Experiences as Servants in England'. Service formed part of Hajnal's European marriage pattern: 'European Marriage Patterns'. See also Smith, 'Some Reflections

Pattern (EMP) was young men and women delaying marriage to work (often as servants) and save up for marriage, but Humphries and Wesidorf have demonstrated that the wages women received were not sufficient to encourage such a delay, calling that hypothesis into serious question.[47]

Evidence for servants in Durham is patchy but provides some insight into this debate. Male servants generally appear for agricultural trespass or affrays. Robert the servant of Robert Smith of Sedgefield was involved in five separate quarrels in 1406 (Smith was in his fair share of fights as well). One of these tussles left Robert the servant so injured that Smith was awarded 12d. in damages for lost service.[48] Marriage records provide more evidence for women in service than men. Of the thirty-three merchet fines recorded between 1388 and 1443, nine were explicitly for servants while in an additional five instances a woman paid her own merchet, which Bennett interpreted as women who worked and saved up their pay.[49] That would suggest that about 40 per cent of medieval Durham marrying for the first time were servants, which undoubtedly undercounts the number of servants thanks to scribal practices relating to women's names. In addition, thirteen of the thirty-five women fined for leyrwite were servants, and another five likely were servants, indicating servants were sexually active.[50]

By the seventeenth century, service had transformed from a stage in the life cycle to a position a woman might hold her entire life. The only certain example of a servant in the parishes marrying is Jane Hilton, who received a bequest in 1602 from Ralph Hilton (relationship unknown) of 20s., equalling two years' wages, and she married the following year.[51] However, there are few references to servants and matching individuals in parish registers is tricky. For example, in 1625 Anne Farrow's servant Elizabeth Johnson died. Women of the same name were born in 1598 and 1601, so if one of those was the same Elizabeth Johnson who died in 1625, then she was between twenty-four and twenty-six years old.[52] The Jane Scathlock (or Shacklock) who received 2s. 6d. in wages in the will of Lancelot Richardson in 1640 may have been around thirty-eight.[53] John Machell lost three servants to the plague in the spring of 1606, Elizabeth Granger, Margaret Trumble, and Anna. Their ages are unknown; the parish register described all of them as *ancillae* (female servants but usually older female servants).[54] The average age at first marriage in the seventeenth century meant marriage remained a

---

on the Evidence for the Origins of the "European Marriage Pattern" in England'. Goldberg argues that this can be applied to the late medieval period: *Women, Work, and Life Cycle*.

[47] Humphries and Wesidorf, 'Wages of Women'.   [48] TNA: PRO DURH 3/14 ff. 21v, 26r, 42v.

[49] TNA: DURH 3/13 ff. 139r, 365r, 445v; 3/14 ff. 21v, 26r, 87v, 123r, 174r, 186r, 229v, 333r, 427v, 622r; 3/15 f. 118v. Of the 186 merchet fines for the entire bishopric, 16 were specifically for servants and another 72 were paid by the woman: see Appendix B: Baptism, Fornication, Marriage, and Funeral Databases; Bennett, 'Medieval Peasant Marriage'.

[50] Appendix B: Baptism, Fornication, Marriage, and Funeral Databases.

[51] DPRI/1/1602/H7/1.   [52] Sedgefield Parish Registers, 22.1, 26.1, 69.2.

[53] DPRI/1/1640/R1/1; Sedgefield Parish Registers 29.3.   [54] Sedgefield Parish Registers 35.3.

possibility for Elizabeth Johnson before death took her, but the economy meant more and more women were likely to remain unmarried.[55] Service may have been the most attractive option remaining.

We are left in the dark about much of the day-to-day life of servants and labourers. Wills and inventories provide additional insights. Inventories leave references to maids' rooms and servants' beds. Other studies help fill in some of the gaps. The length of service could vary. Although Kussmaul concluded that servants typically contracted for a year at a time, from Michaelmas to Michaelmas, Whittle and Mansell noted significant flexibility in the period 1540–1640, with servants rarely working for a single year.[56] Based on wills of parishioners, some servants stayed with a master for years. In his study of seven households in Cheshire and Lancashire, Foster uncovered more details about the lives of servants and labourers than normally survive. In the sixteenth and seventeenth century, wages for labourers there sometimes included food and lodging, either with the master or with tenants (who were compensated), and clothing might be included as well. In periods of high or rising grain prices, those workers who received food were better off than those who worked solely for a cash wage.[57]

What these servants did is unsaid. Cooking, laundering, and working in the fields would have been normal tasks; servants in some households assisted with spinning, weaving, brewing, and dairying, based on the capital goods in the house. Labourers assisted the servants in the fields at key times of the year; sadly, labourers left even less of a trace in the records. They mainly appear collectively and anonymously in debts owed by the decedent, and this was almost exclusively for agricultural work with some carrying of goods.

Probate records provide occasional specifics about wages, permitting some general assessment but no thorough study. Cuthbert Conyers of Layton, Esq., was buried in Sedgefield in 1559; he willed that back wages be paid to his servants plus additional sums depending on their length of service, from half a crown for those who had served him three years or less up to a whole year's wages for those who had been with him seven years. Robert Hilton of Butterwick, gent., willed 12s. to every servant there, both men and women; a former servant received 10s. and to one servant in particular, clothes and a whole year's worth of wages.[58] Grain and animals also featured in bequests to servants. There are few instances of specific wages. There is Jane Hilton, who earned 10s. per year in 1602. If the wages for Jane Scathlock were her quarterly pay, she also earned 10s. thirty-eight years later. Thomas Chapman's inventory included the quarter's wages for a manservant and maidservant, at 10s. and 5s. per quarter, or 40s. and 20s. annually.

---

[55] Wrigley and Schofield, *Population History of England*, pp. 255–6.
[56] Kussmaul, *Servants in Husbandry*, p. 97; Whittle, 'A Different Pattern of Employment', pp. 58–9; Mansell, 'Female Service and the Village Community', pp. 91–3.
[57] Foster, *Seven Households*, pp. 14–16, 126.
[58] *Wills and Inventories* I, pp. 184–6; *Wills and Inventories* II, p. 39–40.

A few years later, another inventory recorded that a maid was due 12s. at Martinmas next; if that were prorated (as the inventory was drawn up in June) the annual wage would be about 29s.[59] These examples fall into the range Foster found in Cheshire and Lancashire: 23s. 4d. to 26s. 8d. in the late sixteenth century for men, and in the 1670s, 40–55s. for men and 12–40s. for women. The examples cited by Humphries and Weisdorf are similar, ranging from 15s. to 33s. 4d. for women. Those examples all include room and board, and possibly some livery. Applying their method to convert the salary and room and board into daily wage rates yields Durham rates of 3.9d., 4.3d., and 4.7d, conforming to the national average they calculated.[60]

The number of servants is harder to estimate based on information from Durham. Bryan Lamb died in 1614 and his inventory included 43s. for the half year's wages for the servants, or an annual bill of 86s. Was that for two men, eight women, or some combination?[61] Foster estimated that tenants in Cheshire with around 90 acres of land likely employed three servants in the sixteenth century. For the sake of argument, if we assume that every bovate over two required a servant—giving a holding of five bovates (75–108) three servants, in line with Foster's estimate—there could have been around fifty servants in the three villages during mid-seventeenth century.[62] The unknown factor is the cultivation of the surrounding manors and farms, such as Layton and Embleton. Embleton contained at least eighty bovates of arable c.1400 and Layton over 1,000 acres in the early seventeenth century.[63] Depending on how these and other former settlements were used for stock or crops would greatly affect the number of servants in the parishes, with some residing in the villages.[64]

Did service and EMP contribute to economic development in Durham? For De Moor and Van Zanden, the result of delayed marriage with increased wage labour was 'a demographic regime embedded in a highly commercial environment, in which households interacted frequently with labour, capital, and commodity markets'.[65] They saw service as contributing to social capital as well. Their hypothesis has been challenged.[66] Legislation limiting the movement and wages of workers fell especially hard on women and reinforced the patriarchal order.[67] Humphries

---

[59] DPRI/1/1606/C2/2; 1608/R7/1.

[60] Foster, *Seven Households*, p. 126; Humphries and Weisdorf, 'Wages of Women', pp. 412–7.

[61] DPR I/1/1614/L1/3.

[62] Foster, *Capital and Innovation*, p. 128; *Parliamentary Surveys*, pp. 189–201, 212–13.

[63] Curtis, 'Sedgefield', pp. 326–27; Baker Baker BAK.72/249 f. 11v.

[64] The names given to closes and fields in Layton reflect residents of the main villages, such as Chipchase, Denom, Wheatley, and Wilkinson: Baker Baker BAK.72/249 f. 11v.

[65] De Moor and Van Zanden, 'Girl Power', p. 1.

[66] Humphries and Weisdorf, 'Wages of Women', pp. 424–28; Dennison and Ogilvie, 'Does the European Marriage Pattern Explain Economic Growth?'; see also Bardsley, 'Women's Work Reconsidered', and Bardsley and Hatcher, 'Debate: Women's Work Reconsidered'.

[67] Bennett, 'Compulsory Service in Late Medieval England'; Poos, 'The Social Context of Statute of Labourers Enforcement'.

and Weisdorf found that casual wages for women did see a boost following the Black Death but then declined to the late sixteenth century, while annual wages (for servants on an annual contract) remained largely flat. The limited data for servant's wages in the parishes accords with their findings and supports their conclusion that female wage rates did not encourage growth or later marriage.

Women did have other opportunities. As expected for a group that made up half of the population, women were everywhere in the parish, but over time their identities and economic activities became less visible in the records. Some activities can be inferred from wills and inventories; spinning was one such, laundry another. Although women consistently made up 10–20 per cent of the tenants throughout the period, female tenants were left behind in agrarian and economic change. Only men engrossed land and dwellings, leased holdings, and expanded or experimented with their agriculture.[68] Likewise, even though women brewed the ale crucial to the rural diet for centuries, men leased the rights to the malt kilns and bread ovens. As the scale of production rose, it became more of a men's task.[69] As women's activities changed, the nature of the records hides much of what they did.[70]

Local Industry

While farming dominates the records, there was more to the local economy in the parishes, but not coal; coal mining of any scale was not undertaken in these villages until the nineteenth century.[71] Some coal was dug: there was a mine near Thrislington in 1328/29, and in 1401. John Pierson of Hett leased a coal mine in Cornforth for three years at 6s. 8d. per annum, and in 1454, two men leased a mine there for 20s.[72] These were all short, small operations. There were limekilns in the villages in the fourteenth century, indicating a regular if small at least small-scale extraction and burning. The tenants of Cornforth were ordered to build a communal kiln in 1381 in similar terms used for common ovens and malt kilns, implying that some had to have been doing this on their own in such a way

---

[68] Women made up a similar proportion of landholders in the four Norfolk manors studied by Whittle: 'Inheritance, Marriage, Widowhood and Remarriage', pp. 35–6. Other studies found higher concentrations in the fourteenth century: Bennett, *Women in the Medieval English Countryside*, p. 33; Franklin, 'Peasant Widows' "Liberation" and Remarriage', p. 188; Russell, *British Medieval Population*, pp. 62–4; Titow, *English Rural Society*, p. 87. Bardsley concluded 'that women's ownership of land...changed little, if at all, after the Black Death': 'Peasant Women and Inheritance of Land', p. 297.

[69] See Bennett, *Ale, Beer, and Brewsters*.

[70] Bennett has argued that while the activities that women carried out may have changed, their nature did not: see *Ale, Beer, and Brewsters*, and *History Matters*. That would seem to be the case here, though again, much is hidden.

[71] 'Local History: Bishop Middleham', 'Local History: Cornforth', 'West Cornforth (Cornforth)'; 'Bishop Middleham Colliery' and 'Cornforth Colliery', *Durham Mining Museum*.

[72] Austin, *Deserted Medieval Village*, p. 4; TNA: DURH 3/13 f. 364r; 15 f. 356r.

that the lord was losing revenue.[73] Campbell noted that lime was increasingly used as a fertilizer in sixteenth- and seventeenth-century England, and Brassley found evidence of lime spread as fertilizer in Northumberland in the 1670s. Green found that eighteenth-century adverts for Durham farms 'emphasized the proximity of limestone and coal'.[74] In 1622, the men inventorying the goods of Robert Farrow the elder noted that he had lime in his barn, so it is possible lime was being used as fertilizer in Durham even earlier.[75]

Unlike coal, the cattle trade and cloth and leather industries had a strong influence in these parishes.[76] Newman has shown that despite the general economic depression of the fifteenth century, the profits of the Darlington market remained steady, and the borough's four fairs continued to be popular. Darlington's position on the road from York and on the main east–west road of the Tees valley were a major factor, as were its connections with Newcastle and Hull.[77] Sedgefield had a market representing a node of the county's trade network, benefitting from the prominence of larger towns. Consequently, butchers featured prominently in the parishes. Leases for butchers' stalls and other spaces in Sedgefield market were recorded in the halmote books a handful of times, in 1392 and 1410, and a few noted as vacant in 1423. Others are mentioned in the collectors' rolls, often eight feet in size for 2s. John Pereson of Newton Hampstead rented a space for six years at 8d., for two butchers' stalls.[78] Centuries later, Edwin Linton, butcher, was brought before the assizes for stealing an ewe in 1601, while the following year John Thompson and William Richeson were charged for practising the trade of butcher without a sufficient apprenticeship.[79] The surviving quarter session rolls for Durham indicate a thriving trade particularly in cattle. Men bought and sold cattle in Darlington and elsewhere, legally and illegally. John Shaw of Cornforth, in trouble for an enclosure, purchased twenty oxen and ten cows contrary to statute at Elwick, about three-quarters of the way from Cornforth to Hartlepool.[80] In 1612 William Guy of Mordon was charged with buying and selling twenty oxen, and Marmaduke Myers, vicar of Middleham, bought thirty-three head of cattle at

---

[73] TNA: DURH 3/135 m. 1. The fine for failing to do so was 20s.

[74] Green, 'Houses and Households', p. 228. Thomas Haswell of Cornforth was 'slain at a lime-kilne' in 1666: Surtees, *History and Antiquities, Vol. 3*, p. 14.

[75] Campbell, *English Yeoman*, pp. 173–5; Brassley, *Agricultural Economy of Northumberland*, p. 156; DPRI/1/1622/F3/3. A by-law on burning lime, and quantities needed, was issued in 1654: DHC1/I/81 f. 486r/501r.

[76] Earls Colne was similarly situated relative to the East Anglian cloth industry, unlike Terling which was more isolated: French and Hoyle, *Character of English Rural Society*, p. 52. Kowaleski discussed the regional cattle, leather, and hides trades and links to a town, in *Local Markets and Regional Trade in Medieval Exeter*, pp. 293–307.

[77] On Darlington's trades, see Newman, 'Economy and Society in North-Eastern Market Towns', pp. 136–9, and 'Marketing and Trade Networks in Medieval Durham', pp. 135–8. A sixteenth-century observer declared Darlington the second most important market town after Durham: Cookson with Newman, 'Trade and Industry', p. 109.

[78] TNA: DURH 3/13 ff. 52v, 70r, 185v–186r; 3/14 f. 619r; CCB B/65/1, Collectors' Accounts, m. 2.

[79] *Durham Quarter Session Rolls*, pp. 129, 132.   [80] *Durham Quarter Session Rolls*, p. 188.

Darlington and resold them 'contrary to statute'.[81] Darlington also had a substantial leather industry.[82] Locally, raising cattle was profitable.

Clothmaking was another important trade. Underwater archaeologist Gary Bankhead discovered more than 300 lead cloth seals in the River Wear by the city of Durham.[83] Darlington merchants supplied Durham priory and traded internationally. Darlington suffered with the rest of England in the fifteenth century, and in the sixteenth century the weavers at Darlington moved to linen and worsted, and eventually to a variant of the new draperies.[84] In the Darlington probate inventories between 1600 and 1625, Atkinson et al. found three weavers and fourteen spinning wheels, concluding that the quantities of wool, flax, and cloth were small.[85] Many villagers in Sedgefield and Bishop Middleham were involved in the cloth trades throughout the period. Men and women in the villages were amerced in the halmote court for putting linen and hemp in the mill chase in Bishop Middleham; in one instance, thirty people were so amerced in one session.[86] A fulling mill in Cornforth was valued at 33s. 4d. per annum but was considered waste in 1397–98. As with milling, baking, and other products, tenants preferred to approach these tasks on their own rather than pay to use the bishop's facility; William Person was fulling cloth in 1420.[87] Probate inventories show that spinning wheels (for linen, hemp, and wool) were common, sometimes multiple wheels in one household. Robert Hyndmer had 180 stone of wool worth £30 at his death in 1558 as well as fifteen yards of linen, fifty-one yards of harden cloth, and nineteen ells of canvas.[88] Thirty years later, Thomas Hutcheson (d.1587) owned forty-two yards of various cloth. Ralph Mason (d.1662) owned three spinning wheels (one for wool, two for linen), and Richard Mason's (d.1670) possessions included £21 of yarns.[89] There were even a few looms. This suggests that some of the cloth production in Darlington had moved into the countryside, at least for spinning.

Beyond production for sale beyond the parishes, there were local artisans in the villages. Blacksmiths played an important if little-remarked role in village agriculture. In *Boldon Book*, many villages had a special holding for the smith, which he held for blacksmithing services in lieu of rent. The connection between service and holding continued into the fifteenth century and was taken seriously. In 1359, John Smith of Sedgefield was stripped of a forge for failure to carry out his duties, and it was given to William de la Smith.[90] By the later fourteenth century, some villages had more than one forge. Thomas Smith held a forge in

---

[81] *Durham Quarter Session Rolls*, pp. 212, 223.
[82] Cookson with Newman, 'Trade and Industry', pp. 112, 147–8.
[83] Durham River Wear Assemblage Project; Ravilious, 'A River Runs Through It', pp. 38–43.
[84] Cookson with Newman, 'Trade and Industry', pp. 111–12, 150–3.
[85] *Darlington Wills*, pp. 37–40, 104.
[86] TNA: DURH 3/13 ff.35r-v, 349r, 446r; 3/14 ff. 94, 95r.   [87] TNA: DURH 3/14 f. 523r.
[88] *Wills and Inventories*, I, pp. 160–64.   [89] DPRI/1/1587/H13, 1662/M6, 1670/M8.
[90] TNA: DURH 3/12 f. 224r.

Bishop Middleham as part of a messuage and 7 acres called Smithesland (later Smithyplace) valued at 8s. rent per annum in exchange for upkeep of the manor's ploughs and for shoeing three horses but had to provide his own iron. He also held another cottage, forge, and 9.5 acres for a total of 7s. 6d. of rent. He may have been the same Thomas Smith who held the common forge in Sedgefield for 20d. per annum; there was another forge as well, held by Robert Pollard for 8d. per annum.[91] Decades later, in 1408, William Erby of Sedgefield leased land for a forge and paid for a licence to occupy Robert Pollard's forge with renewals, and Robert Smith took a parcel of waste north of the king's highway to erect a new forge in 1415.[92] The latter was leased for twelve years by four men in 1422.[93] Late in the sixteenth century, the forge was bundled up with other lands by the Mason family and presumably sublet.[94]

Each village had a common oven or bakehouse where tenants were expected to bake their bread. By the mid-seventeenth century, the cost of baking was 2d. per bushel of grain, paid in dough or coin.[95] These ovens were leased out to enterprising men or sometimes to the village as a collective. Henry Pillok, who acquired a small freehold and four bovates in Sedgefield and whose wife Joan briefly held a moiety of Butterwick, leased the oven at Sedgefield in 1397–98 for half a mark, when it was valued at four times that amount. The lease was important enough to be recorded in Bishop Skirlaw's chancery roll. Like many men of the time, Pillok was an official in the bishopric, and served as bailiff of Sadberge and a commissioner of array.[96] Bishop Middleham and Cornforth shared a common oven, held by the tenants of Cornforth for a half mark per annum.[97]

Brewing was just as important, and one of the few activities in which women were prominent in the records, at least in the later medieval period. As the second-longest data series in the records after land transfers and the one most consistently linked to women, brewing also acts as something of a barometer of patriarchal attitudes. Ale and later beer formed a major component of the diet. Each village had at least one malt kiln, often leased to local entrepreneurs or to the village who were paid in malt or coin. In 1607, a kiln belonging to Ralph Mason set fire to the house of Anthony Henman which was destroyed to the value of £55.[98] Each tourn, the halmote court amerced several persons for 'breaking' the Assize of Ale, and the regularity of amercements demonstrate a licence or fine

[91] *Hatfield's Survey*, pp. 181–2, 188–9.

[92] TNA: DURH 3/14 ff. 105v, 117r, 143v, 186r, 204r, 229r, 346r. There is one instance of a daughter taking her father's smithy, in 1409: 3/14 f. 123r.

[93] TNA: DURH 3/14 f. 582v.   [94] TNA: DURH 3/24, p. 861.

[95] DHC1/I/83 f. 79v.

[96] CCB B/65/1 Collectors' Accounts, m. 1. It had been held for that rent in Hatfield's Survey, by William de Broghton; *Hatfield's Survey*, p. 188; Arvanigian, 'The Nevilles and the Political Establishment in North-Eastern England', p. 268; 'No. 2. Durham Records: Calendar of the Curistor's Records', p. 75.

[97] *Hatfield's Survey*, p. 185.   [98] CCB B/23/25/4, Miscellanea on Accounts.

more than an amercement.[99] Women sold the ale from their houses for consumption there or to take away. These informal and later formal alehouses could be disruptive to the peace, and some of our evidence for conflict in the villages comes from the refusal to sell ale to certain persons.[100]

Much of the brewing for sale was done by the wives of leading tenants, presumably as they had more capital or supply, which would suggest barley and oats were being grown for commercial production of ale. One such example is Annabilla Headlam, who first appeared in the records in 1388. She brewed ale regularly and several times was assessed an additional penalty for not summoning the ale-tasters. Her first husband Thomas held more than 70 acres of land and a lime kiln, and he had leased a stall in the market; this put him among the wealthiest tenants of the village.[101] After Thomas's death, Annabilla married the smith William Erby in 1409 and continued to brew regularly until her death. Many other late medieval women were like her.

The regularity of brewing amercements lets historians use women like Annabilla to study changing attitudes about women. In these villages, the ways in which women were identified changed over time. Late in the fourteenth century, the brewers of the parish could be recorded three different ways: by her first and surname; as 'wife of' with no first name; or simply by her husband's name.[102] Widows were given their first and last names consistently enough that it permits their identification.[103] Starting in 1418, however, only men were listed as brewing for more than century, until 1522 when Elizabeth alias Isabella Kant was listed among the brewers for Bishop Middleham.[104] She continued brewing regularly until 1540. Never described as a widow or a wife, the absence of marital status indicates she was a single woman.[105] Otherwise, the names of men dominated the list, but many wives continued to be involved in brewing; the erasure of women was true only in the parchment halmote books, not the paper drafts.[106] The last appearance of brewing in the parchment books was in 1554 and 1596 for the paper books.

[99] On brewing, see Bennett, *Ale, Beer, and Brewsters*, pp. 4, 160–3; on the practice on the Durham estates, see Larson, *Conflict and Compromise*, pp. 155, 180, 214.

[100] Janet Gregson, widow, charged with operating an alehouse without authority in 1606: *Durham Quarter Session Rolls*, p. 151.

[101] TNA: DURH 3/13 f. 70r; 3/14 f. 56r.

[102] For example, see these tourns from 1391–93: TNA: DURH 3/13 ff. 15r, 71v, 89r, 105v-106r, 118r.

[103] TNA: DURH 3/14 ff. 9r, 21r-22r, 26r-v, 42r-43r, 57r, 65v-66r, 74v, 87r-88r, 106r, 116v, 123r, 143r, 155r-156r, 165v-166r, 174r-175r, 186r-v, 204r-v, 1210v-212r, 229r-v, 235r, 251v-252v, 256v-257r, 269v-270r, 287v-288v, 293r-294r, 313v-315r, 327r-v, 333r-334r, 345v-346v, 365v-366r, 372v, 383r-v, 399r-v, 405r-v, 417r-v, 427r-428r, 444r-v. Bennett observed similar inconsistencies in her study of brewing throughout late medieval England: *Ale, Beer, and Brewsters*, pp. 163–6.

[104] TNA: DURH 3/14 ff. 455v-456v and following to 3/21 f. 266r.

[105] TNA: DURH 3/21 266r; 3/22 pp. 28, 43, 63, 75; 3/23 ff. 2r, 154r. She was not listed in every tourn, and in some tourns no one was amerced for brewing. Before Elizabeth's appearance but still in 1519, Thomas Kant and others leased the common oven, malt kin, and brewing rights for the year: DHC1/I/1 f. 12v.

[106] TNA: DURH 3/22 p. 15. The paper drafts survive from 1519: DHC1/I/4 f. 1r, 51v; DHC1/I/23 f. 28r.

Brewing certainly continued, as the quantities of malt, hops, and brewing equipment in probate records attests, but it is less visible to us.

That is true of many trades. In the sixteenth and seventeenth centuries, and likely earlier, many villagers combined farming and a trade. However, few specialists appeared or at least left records. Although focused on grain and stock production, the villagers had access to artisans in the parishes as well as markets. The ready availability of lime in the parishes was another boon to agriculture. A farmer needed more to succeed, however.

Credit and Debt

A steady supply of credit was necessary for capital expenditures and for getting by until the next harvest or fair. This was true particularly in the later Middle Ages, when coin (especially small coins) was scarce.[107] Briggs's analysis of late medieval village credit applies equally well to these Durham villages, in the types of credit and debt and the relationships between creditors and debtors.[108] For the later Middle Ages, we can see a portion of the local network of credit and debt in the halmote court records. Although in theory limited to debts under 40s., some larger debts were litigated in the halmote for convenience.[109] Pleas of broken covenant were much rarer, averaging three per year in the same period. Pleas of debt and detinue in the halmote courts began to decline from 1430, but from 1390 to 1424 there was an average of twenty pleas per year for the three villages.[110] The average debt was just under 7s. 9d., but the median was only 18d., in line with Brigg's findings; one of the larger cases was for 35s. 4d., for two oxen, two horses, and seven sheep.[111] Many debts were over unpaid wages. Some debts appear to be over the settling of accounts, as when John Stryngs sued Robert Atkinson for 10s. resulting from the exchange of horses.[112] Village collectors and millers sued for what was owed them; John Blakett sued thirteen tenants in 1391 for grain they had withheld, worth more than 10s. Nearly all the debts were to people in the same village or villages nearby. These represent the informal network of lending and exchange underpinning everyday activities.[113] The few debts involving men further away, such as Barnard Castle or Hartlepool, reveal some broader market

---

[107] Day, 'The Great Bullion Famine'.
[108] Briggs, *Credit and Village Society*, esp. pp. 30–56, 102–111; see also his 'Introduction: Law Courts, Contracts and Rural Society in Europe'.
[109] Larson, *Conflict and Compromise*, p. 35.
[110] Harvey concluded that manorial courts were in serious decline in the sixteenth century: Harvey, *Manorial Records*, p. 57. Waddell challenged that conclusion, arguing that 'it would be more useful to think of this era as one in which communities adapted the role of these courts to suit their evolving needs'; 'Governing England through the Manor Courts', p. 301.
[111] TNA: DURH 3/13 f. 88v; Briggs, *Credit and Village Society*, pp. 57–60.
[112] TNA: DURH 3/13 f. 28r.   [113] Briggs, *Credit and Village Society*, pp. 105–7.

connections in the county and Sedgefield's place in that network. Yet in the end, many medieval creditors and debtors remain unknown to us, and Briggs warns against assuming the court evidence provides information about typical credit and debt.[114]

From the 1430s onwards, debts appear in far fewer numbers and with less detail. The amounts are somewhat higher due to inflation, but still relatively small. The detail provided conforms to the earlier pattern, with the addition of some suits over rent due from sublet lands. The one major change, although not a debt per se, was the command to pay the common servant or herder their wages. Far more information on early modern credit and debt comes from probate records, as the men inventorying the deceased's goods often included the debts owed and owing. Most debts were to people in nearby parishes but there were regular connections with merchants in Durham, Gateshead, and Newcastle. Yeoman Robert Cooke (d.1663) instructed his executor to collect money from men all over the south and east of the county, while Ralph Ord (d.1685) of Sedgefield had local debtors in Carlton, Embleton, Great Stainton, Norton, Stockton, and Tudhoe as well as in the cities of Durham and Newcastle. Some of these were clients for his cattle, such as Thomas Danby of Durham, chandler; Thomas Thompson of Norton, innkeeper; and George Swainston of Stockton, butcher.[115] Some people died with very little debt, but credit and debt were common, even for the poor.

Large debts were secured through mortgages, and the examples in the parishes follow many of the patterns that Juliet Gayton identified in her study of copyhold mortgages in Hampshire, in particular that mortgages were not instances of crisis borrowing.[116] In 1653, James Cook, merchant adventurer, took a cottage, close, and 58 enclosed acres as copyhold from Thomas Middleton and immediately sublet it back to him for eight years at £20 per year until £160 had been repaid. Anthony Dale, an alderman of Durham, was also involved in the land market.[117] Ralph Mason and Sir Anthony Young (lately Esq) conveyed nearly 67 acres of copyhold in 1656 to Edward Nicholson of Burne (Yorks.), yeoman, then took it back for £12 a year in a 200 year lease.[118] The terms clearly mark some of these as mortgages, or the use of land as collateral for a loan. Take for example this agreement in 1642:

Memo it is agreed betwixt the said parties that is the said John Harreson his heirs or assignes doe pay or cause to be paid to the said John Johnson his heirs and assigns the sum of £10 yearly to begin at the Feast of Pentecost which shall

[114] Briggs, *Credit and Village Society*, p. 102.
[115] DPRI/1/1663/C11/1–2, 1685/O2/1. Nair found a more restricted range of credit: *Highley*, p. 62.
[116] Gayton, 'Mortgages Raised by Rural English Copyhold Tenants'.
[117] DHC1/I/81 ff. 436r, 489r, 567v; see also/82 ff. 687v, 828r, 1011v;/83 f. 15v.
[118] DHC 82 ff. 596r–v.

in the yeare of 1643 during the [illeg.] of two years and at the two years' end do
pay or cause to be paid to the said John Johnson his heirs or assignes the sum of
125 pounds then he the said John Johnson his heirs or assignes shall resurrender
the premises to the said John Harreson to hould to him and his sequelis in jure
But for defalt of payment of any of the said sommes he the said John Johnson to
hold the premises according to the purportt of this Surrender.[119]

These agreements quickly became terse, such as this 1653 entry:

Memo that the surrender above mentioned and the matter and thing therein
concerned are upon condition that if the above named John Harreson etc. pays
etc. to Robert Young etc. £140 on or before the [blank] day of August 1660 and
yearly £11 the surrender is void and the land resurrendered to John Harreson
etc. If default etc.[120]

Most agreements were for sums ranging from £1 to £300, usually for terms of two,
five, or eight years. Some required a lump sum payment on a specific date in addition to yearly payments, as when Ralph Mason agreed to pay John Pilkington,
gentleman, £8 annually and £100 at the end of the seventh year or with notice for
a 'lease' of 62 acres.[121] Some men, such as John Harrison, made multiple agreements. Men such as he could raise cash easily and repay quickly, though one can
only wonder if some loans were taken out to pay others, postponing a final
reckoning.

While Allen found that mortgages benefitted large landholders and contributed to the elimination of yeomen in the south Midlands, these were among the
more substantial copyholders in the parishes, and the creditors mainly were merchants from Durham, Gateshead, and Newcastle.[122] There is little evidence as to
the reason for the mortgages, but most do not seem to be connected to financial
difficulty.[123] It could be that these were used to acquire lands elsewhere. In the
case of the loan taken by Roland Hixon in 1650, he may have used the money to
acquire leasehold lands in the nearby Dean and Chapter village of Aycliffe.[124] The
timing of many of these mortgages could be connected to purchasing estates during the Interregnum; six of them occurred between 1650 and the Restoration.
Rebuilding houses may have been another reason. Yeomen like these taking
mortgages leads to three important observations: they had something expensive
to purchase; their lands could be let for more than the rents due to the bishop;

---

[119] DHC1/I/79 f. 887r.   [120] DHC 81 f. 327r.   [121] DHC1/I/83 f. 163v.
[122] Allen, *Enclosure and the Yeoman*, pp. 102–4.
[123] Gayton suggested six main reasons for mortgages: purchase of new property; renovation or
rebuilding; investment; providing for children; paying off inherited debts; and financial difficulty:
'Mortgages Raised by Rural English Copyhold Tenants', p. 58.
[124] DHC1/I/81 f. 33r; DPRI/1/1665/H10/1.

and there were lessees confident that they could produce enough to cover those higher rents.

One of the major arguments of this book is that rural Durham was part of the broader economic development in England, supporting industrial development in the northeast, itself directly tied to London. Likewise, the farming examined so far emerged in a broader economic context. Although lacking in self-identified artisans, brewing, dairying, and other trades were occurring at a commercial rather than a household supply level. The trade networks of Durham permitted specialization, particularly in cattle, while the cloth industry provided useful by-employment. Credit was available, with seventeenth-century yeomen able to raise and repay hundreds of pounds, while serving as creditors to lesser tenants. This is not to ignore the poverty in County Durham; in fact, the greater scale of production depended on both available labour and a demand for foodstuffs by those with little or no land. Perhaps the one positive was that the trade connections in the parish provided some avenues for employment, while credit may have eased access to necessities.

8

Individuals and Communities

Studies such as this are predicated on a coherent relationship between people and the area studied. Identities, however, overlap and change, are acquired and imposed. Scholars of the social and economic history of England have grappled with the challenge of community and identity in studies of a village, manor, county, or estate. The joy of a study such as this one is the deep immersion in one community, in this case an administrative unit of the bishopric of Durham. That community is one created by the bishopric administration, drawing on village communities but existing separately from the parish communities, which included settlements and thus people who were part of the parish and sometimes but not always part of the administrative unit or the other villages. And this complexity is in a region where manor and village tend to be coterminous rather than having multiple manors in a village. An examination of community, and the place of individuals within it, is critical in understanding change—more so when one of the supposed changes is the decline of the community and the rise of individualism. One of the lessons from this study of one administrative unit, two parishes, and three villages is that a single village or parish is insufficient. Ideally, this study would have included another parish, such as Aycliffe or Merrington, but that would be too unwieldy for a broad study.

A second lesson is that change did not have to destroy communities.[1] It no doubt helped that holdings remained intact and there was a small population in the later Middle Ages. Some of the smaller settlements in the parish became enclosed farms; those settlements were tiny to begin with, and at least some of those tenants were tenants or residents in the larger villages. The medieval period witnessed plenty of conflict over agriculture, and village oligarchies existed even then. The communal structure allowed men to pursue wealth on their own; the enclosures of the seventeenth century were driven by tenants, large and small, and smallholders continued to be found alongside husbandmen, yeomen, and gentlemen in the seventeenth century.[2] The communities changed but were not lost, remaining one of the constants alongside changes in population, farm size, dynasties, and religion.

---

[1] For examples of the loss of communities, see Goodacre, *Transformation of a Peasant Economy*, pp. 99–100, 141, 239.
[2] This was not the case elsewhere. Goodacre writes 'It is also surprising to find that these early enclosures were not always incompatible with the survival of common husbandry', *Transformation of a Peasant Economy*, pp. 114, 121.

Rethinking the Great Transition: Community and Economic Growth in County Durham, 1349–1660. Peter L. Larson, Oxford University Press. © Peter L. Larson 2022. DOI: 10.1093/oso/9780192849878.003.0009

The ever-growing number of local studies thwarts the propensity to generalize; there is no single pattern of development even with a region of a county. The village and parish community has been a major and often debated topic in premodern English history, even though the view of the idyllic community was jettisoned long ago. Medieval scholars of a Marxist persuasion focused on community solidarity in conflicts with the lord while others, notably Raftis and the 'Toronto School', studied the stratification of peasant communities and argued that their relationships were far more significant. As Hatcher and Bailey noted, '[s]uch disagreements are difficult to resolve because they flow from fundamentally different conceptions of the way medieval rural society operated, which leads historians to make contrasting interpretations of the same evidence'.[3] That has led later generations of scholars to move to a more complex understanding of community and how it could unite or divide.[4]

Scholars looking at early modern communities run into different instances of landlord–tenant conflict, often manifesting in lawsuits as landlords tried to profit from rising prices, such as a conflict between the Dean and Chapter and their tenants.[5] Others have examined the transitions from medieval to early modern, particularly the effect on local society. French and Hoyle deliberately returned to the transition debate in their study of Earls Colne, examining the changes wrought by the arrival of a resident landlord. Here the conflict was over rights and control of land, with the incoming Harlakendens attempting to transform the village and failing, becoming farmers rather than manorial lords. Early modern England transformed Earls Colne as well, as outsiders with capital sought to invest in land, and resident copyholders became tenants, although the general tenurial structure persisted.[6] Others studies of early modern communities explore the effects of capitalism or the Reformation in the rise of the 'middling sort', and the fate of the poor or landless.[7] The connections between the rising middle 'class' with puritanism in particular has been a point of scholarly conflict. This was the focus of Wrightson and Levine's famous work on Terling, which inspired a range of further research on social control, misbehaviour, and cultural transformations.[8]

---

[3] Hatcher and Bailey, *Modelling the Middle Ages*, p. 101.

[4] For examples in Durham, see Larson, *Conflict and Compromise*.

[5] Morrin, 'Transfer to Leasehold', and Marcombe, 'Dean and Chapter of Durham'; Brown, *Rural Society and Economic Change*, pp. 90–1.

[6] French and Hoyle, *Character of English Rural Society*; see also Hoyle, 'Tenure and the Land Market'. McIntosh found that new gentry displaced yeomen in the royal manor of Havering (Essex): *A Community Transformed*.

[7] For example, Everitt, 'Social Mobility in Early Modern England'; Kent, 'The Rural "Middling Sort" in Early Modern England'; H. French, 'Social Status, Localism and the "Middle Sort of People"'; Hindle, *On the Parish*; Kümin, *Shaping of a Community*; K. French, *People of the Parish* and *Good Women of the Parish*; Duffy, *Stripping of the Altars*.

[8] Wrightson and Levine, *Poverty & Piety*; on social control, see McIntosh, *Controlling Misbehavior*.

Some have tried to map allegiances in the English onto different social, cultural, and religious groups to explain the Civil War.[9]

Then, there is the great question of individuality. The needs of communal agriculture, the nucleated village, a single religion, and lord–peasant relations supposedly necessitated strong, self-regulating communities; economic change, enclosure, and Protestantism supposedly broke these apart. Macfarlane challenged that and argued that there were no true English peasants to begin with. Very few would go as far as that but many scholars have identified strong individualist streaks in the rural countryside of late medieval England.[10] Croot pointed out that part of the issue is the assumption that peasants were only subsistence farmers, and uninterested in being anything but—and this despite considerable research on the medieval English peasant.[11] Allen argued that the sixteenth-century yeomen were the true peasants, as owner-occupiers, although this fails to account for yeomen holding land in multiple locations as seen in south-eastern Durham.[12] As has been argued throughout this book, the transformation in economy and society involved a strong stream of continuity—evolution rather than revolution—and that is true of community and individuals. Interpreting evidence to discern individual and community is difficult. Even the most conscientious historian runs the risk of reading too much into the sources. The answer seems to be local and situational, requiring analysis of association and action.

Variety of Community

The people we have met in this book associated with several different communities. Most basic was what they considered 'home'. With close villages such as Bishop Middleham, Cornforth, and Sedgefield, 'home' could refer to more than one; that is, they may not have thought too much on one or the other, perhaps identifying more with parish, or being able to move from one settlement to the other. Then there was their religious affiliation, where they married, baptized their children, and wished to be buried, although the last could be different depending on family ties. For recusant families, this was even more complex. There are tenurial communities: the tenants in any given village or manorial unit. Even this is ambiguous, as men with lands in one village field might owe works at a manor farm attached to another village. Such connections could see families moving from one village to another, as when a child married into another village,

---

[9] For example, David Underdown, *Fire from Heaven* and *Revel, Riot, and Rebellion*; Stoyle, *Loyalty and Locality*.
[10] Macfarlane, *Origins of English Individualism*.
[11] Croot, *World of the Small Farmer*, pp. 5–7, 194–5.
[12] Allen, *Enclosure and the Yeoman*, pp. 14, 56–64, 81–5.

or someone used an acquaintance to acquire more or better land in the new village. While there are few instances that could be termed a true family-land bond, many families demonstrated a deep rootedness in village, parish, and wider community. The Headlam family of Sedgefield is one example of a long connection between family and holding. With ancestors in the village as early as at least 1352 and perhaps before, John Headlam left sometime after his father's death in 1406/07, not to return and claim his copyhold inheritance until 1443. The family still held the same 70-plus-acre holding into the seventeenth century, even surviving involvement in the 1569 northern rebellion.[13] Some other families kept a holding in their hands over a few generations. But many more families, such as the del Gates, Widdifields, and Reas, shifted from holding to holding and village to village while remaining in the neighbourhood. Beyond this, connections were made to some major towns and cities, including Darlington, Durham, Hartlepool, Newcastle, and Sunderland.

The village community, which in Durham often was synonymous with a manorial community, is most evident in agricultural affairs and in law and order.[14] Villages had one or more constables charged with keeping order, something that they did not always do. Likewise, the ale tasters were tasked with enforcing the quality and price of ale, although the Assize of Ale was more a licence to brew rather than a fine for an infraction.[15] In Sedgefield, the stocks for punishing minor offences were outside the bakehouse, which was known as the '[sic] Parlament house', suggesting its use for village meetings; however, the agricultural by-laws were set outside of the church.[16] The latter were enforced by the reeve and jurors of each village, with the reeve often noted as the first juror in the halmote records. Those men also presented infractions at the halmote court. The village, or at least its main tenants, acted as a community to manage the common fields. They also leased land collectively, and some villages even leased themselves from the bishop. In the seventeenth century, these communities sought enclosure. The tenants of Sedgefield sought permission to enclose lands 'for the most parte waisted and worne with continuall ploweinge and thereby made to bare barren and unfruitful as small or no benefitt or profit could be made thereof'.[17] The tenants even created a by-law allowing the reeve to levy funds for the project. These major projects did not go smoothly. Twenty-five men and women of Sedgefield sued four others in the bishop's chancery for failing to go along with the division. The defendants argued, successfully, that they were not dealt with fairly. John

---

[13] TNA: DURH 3/12 f. 61r; 3/14 f. 56r; 3/15 f. 111v.

[14] On the continued importance of manorial courts, see Waddell, 'Governing England through the Manor Courts'.

[15] Bennett, *Ale, Beer, and Brewsters*, pp. 4, 160–3.

[16] *Depositions and Other Ecclesiastical Proceedings*, pp. 298–9.

[17] DHC 6/IV/39 (254575/1/2), 16 July 1636; quotation is from p. 2. For Bishop Middleham, DHC 6/IV/10 (187614), 24 February 1693; for Cornforth, DHC1/M.76, a transcription of the original (4 September 1626).

Woodhouse sued sixteen other tenants of Cornforth over the allotment he was promised for organizing the enclosure. None of these was protracted, however, and the disputes were settled through arbitration.

The parishes overlapped the settlements, though the latter would have dominated the former population-wise. Although the parish is an ecclesiastical unit, it had important secular and quasi-religious functions that united the smaller settlements and farms with the larger village(s). One such instance was education. In 1633, twenty-four 'upstanding and legal parishioners' including two esquires and several gentlemen set up a grammar school.[18] Another function was poor relief, although the sources are quiet about how this worked. Above all, the parish was a religious community. Sedgefield had chantries to St Thomas and St Katherine, and a guild (and a 'gildhouse') of St Mary. Bishop Fox granted an indulgence for the repair of the latter and its altar in 1500.[19] Chapels of ease existed at various times in Bradbury, Embleton, Fishburn, Hardwick, and Thrislington.[20]

Despite the introduction of new beliefs and practices during the Reformation, Catholicism persisted in Sedgefield parish. Kesselring saw Sedgefield as a place where different conservative values clashed, specifically order versus Catholicism, in her study of the 1569 rebellion.[21] After the vicar rearranged the church in 1567 according to the bishop's order of 1563, one of the wardens, John Hutcheson, repeatedly threatened to remove the communion table. On 17 November, he and the other wardens, John Bellerby, Robert Denton, S[blank] Wryght, and Thomas Morland, entered the church and dismantled the new arrangements.[22] Exactly one year later, 17 November 1568, a Sunday, Brian Headlam was accused of threatening the churchwardens and others when they tried to fine him for failing to remove his cap during the service. The timing was, religiously, doubly significant in Sedgefield: 16 November was the feast day of St Edmund of Abingdon, patron saint of Sedgefield's parish church, while 17 November was the feast of a popular north-eastern saint, Hilda, Abbess of Whitby. The Northern Rising began at the same time the following year, around 14 November, with mass celebrated in

---

[18] The men were Cuthbert Conyers, Esq., Nicholas Freville, Esq., Jerrard Salvin, Esq., Henry Blakiston, Charles Elstob, Ralph Butler, Robert Farrow, Humphrey Mason, Robert Johnson, Thomas Smith, Henry Wardell, John Harrison, Robert Browne, John Chapman, Charles Rutter, William Mason, Robert Mason, Thomas Ky, Leonard Middleton, Thomas Wright, Thomas Robinson, James Wood, William Elstob, and William Lyn: DHC1/I/77 f. 834r.

[19] Page, 'A List of the Inventories of Church Goods made temp. Edward VI', p. 215; Mackenzie and Ross, *An Historical, Topographical, and Descriptive View*, vol. I, p. 429; *Register of Richard Fox*, p. 32.

[20] Curtis, 'Sedgefield', pp. 321–43. On laity and religion in late medieval Durham, see Harvey, *Lay Religious Life in Late Medieval Durham*.

[21] Kesselring, *The Northern Rebellion of 1569*, p. 71. See also Tenno, 'Religious Deviance in the Elizabethan Diocese of Durham', pp. 34–41, 79. On Catholicism in Durham, see Oates, 'Catholicism, Conformity and the Community in the Elizabethan Diocese of Durham', pp. 53–76, and Hilton, 'Catholicism in Jacobean Durham', pp. 78–85.

[22] Fordyce, *History and Antiquities of the County Palatine*, vol. 2, p. 334.

many churches including Sedgefield's St Edmunds. Sunday, 16 November, would have been the feast of St Edmund and the eve of the feast of St Hilda. Roland Hixon, one of the churchwardens in 1569, helped oversee the return of Catholicism in Sedgefield during the rebellion. The high altar was restored, the stone having been hidden under a rubbish heap in a garth, with the holy water font hidden in a dunghill. Hixon supposedly burned the Protestant books, saying 'lowe where the Homilies flees to the devyll'. In his deposition, Hixon explained that the parish met to discuss what to do and decided to re-place the altar and holy water font, which together took some thirty persons to do, and tried to shift the blame from himself to Brian Headlam. Following the suppression of the rebellion, twenty-four members of the parish were accused of assisting or hearing mass. The five men who reassembled the altar, including John Newton the parish clerk, were sentenced to process around the church barefoot. Hixon's sentence was not recorded.[23] Thirty-one persons from Sedgefield parish and twenty-one from Bishop Middleham were among the over two hundred men from Stockton Ward who joined the northern earls in rebellion, and eight from Sedgefield and five from Bishop Middleham were executed.[24] Several prominent men had lands in Sedgefield seized on account of their treason, including Anthony Hebburn, Esq., of Hardwick (fled), Ralph Conyers of Layton (pardoned), Robert Lambert (pardoned), Robert Tempest of Holmside (fled), and John Bellerby.[25] Kesselring thought that Brian Headlam 'was quite probably among the Sedgefield men chosen for death', yet he appears again in Sedgefield as a halmote juror in 1571, after being absent since the rebellion.[26] His family remained in the parish into the seventeenth century, as did Roland Hixon's. Other than the gentry, there was little long-term disruption.

It is difficult to get at what individuals felt about the Reformation and the new religious practices. There were notable incidents and recusants, but in the seventeenth century most men took the Protestation Oath. The pro-Catholic incidents leading up to the 1569 rebellion could indicate conformity and peer pressure as much as personal belief. The conclusion that must be drawn, then, is that

---

[23] Fordyce, *History and Antiquities of the County Palatine, vol. 2*, pp. 331–2; *Depositions and Other Ecclesiastical Proceedings*, pp. 183–93.

[24] *Memorials of the Rebellion of 1569*, pp. 140, 250, 259.

[25] DCD/D/EPB/1, f. 39r; *Depositions and other Ecclesiastical Proceedings*, pp. 110–20; *Memorials of the Rebellion*, p. 250; TNA: DURH 3/24 pp. 557, 622, 645. Kesselring's numbers are smaller as she examined the village of Sedgefield only and not the broader parish: *The Northern Rebellion of 1569*, p. 143. Although not as obviously pro-Catholic, in May or June 1575 there was another altercation. John Johnson, a constable, Robert Walker, and John Clerk were accused of assaulting clerk John Martyn. They said Clerk had been in a fight with Robert Crampton, and when trying to take sureties or take him to the stocks, the clerk refused, saying '[t]he Quene haith knaves to hir officers, and thou ar one of them, being the worst': *Depositions and Other Ecclesiastical Proceedings*, pp. 297–300; *Memorials of the Rebellion of 1569*, pp. 250–59, 268.

[26] Kesselring, *The Northern Rebellion of 1560*, p. 143; DHC1/I/32 f. 167r. By 1601, the Headlam holding was in Richard Swinburn's hands, but how is not recorded; TNA: DURH 3/26 f. 38r.

most people in the parish accepted and conformed to the new practices, before and after the rebellion of 1569. Catholicism disappeared less because of oppression than time and forgetfulness; as Duffy explains 'a generation was growing up which had known nothing else [than Protestantism]…which did not look back to the Catholic past as their own'.[27] Among this generation was theologian Samuel Ward, born *c*.1571, and he surely heard stories of the events. He became an establishment puritan; whether his religious leanings had their origins in Durham or after his matriculation at Christ's College in Cambridge *c*.1588 is unknown.[28] The Protestant controversies of the day were not unknown in Durham or these parishes. The vicar of the nearby parish of Aycliffe and cathedral prebendary Peter Smart became embroiled in a puritan–Arminian dispute beginning in 1628 with fellow prebendary and future bishop, John Cosin, one of Archbishop Laud's allies.[29] One of Cosin's fellow Arminians was his father-in-law, Marmaduke Blakiston, rector of Sedgefield.[30] While the Smart–Cosin conflict was limited largely to the cathedral and city, the men and women of the parishes would have been as aware of the tensions as their counterparts elsewhere in England.

As for the old religion, J. Hilton wrote '[t]he reign of James I saw the recovery of Catholicism in Durham', as several Durham men became priests, and Catholic priests were secretly operating in the north.[31] Catholicism persisted among some parish families into the seventeenth and eighteenth centuries, supported by local gentry, the Conyers of Layton and Salvins of Butterwick. The Masons were one of the prominent yeomen families associated with recusancy; Lancelot Mason lost his lands in Sedgefield in 1608 following his conviction for recusancy.[32] He may have been among the 'vulgar people' claimed to be recusants in lists made *c*.1608 and *c*.1615; seventeen Sedgefield residents were noted in the latter, and then forty-seven in a 1624 list.[33] Those lists named only those of middling status and higher, including Robert, Grace, and Christopher Maire.[34] In 1641, ten men in Sedgefield parish refused to take the Protestation Oath: Ralph Catrick, John Heighington, William Stoddart, John Iley, Robert Smith, George Heddan, Thomas Wright, James Wheatly, Thomas Chambers (who said he had taken it earlier), and Sir Ralph Conyers. Robert Mason Sr and Jr, William Mason, and Richard and Nicholas Freville all took the oath, as did four other Catrick men.[35]

---

[27] Duffy, *The Stripping of the Altars*, p. 593.   [28] *Cambridge Alumni Database.*

[29] Brautigam, 'Prelates and Politics', pp. 56–7; Hoffman, 'The Arminian and the Iconoclast'.

[30] Hoffman, 'The Arminian and the Iconoclast', p. 281.

[31] J. Hilton, 'Catholicism in Jacobean Durham', pp. 78–9.   [32] TNA: DURH 3/16 f. 247v.

[33] Lambeth Palace ms. 663.11, ms. 930.123; J. Hilton, 'Catholicism in Jacobean Durham', p. 81.

[34] Lambeth Palace ms. 663.11, ms. 930.123. A Francis Mason from Durham entered seminary on the Continent and was ordained as a Jesuit priest in 1619, but he does not seem to be closely related: Hilton, 'Catholicism in Jacobean Durham', p. 79; Leech and Whitehead, '"IN PARADISE AND AMONG ANGELS"', pp. 64–5; Gooch, 'From Jacobite to Radical', p. 124; Foley, 'The Residence of St. John the Evangelist', p. 1.

[35] *Durham Protestations*, pp. 180–3.

Only Christopher Chilton refused the oath in Bishop Middleham.[36] Grace Maire, née Smith, was an example of the stubbornness of Catholicism in the parish. She had married Robert Maire of Hardwick and converted to Catholicism, greatly upsetting her father, Henry Smith of Durham. He had not seen her in years and all but disinherited her in his will; he did leave her £20 per annum from his coal pits if she would attend service at the cathedral.[37] In her will of 1630, Dame Elizabeth Freville threatened to disinherit her niece Mary Jenson if she became 'a popish recusant', and Jane Mason (d.1663) instructed her executor to disinherit any of her three daughters who apostatized from the Church of England, suggesting continued sympathy to Catholicism in her family and the parish.[38] These are the more fascinating because women have been seen as influencing husbands to convert to Catholicism and here the dynamic was reversed.[39]

The records of the Parliamentary Commissioners provide a glimpse on Catholicism in the middle of the century as aligned with royalist sympathies. Tenants in both parishes had lands sequestered by Parliament, including Sir Ralph Conyers and his son Col. Cuthbert Conyers, Nicholas Freville, Jerrard Salvin, Sir Thomas Tempest, Augustine Hixon, William Frizell, Thomas Maire (Grace's son), and the rector of Sedgefield, Joseph Naylor. The Conyers were recusants; the widow of Col. Cuthbert Conyers bought back his goods for £86 10s, while Lady Mary, Sir Ralph's widow, was allowed £26 6s. 8d out of the £76 brought in from leasing her portion at Layton.[40] Others interacted with 'papists' and fell under suspicion. John Rawling and John Harrison stood bond for Katherine Conyers to pay off the purchase of her late husband's goods. Blacksmith Robert Smith of Bradbury had a warrant issued against him, for failing to aid the sequestrators in Sedgefield parish.[41]

Some profited from the sequestration, or at least collaborated, including Thomas Middleton, Ralph Mason, Richard Mason, and John Widdifield; Ralph Mason, who leased some of the Sedgefield tithes, was a sequestrator of the goods and property of Rev. Naylor and Col. Conyers; some of his activity in the land market in this time likely was connected to these roles. Thomas Welfoot, gent., was given permission to take 1,800 sheep and 160 cattle purchased from the sequestrators into Yorkshire. He is not otherwise associated with the parish, but the inclusion of this entry among a series of Sedgefield entries suggests that at least some of those animals had come from the parish. Other men of families associated with the parishes, such as William Chipchase, Lancelot Lamb, and

---

[36] *Durham Protestations*, pp. 157–8.

[37] *Wills and Inventories*, vol. II, pp. 331–3; Forster, 'The Maire Family of County Durham'; J. Hilton, 'Catholicism in Jacobean Durham', p. 82.

[38] *Wills and Inventories*, vol. IV, p. 225; DPRI/1/1663/M7/1–2.

[39] See J. Hilton, 'Catholicism in Jacobean Durham', pp. 82–3.

[40] *Records of the Committees for Compounding*, pp. 5–8, 11–13, 25, 27, 32–37, 175–6, 185, 210–11, 281–2, 310, 354, 357, 385.

[41] *Records of the Committees for Compounding*, pp. 11–13.

Charles Elstob, were involved in administration of sequestered property in neighbouring parishes.[42] Their motivations are unknown. The engagement of the usual leaders of the parish in these activities could be yet another instance of the community (or its leaders) acting as such rather than openly profiteering.

Village, Parish, and Locality

Membership in these communities could be fluid, with men and women moving for land, employment, or marriage. Within the general mobility, there are distinct patterns revealing a wider community.[43] Many long-term families in these two parishes moved but remained in a broad, thin oval stretching about twelve miles from Kirk Merrington in the west to Embleton in the East, and about six miles from Cornforth in the north to Bradbury and Mordon in the south. This includes the villages of Kirk Merrington, Middlestone (Middle Merrington), Westerton (West Merrington), Ferryhill, and Chilton, all Dean and Chapter villages. Elstob, Great Stainton, and Aycliffe add another layer to this locality, not surprising as they are on the road to Darlington (Figure 8.1).

These local roots are evident among the gentry and rising gentry. George Scurfield (d.1640) of Sedgefield came from Elstob in the parish of Great Stainton, where his father William Scurfield, gent. (d.1626) resided. George also had lands in Sheraton, Sheraton Grange, and Wheatley, to the north and east, and his father held lands in Bradbury (which went to George's younger brother Matthew). George's aunt had married John Harrison while his sister Katherine married Robert Johnson, both of Sedgefield.[44] James Hall of Bishop Middleham (d.1613) named John Lee of Fishburn his executor, and one of the supervisors was Edward Blakiston of Chilton. The local connections are seen in other families as well. There had been a Heighington family holding land and active in Bishop Middleham since the fourteenth century and Richard Heighington was one of the churchwardens in the 1570s or 1580s, but they were resident in Kirk Merrington by 1611.[45] The Hixon family had been present in Sedgefield since at least 1517 with John Hixon, Jr, buried in the church in 1597. Roland Hixon had been churchwarden of Sedgefield in 1569 and involved in restoring the Catholic mass. Following the enclosure of Sedgefield, another Roland Hixon held more than 100 acres, but by 1665 he was describing himself of Nun Stainton, Aycliffe. The Hixon family was scattered across this subregion in this period, with family members buried in Wolviston, Kirk Merrington, Ferryhill, Middlestone, and Auckland

---

[42] *Records of the Committees for Compounding*, pp. 4–12, 14–15, 25–26, 32–7.

[43] Hare noted significant local mobility in the late medieval period although not in a subregional context: *Prospering Society*, pp. 122–3.

[44] *Wills and Inventories*, vol. IV, pp. 200–4. One of the witnesses to William's will was William Rickaby, of another local family, though perhaps a more recent one.

[45] *Injunctions and Other Ecclesiastical Proceedings*, p. 54; DPRI/1/1611/H12.

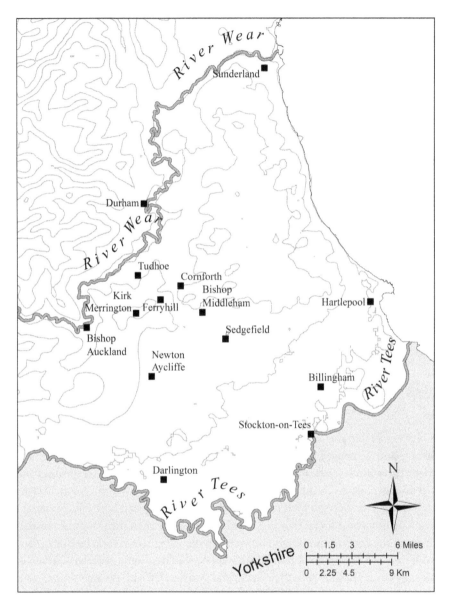

Figure 8.1 Map of major settlements in south-eastern Durham

Source: Ordnance Survey GIS datasets, Boundary-Line v.2020–05 and OS Open Places v.2020–07.
Contains OS data © Crown copyright and database right 2020.

St Andrew's, and even Sunderland and the city of Durham at the end of the seventeenth century. In the early eighteenth century, the family was back in Sedgefield.[46] The Widdifield family, mainly resident in Sedgefield provides a

---

[46] DPRI/1/1597/H17, 1613/H14, 1630/H5, 1630/H6, 1665/H10/1, 1670/H25, 1679/H15, 1690/H10, 1710/H10, 1731/H7. Several were buried in Sedgefield in the eighteenth century.

smaller example; Richard Widdifield (d.1567/8) lived in Fishburn, but William Widdifield lived in Ferryhill.[47] This broader community is remarkably like the Nottinghamshire parishes studied by Mitson, who found that 75 per cent of families moved at least once in their lifetime, but largely within a fifteen-mile radius of their home parish.[48]

For Mitson, the local migration was evidence of community and 'contained the effective day-to-day social hierarchy' defining social status. However, French questioned whether Mitson's subregional society derived from limited opportunities rather than an intentional community.[49] The Durham evidence shows his concerns to be well-founded. That same evidence also agrees with the work he and others have done on local parish officers, who have been used to approach the middling sort of early modern England.[50] Kent looked at these men and argued that their tasks, including working with the poor, created a common set of values and perspectives, although these ideas may not have been shared by others.[51] French took up the question of how far such men represented a 'middling sort' or 'middle class' in Essex and Lancashire, finding that definitions of status were more local than national. That difference was not only about wealth but also about lineage.[52] Sadly, there is little evidence of how the people of these Durham parishes thought about themselves in those terms, but the characteristics are reflected in the leadership of parish and village.

Community Leaders

Local leadership was split among five often overlapping groups. The first two, the gentry and yeomanry, exercised power through deference, landholding, and service. The church leadership, clerical and lay, were concerned with spiritual and eventually political conformity. The village and administrative officers such as the reeve, collector, derived their authority from the bishop and buttressed or weakened by their own social standing. The halmote jurors had the power of presentment in the courts, but they also represented the village (or at least its elite). Many of these men came from families that were or would become yeomanry. Much of the day-to-day authority in the villages and parishes lay with the wealthy peasants and later yeomen with a combination of land, administrative, religious, and social authority, and it may be moot to ask where a man's authority began and ended if

---

[47] *Wills and Inventories* III, p. 40.
[48] Mitson, 'The Significance of Kinship Networks in the Seventeenth Century'.
[49] French, 'Social Status, Localism and the "Middle Sort of People"', pp. 87–8.
[50] Underdown, *Fire from Heaven*; Wrightson and Levine, *Poverty and Piety*; Allridge, 'Loyalty and Identity in Chester Parishes'. French explores this in 'The Search for the "Middle Sort of People"', pp. 277–94.
[51] Kent, 'Rural "Middling Sort" in Early Modern England', esp. p. 42.
[52] French, 'Social Status, Localism and the "Middle Sort of People"', pp. 75, 96–7.

he happened to be reeve, juror, churchwarden, and rentier. Gentlemen certainly possessed power and authority, but their influence was seen primarily through service and rebellion, rather than everyday affairs.

Only twenty-one churchwardens are known, four from Bishop Middleham (for 1578) and seventeen from Sedgefield (for 1578 and 1597/8).[53] Richard Heighington, Richard Hutcheson, and Brian Headlam hailed from families that had been in the area for more than a century. John Harrison, Roland Hixon, and Robert Scathlock were at least third generation; Roland's son John was a churchwarden as well, in 1597. Robert Elstob, Lionel Ord, and Richard Swinburne came from old families in the parish though not ones frequently active in the Sedgefield land market; Robert Johnson and Robert Smyth likely were from long-established families as well. Lancelot Selby did not appear in the halmote court records for several years following the 1569 revolt but was reeve of Cornforth by 1584. John Johnson was at least second generation in Sedgefield and the family may have been there even longer. John Bellerby was second generation; his family took up land in Sedgefield forfeited following the 1569 rebellion, at the direction of the bishop.[54] Robert Younge may have been second generation or may have been like his co-warden Leonard Middleton, possibly new to the parish.[55] Evan Olivant sublet a bovate of land in Sedgefield several years after his appearance as churchwarden, suggesting that he may have been from one of the smaller settlements in the parish, as may have been the case for Henry Cowley, Richard Trowhat, and Adam Wheatly, who could not be traced.[56]

The extensive series of halmote records permits us to learn more about the jurors.[57] These four to six men enforced estate and village regulations and by-laws, but often acted as village elders or representatives: leasing land on behalf of the entire village and representing the village in other ways as needed. The authority, wealth, and length in office further demonstrate how they were or represented the chief inhabitants of each village. It was not uncommon in bishopric and priory villages for men to serve nearly continuously for a decade or more. Robert Mason served as juror in Sedgefield from 1546–75, Nicholas Stelling of Bishop Middleham served from 1558–83, and Lancelot Aytes of Cornforth served from 1546–78.[58] Not all men served so long, but there was a clear core who reappeared year after year and changed only slowly. Certain families were all but continuously represented. Richard Ayre of Bishop Middleham served from 1439–50 for thirty-four sessions, at times alongside Robert Ayre who served three

---

[53] *Injunctions and Other Ecclesiastical Proceedings*, pp. 54–; Baker Baker Papers, BAK.72/249, f. 7r. Most could be traced through landholding: Appendix A: Landholding Database.

[54] TNA: DURH 3/24, p. 557.

[55] DHC1/I/76 f. 20v. There were Middletons in the parish earlier.

[56] TNA: DURH 3/24, p. 988; Sedgefield Parish Registers 65.3.

[57] On the halmote jury in medieval Durham, see Larson, 'Village Voice or Village Oligarchy?'

[58] TNA: DURH 3/23 f. 248r to 3/24, p. 378.

times from 1441–67. They were followed by another Richard from 1461–96 at one hundred sessions, and another Robert who sat forty-three sessions from 1498–1514, then John from 1548–55; the Lancelot Aytes above was proceeded by Henry Aytes from 1515–22 and then another Lancelot Aytes in 1520–30.[59] Three Mowbrays sat between 1438 and 1474; Thomas Headlam was on the Sedgefield jury from 1388–1401, and then there were three Headlams on the jury between 1501 and 1587, with more than one hundred sessions combined.[60] The Laburn family had four men serve between 1522 and 1661: John from 1522–48; William from 1584–95; Nicholas from 1597–1610; and another William from 1639–61.[61] While not a closed group, the jurors often hailed from families that had been in the parish for generations. Those who served less frequently also tended to come from such families: Hardgill, Rawlyn, Scathlock, Mason, Middleton, and the like. Why they served less often is unclear.

How or if these groups restricted access to village lands is unknown. There is no explicit reference to gatekeeping by anyone but the steward, and then only in the decades following the Black Death. The low rents and fines alongside what appeared to be a relatively closed community implies that not just anyone could take up land in these villages. In the 1350s and 1360s, the jurors collectively served as pledges for new tenants. That practice had ended by the 1380s, although there were instances where the jurors or the 'entire village' stood as pledge.[62] From the 1380s there are no patterns with pledging, beyond the fact that the preponderance (more than 70 per cent between 1388 and 1569) of pledges came from families already in the parish, with some of the remainder connected already by blood, marriage, or association.[63] The latter exemplifies how some 'new' men entered these villages. William Hardgill, William Trotter, and Henry Eure did so with a marriage connection. That may have been how the Tempest family acquired a landed connection in the area, as John Hall of Bishop Middleham had married a daughter of Robert Tempest (grandfather of the Robert Tempest involved in the rebellion) in 1500.[64] Others such as Robert Forman and Richard Fery had connections to an important tenant, in both their cases Richard Croud, a very active tenant in Sedgefield; William Hardgill also was connected to Fery and to Croud.[65] Existing tenants would have found it in their interest to limit those taking up tenures, and the slow turnover of tenures, plus the intercon-

---

[59] TNA: DURH 3/15 ff. 21r- 260v; 3/16 ff. 77r-311r; 3/17 ff. 6r-178r; 3/18 ff. 6r-64r *passim*; 3/19 f. 3v-164r *passim*; DHC/1/I/1–2.

[60] TNA: DURH 3/15 ff. 6r-402v; 3/16 ff. 5r-86r, 272r-287r *passim*; 3/19 ff. 3v-266v *passim*; DHC/1/I/1–2.

[61] DHC/1/I/2.

[62] For example, to Robert Hett who took 35 acres in Cornforth in 1391: TNA: DURH 3/13 f. 35r.

[63] Appendix A: Landholding Database. The year 1388 was the first surviving of records following *Hatfield's Survey*, while 1569 witnessed rebellion and some related upheaval in landholding.

[64] *Testamenta Eboracensia*, p. 362.

[65] TNA: DURH 3/14 f. 456v; 3/15 ff. 105v, 267v; 3/16 f. 310v; 3/24 p. 87; 3/26 f. 114r.

nection of major tenants, imply that this was the case. It may not have been an ideal community, and certainly this caused problems, but it was a community of shared interest.

The men who witnessed wills and compiled probate inventories provide another window onto this group. In a sample of twenty-one wills and inventories between 1573 and 1645, all but two involved at least one juror (or frequent juror), and half of the inventories involved two jurors (out of the normal four apprais-ers). One of the exceptions, with no jurors, was the inventory of Robert Blakiston (d.1634), a prebendary of Durham Cathedral.[66] These men served for the same reasons that they were jurors, although not all appraised inventories or witnessed wills while currently a juror. Some other appraisers came from the same long-standing families as jurors, while others were clergy, kin, and gentry.

The connection between socio-economic status and leadership in these Durham villages reflects what French observed in Essex and Suffolk using tax and ship money assessments. He concluded that '[s]uch bodies wielded oligarchic power, yet they drew their authority from their ability to represent and incorpor-ate the "major part of the chief inhabitants" in their settlements'.[67] Looking at the vestry of Earls Colne in the mid-eighteenth century, he found that the vestry drew on those holding 40–60 acres. As in Durham, their ranks were not completely closed even though many came from old families.[68] Mitson found a similar pat-tern of 'dynastic families' dominating the office of churchwarden, above the rank of labourer but below that of gentleman.[69] In Bishop Middleham and Sedgefield, the evidence comes from halmote jurors but the pattern is similar, including socio-economic status and geographical limitation. It seems likely that their atti-tudes and morals reflected those reconstructed for other English villages in the period.

Communities in Crises

The change discussed in this book has been gradual, but there were two periods that could have altered the dynamics radically: the Reformation and the Civil War. The gentry felt the disruption most keenly, in both periods. The yeomen and others in the village, while involved, weathered the storms, and overall, the par-ishes and villages did too. Landholding and tenure patterns continued, as did local families and leadership. If anything, the records for this period shed more light on regular activities at that the time.

---

[66] DPRI/1/1634/B7/4.
[67] French, 'Social Status, Localism and the "Middle Sort of People"', pp. 78–84.
[68] French, 'Social Status, Localism and the "Middle Sort of People"', pp. 88–92.
[69] Mitson, 'The Significance of Kinship Networks in the Seventeenth Century'.

The Reformation could have been divisive or introduced new attitudes in these villages and parishes as it did elsewhere in England. Instead, the community continued and adapted, following a pattern of compliance not so different from what Duffy found in Morebath, though perhaps luckier in the aftermath of rebellion.[70] There were differing religious preferences in Sedgefield. There was the altercation over the communion table, and the incidents related to the rebellion. In both of those, there was little to no evidence of dissension within the parish. Instead, they worked together, without coercion. Brian Headlam's run-in with the churchwardens seems to be a case of a recalcitrant individual. In the aftermath of the rebellion, at least in the three bishopric villages, only gentlemen lost lands. Non-rebellious recusants would not lose land until the early seventeenth century. The entrance of the Freville family had little effect, at least as can be seen in the records, and the family became part of the community. Once again, a potentially major change was moderated by local society and culture.

The English Civil War was far more disruptive. The North was largely royalist, more so than a simple case of royalist sympathies mapping onto Catholic beliefs; only Sunderland sided with Parliament, with puritan Newcastle remaining loyal to Charles I.[71] The Scottish occupation of Durham in 1644 was expensive both in authorized extortion and in plundering. Sequestrations occurred in both Bishop Middleham and Sedgefield parishes, and Thomas Hazelrigg purchased the manor of Bishop Middleham for £3306 6s. 6d. ob.[72] Captain John Shaw of Ferryhill, son of William Shaw of Thrislington, had his lands sequestered because he issued warrants against Parliament in his office of High Constable of Darlington Ward. Among those testifying against him were Thomas Hixon. An equal number of men, including several officers, testified that Shaw's actions were half-hearted and had resulted in his arrest. He switched sides and had his lands plundered by the forces of the Earl of Newcastle, and Peter Hutchinson of Bishop Middleham and four others testified to his loyalty to Parliament.[73] Did others attempt to protect neighbours, or lessen the blow? The inventories of royalists and Catholics are valued suspiciously low, even accounting for the devastation of the county. Katherine Conyers had her goods assessed at £86 10s., while widow Elizabeth Smith's goods were valued at £8.[74] The inventory total for John Trollop, Esq., of Thornley was

---

[70] Duffy, *Voices of Morebath*. Wrightson and Levine's *Poverty & Piety* is the classic example of the effects of a Puritan middling sort on a community. For other studies of reformation and communities, see Underdown, *Fire from Heaven*; Stoyle, *From Deliverance to Destruction*; Walter, *Understanding Popular Violence in the English Revolution*.

[71] Howell, Jr 'The Structure of Urban Politics in the English Civil War', pp. 112–3, and *Newcastle Upon Tyne and the Puritan Revolution*. On Sunderland, see Meikle, 'The Scottish Covenanters and the Borough of Sunderland'.

[72] Saywell, *History and Annals of Northallerton*, p. 92; for an example of the halmote court held in his name, see DHC I/1/81 f. 141r.

[73] *Records of the Committees for Compounding*, pp. 339–40.

[74] *Records of the Committees for Compounding*, pp. 5–8, 11–13, 25, 27, 32–37, 175–76, 185, 210–11, 281–82, 310, 354, 357, 385. Fines for some delinquents in the parishes ranged from £20 for Nicholas Woodhouse of Cornforth to £305 9s. for John Tempest, pp. 44–5.

£10 9s. 8d.; William Rickaby's was £25 5s. 4d. The inventories were rather mean: mainly household utensils, beds (not many featherbeds), some pewter, and limited amounts of animals and grain.[75] On the other hand, many of the lands were valued at or close to market rates.

Throughout the county, most gentry remained aloof from the new administration, and the Restoration largely restored the status quo ante. Several of those who had their lands sequestered compounded with the new Parliamentary regime, and many were able to restore their fortunes. Probably the greatest change was the installation of puritan divines as rectors of Sedgefield: John Vincent in 1644 and Anthony Lapthorne in 1647.[76] The long-time vicar of Bishop Middleham, Thomas Bedford, was left in his living and died in 1660.[77] The market in copyhold and leasehold following the Restoration reflects the reversion to the way things were, involving familiar names: Freville, Chipchase, Mason, Tempest, Elstob, and so forth. Were it not for the switch from Latin to English in the records, and Thomas Hazelrigg's identification as lord of the manor, the halmote court books and parish registers would have one think nothing had happened.

Community and Change

The major question for this chapter, more than finding individuals and communities, is: how did these relate to the economic and other changes examined thus far? The answer is the community provided a structure that shaped options and afforded stability. It also enabled a peasant-yeomen oligarchy to enlarge their holdings. The effects of the changing tenurial structure must have had profound but gradual consequences in the community. The number of tenants shrank by a third although the tenantry remained stratified, unlike the levelling that was seen in Dean and Chapter villages.[78] This was both negative and positive. Smallholders and cottagers were not able to join in the growing wealth in the county, but with low rents, secure title, and an active regional economy they could participate and were better off than those without land. It is nice to believe they would have had a voice in the plebiscites that created village by-laws, until enclosure changed the landscape. Yet, the villages seemed to have been dominated by a relatively small segment of the tenant population throughout the period: the ten or so families with men consistently on the jury in any given period. Jurors were not immune from amercement, but the consistency of families in membership and in landholding imputes a certain level of authority. Their relative wealth in the sixteenth

---

[75] *Records of the Committees for Compounding*, pp. 25–30.
[76] Dumble, 'Government, Religion and Military Affairs in Durham', esp. pp. 234, 313–21.
[77] Surtees, *History and Antiquities*, vol. 3, pp. 6–7.
[78] Brown, 'Church Leaseholders', and *Rural Society and Economic Change*, pp.197–249.

and seventeenth centuries, and the employment of other villagers as servants, would have strengthened that authority further. There were few signs in the records of widespread conflict within the village, as opposed to the late fourteenth-century Durham priory villages.[79] Failure to come to the plebiscite resulted in a fine. When a man lost his wain in service to Sedgefield, a levy of 10d. per oxgang was made in 1643 'by a general consent of the town' to compensate him.[80] The temporary restoration of Catholicism in Sedgefield and the tenant-driven enclosures of all three main villages show cooperation in important matters. Conflict, when present, appeared to be between individuals, or more importantly for present purposes, between the community and specific individuals.

The halmote books and other records reveal certain individuals as lightning rods for conflict. In the fifteenth century, it was William Newcomer, who clashed violently with other men over agriculture. In the sixteenth century, Brian Headlam's headstrong opposition to the new Protestant order put him at odds with others in the parish, even though many sympathized with Catholicism. In noting the conflict between order and religious belief in Sedgefield, Kesselring hit on a deeper truth within that village: the need for order and stability. The community did not reject change; they rejected resistance to the community order. Piecemeal enclosure occurred without conflict but wandering animals and broken fences were a problem. The halmotes are full of instances where tenants failed to contribute to a common task, mend their hedges, or ring their pigs; but while some persons were frequent offenders, they were not consistent offenders. There was an emphasis on compliance and conformity, of an acceptance of authority, even if one were taking a very different path. Much has been made about the emphasis on *conformity* rather than belief within English Protestantism, but this may reflect deeper values of late medieval and early modern English society. It is telling that the halmotes continued to be held even as the plague ravaged Durham in 1349.

All this demonstrates that certain types of individualism were tolerated. Those who went their own way but cooperated (more or less) encountered few problems. Those who stood out, who rejected the authority of community, those were the true troublemakers. The communities in these villages and parishes are significant because they persisted for centuries without being pulled apart by individualism, Protestantism, or economic change, and with many families remaining in the area and even holding the same tenures for generations. This was not stagnation, as the communities did change, nor was it an idyllic communism. As change certainly occurred, these communities insisted on a level of compliance: individuals and innovators were fine, rebels and troublemakers were not. Their seemingly ordinary tradition makes them significant. And yet, individualism, and

---

[79] Larson, *Conflict and Compromise*, pp. 171–98.   [80] DHC I/1/80 f. 985r.

attitudes consistent with modernism and development, can be seen in the fourteenth century. These communities were durable and adaptable, surviving rebellion, civil war, and economic change. One must wonder, then, had other villages not been touched by industry or by revolutionary agricultural change, would our narrative about community, individualism, and modernity be different?

Conclusion

One of the tenants listed in *Bishop Hatfield's Survey*, if hurled three centuries forward in time, would have found a radically different religion and nation. The number of people in the parishes would be astonishing. Agrarian and economic changes would have been more about scale than nature: bigger farms and flocks, more enclosed lands, and greater commercialization. The tools of farming would be much the same, as would the crops. Everyday living would be more comfortable, even for the poor, and our time traveller might be shocked at how many farmers lived like knights.

And yet, much would have been familiar. The house might be furnished differently, but many would contain a similar size household. The population had swelled but there was a stratified tenantry like the late fourteenth century. A handful of families—including some familiar names—dominated villages. The local gentry had changed but such change had long been common, especially if one chose the losing side. Households, village, parish, community all would have been familiar. Even the halmote court, with its jury and by-laws, had changed little (unless our traveller arrived during the Interregnum when English replaced Latin). The village of Sedgefield still played football on Shrove Tuesday, as they still do today.[1]

But what do we, as modern observers, make of the changes? The change in wealth and material culture looms large. Local society had become more stratified, with more ways to distinguish between layers of wealth. A major factor here was the combination of local desire and seigneurial indifference that saw holdings amalgamated rather than fragment. A small number of families controlled access to land in the villages, adding to the possibility of stability within communities. This also gave them control over agriculture and freedom to pursue their own approaches within reason. The result was the ability to intensify production or modify their farming when there was demand, desired consumer goods, or opportunities for investment. Local attitudes shaped agrarian and economic development, and were flexible enough to adapt to changing circumstances, needs, and wants.

---

[1] There are numerous videos on YouTube including some embedded in newspaper articles; for example, Lunn, 'Highlights from Sedgefield Shrove Tuesday Ball Game with Usual Mix of Fun and Mayhem', *TeessideLive*, 5 March 2019.

Rethinking the Great Transition: Community and Economic Growth in County Durham, 1349–1660. Peter L. Larson, Oxford University Press. © Peter L. Larson 2022. DOI: 10.1093/oso/9780192849878.003.0010

The most significant transformation, particularly from our viewpoint, was economic. In central and southern England, in the traditional narrative, change was sharp and disruptive. Engrossment, commercialized agriculture, and capitalism disrupted communities, resulting in a large landless population and a broader divide between haves and have-nots. If Durham were matched along this paradigm, we would conclude that south-eastern Durham started along this path earlier than the rest of England with the development of 45–60-acre farms in the fourteenth and early fifteenth century, but then fell behind and stagnated, not fully developing until the nineteenth century. It would be a case of an auspicious start and then failed development. But that assumes only one true path, and that is not the case. In rural Durham, change was slower and evolutionary in response to population growth and later the additional demands of industry. Medieval techniques were adapted, expanded, and transformed, proving sufficient for the demands made upon the farmers. Greater specialization in specific crops or stock was another result, again not a radical departure due to need but experimentation made possible by comfortable wealth. Independent enclosures proliferated, and the organized townfield enclosures of the seventeenth century were a natural development. It would take another surge in population growth to cause farmers to turn to new crops to boost yields. These changes occurred within and because of traditional community structure. These entrepreneurs were not rebels, but leading men of the community from old families. Change was gradual. New imports may have caused a stir, but it would take decades for them to transform daily life. The development of agrarian capitalism, and of an agrarian revolution, need not have been as disruptive as elsewhere in England.

That is not to say that the experience of these villages was utopian. Better is not the same as good. More people profited, fewer people suffered, but overall, many did suffer. Allen concluded that 'most English men and women would have been better off had the landlords' revolution [of the eighteenth century] never occurred'.[2] 'Most' might be taking the sentiment too far. Some men clawed their way up, amassing larger farms and flocks. Many more were left behind as husbandmen and cottagers—but at least they were not dispossessed by external entrepreneurs buying out their holdings. In a way, they may have been the true winners in this model of change. Those without land had little choice but to labour, in households, fields, or mines; they likely faced worse prospects than before, with fewer chances to marry into land, and more competition for work. Women too did not benefit; the new opportunities were for men. Women continued to brew ale and work as servants. Perhaps the growing economy provided new opportunities in the local cloth industry, but these were not high-status jobs.

[2] Allen, *Enclosure and the Yeoman*, p. 21.

Wives and widows may have benefitted from enterprising husbands, but few had the opportunity to better themselves as Elena Hall Eure did.

Transition

Returning to the questions raised in Chapter 1 about prerequisites and causation for agrarian development and capitalism, several important conclusions can be drawn. The first is that, as so many have argued, secure tenure and personal freedom were necessary. On the Durham bishopric estate, both existed at the beginning of the period examined here; what few serfs there were quickly disappeared. Copyhold was popular, more so than leasehold. Durham priory was more assiduous in tracking its servile families, but that does not seem as significant as their preference for leasehold. With both freedom and copyhold (and leasehold), Durham was a generation or more ahead.

What Durham lacked was a continuing reason to expand production or to innovate. This might seem obvious but it is not. Large demesnes existed but these were not the testbeds of agrarian capitalism. In Durham, land was available in the fourteenth and fifteenth centuries but those with access did not seek it beyond a certain point: 45–60 acres was an optimal size for ambitious husbandmen. The next wave of engrossment came in the sixteenth century as population expanded and more hands turned to mining and expanded enclosure came with it. Greater specialization likely accompanied this or followed soon after. It was in this period that small houses were replaced with two-storey structures filled with pewter, fine linens on feather beds, and furniture. Major departures, such as new crops, were not needed in Durham until the eighteenth and nineteenth centuries. This contrasts strongly with the intense demand from London that would be so transformative of the Midlands and East Anglia. Newcastle and Sunderland were hungry and growing, but London was in a different league.

Demand, however, was insufficient on its own. Expanded agrarian production came from rising yeomen and husbandmen, but they needed incentives. Even 100 acres was not enough to make them gentlemen, though they might dream of that for their sons and grandsons. Larger and better houses were an incentive, as was the increasing variety and quality of consumer goods. The development of coal mining, salt panning, and other industries in the late sixteenth and seventeenth centuries may have offered investment opportunities, but if any entered into them, they left and moved to the towns. Wealth and finer goods boosted the chances of future generations of moving into the gentry, or simply of living better.

Institutional and structural factors were important. The absence of serfdom removed one reason for potential emigration. Durham's low population, or perhaps underpopulation, let aspiring farmers acquire land more easily, and the communities appear to have helped keep those lands in local hands. The low rents and entry fines—consequences of the bishopric administration's choice to accept lower income in exchange for less effort, instead focusing their energy elsewhere—allowed tenants to get by in lean years and expand in good ones. The strong preference for intact holdings, easy subleasing, and widow-right made it easier for enlarged holdings to pass intact from one generation to the next. These factors together put bishopric tenants on the path to yeomanry before much of England. The higher population and rents and smaller holdings in the south did not prevent engrossment and promotion, but they did make it harder. In all, large parts of Durham were precocious relative to southern England for a mix of exogenous factors and collective choices.[3]

Was this path set, or could it have been altered? Brown made a strong argument for path dependency in explaining early modern Durham.[4] The humanist approach demands that contingency be acknowledged: trends are just a bird's eye view of individual choices. That said, some people's choices mattered more. Gentry represented a potential vector for change. Local gentlemen were converting smaller settlements (if they could be called that by the late Middle Ages) into large farms; elsewhere in England, wealthy men snapped up lands and rented them out. Southern gentry like the Frevilles were not required; there was wealth in the county that could have been converted to land. Two other possible turning points were the rebellion of 1569 and the English Civil War. Both could have resulted in changes among families below the gentry through death and forfeiture.

The true 'what if', though, centres on the bishopric administration: could a new bishop or steward have raised rents and entry fines as other lords did? The answer must be yes, at least from the sixteenth century. The low population tied the administration's hands, but once population grew the option was available: where else would tenants find land so cheaply? Tradition, inertia, whatever one wishes to call it, was not immutable. There are other possible reasons. Low rents, indivisible holdings, and stable tenant families had advantages; a certain level of rent was guaranteed no matter the ups and downs of the immediate economy. Long-term residents also contributed to the stability of the locality and the county (1569 excepted). The low rents and entry fines may be akin to the discounts later landlords gave reputable farmers. Other explanations are possible, and worthy of investigation; to the bishops, rack renting may not have been the rational approach. Bishopric tenants had many reasons to build up their holdings and increase production; we must also acknowledge that, once they had land, they faced fewer constraints.[5]

---

[3] The contrast is even stronger with parts of Europe, which experienced a 'second serfdom'; for example, see Klein and Ogilvie, 'Occupational Structure'.

[4] Brown, *Rural Society and Economic Change*.

[5] See again Ogilvie's 'Choices and Constraints'.

Divergence

The preceding chapters demonstrate the economic vitality of early modern Durham and its late medieval roots. This offers the possibility of finding similar vitality in other 'peripheral' regions of England. Can it also help explain England's rise to economic dominance in the seventeenth century? Conflict destabilized the economy of the Low Countries; meanwhile England's GDP was rising, and a growing population contributed to urbanization. The story of the parishes told here suggests that it was England's *rural* economy that was fostering growth in the sixteenth and early seventeenth century. An increasing rural population migrated to towns and mines for work, fed by ever-larger farms.

The region had an institutional framework to build on. The shock of the plague did not undo commercialization in the region; the markets and trade networks contracted but remained. The same is true of farming in the region; production shifted towards cattle and sheep instead of grain, but the switch was reversible. Copyhold and leasehold aided in that, as did estate and village administration. The change in population and production may have rendered the region more commercialized. Newcastle's national and international trade continued to be diverse, exporting raw and basic materials and importing groceries, spices, and durable consumer goods.

This supports the argument by Broadberry et al. on economic growth.[6] There was more to the late medieval economy than rents, wages, and wool. The northeast's late medieval economy may have been small, but the factor markets in the county were favourable for rapid expansion. Food, raw materials, labour, credit, and an integrated market network were on hand. The region's ports, notably but not only Newcastle, provided an outlet for production while bringing in items for consumption. Their trading connections to London and the Low Countries offered access to the benefits of wealthy international trade. The region was prospering in the sixteenth century but the rising demand for coal took the economy to another level. The fruits of that trade, particularly cloth and durable consumer goods, helped the region's industries expand to provide cheaper local versions of imported goods.

This assisted England in surpassing the Netherlands in the seventeenth century. The development of the new draperies and the growth of London was a major factor, as was increasing colonial trade. The ability of the northeast to ramp up not only coal mining but associated industries such as shipbuilding also was significant. So was the ability to develop other local industries using local resources; one example is how Newcastle's participation in the broader trade fostered a demand for tobacco pipes, met through the region's glass production.

---

[6]   Broadberry et al., *British Economic Growth*.

England's late medieval economy was uneven and, in many ways, regional. London's increasing dominance as England's major port was a sign of an increasingly national, then imperial, economy; the parishes of Bishop Middleham and Sedgefield reveal how that economy had become more even and integrated by the seventeenth century.

Local, National, and Global History

All of this resulted from choices made by ordinary people such as Annabilla Headlam, John Hall, Roland Hixon, and Ralph Mason. Individually, their choices might not have been so significant. Collectively, their production and consumption, belief and obedience, actions and inaction, all shaped society, culture, and economy. There is much we do not know about their lives, and questions we cannot answer: Thomas Chipchase married Gurchian Mayer in 1670; how did they meet?[7] Was she a religious refugee, or the daughter of a merchant, or was Thomas or one of his relatives a merchant, or traveller? We do not know. When Thomas Hutcheson outlined in his will what his wife should deliver to his father for the latter's support, was this because of bad blood between them or some other reason? These nuggets provide the basis for speculation, little more, yet they remind us that beneath price series of grains, median inventory values, and mean numbers of children were men and women acting within the world they knew.

The conclusions offered here are as much a beginning as an end. There is more work that can be done on the northeast, and the sources to undertake it. The material culture and credit networks of the region offer one avenue to exploring its economic and social history.[8] The strength of farming in the county may explain the relatively small share for non-agricultural occupations in the seventeenth century based on probate documents; perhaps an alternative approach is needed, examining inventoried goods for signs of alternative occupations.[9] Recent underwater archaeology on the River Wear has offered new information on Durham's cloth industry, corroborating evidence from court records and probate inventories.[10] The argument here about two Durhams, one wealthy and one not, exposes the region's reputation as a cultural construct. Many other

---

[7] Sedgefield Parish Register, 'Index to Sedgefield, Marriages 1581-1982', p. 23.

[8] In a study of the woollen industry and credit around London, Zell found that while credit was in the hands of the London merchants, the entrepreneurs in the countryside had the capital: 'Credit in the Pre-Industrial English Woollen Industry'. This demonstrates, like many other studies, a more complicated relationship between urban and rural.

[9] See Clark et al., 'Malthus, Wages, and Preindustrial Growth'. This possibility sets up an interesting comparison with the work of Klein and Ogilvie on Bohemia, where they found lower non-agricultural activity than expected, that villages with less seigneurial presence were more diverse (unlike the parishes examined here), but also that towns did not benefit rural areas: 'Occupational Structure'.

[10] Durham River Wear Assemblage Project.

historians—Thirsk, Zell, Yates, and Hare to name but a few—have demonstrated the difference between regions; but they still focused on areas close to central England. There has been work on the southwest and northwest, but potential for much more.[11] 'Smoking guns' and conclusive proof are rare for studies of the pre-modern world but decentring the narrative of change will paint a fuller picture of England's transition from the Middle Ages to modernity.

---

[11] I would include Wales and Scotland, except that I am not well-versed in their history or pre-modern regional characteristics.

APPENDIX A

Landholding Database

A database of land transfers and related entries for the period 1349–1660 was compiled from the Durham bishopric halmote books, using:

- DHC/1/I/1–83 Halmote Court Books (all divisions)

Durham University Library, Archives & Special Collections, Durham Bishopric Halmote Court Records.
http://reed.dur.ac.uk/xtf/view?docId=ark/32150_s1h415p952q.xml#qxj-236

- DURH 3/12–28 Halmote Court Books

The National Archives Public Record Office, Kew, London, Records of the Palatinate of Durham: Chancery Court: Cursitor's Records.

The two series contain approximately 17,680 folios or the equivalent. Fortunately, many tourns had a contemporary index of villages. The surviving books are generally in good condition with minor loss or illegibility; the gaps in the series are due to lost books rather than damage.

The DHC/1/I series appear to be original paper records from the court session, while the DURH 3/series are later parchment copies, likely made following the end of a tourn. The DURH series includes later annotations and is less likely to include duplicate entries.

A search of the books yielded a total of 2,898 entries, including calls for heirs, memoranda, and orders directly relating to landholding in Bishop Middleham, Cornforth, Mainsforth (under Bishop Middleham), and Sedgefield. That total includes entries that were cancelled or duplicated in the records; such entries were noted as such and accounted for in calculations. From those entries, the following information was entered from the records if available:

- Date (Year and Month);
- Village;
- Names of past, current, new landholders, and their relation (if any);
- Land, acreage, and any details (such as holding name);
- Whether the land was surrendered;
- Type of tenure (and length of term, if relevant);
- Entry fine;
- Rent;
- Any recusal of rights;
- Pledges;
- Any relevant information on the holding or tenure (e.g., timber for repairs, previous rent).

A very few entries were made under other villages when there was space available in the books.

Multiple holdings in a single entry were not separated out when entering the data; for example, if someone took a husbandland, a cottage, and 5 acres of meadow, that was entered as one entry rather than three. Scribal errors were corrected when certain; names of persons, tenures, and buildings were standardized. Notes were made when a court session had no land transfers or related business.

From the data extracted from the books, the following were determined and added to the database:

- Category of entry (e.g., inter vivos, post mortem, new);
- Descent of land (e.g., to the widow, to the son);
- Acreage;
- Number of dwellings.

There are important limitations, however:

- Rents were recorded irregularly;
- Holdings often referred to as 'the tenure of X,' with type of dwelling, acreage, and other details omitted, even with a composite holding;
- In some cases of father to son inheritance, the occupation of the land by the widow was omitted. This has been corrected where possible.

The available data and limitations make the database an excellent tool to study tenure and the land market, as well as certain themes (such as widow-right). Constructing landholding histories such as those by French and Hoyle was more limited and so was approached anecdotally rather than statistically; their approach should however be possible for these villages following enclosure.[1]

---

[1] French and Hoyle, *Character of English Rural Society*, pp. 180–4.

Baptism, Fornication, Marriage, and Funeral Databases

A set of four databases was compiled using halmote court records and parish registers:

- DURH 3/12–15 Halmote Court Books

The National Archives Public Record Office, Kew, London, Records of the Palatinate of Durham: Chancery Court: Cursitor's Records

- EP/SE 1/1–2 (Microfilm M42/152)

Durham County Record Office, Sedgefield Parish Registers
Much of this has been accessed from transcriptions (baptisms, burials) and an index (marriages 1581–1982) produced by K. G. and I. J. Walker in 2004, held in the Durham County Record Office.

- *The Registers of Bishop Middleham, in the County of Durham*, ed. Reginald Peacock (Sunderland, 1906).

Additional data were collected from Familysearch.org and collated with surviving sources.

Mortality Database

This was built from the halmote books and parish registers. Most of the information from the halmote books related to the death of tenants (mostly men) taken from the Landholding Database, whereas the funerals recorded in the registers are more inclusive. When possible, the following data were collected:

- Name of the deceased;
- Parents, spouse, or other relatives, as named.

Medieval Marriage and Fornication Database, 1349–1450

This was built from merchet and widows' fines recorded in the halmote books. When possible, the following data were collected:

- Woman's name;
- Man's name;
- Former husband's name (for widows);
- Woman's father's name;
- Name of pledge(s);
- Type and amount of fine;
- Connected land transfers.

Early Modern Marriage Database, 1559–1701

When possible, the following data were collected from the parish registers:

- Bride's name;
- Groom's name;
- Former husband's name (for widows);
- Bride's father's name;
- Number and dates of children (from Baptism Database).

Baptism Database, 1559–1701

When possible, the following data were collected from the parish registers:

- Name;
- Father's name;
- Mother's name.

With information on illegitimacy, or being a twin, entered when recorded. When possible, individuals were cross-linked between databases.

Probate Inventories

The North East Inheritance Project created a searchable database of pre-1858 Durham Probate Records, http://familyrecords.dur.ac.uk/nei/ (accessed 4/09/21). Searching of the records for inventories in County Durham, excluding soldiers, royal navy, and persons for which no inventory value was provided or could be determined, yielded 8,242 inventories (1,139 women, 7,103 men) for the period 1542–1699. The following data were entered into an Excel spreadsheet: Date of Probate (using modern calendar); Name; Parish; Occupation/Status (if given); Marital Status (if given); Recorded Value of Inventory (using corrected or fullest totals if more than one inventory were recorded).

There are many caveats with using probate inventories to investigate wealth.[1] First is what is or is not recorded in the inventories. Items for consumption, such as everyday foods as opposed to those in bulk, were omitted; this includes items such as sugar, pepper and other spices, fruits, and vegetables. The Recorded Value in the Inheritance Project database includes debts owing to the deceased, what might be termed the gross value; debts owed, legacies, and funeral experiences are listed separately in the database where available. This affects the comparability of inventories and has been factored in wherever possible.

Second, these inventories present value rather than a price—what the executor or executrix could sell them for to settle accounts. The appraisers could over- or under-value goods, intentionally or not, and the status of the deceased could affect their valuations. The Durham appraisers tended to assign round values when they could (for example, they valued frying pans at an even shilling far more often than 10d., 11d., or 13d.) and sometimes grouped disparate items together to do so. The condition, size, and quality of an item were stated irregularly. Some inventories have detailed lists but assign a single value for a category or even the entire room. At other times, particularly for plough gear, no sense of quantity or scope was provided, and those values reflect levels of capital investment more than individual value. The value of some items was sticky throughout the period; for example, Flanders chests were usually valued at 5s., no matter the date. Debts owed to and by the decedent are not always recorded.

Third is the question of comparability of nominal vs real value because the purchasing power of English money changed. This is a particular concern of those studying real wages and standards of living; the solution has been to create a price index based around a standardized 'basket of consumables' to assess the purchasing power of a worker at any given time.[2] As the inventories provide values and not prices, an inventory basket was used here, following the lead of Overton et al. The vagaries of valuation noted above put important constraints on what value series could be derived to build this basket. Weighting the items was tricky, as there is little outside information that can be used, so the weights were chosen

---

[1] The following paragraphs explain concerns with the Durham inventories specifically; see above, Chapter 6, p. C6.P21, for discussion of the literature on probate inventories generally.

[2] De Vries has an interesting discussion of these indices, and also wage indices, from the viewpoint of someone working with inventories: 'Between Purchasing Power', pp. 210–14.

to reflect common amounts of items; several weights were tried before arriving at the following:

- 4bu. of wheat, 4 of rye, 6 of barley, and 12 of oats (in the house or garth, not sown);
- 1 beehive;
- 1.5 iron chimneys (excluding those listed in kitchens);
- 6 brass candlesticks and 12 ordinary candlesticks;
- A frying pan, dripping pan, and chafing dish;
- 6 pairs of coarse sheets, 6 pairs of linen sheets, 12 pillowcases, 6 pairs of blankets, 6 coverlets, 2 dozen ordinary napkins, 1 dozen diapered napkins;
- 6 silver spoons;
- 8 cushions;
- 2 spinning wheels (wool or linen).

This basket omits wooden furniture because of the great variety of sizes and decorations, and because the value sometimes included the goods within. Brass and pewter likewise are excluded as appraisers increasingly gave a value and no indication of number or type of vessels. Except for spinning wheels, there was little consistency in listing other capital items.

It was not possible to construct a separate statistically-valid series for Bishop Middleham and Sedgefield due to the low number of values recorded for individual items. Generally, values for items in these two parishes corresponded with those seen elsewhere and fell comfortably within the standard deviation for the item in the entire county; the exceptions (other than foodstuffs, where value depended on season and condition) were instances of a single item with an unusually high value that could indicate a larger or better-quality item. This illustrates the need for care with a small sample.

To assess the accuracy of this Durham inventory basket, Pearson coefficients were calculated against several other indices, either as a whole or broken down into subgroups. The correlation between the foodstuffs in the Durham basket and the Agricultural series by Overton was a reassuring 0.9096, and for Textiles 0.7557—lower than hoped but this could be explained through local cloth production and imported linen. The correlation between the metal objects above and the Overton's Metal A index was -0.5719, the main divergence coming between 1590 and 1639 as values dropped in Durham and rose elsewhere.[3] The coefficient for the overall Durham series compared to Allen's London Consumer Price index was 0.72, and against Clark's GDP and Cost of Living price indices, 0.73 and 0.74.[4] The growing value of the Durham basket from the 1570s to the 1630s, when it plateaued, follows the arguments of this book.

---

[3] Overton, 'Prices from Probate Inventories', p. 240.
[4] Allen, 'Craftsmen's Relative Wages.xlsx', from the 'Global Price and Income History Group', University of California-Davis, https://gpih.ucdavis.edu/Datafilelist.htm (accessed 5/12/2021); Clark, 'National Income' series, http://faculty.econ.ucdavis.edu/faculty/gclark/data.html (accessed 5/12/2021).

Bibliography

Archival Sources

Durham County Record Office, Durham, UK

EP/SE 1/1–2 (Microfilm M42/152), Sedgefield Parish Registers.

Walker, K.G. and Walker, I.J., 'Sedgefield, Baptisms 1580–1672', unpublished index and transcript, 2004.

Walker, K.G. and Walker, I.J., 'Sedgefield, Burials, 1580–1765', unpublished index and transcript, 2004.

Walker, K.G. and Walker, I.J., 'Sedgefield, Marriages 1580–1982', unpublished index, 2004.

Durham University Archives & Special Collections, Durham, UK

Additional Manuscripts

Add.MS. 1930 Photostat copy of Durham Cathedral Library, MS Sharpe 167.

Baker Baker Papers, Mischellaneous Books c.1581–1858

BAK 72/249.

Church Commission Deposit of Durham Bishopric Estate Records: Financial and Audit Records to 1649

CCB B/23/25/4.
CCB B/50/1, 3, 6, 11, 18, 20, 23, 28, 35–38.
CCB B/65/1–16, 18–25, 27, 34, 40.
CCB B/73/9.

Durham Bishopric Halmote Court Records

DHC 1 I/1–83, Halmote Court Books (all divisions).
DHC 1 M64, Court and miscellaneous books.
DHC 1 M84, List of Prisoners and Recusants.
DHC 4/194253–194263, Rentals.
DHC 6 IV/10, 39, Inclosure Material.
DHC 11 I/35–36, 43–44, Maps.

Mickleton and Spearman Manuscripts

MSP 7–9, 25.

Durham Cathedral Archive

Spiritual jurisdiction of Durham dean and chapter and of other persons: Ecclesiastical Precedent Books, DCD/D/EPB/1.

Halmote Court Rolls, 1295–1534.
Miscellaneous Charters 2640.

Durham Probate Records Collection
Wills and Inventories: DPR I/1/: 1558/H3; 1573/H5; 1584/M4; 1587/H13; 1588/W11;
   1596/G1, G2; 1597/G4, H17; 1602/H7; 1603/E1; 1604/S1; 1606/C2; 1608/R7; 1609/C11,
   E1; 1611/H12; 1613/H3, H14; 1614/L1; 1615/E1; 1621/G1; 1622/F3, W8; 1625/S4; 1627/
   M1, M6; 1628/B2; 1629/H16; 1630/H5, H6; 1633/J10; 1634/B7, C2; 1636/S9; 1639/F2,
   M3; 1640/R1, S1; 1655/W4; 1662/M6; 1663/C11, M7; 1664/D6; 1665/H10, J5, W4;
   1666/E2, S5, W13, W25; 1669/R6, W19; 1670/H25, M7, M8; 1671/D5; 1672/O1; 1673/
   F10, H27; 1675/S7; 1676/S7; 1677/W22; 1679/G9, H15; 1681/L2; 1682/S21; 1685/O2;
   1690/H10; 1696/M6/3; 1710/H10; 1731/H7.
Bonds: DPR1/3/1586/B12,/1587/B486, 1619/B210,/1693/B114.

Lambeth Palace Library, London, UK

MSS 663.11, 930.123.

London School of Economics, Archives and Special Collections, London, UK

Beveridge Price History, C/8/1–2.

The National Archives of the UK (TNA), London, UK

C/25/58, Middleton v. Middleton, Chancery: Examiners Office: Interrogatories.
DURH 3/12–28, Palatinate of Durham: Chancery Court: Cursitor's Records.
DURH 8/77/2, Palatinate of Durham: Chancery Court: Cursitor's and Registrar's Miscellanea.

Printed Primary Sources

'Appendix No. 2. Durham Records: Calendar of Chancery Enrolments: Cursitor's Records,'
   in *The Thirty-Third Annual Report of the Deputy Keeper of the Public Records* (London:
   George E. Eyre and William Spottiswoode, 1872).
Bishop Hatfield's Survey, ed. by William Greenwell, Surtees Society, vol. 32 (Durham:
   George Andrews, 1857; reprinted London: W. Dawson and sons, 1967).
Brereton, William, *Travels in Holland, the United Provinces, England, Scotland, and Ireland,
   M.DC.XXXIV.-M.DC.XXXV*, ed. by Edward Hawkins (London: Chetham Society, 1844).
Calendar of State Papers, Domestic Series, Elizabeth, 1595–97, ed. by Mary Anne Everett
   Green (London: HMSO, 1869).
The Customs Accounts of Newcastle Upon Tyne 1454–1500, ed. by F. J. Wade, Surtees Society,
   vol. 202 (Woodbridge: Boydell, 1995).
The Correspondence of John Cosin, D.D., Lord Bishop of Durham, vol. I, ed. by George
   Ornsby, Surtees Society, vol. 52 (Durham: Andrews, 1869).
The Correspondence of Reginald Pole, vol. 4, ed. by Thomas F. Mayer (Aldershot:
   Ashgate, 2008).

County Durham Hearth Tax Assessment, Lady Day 1666, ed. by Adrian Green, Elizabeth Parkinson, and Margaret Spufford (London: British Record Society, 2006).

Darlington Wills and Inventories, ed. by J. A. Atkinson, Surtees Society, vol. 201 (Newcastle upon Tyne: Athenaeum Press, 1993).

Depositions and Other Ecclesiastical Proceedings from the Courts of Durham, Extending from 1311 to the Reign of Elizabeth, ed. by James Raine (London: J.B. Nichols, 1845).

The Diocesan Population Returns for 1563 and 1603, ed. by Alan D. Dyer and David M. Pallier (London: British Academy, 2005).

Domesday Book Supplementary, vol. 35: Boldon Book, Northumberland and Durham ed. by David Austin (Stroud: Phillimore & Co., 1982).

Durham Cathedral Priory Rentals: Bursars Rentals, ed. by R. A. Lomas and A. J. Piper, Surtees Society, vol. 198 (Newcastle upon Tyne: Athenaeum Press, 1989).

Durham Protestations, ed. by H. M. Wood, Surtees Society, vol. 135 (Durham: Andrews, 1922).

Durham Quarter Session Rolls, 1471–1625, ed. by C. M. Fraser, Surtees Society, vol. 199 (Newcastle upon Tyne: Athenaeum Press, 1988).

Feodarium Prioratus Dunelmensis, ed. by William Greenwell, Surtees Society, vol. 58 (Durham: Andrews, 1872).

Historia de Sancto Cuthberto, ed. by Ted Johnson South (Rochester, N.Y.: D.S. Brewer, 2002).

Historiae Dunelmensis Scriptores Tres, ed. by James Raine (London: J.B. Nichols, 1839).

The Injunctions and Other Ecclesiastical Proceedings of Richard Barnes, Bishop of Durham, from 1575 to 1587, ed. by James Raine, Surtees Society, vol. 22 (Durham: Andrews, 1850).

Letters and Papers, Foreign and Domestic, Henry VIII, vol. 4, 1524–1530, ed. by J. S. Brewer (London: Longman, Green, Longman, and Roberts, 1875).

Letters and Papers, Foreign and Domestic, Henry VIII, vol 4, 1524–1530, ed. by J. S. Brewer (London: Her Majesty's Stationery Office, 1875). British History Online, accessed October 8, 2021, http://www.british-history.ac.uk/letters-papers-hen8/vol4.

Memorials of the Rebellion of 1569, ed. by Cuthbert Sharp (London: J.B. Nichols, 1840).

More, Thomas, *Utopia*, ed. by George M. Logan and Robert M. Adams (Cambridge: Cambridge University Press, 1989; rev. edn, 2002).

Parliamentary Surveys of the Bishopric of Durham, vol. II, ed. by David Kirby, Surtees Society, vol. 185 (Gateshead: Northumberland Press, 1929).

The Poll Taxes of 1377, 1379 and 1381, Part 1: Bedfordshire-Lincolnshire, ed. by Carolyn Fenwick (Oxford: Oxford University Press, 1998).

Records of the Committees for Compounding, etc. with Delinquent Royalists in Durham and Northumberland During the Civil War, etc. 1643–1660, ed. by Richard Welford, Surtees Society, vol. 111 (Durham: Andrews, 1905).

Records of the English Province of the Society of Jesus, vol. III, ed. by Henry Foley (London: Burns and Oates, 1878).

The Register of Richard Fox, Lord Bishop of Durham, 1494–1501, ed. by Marjorie Peers Howden, Surtees Society, vol. 147 (Durham: Andrews, 1932).

The Register of Thomas Langley, Bishop of Durham 1406–1437, vol. III, ed. by R. L. Storey, Surtees Society, vol. 159 (Durham: Andrews, 1954).

The Registers of Bishop Middleham, in the County of Durham, ed. by Reginald Peacock (Sunderland: Durham and Northumberland Parish Record Society, 1906).

The Registers of Cuthbert Tunstall, Bishop of Durham 1530–39 and James Pilkington, Bishop of Durham 1561–76, ed. by Gladys Hinde, Surtees Society, vol. 161 (Durham: Andrews, 1952).

Scott, Walter, *The Bridal of Triermain, Harold the Dauntless, Field of Waterloo, and Other Poems* (Edinburgh: Cadell, 1836).

Select Cases in Manorial Courts 1250–1550: Property and Family Law, ed. by L.R. Poos and Lloyd Bonfield, Selden Society, vol. 114 (London: Selden Society, 1998).

The Statutes of the Realm, ed. by Alexander Luders et al., vol. III (London: HMSO, 1817, reprinted London: Dawsons, 1963).

Testamenta Eboracensia: A Selection of Wills from the Registry at York, vol. III, ed. by James Raine and John William Clay, Surtees Society, vol. 106 (Durham: Andrews, 1865).

Thirty-third Annual Report of the Deputy Keeper of the Public Records (London: HMSO, 1872).

Wills and Inventories from the Register at Durham, vol. I, ed. by James Raine, Surtees Society, vol. 2 (London: J.B. Nichols, 1835).

Wills and Inventories from the Register at Durham, vol. II, ed. by William Greenwell, Surtees Society, vol. 38 (Durham: Andrews, 1860).

Wills and Inventories from the Register at Durham, vol. III, ed. by J. C. Hodgson, Surtees Society, vol. 112 (Durham: Andrews, 1906).

Wills and Inventories from the Register at Durham, vol. IV, ed. by Herbert Maxwell Wood, Surtees Society, vol. 142 (Durham: Andrews, 1929).

Secondary Sources

Albritton, Robert, 'Did Agrarian Capitalism Exist?' *Journal of Peasant Studies* 20:3 (1993): 419–41, doi:10.1080/03066159308438516.

Allen, Robert C., *Enclosure and the Yeoman: The Agricultural Development of the South Midlands* (Oxford: Clarendon Press, 1992).

Allen, Robert C., 'The Great Divergence in European Wages and Prices from the Middle Ages to the First World War', *Explorations in Economic History* 38:4 (2001): 420–4, doi:10.1006/exeh.2001.0775.

Allen, Robert C., 'Progress and Poverty in Early Modern Europe', *Economic History Review* 56:3 (2003): 403–43, doi:10.1111/j.1468-0289.2003.00257.x.

Allen, Robert C., *The British Industrial Revolution in Global Perspective* (Cambridge: Cambridge University Press, 2009).

Allen, Robert C., and Jacob Weisdorf, 'Was There an "Industrious Revolution" before the Industrial Revolution? An Empirical Exercise for England, 1300–1830', *Economic History Review* 64:3 (2011): 715–29, doi:10.1111/j.1468-0289.2010.00566.x.

Allridge, N., 'Loyalty and Identity in Chester Parishes, 1540–1640', in *Parish, Church and People: Local Studies in Lay Religion, 1350–1750*, ed. by S. J. Wright (London: Hutchinson, 1988), pp. 85–124.

Arkell, Tom, 'Multiplying Factors for Estimating Population Totals from the Hearth Tax', *Local Population Studies* 28 (1982): 51–7.

Arkell, Tom, 'Interpreting Probate Inventories', in *When Death Do Us Part: Understanding and Interpreting the Probate Records of Early Medieval England* (Oxford: Leopard's Head Press, 2006), pp. 72–102.

Aston, Mick and Chris Gerrard, *Interpreting the English Village: Landscape and Community at Shapwick, Somerset* (Oxford: Oxbow Books, 2013).

Aston, Mick and Chris Gerrard, *The Shapwick Project, Somerset: A Rural Landscape Explored* (London: Routledge, 2017).

Aston, T. H., and C. H. E. Philpin, eds, *The Brenner Debate: Agrarian Class Structure and Economic Development in Pre-Industrial Europe* (Cambridge: Cambridge University Press, 1985).

Austin, D., *The Deserted Medieval Village of Thrislington, County Durham, Excavations 1973–74*, Society for Medieval Archaeology Monograph 12 (Lincoln: Society for Medieval Archaeology, 1989).

Bailey, Mark, *A Marginal Economy? East Anglian Brecklands in the Later Middle Ages* (Cambridge: Cambridge University Press, 1989).

Bailey, Mark, 'Peasant Welfare in England, 1290–1348', *Economic History Review* 51:2 (1998): 223–51, doi:10.1111/1468-0289.00089.

Bailey, Mark, *Medieval Suffolk: An Economic and Social History 1200–1500* (Woodbridge: Boydell & Brewer, 2007).

Bailey, Mark, *The Decline of Serfdom in Late Medieval England: From Bondage to Freedom* (Woodbridge: Boydell & Brewer, 2014).

Bailey, Mark, 'The Transformation of Customary Tenures in Southern England, c. 1350 to c. 1500', *Agricultural History Review* 62:2 (2014): 210–30, https://www.jstor.org/stable/43697978.

Bailey, Mark, 'The Myth of the "Seigniorial Reaction" in England after the Black Death', in *Peasants and Lords in the Medieval English Economy* (2015).

Bailey, Mark and S. H. Rigby, eds, *Town and Countryside in the Age of the Black Death: Essays in Honour of John Hatcher* (Turnhout: Brepols, 2012).

Baker, J. H., *The Oxford History of the Laws of England, 6: 1348–558* (Oxford: Oxford University Press, 2003).

Bardsley, Sandy, 'Women's Work Reconsidered: Gender and Wage Differentiation in Late Medieval England', *Past & Present* 165 (1999): 1–29, doi:10.1093/past/165.1.3.

Bardsley, Sandy, 'Missing Women: Sex Ratios in England, 1000–1500', *Journal of British Studies* 53:2 (2014): 273–309, doi:10.1017/jbr.2014.9.

Bardsley, Sandy, 'Peasant Women and Inheritance of Land in Fourteenth-Century England', *Continuity & Change* 29:3 (2014): 297–324, doi:10.1017/S0268416014000253.

Bardsley, Sandy, and John Hatcher, 'Debate: Women's Work Reconsidered: Gender and Wage Differentiation in Late Medieval England', *Past & Present* 173 (2001): 191–202, doi:10.1093/past/173.1.191.

Barlow, Frank, *Durham Jurisdictional Peculiars* (London: Oxford University Press, 1950).

Bean, J. M. W., *The Estates of the Percy Family 1416–1537* (London: Oxford University Press, 1958).

Beckett, John V., and Michael E. Turner, 'Freehold from Copyhold and Leasehold. Tenurial Transitions in England between the 16th and 19th Centuries', in *Landholding and Land Transfer in the North Sea Area (Late Middle Ages – 19th century)*, Comparative Rural History of the North Sea Area 5 (Turnhout: Brepols, 2004), pp. 282–292. https://doi.org/10.1484/M.CORN-EB.4.00150.

Bennett, Judith M., 'Medieval Peasant Marriage: An Examination of Marriage License Fines in The *Liber Gersumarum*', *Pathways to Medieval Peasants*, ed. by J. A. Raftis (Toronto: Pontifical Institute of Medieval Studies, 1981), pp. 193–246.

Bennett, Judith M., *Women in the Medieval English Countryside: Gender & Household in Brigstock before the Plague* (Oxford: Oxford University Press, 1987).

Bennett, Judith M., 'Widows in the Medieval English Countryside', in *Upon My Husband's Death: Widows in the Literature and Histories of Medieval Europe*, ed. by Louise Mirrer (Ann Arbor: University of Michigan Press, 1992), pp. 69–114.

Bennett, Judith M., *Ale, Beer, and Brewsters in England: Women's Work in a Changing World, 1300–1600* (Oxford: Oxford University Press, 1996).

Bennett, Judith M., *A Medieval Life: Cecilia Penifader of Brigstock, c. 1295–1433* (Boston: McGraw-Hill, 1998).

Bennett, Judith M., 'Writing Fornication: Medieval Leyrwite and Its Historians', *Transactions of the Royal Historical Society* 13 (2003): 131–62, doi:10.1017/S0080440103000069.

Bennett, Judith M., *History Matters: Patriarchy and the Challenge of Feminism* (Philadelphia: University of Pennsylvania Press, 2006).

Bennett, Judith M., 'Compulsory Service in Late Medieval England', *Past & Present* 209 (2010); 7–51, doi:10.1093/pastj/gtq032.

Bennett, Judith M., 'Wretched Girls, Wretched Boys and the European Marriage Pattern in England (c. 1250–1350)', *Continuity and Change* 34 (2019): 315–47, doi:10.1017/S0268416019000328.

Bennett, Judith M., and Amy Froide, eds, *Singlewomen in the European Past* (Philadelphia: University of Pennsylvania Press, 1999).

Beresford, M. W., 'East Layton, Co. Durham, in 1608: Another Early Cartographic Representation of a Deserted Medieval Village Site', *Medieval Archaeology* 11 (1967): 257–60.

Blanchard, Ian, 'Population Change, Enclosure, and the Early Tudor Economy', *Economic History Review* 23:3 (1970): 427–45, doi:10.2307/2594614.

Blanchard, Ian, 'The Miner and the Agricultural Community in Later Medieval England', *Agricultural History Review* 20:2 (1972): 93–106, https://www.jstor.org/stable/40273487.

Bolton, J. L., *Money in the Medieval English Economy 973–1489* (Manchester: Manchester University Press, 2012).

Bradshaw, Frederick, 'Social and Economic History', in *Victoria History of the County of Durham*, vol. II, ed. by William Page (London: Dawsons, 1907; reprinted 1968), pp. 175–274.

Brassley, Paul, 'Northumberland and Durham', in *The Agrarian History of England and Wales, vol. V 1640–1750, part I: Regional Farming Systems*, ed. by Joan Thirsk (1984), pp. 30–58.

Brassley, Paul, *The Agricultural Economy of Northumberland and Durham in the Period 1640–1750* (New York: Garland Pub., 1985).

Brautigam, Dwight, 'Prelates and Politics: Uses of "Puritan," 1625–40', in *Puritanism and Its Discontents*, ed. by Laura Lunger Knoppers (Newark, Del: University of Delaware Press, 2003), pp. 49–66.

Bridbury, A. R., *Economic Growth: England in the Later Middle Ages* (London: Allen and Unwin, 1962).

Briggs, Chris, *Credit and Village Society in Fourteenth-Century England* (Oxford: Oxford University Press, 2009).

Briggs, Chris, 'Introduction: Law Courts, Contracts and Rural Society in Europe, 1200–1600', *Continuity and Change* 29:1 (2014): 3–18, doi:10.1017/S026841601400006x.

Briggs, Chris, Alice Forward, Ben Jervis, and Matthew Tompkins, 'People, Possessions and Domestic Space in the Late Medieval Escheators' Records', *Journal of Medieval History* 45:2 (2019): 145–61, doi:10.1080/03044181.2019.1593624.

Britnell, Richard H., *Growth and Decline in Colchester: 1300–1525* (Cambridge: Cambridge University Press, 1986).

Britnell, Richard H., 'The Langley Survey of Durham Bishopric Estates, 1418–21', *Archæologia Æliana* 5th ser. 16 (1988): 213–21, https://doi.org/10.5284/1060834.

Britnell, Richard H., 'Feudal Reaction after the Black Death in the Palatinate of Durham', *Past & Present* 128 (1990): 28–47, doi:10.1093/past/128.1.28.

Britnell, Richard H., *The Commercialisation of English Society 1000–1500* (Manchester: Manchester University Press, 1993; 2nd edn Cambridge: Cambridge University Press, 1996).

Britnell, Richard H., 'Urban Demand in the English Economy, 1300–1600', in *Trade, Urban Hinterlands and Market Integration c. 1300–1600*, ed. by J. A. Galloway (London: University of London Institute for Historical Research, 2000), pp. 1–22.

Britnell, Richard H., 'English Agricultural Output and Prices, 1350–1450: National Trends and Regional Divergences', in *Agriculture and Rural Society after the Black Death: Common Themes and Regional Variations*, ed. by Richard Britnell and Ben Dodds (Hatfield: University of Hertfordshire Press, 2008), pp. 20–39.

Britnell, Richard H., 'The Coal Industry in the Later Middle Ages: The Bishop of Durham's Estate', in *Town and Countryside in the Age of the Black Death: Essays in Honour of John Hatcher*, ed. by Mark Bailey and S.H. Rigby (Turnhout: Brepols, 2012), pp. 439–472.

Broadberry, Stephen, Bruce M. S. Campbell, and Bas van Leeuwen, 'When Did Britain Industrialise? The Sectoral Distribution of the Labour Force and Labour Productivity in Britain, 1381–1851', *Explorations in Economic History* 50:1 (2013): 16–27, https://doi.org/10.1016/j.eeh.2012.08.004.

Broadberry, Stephen, Bruce M. S. Campbell, Alexander Klein, Mark Overton, and Bas van Leeuwen, *British Economic Growth, 1270–1870* (Cambridge: Cambridge University Press, 2015).

Broadberry, Stephen, Hanhui Guan, and David Daokui Li, 'China, Europe, and the Great Divergence: A Study in Historical National Accounting, 980–1850', *The Journal of Economic History* 78:4 (2018): 955–1000, doi:10.1017/S0022050718000529.

Brown, A. T., *Rural Society and Economic Change in County Durham: Recession and Recovery, c.1400–1640* (Woodbridge: Boydell & Brewer, 2015).

Brown, A. T., 'Church Leaseholders on Durham Cathedral's Estate, 1540–1640', in *Economy and Culture in North-East England, 1500–1800* (Woodbridge: Boydell & Brewer, 2018), pp. 21–42.

Burn, Andy, 'Seasonal Work and Welfare in an Early Industrial Town: Newcastle upon Tyne, 1600–1700', *Continuity & Change* 32:2 (2017): 157–82, doi:10.1017/S0268416017000182.

Buxton, Anthony, *Domestic Culture in Early Modern England* (Woodbridge: Boydell & Brewer, 2015).

Campbell, Bruce M. S., 'Population Pressure, Inheritance and the Land Market in a Fourteenth-Century Peasant Community', in *Land, Kinship and Life-Cycle* (Cambridge: Cambridge University Press, 1984), pp. 87–134.

Campbell, Bruce M. S., *English Seigniorial Agriculture, 1250–1450* (Cambridge: Cambridge University Press, 2006).

Campbell, Bruce M. S., 'Factor Markets in England before the Black Death', *Continuity and Change* 24:1 (2009): 79–106, doi:10.1017/S0268416009007036.

Campbell, Bruce M. S. 'Grain Yields on English Demesnes after the Black Death,' in *Town and Countryside in the Age of the Black Death: Essays in Honour of John Hatcher*, ed. by Mark Bailey and Stephen Rigby (Turnhout: Brepols, 2011), pp. 121–74. doi:10.1484/M.TMC-EB.6.09070802050003050305010703.

Campbell, Bruce M. S., 'Unit Land Values as a Guide to Agricultural Land Productivity in Medieval England', in *Measuring Agricultural Growth: Land and Labour Productivity in Western Europe from the Middle Ages to the Twentieth Century (England, France and Spain)*, ed. by Jean-Michel Chevet and Gérard Béaur,), Comparative Rural History of the North Sea Area 15 (Turnhout: Brepols, 2014), pp. 25–50.

Campbell, Bruce M. S., *The Great Transition: Climate, Disease and Society in the Late-Medieval World* (Cambridge: Cambridge University Press, 2016).

Campbell, Mildred, *The English Yeoman under Elizabeth and the Early Stuarts* (New Haven: Yale University Press, 1942; reprinted London: Merlin Press, 1983).

Cannon, John, *Parliamentary Reform 1640–1832* (Cambridge: Cambridge University Press, 1973).

Carlisle, Nicholas, *A Concise Description of Endowed Grammar Schools of England and Wales*, vol. 1 (London: Bulmer, 1818).

Chayanov, A. V., *The Theory of Peasant Economy*, ed. by D. Thorner, B. Kerblay, and R. E. F. Smith (Homewood, Ill.: American Economic Association, 1966).

Chaytor, Miranda, 'Household and Kinship: Ryton in the late 16th and early 17th centuries', *History Workshop Journal* 10:1 (1980): 25–60, doi:10.1093/hwj/10.1.25.

Clark, Gregory, 'The Price History of English Agriculture, 1209–1914', *Research in Economic History* 22 (2003): 60–79, doi:10.1016/S0363-3268(04)22002-x.

Clark, Gregory, 'The Long March of History: Farm Wages, Population, and Economic Growth, England 1209–1869', *The Economic History Review* 60:1 (2007): 97–135, doi:10.1111/j.1468-0289.2006.00358.x.

Clark, Gregory, 'Microbes and Markets: Was the Black Death an Economic Revolution?' *Journal of Demographic Economics* 82 (2016): 139–65, doi:10.1017/dem.2016.6.

Clark, Gregory, and David Jacks, 'Coal and the Industrial Revolution, 1700–1869', *European Review of Economic History* 11:1 (2007): 39–72, https://www.jstor.org/stable/41378456.

Clark, Gregory, Joseph Cummins, and Brock Smith, 'Malthus, Wages, and Preindustrial Growth', *Journal of Economic History* 72:2 (2012): 364–92, https://www.jstor.org/stable/23256942.

Cookson, G., ed., *A History of the County of Durham, vol. IV: Darlington* (Woodbridge: Boydell & Brewer, 2005).

Cookson, G., ed., *A History of the County of Durham, vol. V: Sunderland* (Woodbridge: Boydell & Brewer, 2015).

Cookson, G., with C. M. Newman, 'Trade and Industry', in *A History of the County of Durham, vol. IV*, ed. By G. Cookson (Woodbridge: Boydell & Brewer, 2005), pp. 107–192.

Courtney, William Prideaux, 'Grenville, Denis', in the *Dictionary of National Biography*, vol. 23, ed. by Leslie Stephen and Sidney Lee (New York: Macmillan and Co., 1890), p. 112.

Croot, Patricia, *The World of the Small Farmer: Tenure, Profit and Politics in the Early Modern Somerset Levels* (Hatfield: University of Hertfordshire Press, 2017).

Croot, Patricia, and David Parker, 'Agrarian Class Structure and the Development of Capitalism: France and England Compared', in *The Brenner Debate*, eds. by Aston and Philpin, pp. 79–90.

Curtis, Myra, 'Bishop Middleham', in *A History of the County of Durham, vol. 3* (1928).

Curtis, Myra, 'Sedgefield', in *History of the County of Durham, vol. 3* (1928).

Davis, Ralph, *English Overseas Trade, 1500–1700* (Macmillan, 1973).

Day, John, 'The Great Bullion Famine of the Fifteenth Century', *Past & Present* 79 (1978): 3–54, doi:10.1093/past/79.1.3.

De Moor, Tine, and Jan Luiten Van Zanden, 'Girl Power: the European Marriage Pattern and Labour Markets in the North Sea Region in the Late Medieval and Early Modern Period', *Economic History Review* 63:1 (2010): 1–33, doi:10.1111/j.1468-0289.2009.00483.x.

De Pleijt, Alexandra, and Jan Luitenvan Zanden, 'Accounting for the "Little Divergence": What Drove Economic Growth in Pre-Industrial Europe, 1300–1800?' *European Review of Economic History* 20 (2016), pp. 387–409, doi:10.1093/ereh/hew013.

De Vries, Jan, 'Between Purchasing Power and the World of Goods: Understanding the Household Economy in Early Modern Europe', in *Consumption and the World of Goods*, ed. by John Brewer and Roy Porter (London: Routledge, 2013), pp. 85–132.

De Vries, Jan, *The Industrious Revolution: Consumer Behavior and the Household Economy, 1650 to the Present* (Cambridge: Cambridge University Press, 2008).

Dennison, Tracy, and Sheilagh Ogilvie, 'Does the European Marriage Pattern Explain Economic Growth?' *Journal of Economic History* 74:3 (2015), doi:10.1017/s0022050714000564.

DeWindt, Edwin Brezette, *Land and People in Holywell-cum-Needingworth: Structures of Tenure and Patterns of Social Organization in an East Midlands Village, 1252-1457* (Toronto: Pontifical Institute of Medieval Studies, 1972).

Dimmock, Spencer, *The Origin of Capitalism in England 1400-1600* (Chicago: Haymarket Books, 2014).

Dobb, Maurice, *Studies in the Development of Capitalism* (New York: International Publishers, 1946).

Dobson, R. B., *Durham Priory 1400-1450* (Cambridge: Cambridge University Press, 1973).

Dodds, Ben, 'Estimating Arable Output Using Durham Priory Tithe Receipts, 1341-1450', *Economic History Review* 57:2 (2004), doi:10.1111/j.1468-0289.2004.00278.x.

Dodds, Ben, *Peasants and Production in the Medieval North-East: The Evidence from Tithes, 1270-1536* (Woodbridge: Boydell & Brewer, 2007).

Dolan, Loretta A., *Nurture and Neglect: Childhood in Sixteenth-Century Northern England* (New York: Routledge, 2017).

Drury, Linda, 'More Stout than Wise: Tenant Right in Weardale in the Tudor period', in *The Last Principality: Politics, Religion and Society in the Bishopric of Durham 1494-1660* ed. by David Marcombe (Nottingham: University of Nottingham, 1987), pp. 71-100.

Duffy, Eamon, *The Stripping of the Altars: Traditional Religion in England c. 1400-c.1580* (New Haven: Yale University Press, 1992).

Duffy, Eamon, *The Voices of Morebath: Reformation and Rebellion in an English Village* (New Haven: Yale University Press, 2003).

Dunsford, Helen, and Simon Harris, 'Colonization of the Wasteland in County Durham, 1100-1400', *Economic History Review* 56:1 (2003): 34-56, doi:10.1111/1468-0289.00241.

Durham County Record Office, 'Subject Guide 1: Records Relating to Inclosure', Issue 18, November 2018.

Dyer, Christopher, *Lords and Peasants in a Changing Society: The Estates of the Bishopric of Worcester, 680-1540* (Cambridge: Cambridge University Press, 1980).

Dyer, Christopher, *Standards of Living in the Later Middle Ages* (Cambridge: Cambridge University Press, 1993).

Dyer, Christopher, *Making a Living in the Middle Ages: The People of Britain 850-1250* (New Haven: Yale University Press, 2002).

Dyer, Christopher, *An Age of Transition? Economy and Society in the Later Middle Ages* (Oxford: Clarendon Press, 2005).

Dyer, Christopher, 'Did Peasants Need Markets and Towns? The Experience of Late Medieval England', in *London and Beyond: Essays in Honour of Derek Keene*, ed. by Matthew Davies and J. A. Galloway (London: University of London Institute of Historical Research, 2012), pp. 25-48.

Dyer, Christopher, 'Trade, Urban Hinterlands and Market Integration, 1300-1600: a Summing up', in *London and Beyond: Essays in Honour of Derek Keene*, ed. by Matthew Davies and J. A. Galloway (London: University of London Institute of Historical Research, 2012), pp. 103-109.

Dyer, Christopher, 'The Agrarian Problem, 1440-1520', in *Landlords and Tenants in Britain, 1440-1660: Tawney's Agrarian Problem Revisited* ed. by Jane Whittle (Woodbridge: Boydell & Brewer, 2013), pp. 19-34.

Dyer, Christopher, 'Peasant Farming in Late Medieval England: Evidence from the Tithe Estimations by Worcester Cathedral Priory', in *Peasants and Lords in the Medieval English Economy: Essays in Honour of Bruce M.S. Campbell*, ed. by Maryanne Kowaleski, John Langdon, and Phillipp R. Schofield (Turnhout: Brepols, 2015), pp. 83–109. doi:10.1484/M.TMC-EB.5.109810.

Dyer, Christopher, 'Open Fields in Their Social and Economic Context: the West Midlands of England', in *Peasants and Their Fields: The Rationale of Open-Field Agriculture, c. 700–1800*, ed. by Christopher Dyer, Erik Thoen, and Tom Williamson, Comparative Rural History of the North Sea Area 15 (Turnhout: Brepols, 2016), pp. 29–47.

Edwards, Jeremy Edwards, and Sheilagh Ogilvie, 'What Can We Learn from a Race with One Runner? A Comment on Foreman-Peck and Zhou, 'Late Marriage as a Contributor to the Industrial Revolution in England', *Economic History Review* 72:4 (2019): 1439–46, doi:0.1111/ehr.12785.

Emsley, Kenneth, and C. M. Fraser, *The Courts of the County Palatine of Durham from Earliest Times to 1971* (Durham: Durham County Local Historical Society, 1984).

Epstein, Stephan R., *Freedom and Growth: The Rise of States and Markets in Europe, 1300–1750* (Routledge, 2000).

Erickson, Amy, *Women and Property in Early Modern England* (London: Routledge, 1995).

Everitt, Alan, 'Social Mobility in Early Modern England', *Past & Present* 33 (1966): 56–73, https://www.jstor.org/stable/649802.

Faith, Rosamond, 'Peasant Families and Inheritance Customs in Medieval England', *Agricultural History Review* 14:2 (1967): 77–95, https://www.jstor.org/stable/40273202.

Faith, Rosamond, 'Berkshire: Fourteenth and Fifteenth Centuries', in *The Peasant Land Market in Medieval England*, ed. by P.D.A. Harvey (Oxford: Clarendon Press, 1984), pp. 106–177.

Faith, Rosamond, *The English Peasantry and the Growth of Lordship* (London: Leicester University Press, 1997).

Fenoaltea, S., 'Risk, Transaction Costs, and the Organization of Medieval Agriculture' *Explorations in Economic History* 13:2 (1976): 129–51, doi:10.1016/0014-4983(76)90022-X.

Fenoaltea, S., 'Fenoaltea on Open Fields: a Reply [to McCloskey]', *Explorations in Economic History* 14:4 (1977): 405–10, doi:10.1016/0014-4983(77)90025-0.

Fisher, F. J., 'Influenza and Inflation in Tudor England', *Economic History Review* 18:1 (1965): 120–9, https://www.jstor.org/stable/2591877.

Fleming, Peter, *Family and Household in Medieval England* (New York: Palgrave, 2001).

Fordyce, William, *The History and Antiquities of the County Palatine of Durham*, vol. 2 (Newcastle upon Tyne: A. Fullarton, 1857).

Foreman-Peck, James, and Peng Zhou, 'Late Marriage as a Contributor to the Industrial Revolution in England', *Economic History Review* 71:4 (2018): 1073–99, doi:10.1111/ehr.12651.

Foreman-Peck, James, and Peng Zhou, 'Response to Edwards and Ogilvie', *Economic History Review* 72:4 (2019): 1447–50, doi:10.1111/ehr.12819.

Forster, Ann M. C., 'The Maire Family of County Durham', *Recusant History* 10:6 (1970): 332–46, doi:10.1017/S0034193200000431.

Foster, A. W., 'The Struggle for Parliamentary Representation for Durham, c.1600–41', in *The Last Principality: Politics, Religion and Society in the Bishopric of Durham 1494–1660* ed. by David Marcombe (Nottingham: University of Nottingham 1987), pp. 176–201.

Foster, Charles F., *Cheshire Cheese and Farming in the North West in the 17th and 18th Centuries* (Northwich: Arley Hall Press, 1998).

Foster, Charles F., *Seven Households: Life in Cheshire and Lancashire 1582–1774* (Northwich: Arley Hall Press, 2002).

Foster, Charles F., *Capital and Innovation—How Britain became the First Industrial Nation: A Study of the Warrington, Knutsford, Northwich and Frodsham Area 1500-1780* (Northwich: Arley Hall Press, 2004).

Foster, Joseph, *Alumni Oxonienses: The Members of the University of Oxford, 1500-1714*, vol. 2 (Oxford: Parker & Co., 1891-2).

Frank, Andre Gunder, *ReOrient: Global Economy in the Asian Age* (Berkeley: University of California Press, 1998).

Franklin, Peter, 'Peasant Widows' "Liberation" and Remarriage before the Black Death', *Economic History Review* 39:2 (1986): 186-204, doi:10.2307/2596149.

Fraser, Constance, *A History of Antony Bek, Bishop of Durham 1283-1311* (Oxford: Clarendon Press, 1957).

French, Henry R., 'The Search for the "Middle Sort of People" in England, 1600-1800', *Historical Journal* 43:1 (2000): 277-94, https://www.jstor.org/stable/3021022.

French, Henry R., 'Social Status, Localism and the 'Middle Sort of People' in England 1620-1750', *Past & Present* 166 (2000): 67-99, doi:10.1093/past/166.1.66.

French, Henry R., and Richard Hoyle, *The Character of English Rural Society: Earls Colne 1550-1750* (Manchester: Manchester University Press, 2007).

French, Katherine, *The People of the Parish: Community Life in a Late Medieval Diocese* (Philadelphia: University of Pennsylvania Press, 2000).

French, Katherine, *The Good Women of the Parish: Gender and Religion After the Black Death* (Philadelphia: University of Pennsylvania Press, 2007).

French, Katherine, *Household Goods and Good Households in Late Medieval London: Consumption and Domesticity After the Plague* (Philadelphia: University of Pennsylvania Press, 2021).

Froide, Amy, *Never Married: Singlewomen in Early Modern England* (Oxford: Oxford University Press, 2005).

Fuller, Thomas, ed., *History of the Worthies of England* (London: T. Tegg, 1840).

Galor, Oded, *Unified Growth Theory* (Princeton: Princeton University Press, 2011).

Galor, Oded and Omer Moav, 'From Physical to Human Capital Accumulation: Inequality and the Process of Development', *The Review of Economic Studies*, 71:4 (2004): 1001-26, https://www.jstor.org/stable/3700726.

Garret-Goodyear, Harold, 'Common Law and Manor Courts: Lords, Copyholders and Doing Justice in Early Tudor England', in *Landlords and Tenants in Britain, 1440-1660: Tawney's Agrarian Problem Revisited*, ed. by Jane Whittle (Woodbridge: Boydell & Brewer, 2013), pp. 35-51.

Gates, Lori A., 'Widows, Property, and Remarriage: Lessons from Glastonbury's Deverill Manors', *Albion* 28 (1996): 19-35, doi:10.2307/4051952.

Gayton, Juliet, 'Mortgages Raised by Rural English Copyhold Tenants 1605-1735', in *Land and Credit: Mortgages in the Medieval and Early Modern European Countryside*, ed. by Chris Briggs and Jaco Zuijderduijn (London: Palgrave, 2018), pp. 47-80.

Goldberg, P. J. P., *Women, Work and Life Cycle in a Medieval Economy: Women in York and Yorkshire c. 1300-1520* (Oxford: Clarendon Press, 1992).

Goldstone, Jack A., 'Efflorescences and Economic Growth in World History: Rethinking the "Rise of the West" and the Industrial Revolution', *Journal of World History* 13:2 (2002): 323-89, https://www.jstor.org/stable/20078976.

Goodacre, John, *The Transformation of a Peasant Economy: Townspeople and Villagers in the Lutterworth Area 1500-1700* (Aldershot: Scolar Press, 1994; reprinted London: Taylor and Francis, 2017).

Gray, C. M., *Copyhold, Equity and the Common Law* (Cambridge, MA: Harvard University Press, 1963).

Green, Adrian, 'County Durham at the Restoration: A Social and Economic Case Study', in *County Durham Hearth Tax Assessment, Lady Day 1666*, ed. by Adrian Green, Elizabeth Parkinson, and Margaret Spufford (London: British Record Society, 2006), pp. xv–cxl.

Green, Adrian 'Durham Ox: Commercial Agriculture in North-East England, 1600–1800', in *Economy and Culture in North-East England, 1500–1800*, ed. by Adrian Green and Barbara Crosbie (Woodbridge: Boydell & Brewer, 2018), pp. 44–67.

Green, Adrian, 'Law and Architecture in Early Modern Durham', in *Law, Lawyers and Litigants in Early Modern England: Essays in Memory of Christopher W. Brooks*, ed. by Michael Lobban, Joanne Begiato, and Adrian Green (Cambridge: Cambridge University Press, 2019), pp. 265–291.

Hajnal, John, 'European Marriage Patterns in Perspective', in *Population in History: Essays in Historical Demography*, ed. by D. V. Glass and D. E. C. Eversley (London: Edward Arnold, 1965), pp. 101–43.

Hanawalt, Barbara, *The Ties That Bound: Peasant Families in Medieval England* (Oxford: Oxford University Press, 1986).

Hanawalt, Barbara, *The Wealth of Wives: Women, Law, and Economy in Late Medieval London* (Oxford: Oxford University Press, 2007).

Hare, John, *A Prospering Society: Wiltshire in the later Middle Ages* (Hatfield: University of Hertfordshire Press, 2012).

Harris, Simon J., 'Wastes, the Margins and the Abandonment of Land: The Bishop of Durham's Estate, 1350–1480', in *North-East England in the Later Middle Ages*, ed. by Christian D. Liddy and Richard H. Britnell (Woodbridge: Boydell & Brewer, 2005), pp. 197–220.

Harvey, Barbara, *Westminster Abbey and Its Estates in the Middle Ages* (Oxford: Clarendon Press, 1977).

Harvey, Margaret, *Lay Religious Life in Late Medieval Durham* (Woodbridge: Boydell & Brewer, 2006).

Harvey, P. D. A, *A Medieval Oxfordshire Village: Cuxham 1200–1400* (Oxford: Oxford University Press, 1965).

Harvey, P. D. A., ed., *The Peasant Land Market in Medieval England* (Oxford: Clarendon Press, 1984).

Harvey, P. D. A., *Manorial Records* (London: HMSO, 1984; rev. edn, 1999).

Hatcher, John, *Rural Economy and Society in the Duchy of Cornwall, 1300–1500* (Cambridge: Cambridge University Press, 1970).

Hatcher, John, *The History of the British Coal Industry, vol. I: Before 1700: Towards the Age of Coal* (Oxford: Clarendon Press, 1993).

Hatcher, John, 'The Great Slump of the Mid-Fifteenth Century', in *Progress and Problems in Medieval England: Essays in Honour of Edward Miller*, ed. by Richard Britnell and John Hatcher (Cambridge: Cambridge University Press, 1996), pp. 237–272.

Hatcher, John, 'Unreal Wages: Long-Run Living Standards and the "Golden Age" of the Fifteenth Century', in *Commercial Activity, Markets and Entrepreneurs in the Middle Ages*, ed. by Ben Dodds and Christian D. Liddy, (Woodbridge: Boydell & Brewer, 2011), pp. 1–24.

Hatcher, John, 'Seven Centuries of Unreal Wages', in *Seven Centuries of Unreal Wages: The Unreliable Data, Sources and Methods that Have Been Used for Measuring Standards of Living in the Past*, ed. by John Hatcher and Judy Z. Stephenson (London: Palgrave, 2018), pp. 15–69.

Hatcher, John, and Mark Bailey, *Modelling the Middle Ages: The History and Theory of England's Economic Development* (Oxford: Oxford University Press, 2001).

Heller, Henry, *The Birth of Capitalism: A 21st Century Perspective* (London: Pluto Press, 2011).

Heley, Gwendolynn, 'The material culture of the tradesmen of Newcastle upon Tyne 1545-1642: The Durham probate record evidence', 2 vols., Ph.D. thesis, Durham University (2007).

Hill, Christopher, *The English Revolution, 1640* (London: Lawrence and Wishart, 1942).

Hilton, J. A., 'Catholicism in Jacobean Durham', *British Catholic History* 14:2 (1977): 78–85, doi:10.1017/S0034193200004908.

Hilton, R. H., 'Rent and Capital Formation in Feudal Society', in *The English Peasantry in the Later Middle Ages* (Oxford: Oxford University Press, 1975), pp. 174–214.

Hindle, Steve, *On the Parish? The Micro-Politics of Poor Relief in England, c. 1550–1750* (Oxford: Oxford University Press, 2004).

Hobsbawm, Eric, 'The Crisis of the Seventeenth Century, II', *Past & Present* 6 (1954): 44–65, www.jstor.org/stable/649814.

Hobsbawm, Eric, 'The General Crisis of the European Economy in the Seventeenth Century', *Past & Present* 5 (1954): 33–53, https://www.jstor.org/stable/649822.

Hodgson, R. I., 'Demographic Trends in County Durham, 1560–1801', *University of Manchester School for Geography Research Papers* 5 (Manchester: University of Manchester School of Geography, 1978).

Hodgson, R. I., 'The Progress of Enclosure in County Durham 1550–18070', in *Change in the Countryside: Essays on Rural England*, ed. by H.S.A. Fox and R.A. Butlin (London: Institute of British Geographers, 1979), pp. 83–102.

Hoffman, John G., 'The Arminian and the Iconoclast: The Dispute between John Cosin and Peter Smart', *Historical Magazine of the Protestant Episcopal Church,* 48:3 (1979): 279–301, https://www.jstor.org/stable/42973702.

Holderness, B. A. 'Widows in Pre-Industrial Society: An Essay upon Their Economic Functions', in *Land Kinship and Life-Cycle*, ed. by Richard M. Smith (Cambridge: Cambridge University Press, 1984), pp. 423–442.

Homans, G. C., *English Villagers of the Thirteenth Century* (Cambridge, MA.: Harvard University Press, 1941, 2nd edn 1960).

Hopcroft, Rosemary, 'The Social Origins of Agrarian Change in Late Medieval England', *Journal of Sociology* 99:6 (1994): 1559–95, doi:10.1086/230454.

Hoppenbrouwers, Peter, and Jan Luitenvan Zanden, eds, *Peasants into Farmers? The Transformation of the Rural Economy and Society in the Low Countries (Middle Ages—19th Century) in Light of the Brenner Debate*, Comparative Rural History of the North Sea Area 4 (Turnhout: Brepols, 2001).

Hoskins, W. G. 'The Leicestershire Farmer in the Sixteenth Century', Leicestershire Archaeological Society, *Transactions* 22 1944–45): 34–94, https://www.le.ac.uk/lahs/publications/transactions.html.

Hoskins, W. G., 'The Leicestershire Farmer in the Seventeenth Century', *Agricultural History* 25:1 (1951): 9–20, https://www.jstor.org/stable/3740294.

Howell, Cicely, *Land, Family and Inheritance in Transition: Kibworth Harcourt, 1280–1700* (Cambridge: Cambridge University Press, 1983).

Howell, Jr, Roger,*Newcastle upon Tyne and the Puritan Revolution: A Study of the Civil War in North England* (Oxford: Clarendon Press, 1967).

Howell, Jr, Roger, 'The Structure of Urban Politics in the English Civil War', *Albion* 11:2 (1979): 111–27, doi:10.2307/4048269.

Hoyle, R. W., 'An Ancient and Laudable Custom: the Definition and Development of Tenant Right in North-Western England in the Sixteenth Century', *Past & Present* 116 (1987): 24–55, doi:10.1093/past/116.1.24.

Hoyle, R. W., 'Tenure and the Land Market in Early Modern England: or a Late Contribution to the Brenner Debate', *Economic History Review* 44 (1990): 1–20, doi:10.1111/j.1468–0289. 1990.tb00517.x.

Hoyle, R. W., ed., *Custom, Improvement, and Landscape in Early Modern Britain* (London: Routledge, 2013).

Hoyle, R. W, 'Introduction: Custom, Improvement and Anti-Improvement', in *Custom, Improvement, and Landscape in Early Modern Britain*, ed. by R.W. Hoyle (London: Routledge, 2013), pp. 1–38.

Humphries, Jane, and Jacob Weisdorf, 'The Wages of Women in England, 1260–1850', *The Journal of Economic History* 75:2 (2015): 405–47. https://www.jstor.org/stable/ 24550938.

Hutchinson, William, *The History and Antiquities of the County Palatine of Durham*, vol. III (Newcastle: S. Hodgson & Robinsons, 1794).

Hyams, Paul, 'The Origins of a Peasant Land Market in England', *Economic History Review* 23:1 (1970): 18–31, doi:10.1111/j.1468-0289.1970.tb01011.x.

James, Mervyn, *Family, Lineage, and Civil Society: A Study of Society, Politics and Mentality in the Durham Region 1500–1640* (Oxford: Clarendon Press, 1974).

Jervis, Ben, Chris Briggs, and Matthew Tompkins, 'Exploring Text and Objects: Escheators' Inventories and Material Culture in Medieval English Rural Households', in *Medieval Archaeology* 59:1 (2015): 168–192. doi:10.1080/00766097.2015.1119400.

Jewell, Helen M., *The North-South Divide: the Origins of Northern Consciousness in England* (Manchester: Manchester University Press, 1994).

Jolliffe, J. E. A., Northumbrian Institutions', *English Historical Review* 161 (1926): 1–42, https://www.jstor.org/stable/552327.

Jones, Glanville R. J., 'Basic Patterns of Settlement Distribution in Northern England', *Advancement of Science* 18 (1961): pp. 192–200.

Jones, Oliver R., 'London Mustard Bottles', in *Historical Archaeology* 17:1 (1983): 69–84, doi:10.1007/BF03374032.

Jones, W. K., *Philanthropy in England, 1480–1660: A Study of the Changing Patterns of English Social Aspirations* (New York: Russell Sage Foundation, 1959, reprinted 1964).

Kapelle, William E., *The Norman Conquest of the North*, (London: Croom Helm, 1979).

Kelly, Kelly, and Cormac Ó Gráda, 'Numerare Est Errare: Agricultural Output and Food Supply in England Before and During the Industrial Revolution', *Journal of Economic History* 73:4 (2013): 1132–63, https://www.jstor.org/stable/24551014.

Kent, Joan, 'The Rural "Middling Sort" in Early Modern England, circa 1640–1740: Some Economic, Political and Socio-Cultural Characteristics', *Rural History* 10:1 (1999): 19–54, doi:10.1017/S0956793300001679.

Kerridge, Eric, 'The Movement of Rent, 1540–1640', *Economic History Review* 6:1 (1953), pp. 16–34, doi:10.1111/j.1468–0289.1953.tb01483.x.

Kerridge, Eric, *The Agricultural Revolution* (London: Allen and Unwin, 1967).

Kerridge, Eric, *Agrarian Problems in the Sixteenth Century and After* (London: Routledge, 2006).

Kesselring, K. J., *The Northern Rebellion Of 1569: Faith, Politics, and Protest in Elizabethan England* (Basingstoke: Palgrave Macmillan, 2007).

Kilby, Susan, *Peasant Perspectives on the Medieval Landscape: A Study of Three Communities* (Hatfield: University of Hertfordshire Press, 2020).

Kirby, D. A., 'Population Density and Land Values in County Durham during the Mid-Seventeenth Century', *Transactions of the Institute of British Geographers* 57 (1972): 83–98, doi:10.2307/621555.

Kitsikopoulos, Harry, 'Standards of Living and Capital Formation in Pre-Plague England: a Peasant Budget Model', *Economic History Review* 532: (2000): 237–6, doi:10.1111/1468-0289.00159.

Klein, Alexander, and Sheilagh Ogilvie, 'Occupational Structure in the Czech Lands under the Second Serfdom', *Economic History Review* 69:2 (2016): 493–521, doi:10.1111/ehr.12118.

Kowaleski, Maryanne, 'The Grain Trade in Fourteenth-Century Exeter', in *The Salt of Common Life: Individuality and Choice in the Medieval Town, Countryside, and Church: Essays Presented by J. Ambrose Raftis*, ed. by Edwin Breezette DeWindt (1995), pp. 1–52.

Kowaleski, Maryanne, *Local Markets and Regional Trade in Medieval Exeter* (Cambridge: Cambridge University Press, 1995).

Kümin, B., *The Shaping of a Community: The Rise and Reformation of the English Parish c. 1400–1560* (Aldershot: Scolar Press, 1996).

Kussmaul, A., *Servants in Husbandry in Early-Modern England* (Cambridge: Cambridge University Press, 1981).

Landes, David S., *The Wealth and Poverty of Nations: Why Some Are So Rich and Some So Poor* (New York: W.W. Norton, 1999).

Langdon, John, 'Review of *The Development of Agrarian Capitalism: Land and Labour in Norfolk 1440–1580*', *The American Historical Review* 106:4 (2001). https://www.jstor.org/stable/2693088.

Langdon, John, and James Masschaele, 'Commercial Activity and Population Growth in Medieval England', *Past & Present* 190 (2006): 35–81, doi:10.1093/pastj/gtj005.

Lapsley, G. T., *The County Palatine of Durham* (Cambridge, MA.: Harvard University Press, 1900).

Larson, Peter L., 'Local Law Courts in Late Medieval Durham', in *North-East England in the Later Middle Ages*, ed. by Christian D. Liddy and Richard H. Britnell (Woodbridge; Boydell & Brewer, 2005), pp. 97–110.

Larson, Peter L., *Conflict and Compromise in the Late Medieval Countryside: Lords and Peasants in Durham, 1349–1400* (London: Routledge, 2006).

Larson, Peter L., 'Village Voice or Village Oligarchy? The Jurors of the Durham Halmote Court, 1349–1424', in *Law and History Review* 28:3 (2010): 675–709, https://www.jstor.org/stable/25701146.

Larson, Peter L. 'Peasant Opportunities in Rural Durham: Land, Vills and Mills, 1349–1500', in *Commercial Activity, Markets and Entrepreneurs in the Middle Ages: Essays in Honour of Richard Britnell* ed. by Ben Dodds and Christian D. Liddy (Woodbridge: Boydell & Brewer, 2011), pp. 141–164.

Larson, Peter, 'Widow-right in Durham, England (1349–1660), in *Continuity and Change* 32:2 (2018): 173–201. doi:10.1017/S0268416018000127.

Larson, Peter L., 'Tenure and the Land Market in Northeastern England: A Comparative Perspective', in *The Routledge Handbook of Medieval Rural Life*, ed. by Miriam Müller (London: Routledge, 2021).

Laslett, Peter, 'Introduction: The history of the family', in *Household and Family in Past Time,* ed. by Peter Laslett and Richard Wall (Cambridge: Cambridge University Press, 1972), pp. 1–89. *doi:*10.1017/CBO9780511561207.

Laslett, Peter, 'Mean Household size in England since the sixteenth century', in *Household and Family in Past Time,* ed. by Peter Laslett and Richard Wall (Cambridge: Cambridge University Press, 1972), pp. 125–158. *doi:*10.1017/CBO9780511561207.

Lee, John S., 'Feeding the Colleges: Cambridge's Food and Fuel Supplies, 1450-1650', *Economic History Review* 56:2 (2003): 248–51, doi:10.1046/j.1468-0289.2003.00249.x

Leech, Peter, and Maurice Whitehead, '"IN PARADISE AND AMONG ANGELS": Music and Musicians at St. Omers English Jesuit College, 1593–1721', *Tijdschrift van de Koninklijke Vereniging voor Nederlandse Muziekgeshiedenis* 61:1/2 (2011): 57–82. https://www.jstor.org/stable/43738321.

Levett, A. E., *Studies in Manorial History*, ed. by H.M. Cam, M. Coate, and L.S. Sutherland (Oxford: Clarendon Press, 1938).

Levine, David, and Keith Wrightson, *The Making of an Industrial Society: Whickham 1560–1765* (Oxford: Clarendon Press, 1991).

Liddy, Christian D., *The Bishopric of Durham in the Late Middle Ages: Lordship, Community and the Cult of St. Cuthbert* (Woodbridge: Boydell & Brewer, 2008).

Lloyd, Paul S., *Food and Identity in England, 1540–1640: Eating to Impress* (London: Bloomsbury, 2015).

Lomas, R. A., 'Developments in Land Tenure on the Prior of Durham's Estate in the Later Middle Ages', *Northern History* 13:1 (1977): 27–43, doi:10.1179/007817277790176759.

Lomas, R. A., 'The Priory of Durham and its Demesnes in the Fourteenth and Fifteenth Centuries.' *Economic History Review* 31:3 (1978): 339–53, doi:10.1111/j.1468-0289.1978.tb00290.x.

Lomas, R. A., 'A Northern Farm at the End of the Middle Ages: Elvethall Manor, Durham, 1443/4–1513/14', *Northern History* 18:1 (1982): 26–53, doi:0.1179/007817282790176708.

Lomas, R. A., 'The Black Death in County Durham', *Journal of Medieval History* 15:2 (1989): 127–40, doi:10.1016/0304-4181(89)90013-4.

Lomas, Timothy, 'South-East Durham: Late Fourteenth and Fifteenth Centuries', in *The Peasant Land Market in Medieval England*, ed. by P.D.A. Harvey (Oxford: Clarendon Press, 1984), pp. 252–327.

Lunn, Katie, 'Highlights from Sedgefield Shrove Tuesday Ball Game with Usual Mix of Fun and Mayhem', *TeessideLive*, 5 March, 2019, https://www.gazettelive.co.uk/whats-on/whats-on-news/highlights-sedgefield-shrove-tuesday-ball-15926222.

Maddison, Angus, *The World Economy: A Millennial Perspective* (Development Centre of the Organization for Economic Co-Operation and Development, 2001), https://doi.org/10.1787/9789264189980-en.

McCloskey, Donald N., 'The Persistence of English Common Fields', in *European Peasants and Their Markets*, ed. by W.N. Parker and E.L. Jones (Princeton: Princeton University Press, 1975), pp. 73–120.

McCloskey, Donald N., 'English Open Fields as Behavior Towards Risk', *Research in Economic History* 1, ed. by Paul Uselding (Greenwich, CT: JAI Press, 1976), pp. 124–171.

McCloskey, Donald N., 'The Prudent Peasant: New Findings on Open Fields.' *Journal of Economic History* 51 (1991), 343–55, doi:10.1017/s0022050700038985.

Macfarlane, Alan, *The Origins of English Individualism: The Family, Property, and Social Transition* (Cambridge: Cambridge University Press, 1978).

Macfarlane, Alan, 'English Individualism Refuted—and Reasserted: The Land Market of Earls Colne (Essex), 1550–1750', *Economic History Review* 56:4 (2003): 595–622, doi:10.1111/j.1468-0289.2003.00263.x.

McIntosh, Marjorie, *Autonomy and Community: The Royal Manor of Havering, 1200–1500* (Cambridge: Cambridge University Press, 1986).

McIntosh, Marjorie, *A Community Transformed: The Manor and Liberty of Havering, 1500–1620* (Cambridge: Cambrdige University Press, 1991).

McIntosh, Marjorie, *Controlling Misbehavior in England, 1370–1600* (Cambridge: Cambridge University Press, 1998). doi:10.1017/CBO9780511582783.

McKendrick, Neil, 'Home Demand and Economic Growth: A New View of the Role of Women and Children in the Industrial Revolution', in *Historical Perspectives: Studies in English Thought and Society in Honour of J. H. Plumb*, ed. by Neil McKendrick (London: Europa Publications, 1974), pp. 152–210.

Mackenzie, Eneas, and M. Ross, *An Historical, Topographical, and Descriptive View of the County Palatine of Durham* (Newcastle upon Tyne: Mackenzie and Dent, 1834).

MacKinnon, Dolly, *Earls Colne's Early Modern Landscapes* (London: Routledge, 2014).

Mansell, Charmian, 'Female Service and the Village Community in South-West England 1550–1650: The Labour Laws Reconsidered', in *Servants in Rural Europe*, ed. by Jane Whittle (Woodbridge: Boydell & Brewer, 2018), pp. 77–94.

Mansell, Charmian, 'The Variety of Women's Experiences as Servants in England (1548–1649): Evidence from Church Court Depositions', *Continuity & Change* 33:3 (2018): 315–38, doi:10.1017/s0268416018000267.

Masschaele, James, *Peasants, Merchants, and Markets: Inland Trade in Medieval England, 1150–1350* (New York: St. Martin's, 1997).

Mate, Mavis, *Daughters, Wives and Widows after the Black Death: Women in Sussex, 1350–1535* (Woodbridge: Boydell & Brewer, 1998).

Meikle, Maureen M., 'The Scottish Covenanters and the Borough of Sunderland, 1639–1647: A Hidden Axis of the British Civil Wars', *Northern History* 54:2 (2017): 167–88, doi:10.1080/0078172x.2016.1256063.

Miller, Edward, *The Abbey and Bishopric of Ely: The Social History of an Ecclesiastical Estate from the Tenth Century to the Early Fourteenth Century* (Cambridge: Cambridge University Press, 1951).

Milton, Anthony, 'Licensing, Censorship, and Religious Orthodoxy in Early Stuart England', *The Historical Journal* 41:3 (1998): 625–51, doi:10.1017/s0018246x98007948.

Mitson, Anne, 'The Significance of Kinship Networks in the Seventeenth Century: South-West Nottinghamshire', in *Societies, Cultures and Kinship, 1580–1850: Cultural Provinces and English Local History*, ed. by Charles Pythian-Adams (Leicester: Leicester University Press, 1993), pp. 24–76.

Mokyr, Joel, *The British Industrial Revolution: An Economic Perspective* (Routledge, 1999).

Mokyr, Joel, *The Enlightened Economy: An Economic History of Britain 1700–1850* (New Haven: Yale University Press, 2010).

Mokyr, Joel, *A Culture of Growth: The Origins of the Modern Economy* (Princeton: Princeton University Press, 2018).

Moore, John S., '"Jack Fisher's Flu": A Visitation Revisited', *Economic History Review* 46:2 (1993): 280–307, doi:10.2307/2598018.

Moore, John S., 'Population Trends in North-East England, 1548–1563', *Northern History* 45:2 (2008): 239–58, doi:10.1179/174587008x322544.

Moore, John S., 'Demographic Dimensions of the Mid-Tudor Crisis', *Sixteenth Century Journal* 41:4 (2010): 1039–63, https://www.jstor.org/stable/40997601.

Morrin, Jean, 'The Transfer to Leasehold on Durham Cathedral Estate, 1541–1626', in *Landlords and Tenants in Britain, 1440–1660: Tawney's Agrarian Problem Revisited* ed by. Jane Whittle (Woodbridge: Boydell & Brewer, 2013), pp. 117–32.

Mousnier, Roland, et al., 'Discussion of H. R. Trevor-Roper: "The General Crisis of the Seventeenth Century"', *Past & Present* 18 (1960): 8–42, doi:10.1093/past/18.1.8.

Mullan, John, and Richard Britnell, *Land and Family: Trends and Local Variations in the Peasant Land Market on the Winchester Bishopric Estates, 1263–1415* (Hatfield: University of Hertfordshire Press, 2010).

Müller, Miriam, 'Peasants, Lords and Development in Leasing in Later Medieval England', in *The Development of Leasehold in Northwestern Europe, c. 1200–1600*, ed. by Bas von Bavel and Phillipp Schofield, *Comparative Rural History of the North Sea Area 10* (Turnhout: Brepols, 2008), pp. 155–78.

Müller, Miriam, 'Peasant Women, Agency and Status, in Mid-Thirteenth to Late Fourteenth-Century England: Some Reconsiderations', in *Married Women and the Law in Premodern Northwest Europe*, ed. by Cordelia Beattie and Matthew Frank Stevens (Woodbridge: Boydell & Brewer, 2013), pp. 91–113.

Nair, Gwyneth, *Highley: The Development of a Community, 1550–1880* (Oxford: Basil Blackwell, 1988).

Nef, J. U., *The Rise of the British Coal Industry*, vol. I (London: Routledge, 1932, reprinted 1952).

Newman, Christine M., 'Economy and Society in North-Eastern Market Towns: Darlington and Northallerton in the Later Middle Ages', in *North-East England in the Later Middle Ages*, ed. by Christian D. Liddy and Richard H. Britnell (Woodbridge: Boydell & Brewer, 2005), pp. 127–40.

Newman, Christine M., 'Marketing and Trade Networks in Medieval Durham', in *Commercial Activity, Markets and Entrepreneurs in the Middle Ages*, ed. by Ben Dodds and Christian D. Liddy, (Woodbridge: Boydell & Brewer, 2011), pp. 129–40.

Oates, Rosamund, 'Catholicism, Conformity and the Community in the Elizabethan Diocese of Durham', *Northern History* 43:1 (2006): 53–76, doi:10.1179/174587006x86765.

Ogilvie, Sheilagh, '"Whatever Is, Is Right?" Economic Institutions in Pre-Industrial Europe', *Economic History Review* 60:4 (2007): 649–84, doi:10.1111/j.1468-0289.2007.00408.x.

Ogilvie, Sheilagh, 'Choices and Constraints in the Pre-Industrial Countryside', in *Population, Welfare and Economic Change in Britain, 1290–1834*, ed. by Chris Briggs, P.M. Kitson, and S.J. Thompson (Woodbridge, Boydell & Brewer, 2014), pp. 269–305.

Ormrod, David, 'Agrarian Capitalism and Merchant Capitalism: Tawney, Dobb, Brenner, and Beyond', in *Landlords and Tenants in Britain, 1440–1660: Tawney's Agrarian Problem Revisited*, ed. by Jane Whittle (Woodbridge: Boydell & Brewer, 2013), pp. 200–15.

Overton, John Henry, 'Cosin, John', in *The Oxford Dictionary of National Biography 1885–1900*, vol. 12, ed. by Llwyd Mason (New York: Macmillan, 1917), pp. 264–71.

Overton, Mark, 'Re-Estimating Crop Yields from Probate Inventories: a Comment', *Journal of Economic History* 50:4 (1990): 931–5, https://www.jstor.org/stable/2122462.

Overton, Mark, *Agricultural Revolution in England: The transformation of the agrarian economy 1500–1850* (Cambridge: Cambridge University Press, 1996).

Overton, Mark, 'Prices from Probate Inventories', in *When Death Do Us Part: Understanding and Interpreting the Probate Records of Early Medieval England*, ed. by Tom Arkell, Nigel Goose, and Nesta Evans (Oxford: Leopard's Head Press, 2006), pp. 120–43.

Overton, Mark, Jane Whittle, Darron Dean, and Andrew Hann, *Production and Consumption in English Households, 1600–1750* (London: Routledge, 2004).

Page, William, 'A List of the Inventories of Church Goods made temp. Edward VI', in *The Antiquary: A Magazine Devoted to the Study of the Past* 22 (1890): 28–9, 76–9, 120–3, 167–9, 214–6, 256–60.

Piper, A. J., 'The Size and Shape of Durham's Monastic Community, 1274–1539', in *North-East England in the Later Middle Ages*, ed. by Christian D. Liddy and Richard H. Britnell (Woodbridge: Boydell and Brewer, 2005), pp. 153–72.

Pollard, A. J., 'The North-Eastern Economy and the Agrarian Crisis of 1438–40', *Northern History* 25:1 (1989): 88–105, doi:10.1179/nhi.1989.25.1.88.

Pollard, A. J., *North-Eastern England during the Wars of the Roses* (Oxford: Clarendon Press, 1990).

Pomeranz, Kenneth, *The Great Divergence: China, Europe, and the Making of the Modern World Economy* (Princeton: Princeton University Press, 2000).

Poos, L. R., 'The Social Context of Statute of Labourers Enforcement', *Law and History Review* 1:1 (1983): 27–52, doi:10.2307/744001.

Poos, L. R., *A Rural Society after the Black Death: Essex 1350–1525* (Cambridge: Cambridge University Press, 1991).

Poos, L. R., Zvi Razi, and R. M. Smith, 'The Population History of Medieval English Villages: A Debate on the Use of Manor Court Records', in *Medieval Society and the Manor Court*, ed. by Zvi Razi and Richard M. Smith (Oxford: Clarendon Press, 1996), pp. 298–368.

Postan, M. M., ed., *Cambridge Economic History of Europe, v. i: The Agrarian Life of the Middle Ages* (Cambridge: Cambridge University Press, 1966).

Postan, M. M., 'The Fifteenth Century', in *Essays on Medieval Agriculture and General Problems of the Medieval Economy*, ed. by M.M. Postan (Cambridge: Cambridge University Press, 1973), pp. 41–48.

Raftis, J. A, *Tenure and Mobility: Studies in the Social History of the Mediaeval English Village* (Toronto: Pontifical Institute of Medieval Studies, 1981).

Raftis, J. A., *Peasant Economic Development within the English Manorial System* (Montreal: McGill-Queen's University Press, 1996).

Ravensdale, Jack, 'The Transfer of Customary Land', in, *Land, Kinship and Life-Cycle*, ed. by Richard M. Smith (Cambridge: Cambridge University Press, 1984), pp. 197–226.

Ravilious, Kate, 'A River Runs through It: The Twists and Turns of a Medieval English City's History Emerge from an Artifact-Rich Riverbed', *Archaeology* 72:5 (2019): 38–43.

Razi, Zvi, *Life, Marriage & Death in a Medieval Parish* (Cambridge: Cambridge University Press, 1980).

Razi, Zvi, 'The Erosion of the Family-Land Bond in the late Fourteenth and Fifteenth Centuries: a Methodological Note', in *Land, Kinship and Life-Cycle*, ed. by Richard M. Smith (Cambridge: Cambridge University Press, 1984), pp. 295–304.

Razi, Zvi, 'The Myth of the Immutable English Family', *Past & Present* 140 (1993): pp. 28–9, doi:10.1093/past/140.1.3.

Roberts, B. K., *The Green Villages of County Durham: A Study in Historical Geography*, Durham County Library Local History Publication no. 12 (Durham: Durham County Council, 1977).

Roberts, B. K., *Rural Settlement in Britain* (London: Dawson, 1977; reprinted London: Hutchinson, 1979).

Russell, J. C., *British Medieval Population* (Albuquerque: University of New Mexico Press, 1948).

Saywell, J. L., *The History and Annals of Northallerton, Yorkshire* (London: Simpkin, Marshall, & Co., 1885).

Scammell, Lorna, 'Was the North-East Different from Other Areas? The Property of Everyday Consumption in the Late Seventeenth and Early Eighteenth Centuries', in *Creating and Consuming Culture in North-East England, 1660–1830*, ed. by Helen Berry and Jeremy Gregory (Aldershot: Ashgate, 2004), pp. 12–23.

Schofield, Phillipp, *Peasant and Community in Medieval England, 1200–1500* (New York: Palgrave Macmillan, 2002).

Schofield, Phillipp, 'Regional Price Differentials and Local Economies in North-East England, c. 1350-c.1520', in *Agriculture and Rural Society after the Black Death: Common Themes and Regional Variations*, ed. by Richard Britnell and Ben Dodds (Hatfield: University of Hertfordshire Press, 2008), pp. 40–55.

Schuessler, Jennifer, 'Earliest Known Draft of King James Bible Is Found, Scholars Say', *New York Times*, 14 October 2015, https://www.nytimes.com/2015/10/15/books/earliest-known-draft-of-king-james-bible-is-found-scholar-says.html.

Sear, Joanne, and Ken Sneath, *The Origins of the Consumer Revolution in England: From Brass Pots to Clocks* (London: Routledge: 2020).

Shammas, Carole, *The Pre-Industrial Consumer in England and America* (Oxford: Clarendon Press, 1990).

Shaw-Taylor, Leigh, 'The Rise of Agrarian Capitalism and the Decline of Family Farming in England', *Economic History Review* 65 (2012): 26–60, doi:10.1111/j.1468-0289.2010.00585.x.

Shepard, Alexandra, and Judith Spicksley, 'Worth, Age, and Social Status in Early Modern England', *Economic History Review* 64:2 (2011): 493–530, doi:10.1111/j.1468-0289.2010.00533.x.

Slack, Paul, 'Mortality Crises and Epidemic Disease in England (1485–1610)', in *Health, Medicine and Mortality in the Sixteenth Century*, ed. by Charles Webster (Cambridge: Cambridge University Press, 1979), pp. 9–59.

Smith, Richard M., 'Some Reflections on the Evidence for the Origins of the 'European Marriage Pattern' in England', in *The Sociology of the Family: New Directions from Britain*, ed by. C. Harris (Chester: Bemrose Press, 1979), pp. 74–112.

Smith, Richard M., 'Some Thoughts on the "Hereditary" and "Proprietary" Rights in Land under Customary Law in Thirteenth and Early Fourteenth Century England', *Law and History Review* 1 (1983): 95–128, doi:10.2307/744004.

Smith, Richard M., 'Families and Their Land in an Area of Partible Inheritance: Redgrave, Suffolk 1260–1320', in *Land, Kinship and Life-Cycle*, ed. by Richard M. Smith (Cambridge: Cambridge University Press, 1984), pp. 135–196.

Smith, Richard M. 'Some Issues Concerning Families and Their Property in Rural England 1250–1800', in *Land, Kinship and Life-Cycle*, ed. by Richard M. Smith (Cambridge: Cambridge University Press 1984), pp. 1–86.

Smith, Richard M., 'Relative Prices, Forms of Agrarian Labour and Female Marriage Patterns in England, 1350–1800', in *Marriage and Rural Economy: Western Europe since 1400*, ed. by Isabelle Devos and Liam Kennedy, Comparative Rural History of the North Sea Area 3 (Turnhout: Brepols, 1999), pp. 19–48.

Spaeth, Donald, '"Orderly Made": Re-Appraising Household Inventories in Seventeenth-Century England', *Social History* 41:4 (2016): 417–35, doi:10.1080/03071022.2016.1215101.

Spufford, Margaret, *Contrasting Communities: English Villagers in the Sixteenth and Seventeenth Centuries* (Cambridge: Cambridge University Press, 1974).

Spufford, Margaret, 'The Limitations of the Probate Inventory', in *English Rural Society, 1500–1800: Essays in Honour of Joan Thirsk*, ed. by J. Chartres and D. Hey (Cambridge: Cambridge University Press, 1990), pp. 139–174.

Stone, David, *Decision-Making in Medieval Agriculture* (Oxford: Oxford University Press, 2005).

Stone, Lawrence, 'The Educational Revolution in England, 1560–1640', *Past & Present* 28 (1964): 41–80, https://www.jstor.org/stable/649877.

Stoyle, Mark, *Loyalty and Locality: Popular Allegiance in Devon during the English Civil War* (Exeter: University of Exeter Press, 1994).

Stoyle, Mark, *From Deliverance to Destruction: Rebellion and Civil War in an English City* (Exeter: University of Exeter Press, 1996).

Surtees, Robert, *The History and Antiquities of the County Palatine of Durham, vol. 3, Stockton and Darlington Wards* (London: Nichols, 1823).

Swanson, Paul, *An Introduction to Capitalism* (London: Routledge, 2013).

Sweezy, Paul, et al., *The Transition from Feudalism to Capitalism*, (London: Verso, 1976; reprinted 1987).

Tawney, R. H., *The Agrarian Problem in the Sixteenth Century* (London: Longmans, Green and Co., 1912).

Thirsk, Joan, *English Peasant Farming: The Agrarian History of Lincolnshire from Tudor to Recent Times* (London: Routledge, 1957).

Thirsk, Joan, 'Industries in the Countryside', in *Essays in the Economic and Social History of Tudor and Stuart England*, ed. by F. J. Fisher (Cambridge: Cambridge University Press, 1961), pp. 70–88.

Thirsk, Joan, 'The Farming Regions of England: The Northern Province', in *The Agrarian History of England and Wales, vol. IV*, ed. by Joan Thirsk (Cambridge: Cambridge University Press, 1967), pp. 16–27.

Thirsk, Joan, *Economic Policy and Projects: The Development of a Consumer Society in Early Modern England* (Oxford: Clarendon Press, 1978).

Thirsk, Joan, 'Agriculture in Kent, 1540–1640', in *Early Modern Kent*, ed. by Michael Zell (Woodbridge: Boydell & Brewer, 2000).

Threlfall-Holmes, Miranda, *Monks and Markets: Durham Cathedral Priory, 1460–1520* (Oxford: Oxford University Press, 2005).

Titow, J. Z., 'Some Differences between Manors and Their Effects on the Condition of the Peasant in the Thirteenth Century', *Agricultural History Review* 10 (1962): 1–13, www.jstor.org/stable/40272998.

Titow, J. Z., *English Rural Society, 1200–1350* (London: George Allen and Unwin, 1969).

Todd, Barbara, 'The Remarrying Widow: a Stereotype Reconsidered', in *Women in English Society 1500–1800*, ed. by Mary Prior (London: Routledge, 1985), pp. 54–92. doi:10.4324/9780203985342.

Todd, Margo, 'Puritan Self-Fashioning: The Diary of Samuel Ward', *Journal of British Studies* 31:3 (1992): 236–64, doi:10.1086/386007.

Trevor-Roper, H. R., 'The General Crisis of the 17th Century', *Past & Present* 16 (1959): 31–64, doi:10.1093/past/16.1.31.

Turner, M. E., J. V. Beckett, and B. Afton, *Farm Production in England 1700–1914* (Oxford: Oxford University Press, 2001), doi:10.1093/acprof:oso/9780198208044.001.0001.

Tuck, J. A., 'The Occupation of the Land: 1. The Northern Borders', in *The Agrarian History of England and Wales, vol. III 1348–1500*, ed. by Edward Miller (Cambridge: Cambridge University Press, 1991), pp. 34–42.

Underdown, David, *Revel, Riot, and Rebellion: Popular Politics and Culture in England, 1603–1660* (Oxford: Oxford University Press, 1987).

Underdown, David, *Fire from Heaven: Life in an English Town in the Seventeenth Century* (New Haven: Yale University Press, 1994).

van Bavel, Bas, 'Land, Lease and Agriculture: The Transition of the Rural Economy in the Dutch River Area from the Fourteenth to the Sixteenth Centuries', *Past & Present* 172 (2001): 3–43, doi:10.1093/past/172.1.3.

van Bavel, Bas, and Phillipp Schofield, 'Introduction. The Emergence of Lease and Leasehold in a Comparative Perspective: Definitions, Causes and Consequences', in *The development of Leasehold*, pp. 11–30.

van Zanden, Jan Luiten, Sarah Carmichael, and Tine De Moor, *Capital Women: The European Marriage Pattern, Female Empowerment and Economic Development in Western Europe 1300–1800* (Oxford: Oxford University press, 2019).

Voightländer, Nico, and Hans-Joachim Voth, 'How the West "Invented" Fertility Restriction', *The American Economic Review* 103:6 (2013): 2227–64, doi:10.3386/w17314.

Waddell, Brodie, 'Governing England through the Manor Courts, 1550–1850', *The Historical Journal* 55: 2 (2012): 279–315, doi:10.1017/s0018246x12000040.

Walter, John, *Understanding Popular Violence in the English Revolution: The Colchester Plunderers* (Cambridge: Cambridge University Press, 1999).

Weatherill, Lorna, *Consumer Behaviour and Material Culture in Britain, 1660–1760* (London: Routledge, 1988).

Webster, Charles, ed., *Health, Medicine and Mortality in the Sixteenth Century* (Cambridge: Cambridge University Press, 1979).

Whitrow, G. J., *Time in History: Views of Time from Prehistory* (Oxford: Oxford University Press, 1989).

Whittle, Jane, 'Individualism and the Family-Land Bond: A Reassessment of Land Transfer Patterns among the English Peasantry c. 1270–1580', in *Past & Present* 160 (1998): 25–63, doi:10.1093/past/160.1.25.

Whittle, Jane, 'Inheritance, Marriage, Widowhood and Remarriage: A Comparative Perspective on Women and Landholding in North-East Norfolk, 1440–1580', *Continuity & Change* 13 (1998): 33–72, doi:10.1017/s026841609800304x.

Whittle, Jane, *The Development of Agrarian Capitalism: Land and Labour in Norfolk 1440–1580* (2000), doi:10.1093/acprof:oso/9780198208426.001.0001.

Whittle, Jane, and Margaret Yates, ' "Pays Réel or Pays Légal"? Contrasting Patterns of Land Tenure and Social Structure in Eastern Norfolk and Western Berkshire, 1450–1600', *The Agricultural History Review* 48:1 (2000): 1–26.

Whittle, Jane, ed., *Landlords and Tenants in Britain, 1440–1660: Tawney's* Agrarian Problem *Revisited* (Woodbridge: Boydell & Brewer, 2013).

Whittle, Jane., ed., *Servants in Rural Europe 1400–1900* (Woodbridge: Boydell & Brewer, 2018).

Whittle, Jane, 'A Different Pattern of Employment: Servants in Rural England c.1500–1660', in *Servants in Rural Europe 1400–1900*, ed. by Jane Whittle (Woodbridge: Boydell & Brewer, 2018), pp. 57–76.

Whittle, Jane, 'Tenure and Landholding in England 1440–1580. A Crucial Period for the Development of Agrarian Capitalism?' in *Landholding and Land Transfer*, ed. by Beckett and Turner, pp. 237–49.

Williamson, J., 'Norfolk: Thirteenth Century', in *The Peasant Land Market in Medieval England*, ed. by P.D.A. Harvey (Oxford: Clarendon Press, 1984), pp. 31–106.

Williamson, Tom, *The Transformation of Rural England: Farming and the Landscape, 1700–1870* (Exeter: University of Exeter Press, 2002).

Wong, Roy Bin, *China Transformed: Historical Change and the Limits of European Experience* (Ithaca: Cornell University Press, 1997).

Woodward, Donald, *Men at Work: Labourers and Building Craftsmen in the Towns of Northern England, 1450–1750* (Cambridge: Cambridge University Press, 1995).

Wrightson, Keith, 'Household and Kinship in Sixteenth-Century England', *History Workshop Journal* 12 (1981): 151–8, doi:10.1093/hwj/12.1.151.

Wrightson, Keith, *Earthly Necessities: Economic Lives in Early Modern Britain* (New Haven: Yale University Press, 2000).

Wrightson, Keith, and David Levine, *Poverty & Piety in an English Village: Terling, 1525–1700* (New York: Academic Press, 1979; revised ed. Oxford: Clarendon Press, 1995).

Wrigley, E. A., 'Urban Growth and Agricultural Change: England and the Continent in the Early Modern Period', *The Journal of Interdisciplinary History* 15:4 (1985): 683–728, doi:10.2307/204276.

Wrigley, E. A., 'European Marriage Patterns and their Implications; John Hajnal's Essay and Historical Demography during the Last Half-Century', in *Population, Welfare and Economic Change in Britain 1290–1834*, ed. by Chris Briggs, P.M. Kitson, and S.J. Thompson (Woodbridge: Boydell & Brewer, 2014), pp. 15–42.

Wrigley, E. A., *The Path to Sustained Growth: England's Transition from an Organic Economy to an Industrial Revolution* (Cambridge: Cambridge University Press, 2016).

Wrigley, E. A., and R. S. Schofield, *The Population History of England 1541–1871: A Reconstruction* (London: Edward Arnold, 1981).

Yates, Margaret, 'Change and Continuities in Rural Society from the Later Middle Ages to the Sixteenth Century: The Contribution of West Berkshire', *Economic History Review* 52:4 (1999): 617–37, https://www.jstor.org/stable/259932.

Yates, Margaret, *Town and Countryside in Western Berkshire, c. 1327–c. 1600* (Woodbridge: Boydell & Brewer, 2007; eBook Cambridge: Cambridge University Press, 2013).

Yelling, J. A., 'Common Land and Enclosure in East Worcestershire, 1540–1870', *Transactions of the Institute for British Geographers* 45 (1968): 157–68, doi:10.2307/621399.

Yelling, J. A., 'Probate Inventories and the Geography of Livestock Farming: A Study of East Worcestershire, 1540–1750', *Transactions of the Institute of British Geographers* 51 (1970): 111–26, doi:10.2307/621765.

Zell, Michael, 'The Social Parameters of Probate Records in the Sixteenth Century', *Bulletin of the Institute of Historical Research* 57 (1984): 107–13, doi:10.1111/j.1468-2281.1984.tb01264.x.

Zell, Michael, 'Fisher's 'Flu and Moore's Probates: Quantifying the Mortality Crisis of 1556–1560', *Economic History Review* 47:2 (1994): 354–8, doi:10.2307/2598086.

Zell, Michael, *Industry in the Countryside: Wealden Society in the Sixteenth Century* (Cambridge: Cambridge University Press, 1994).

Zell, Michael, 'Credit in the Pre-Industrial English Woollen Industry', *Economic History Review* 49:4 (1996): 667–91, https://www.jstor.org/stable/2597968.

Zell, Michael, 'Landholding and the Land Market in Early Modern Kent', in *Early Modern Kent* (Woodbridge: Boydell & Brewer, 2000), pp. 39–74.

Websites

Abstract of the Answers and Returns, Enumeration Part I: England and Wales (1801), Histpop—The Online Historical Population Reports Website, http://www.histpop.org/ohpr/servlet/Show?page=Home (accessed 17/9/2019).

'ACAD, A Cambridge Alumni Database', http://venn.lib.cam.ac.uk/acad/2018/search-2018.html (accessed 8/7/2019).

'Beresford's Lost Villages', ed. by Helen Fenwick and Michael Turner http://www.dmvhull.org/ (accessed 17/9/2019).

'Bishop Middleham Colliery', *Durham Mining Museum*, http://www.dmm.org.uk/colliery/b002.htm (accessed 17/9/2019).

'Cornforth Colliery', *Durham Mining Museum*, http://www.dmm.org.uk/colliery/c081.htm (accessed 17/9/2019).

'Cracroft's Peerage: The Complete Guide to the British Peerage & Baronetage', http://www.cracroftspeerage.co.uk/online/ (accessed 29/1/2016).

The Durham River Wear Assemblage Project, https://www.dur.ac.uk/archaeology/research/projects/all/?mode=project&id=622 (accessed 18/9/2019).

'Local History: Bishop Middleham', 'Keys to the Past', http://www.keystothepast.info/article/10339/Site-Details?PRN=D6649 (accessed 17/9/2019).

'Local History: Cornforth', 'Keys to the Past', http://www.keystothepast.info/article/10339/Site-Details?PRN=D6769 (accessed 17/9/2019).

'Local History: West Cornforth (Cornforth)', 'Keys to the Past', http://www.keystothepast.info/article/10339/Site-Details?PRN=D158 (accessed 17/9/2019).

National Character Area profile 15. Durham Magnesian Limestone Plateau (2013), http://publications.naturalengland.org.uk/publication/8308038 (accessed 14/9/2019).

'North East Inheritance database', http://familyrecords.dur.ac.uk/nei/data/intro.php (accessed 2/6/2021).

'Online Gazetteer of Markets and Fairs in England Wales to 1516', ed. nby Samantha Letters, http://www.history.ac.uk/cmh/gaz/gazweb2.html (accessed 20/4/2016).

'Taxatio Ecclesiastica', ed. by Jeff Denton et al. (HRI Online, Sheffield, 2014), https://www.dhi.ac.uk/taxatio/forms (accessed 25/5/2021).

Working and Conference Papers

Allen, Robert C., 'Global Price and Income History Group', https://gpih.ucdavis.edu/Datafilelist.htm (accessed 30/5/201).

Boucekkine, Raouf, David de la Croix, and Dominique Peeters, 'Disentangling the Demographic Determinants of the English Take-off: 1530–1680', CORE Discussion Paper No. 2007/33 (April 2007), https://ssrn.com/abstract=1006814.

Broadberry, Stephen, 'Accounting for the Great Divergence', Economic History Working Papers (184/13), London School of Economics and Political Science (2013), http://eprints.lse.ac.uk/id/eprint/54573.

Broadberry, Stephen, 'The Industrial Revolution and the Great Divergence: Recent Findings from Historical National Accounting', Centre for Economic Policy Research, Economic History Working Paper DP15207 (26 August 2020).

Broadberry, Stephen, and Alexandra M. de Pleijt, 'Capital and Economic Growth in Britain, 1270–1870: Preliminary Findings', Centre for Economic Policy Research, Economic History Working Paper DP15889 (6 March 2021), https://ssrn.com/abstract=3805304.

Clark, Gregory, 'The Macroeconomic Aggregates for England, 1209–2008', University of California-Davis, Economics Working Paper 09–19 (October, 2009).

Clark, Gregory, 'Data on the English Economy, 1150–1914', http://faculty.econ.ucdavis.edu/faculty/gclark/data.html (accessed 30/5/2021).

Clark, Gregory, 'National Income, Prices, Wages, Land Rents, Population, England, 1209–1869' series, 'England NNI - Clark - 2015-2.xlsx', from 'Gregory Clark - Professor of Economics, UC-Davis', http://faculty.econ.ucdavis.edu/faculty/gclark/data.html (accessed 12/5/2021).

De Pleijt, Alexandra, and Jan Luiten van Zanden, 'Tale of Two Transitions: The European Growth Experience, 1270–1900', Maddison Project Working Paper WP 14 (February 2020). https://www.rug.nl/ggdc/historicaldevelopment/maddison/publications/wp14.pdf.

Humphries, Jane, and Jacob Weisdorf, 'Unreal Wages? Real Income and Economic Growth in England, 1260–1850', *Center for Economic Policy Research*, Discussion Paper Series, Discussion Paper DP119999 (London, 2017). http://www.ehes.org/EHES_121.pdf.

Ogilvie, Sheilagh, 'Institutions and Economic Growth: Cautionary Tales from History', Thought Experiment Lecture, UK Treasury, 18 October 2019.

Overton, Mark, 'Household Wealth, Indebtedness, and Economic Growth in Early Modern England', presented at the 14th International Economic History Congress (2006), https://www.researchgate.net/publication/237429385_Household_wealth_indebtedness_and_economic_growth_in_early_modern_England

Unpublished Theses and Dissertations

Arvanigian, Mark, 'The Nevilles and the Political Establishment in North-Eastern England, 1377–1413', PhD thesis, Durham University (1999), http://etheses.dur.ac.uk/1469/.

Barker, Nicholas Andrew, ' "If the King Had Asked for an Ass, He Would Have Received His Wish This Time:" a Study of the Career of Thomas de Hatfield, Bishop of Durham (1345–1381), as a Royal Servant, 1336–1357', MA thesis, Durham University (2003).

Clifford, John, 'Settlement and Field Systems in Middleham Manor 1600–1850', MA thesis, Durham University (1977), http://etheses.dur.ac.uk/10021/.

Dumble, W., 'Government, Religion and Military Affairs in Durham during the Civil War and Interregnum', M.Litt. thesis, Durham University (1978), http://etheses.dur.ac.uk/9858/.

Dunkley, Peter James, 'The New Poor Law and County Durham', PhD thesis, Durham University (1971).

Edwards, Lloyd J., 'Tobacco Pipes, Pipemakers, and Tobacconists in Newcastle and Gateshead until c. 1800: an Archaeological Study', PhD thesis, Durham University (1986), http://etheses.dur.ac.uk/6882/.

Foss, D. B. 'The Episcopate of Richard de Kellawe, Bishop of Durham 1311–16', MA thesis, Durham University (1966), http://etheses.dur.ac.uk/9871/.

Gooch, Leopold, 'From Jacobite to Radical: the Catholics of North East England, 1688–1850', PhD thesis, Durham University (1989). http://etheses.dur.ac.uk/1422/.

Green, Adrian, 'Houses and Households in County Durham and Newcastle c. 1570–1730', PhD thesis, Durham University (2000), http://etheses.dur.ac.uk/1600/.

Issa, Christine, 'Obligation and Choice: Aspects of Family and Kinship in Seventeenth Century County Durham', PhD thesis, University of St. Andrews (1988).

Lomas, R. A., '+ Priory as a Landowner and a Landlord, 1290–1540', PhD thesis, Durham University (1973).

Lomas, Timothy, 'Land and People in South-East Durham in the Later Middle Ages', PhD thesis, Teesside Polytechnic University (1976).

Marcombe, David, 'The Dean and Chapter of Durham, 1558–1603', PhD thesis, Durham University (1973).

Morrin, Elizabeth Jean, 'Merrington: Land, Landlord and Tenants 1541–1840: A Study in the Estate of the Dean and Chapter of Durham.' PhD thesis, Durham University (1997), http://etheses.dur.ac.uk/4757/.

Tenno, Siiri, 'Religious Deviance in the Elizabethan Diocese of Durham', MA thesis, Durham University (2009), http://etheses.dur.ac.uk/167/.

Welford, Judith, 'Functional Goods and Fancies: The Production and Consumption of Consumer Goods in Northumberland, Newcastle upon Tyne and Durham c, 1680–1780', PhD thesis, Durham University (2010), http://etheses.dur.ac.uk/327/.

Index

Note: Tables and figures are indicated by an italic "*t*" and "*f*", respectively, following the page number.

For the benefit of digital users, indexed terms that span two pages (e.g., 52–53) may, on occasion, appear on only one of those pages.

agrarian capitalism 1, 5–6, 12–15, 17–19, 22, 62, 87–8, 178, 180
'agrarian fundamentalism,' 15–16, 20, 23, 62, 64–5
Agricultural Revolution 14, 17–18, 23, 64–5, 88, 102–3, 178
ale and beer 32–4, 57, 103, 145–6, 149, 151, 154–7, 159, 163–4, 178
animals, stray 31, 139–42, 145, 176
arable land 32–4, 85–6, 92–4, 101, 103, 141–3, 150
  conversion from pasture. *See* pasture, conversion to arable
  conversion to pasture 137–8, 142
  crop rotation 30–1, 103, 139–40
  regulation of 31, 141, 145
assarts 84, 86–7, 89–91, 139–42
Atkinson, John 46–8
Auckland
  Bishop 13–14, 29, 32–4, 94–5, 102–3
  North 93, 102–3
  St Andrews 168–70
Aycliffe 92, 158–9, 165–6, 168–70
Ayre, Richard 171–2
Ayre, Robert 171–2
Aytes, Lancelot 171–2

Barnard Castle 29, 156–7
beans 103, 139–40
Bedford, Thomas, vicar of Bishop Middleham 175
beds, feather 103, 174–5, 180
beehives 103, 190
Bellerby, John 163–4, 171
Bewley, Cowpen 62–3, 95
Bewley, Newton 95
Billingham 61–3, 90–2, 94–5, 103
Bishopric of Durham 30–1, 35, 37–8, 44–5, 61, 63, 66–72, 92–5, 98–9, 159
  demesnes 25, 32–4, 84
  estate 24–5, 34–7, 44–5, 64–9, 89–91, 94–5, 98–9, 101–3

surveys
  Boldon Book 32–4, 66–7, 90–3, 153–4
  Gilly-Corn 90–1, 94
  Hatfield's Survey 32–4, 41–2, 66–71, 92, 94–5, 141–2, 172–3, 178
  other 88, 94
  Parliamentary 62, 81–4
  villages 62, 64–5, 72, 93–5, 99–101, 141–4
Bishopwearmouth 61–2, 93, 102–3
Black Death 1–2, 5–6, 9–11, 16–17, 19–21, 24–5, 27, 30–1, 37–8, 53–4, 66–9, 90–2, 137–8
blacksmiths 57, 90–2, 153–4, 167
Blackwell 93, 102
Blakett, John 156–7
Blakiston, Edward 168–70
Blakiston, Henry 163–4
Blakiston, Marmaduke 59–60, 165–6
Blakiston, Robert 173
Boldon
  village of 90–1, 103
  West 61
Boldon Book. *See* Bishopric of Durham, surveys, Boldon Book
Bradbury 35–7, 163–4, 167–70
Brancepeth 103
brass goods 103, 190
bread 103, 139–40, 153–4
  ovens 32–4, 151, 154, 163–4
Brenner Debate 17–19
Burdon 93, 102
butchers 103, 152–3, 157
butter 103, 139–40
Butterwick 35–7, 61–2, 103, 149–50, 154, 166–7
by-laws, village 37, 141, 145–6, 152–3, 163–4, 171–2, 175–6, 178

Cambridge University 103, 165–6
candlesticks 103, 190
capital 1–3, 11–12, 17–18, 20–1, 23, 103, 155–7, 161–2, 183–4
capital goods 15, 103, 149, 189–90

Carlisle 103, 190
carpenters 90–2
Cassop 93, 102
Catholicism
    persistence of 103, 163–7, 174–6
    in Sedgefield 163–4, 175–6
    temporary restoration of 163–4, 175–6
cattle 103, 139–40, 143–5, 152–3, 157, 159,
    167–8, 182
chantries and chapels 103, 163–4
cheese 103, 139–40
Cheshire 24–5, 60–1, 144, 149–50
Chester-le-Street 29, 103
Chilton 168–70
china 103
Chipchase, John 84
Chipchase, Nicholas 84
Chipchase, Thomas 183
Chipchase, William 167–8
churchwardens 37, 103, 163–4, 168–71, 173–4
Claxton, Sir William 103
Cleadon 93, 102
clocks 24, 103, 190
cloth 3, 153, 182
    damask 103
    diapered 103
    harden 153
    Holland 103
cloth industry 15, 18–19, 103, 152–3, 159,
    178, 183–4
cloves 103
coal 1–2, 5–6, 22, 29, 34–5, 58, 61–2, 103, 151–3,
    182, 190
coal mining 1–2, 5–6, 24–5, 27, 29–30, 34–5,
    49–52, 102–3, 137–8, 180
    Bishop Middleham 34–5, 151–2, 190
    Cornforth 34–5, 151–2, 190
coal trade 3, 5–6, 12–13, 18–19, 34–5, 37–8,
    103, 190
commercialization 20–1, 58, 103, 178
conformity 19–20
    religious 32, 165–6, 176
Coniscliffe 103
Consumer Revolution 15–16, 103
Consumption Revolution 103, 189–90
Conyers, Cuthbert 149–50, 163–4, 167
Conyers, Katherine 167, 174–5
Conyers, Simon 101
Conyers, Sir Ralph 163–4, 166–7
Conyers, Thomas 103
copyhold 1, 5–6, 27, 66, 70–8, 81–3, 86–8, 99,
    101–3, 143–4, 157, 180
    heritability 68–9, 161–2
copy of the court roll 66–7, 143–4

Cosin, John, Bishop of Durham 31–2, 70–1,
    81–3f, 98, 165–6
cottagers 84, 90–2, 101–3, 175–6, 178
cottages 1, 57, 80–1, 85–6, 90–3, 95–7, 101, 103,
    153–4, 157
Coundon 90–1, 93, 102
courts
    bishop's free 89–90
    halmotes. See halmote court
    other 31, 35–7
    palatinate 27–8
    quarter sessions. See Quarter Sessions
credit 1, 11–12, 22–3, 95–7, 103, 156–7, 159,
    182–4, 190
    networks 103, 156–9, 183–4
crops, new 1–2, 16–17, 20, 22–3, 30–1, 137–8,
    178, 180
Croud, Robert 62–3, 145–6, 172–3
Cumberland 27–8, 43–4t, 103
Cutheard, Bishop of Durham 25

dairy production 143–4
Dalton 92, 103
Darlington 13–14, 29, 32–4, 37–8, 61–2, 102–3,
    152–3, 161–2, 168, 190
    Bondgate 93
daughters 59–63, 68–9, 79–80, 103, 154–5,
    166–7, 172–3
Dean and Chapter 24
    Durham Priory 3, 25, 70–1, 73–5, 89–95,
        98–9, 103
    estate 25, 29–30, 42–3t, 64–7, 72, 87, 90–1, 94,
        99–101, 137–8, 141–2
    tenants 29–30, 72, 95, 100–1, 103, 143–4
    villages 61–5, 86–7, 90–2, 95, 98, 101, 168,
        171–2, 175–6
debt 31, 68–9, 103, 139–40, 149, 156–7, 189
de Bury, Richard, Bishop of Durham 103
del Gate, Alice 66–7
del Gate, John 99
del Gate, Juetta 55–6, 78
del Gate, Robert Sr 1
del Gate family 1, 5–6, 161–2
    demesnes 23, 70–5, 84, 86–7, 89–91, 94, 98,
        100–1, 103
diet. See standard of living, diet
drengage lands 90–1, 103
Durham, city of 29
Durham Priory. See Dean and Chapter

Earls Colne 11–12, 50–2, 64–5, 102–3, 139–40,
    144, 152–3, 161–2, 173
Easington 90–1, 93, 95, 102–3
Elmden 35

Elstob, village of 168–70, 175
Elstob, Charles 103, 163–4, 167–8
Elstob, Ralph 103
Elstob, Robert 171
Elstob, William 163–4
Elwick 152–3
Embleton 35–7, 150, 157, 163–4, 168
EMP. *See* marriage, European Marriage Pattern
enclosure 5–8, 17–18, 20, 62, 101–3, 137–8,
        141–4, 159, 163–4, 175–6, 178
English Civil War 7–8, 14, 16–17, 49–52, 98, 103,
        173, 176–7, 181
engrossment 7–8, 14, 17–18, 20–1, 23, 64–5,
        78–9, 88, 178, 180–1
entry fines 42–3*t*, 64–5, 70–3, 80–8, 180–1
Erby, Annabilla. *See* Headlam, Annabilla
Erby, William 55–7, 153–5
Escomb 93
Eure, Helena 78–80, 178
Eure, Henry 78–9, 172–3
Eure, Sir Ralph 94–5, 97–8
Eure, Sir William 59–60, 79–80
European Marriage Pattern. *See*, marriage,
        European Marriage Pattern
exchequerland 66–7, 95–7, 139–40

fair, St Cuthbert's 91–2
fairs, Darlington 152–3
family
    size 58–60, 103
    structure 50–2, 58–9, 63, 100–1, 173
family-land-bond 73–5*f*, 87, 161–2, 190
farms
    capitalist 5–6, 22, 98, 103
    enclosed 22, 64–5, 159
    family 5–6, 95–7, 103
    larger 1–2, 5–6, 17–20, 24–5, 37–8, 86, 88, 103,
        137–8, 178, 181
Farrow, Robert 103, 151–2, 163–4
Fawdon, Robert 103
Ferryhill 92, 139–40, 168–70, 174–5
fertility 11–12, 32, 62
Fery, Richard 145–6, 172–3
feudal reaction 66–7
fields
    common 15, 19–20, 92, 103, 141–3,
        153–4, 163–4
    open 7–8, 24, 30–4, 101, 139–43, 145
    severalty 139–43
    townfields 1–2, 27, 139–40, 142–4, 150–1
Firbank, Ralph 78–9
fish 103
Fishburn 35–7, 42–4*t*, 103, 139–40, 163–4,
        168–70

Fishburn, Richard. *See* Fysshburn, Richard
flax 3, 153
Flemish refugees 1–2
fodder 103, 139–40
    hay 23, 103, 137–8, 143–5
    turnips 23, 137–8
forges 32–4, 153–4
fornication 50–2, 76–8
Foxton 35–7, 103
freedom, personal 23–4, 64–5, 88, 180
freehold 86–7, 89–93, 141–2, 190
Freville, Dame Elizabeth 84, 103, 166–7
Freville, George 78–80, 100–1, 103
Freville, Nicholas 103, 139–40, 163–4, 166–7
Freville family 100–1, 174–5, 181
Frizell, William 83–4, 167
fruit 3, 14, 103, 182, 189
    prunes 103
    raisins 103
Fulwell 92, 139–40
furniture 103, 180
Fysshburn, Richard 141–2

Gage, John 103, 142–3
gardens/garths 19–20, 66–7, 92, 101, 103,
        139–43, 145–7, 163–4, 190
Garmondsway 35–7
Garry, John 145–6
Gateshead 29, 61–2, 157–9
gentry 94–5, 101–3, 139–40, 159, 163–4, 168–71,
        173–5, 180–1
Gibson, Richard 103, 145–6
ginger 103
glass 103
glassmaking 103, 182–3
grain 1–2, 20, 29–30, 100–1, 103, 137–8, 143–5,
        149–50, 154, 156–7, 182–3
    imported 5–6, 13–14
grammar school 103, 163–4, 190
Grand Lease 103
Great Divergence 9, 24–5
Great Stainton 157, 168–70

Halesowen 11–12, 55–7
Hall, James 60–1, 103, 168–70
Hall, John 85–6, 103, 172–3, 183
Hall, William 14, 78–9, 142
Hall family 100–1
halmote court 31–2, 174–5
    Durham bishopric 25, 31, 37, 57–9, 66–9,
        81–3, 89–91, 103, 141, 143–4, 146–7,
        153, 176
    court books 44–5, 55–7, 66, 68–76, 81–6,
        94, 103, 142, 171–2, 185, 187

halmote court (*cont.*)
  Durham Priory 66–7
    court rolls 1–2, 31, 37–8, 66, 94, 101
    jurors 31, 37, 103, 141, 145–7, 163–4, 170–3,
      175–6, 178
Hamsterley 103
Hardgill, George 62–3
Hardgill, William 62–3, 145–6, 172–3
Hardwick 35–7, 40–1, 61–2, 78–80, 100–1, 103,
  163–4, 166–7
Hardwick, John 94–5, 141–2
Harreson, John 157–8
Harrison, John 83–4, 158, 163–4, 167, 171
Harrison, John Sr 81–3
Hartburn 93
Hartlepool 29, 32–4, 152–3, 156–7, 161–2
Harton 95
Hatfield, Thomas, Bishop of Durham 27–8, 68–9
Haughton-le-Skerne 93, 102
Hazelrigg, Thomas 174–5
Headlam, Annabilla (Erby, Annabilla) 14, 57,
  70–1, 103, 155–6, 183
Headlam, Brian 14, 163–4, 171, 174, 176
Headlam, John 161–2
Headlam, Thomas 95–7, 171–2
Headlam family 62–3, 161–2, 165–6, 171–2
hearths 103
Hearth Tax 5–6, 50, 103
Hebburn, Anthony 79–80, 163–4
Hebburn, John 79–80
hedges 142–3, 145, 176
Heighington, village of 46–8, 57, 61, 90–1, 93, 102–3
Heighington, John 166–7
Heighington, Richard 168–71
Hett 151–2
Hilton, Jane 148–50
Hilton, Ralph 148–9
Hilton, Robert 103, 149–50
hirsell 141, 145
Hixon, Augustine 167
Hixon, John 168–70
Hixon, Robert 59–60
Hixon, Roland 14, 84, 101, 158–9, 163–4,
  168–71, 183
Hixon, Thomas 174–5
Hixon family 163–4, 168–70
hops 3, 103, 143–4, 155–6
horses 103, 139–40, 143–5, 153–4, 156–7
Houghton-le-Side 103
Houghton-le-Spring 93, 103
household consumption 103
households 37–8, 40–52, 58–62, 103, 149–51,
  178, 190
household size 58–61

houses, rebuilding 1–2, 5–6, 103, 158–9, 180
  Great Rebuilding 103
Hull 152–3
human capital 9–11, 53
husbandlands 58–9, 66–9, 71–2, 80–7, 90–3,
  95–9, 102–3, 139–40
husbandmen 62, 68–9, 80–1, 88, 90–2, 95–7,
  101–3, 159, 178, 180
Hutcheson, John 145–6, 163–4
Hutcheson, John Jenkin 139–40
Hutcheson, Richard 171
Hutchinson, Peter 174–5
Hyndmer, Robert 103, 153

imports 1–2, 5–6, 13–14, 103, 182
import substitution 103
Inclosure. *See* enclosure
individualism 14–16, 19–20, 24–5, 63, 71–2,
  159, 176–7
industrialization 1–3, 19–20, 24–5, 34–5, 37–8,
  102–3, 159, 178
Industrial Revolution 1, 3, 7–11, 15–17, 23–5,
  29, 102–3
industrious revolution 14, 103
inflation 86–7, 103, 157
Inheritance 58, 64–5, 72–5
Inner Temple 103
Inns of Court 103
Interregnum 14, 158–9, 178
iron, objects 103, 153–4
iron chimneys 103, 190

Jarrow 92
Johnson, Elizabeth 148–9
Johnson, John 103, 157–8, 165–6, 171
Johnson, Robert 103, 143–4, 163–4, 171
Johnson, Samuel 142–3
Joly, John 103, 139–40

Killerby 61, 93
kinship 31–2, 50–2
kitchen pans and utensils 103, 189–90

labour 1–3, 7–11, 37–8, 46–8, 58, 90–2, 103,
  147–51, 190
labourers 15, 17–19, 93, 101, 103, 147, 149, 173, 190
Lamb, Brian 76–8
Lamb, Bryan 150
Lamb, Lancelot 167–8
Lanchester 94–5, 103
land
  customary 64–9, 76–9, 83–4, 86–7, 89–91, 93,
    98–9, 101, 190
  waste 27, 92, 137–8, 141–2, 153–4

landless population 7–8, 22, 37–8, 42–3, 59, 61–2, 98, 103
  land market 19–21, 44–5, 58, 64–5, 72–6, 78–80, 86–8, 190
Langley, Thomas, Bishop of Durham 68–9, 103
Laud, William, Archbishop of Canterbury 165–6
Layton 35, 142–3, 149–51, 163–4, 166–7
  East 143–4, 190
leasehold 1, 64–7, 70–6, 80–7, 98–100, 103, 137–8, 158–9, 161–2, 180, 190
  beneficial 72–3
  renewals 71, 99–101, 153–4
  syndicates 64–5, 98, 100–1
leather 103, 152–3
leyrwite 50–4, 148
lime 1–2, 103, 151–2, 156
  as fertilizer 151–2
  kilns 32–4, 151–3, 155
linen 103, 153, 190
  fine 103, 180
  imported 190
  table 24, 103, 190
liquorice 103
Little Divergence 3, 9–11, 17, 53–4, 190
London 1–2, 5–6, 11–13, 24–5, 27–8, 79–80, 88, 103, 139–40, 180, 182–4
looking glasses 103

mace (spice) 103
Mainsforth 35–7, 40–1, 42–3t, 103, 185
Maire, Christopher 166–7
Maire, Grace 166–7
Maire, Thomas 167
mallands 57, 80–4, 86–7, 91–2, 95–7, 103, 142–3, 145–6
malmen 68–9, 91–2
malt 103, 139–40, 154–6
  kilns 32–4, 103, 151–2, 154–7
market 15–17, 20, 72–6, 80, 86, 88, 152–3, 155–6
market structures and integration 9–11, 22–3, 34–5, 190
marriage 54–5, 57–63, 76–80, 147–8, 166–8, 172–3
  European Marriage Pattern (EMP) 9–12, 53–4, 58, 147–52, 190
  widow 53–4, 58, 76–9
marriage fine. See merchet
Mason, Francis 166–7
Mason, Humphrey 163–4
Mason, Jane 103, 166–7
Mason, Lancelot 166–7
Mason, Ralph 14, 101, 103, 142–4, 153–5, 157–8, 167–8, 183
Mason, Richard 153, 167–8

Mason, Robert 163–4, 171–2
Mason, Robert Sr 166–7
Mason, William 103, 163–4, 166–7
meadow 32–4, 80–6, 93, 100–1, 103, 139–42, 144
merchants 3, 5–6, 29–30, 103, 157–9, 183
merchet 53–6, 66, 148–9, 187
  licensia vidualis 53–4, 142
Merrington 72–3, 103, 159, 190
Merrington, Kirk 103, 168–70
Middleham manor 30–1, 34–5, 137–8, 174–5
  bailiff 34–5, 100–1, 137–8
  demesnes 84–6, 91–2, 100–1, 137–40
  orchard 32–4, 85–6, 103, 145–6
Middlestone 61, 168–70
Middleton, Leonard 101, 139–40, 143–4, 163–4
Middleton, Thomas, vicar of Bishop Middleham 103
middling sort 103, 161–2, 166–7, 170, 174–5
Middridge 61, 93, 102
migration 14, 20–1, 24–5, 45–8, 50–2, 58, 103, 161–2, 168–70
millers 87, 90–1, 99, 156–7, 190
mills 66, 70–3, 83–4, 103, 145–6, 153, 190
  fulling 32–4, 153
  water 32–4, 145–6
Monk Hesleden 92
Monkton 92
Monkwearmouth 61–2, 92, 103
Moorsley 94–5
Mordon 35–7, 152–3, 168
Morebath 11–12, 174
Moresley 92
Moreton 40–1, 42–4t, 93
mortgages 83–4, 157–9
Mowbray family 62–3, 171–2

Nether Heworth 61–2, 90–2
Netherlands 53, 103, 182–3
Newbottle 90–1, 93, 102
Newcastle-upon-Tyne 1–2, 5–6, 13–14, 24–5, 27–9, 103, 157–9, 161–2, 174–5, 180, 182–3
Newcomer, William 146–7, 176
New Draperies 1–2, 153, 182–3
Newton Capp 93, 102
Norfolk 12–13, 18–19, 73–5, 86–7, 137–8, 151–2
Northern Rebellion 27–8, 78–80, 101, 161–6, 171–4, 181, 190
Northumberland 27–9, 41–2, 42–3t, 102–3, 151–2
Northumbria 27–8
Norton 1, 93, 95–7, 142, 157

oats 80–1, 103, 139–40, 155, 190
Ord, George 139–40

Ord, Lionel 171
Ord, Ralph 157
ovens 72–3, 103, 151–2, 154, 156–7
oxen 103, 139–40, 143–4, 152–3, 156–7
Oxford University 103, 190

Palatinate of Durham 5–6, 25, 27–30, 40–1, 101, 103, 163–6
parish registers, as a source 12, 32, 40–1, 45–6, 148–9
Parliament 29, 103, 167, 174–5
　Commissioners 83–4, 103, 167
　representation in 29–30, 190
　sequestrators 167–8
parlours 103
pasture 27, 32–4, 73–5, 85–6, 92–4, 103, 142–3, 145–6
　conversion to arable 92, 142
　overloading 145
peas 103, 139–40
pepper 103, 189
pewter 24, 103, 174–5, 180, 190
pigs 103, 139–40, 143–4, 176
Pilkington, John 158
Pillok, Henry 154
pinders 90–2, 141, 145
Pittington 92, 103, 139–40
　North 94–5
plague 7–8, 20–1, 37–8, 41–2, 42–3t, 56–8, 64–5, 68–9, 94, 103
Poor Rates 103
poultry 103, 139–40
　turkeys 103
poverty 10–11, 53, 58, 103, 159
　poor relief 163–4, 190
Protestantism 161–6, 176–7
　in Sedgefield 163–4, 174
Protestation Oath 35–7, 40–1, 49–52, 165–7
Proudlok, Joan 60–1
punderlands 91–2, 141–2
puritanism 16–17, 161–2, 165–6, 175

Quarrington 90–1, 93, 142–3
Quarter Sessions 142–3, 152–3, 155–6, 190

Rainton, West 93–5
Rauf, Cecilia 66–9, 103
Rawling, John 167
Raynald, Thomas 145–6
recession, fifteenth-century 18–19, 64–5, 73–5
recusants 32, 101, 103, 165–7, 174, 190
Redworth 93, 102
reeves 37, 91–2, 141, 145–6, 163–4, 170–1
Reformation 3, 7–8, 14, 27–9, 40, 103, 161–6, 173–5, 190

rents 24–5, 64–73, 80–8, 100–1, 103, 143–4, 153–5, 180–1, 185
　ancient 66–7, 70–1
　cash 66–9, 91–2
　　firmarii 68–9, 90–1
　　pennyfarm 68–9, 80–1
　customary 37, 85–6, 103
　　blacksmith 153–4
　　services 37, 66–9, 80–1, 89–92, 137–8, 161–2
　exchequerland 84
　freehold 37, 81–3, 89–90
　husbandland 25, 66–71, 80–3, 90–2, 103, 137–8, 153–4
Restoration 7–8, 40–1, 158–9, 175
rye 103, 139–40, 143–4, 190
Ryhope 93, 95, 102
Ryton 190

Sadberge 25, 154
salt industry 3, 61–2, 103, 180
Scurfield, George 103, 168–70
serfdom 7–8, 14, 16–17, 20–2, 64–7, 87–8, 90–1, 180–1
　servile dues 20–1, 66–7
servants 31–2, 34–5, 37–8, 42–3t, 50–2, 58–63, 101, 103, 147–51, 190
　female 58, 60–1, 63, 103, 148–51, 190
service 147–51
settlements, deserted 35, 142–3
Shaldforth 93, 102
Shaw, John 152–3
Shaw, John Jr 142
Shaw, Robert 103, 139–40
Shaw, William 174–5
sheep 103, 141, 143–4, 156–7, 167–8, 182
sheets 31–2, 103, 190
Sheraton Grange 168–70
Sherburn 93, 102
Shotton 35–7
silver 103, 190
Skirlaw, Walter, Bishop of Durham 154
smallholders 17–18, 88, 93–5, 102–3, 139–40, 159, 175–6
smithland 153–4
Southwick 93, 100–1
spices 3, 103, 182, 189
Spurner, Gilbert 1, 5–6, 95–7
Staindrop 29, 90–1
Stainton 168–70
standard of living
　diet 103, 154–5, 189–90
　peasant budget model 103
Stanely 103
Stanhope 29, 93, 102–3

St Cuthbert
  fair of 91–2
  patrimony 25
St Edmund
  fair of 32–4
  feast of 32–4, 163–4
St Edmunds (Sedgefield) 103, 163–4, 168–70
  clergy 59–60, 83–4, 103, 163–7, 175
  steward of Durham 37, 66–72, 93–4, 99,
    172–3, 181
St Mary, guild house 163–4
St Michaels (Bishop Middleham), clergy 100–1,
    152–3, 175
Stockton-on-Tees 29, 32–4, 61–2, 95, 103,
    157, 190
Stockton Ward 25, 70–2, 81–3, 103, 137–8, 163–4
Streatlam 59–60
subletting 42–3t, 73–5, 83–4, 86–7, 93, 95–8,
    142–3, 180–1
Suffolk 87, 137–8, 173, 190
sugar 103, 189
Sunderland 1–3, 29, 61–2, 102–3, 161–2, 168–70,
    174–5, 180, 187, 190
Swainston 103

taxes 18–19, 29, 37–8, 40–2, 103, 173
  clerical 29, 103, 190
  parliamentary 40–2, 42–3t, 62, 103, 190
  ship money 103, 173
Tele, Robert 145–7
Tempest, Robert 163–4, 172–3
Tempest, Thomas 103
tenant right 29, 80–1, 190
tenure 64–80, 87–8, 99, 103, 141–2, 172–3,
    185–6, 190
  customary 20–2, 64–7, 71–2, 97–8, 190
  security of 87, 175–6, 182
Terling 11–12, 50–2, 54, 59–60, 103, 152–3,
    161–2, 190
Thickley, West 93
Thornley 174–5
Thorpe Thewles 142
Thrislington 34–7, 103, 139–40, 151–2, 163–4,
    174–5, 190
Thrislington Hall 103
Thurstanton. See Thrislington
tithes 20, 29–30, 103, 137–8, 167–8, 190
tobacco 29–30, 182–3
Tose, Juetta 57
transition debate 3, 7–9, 12–13, 15–16, 161–2
transition from medieval to modern 5–8, 14, 17,
    21–5, 66–7, 72–3, 161–2

Trimdon 103
Tudhoe 157
Tudhoe Hall 103
Tunstall 61–2, 93, 102
Tyneside 1–2, 25, 34–5, 37–8, 61–2, 103

vegetables 103, 189
village governance 37, 81–3, 89–90, 139–41, 146,
    156–7, 163–4, 170–1, 175–6, 182
village herdsmen 141, 145

wages 9–11, 103, 147–51, 156–7, 182–4, 190
  female 53–4, 147–52
  real 9–11, 103, 147, 189–90
Wales 103, 183–4, 190
Walker, Samuel 60–1, 103
Ward, Samuel 165–6, 190
Warden Law 93
Warrington 190
Washington 103
Weardale 27–8, 103, 190
weavers 153
Westerton 61, 90–1, 139–40, 168
Westmoreland 43–4t, 103
Westoe 93
wheat 27, 103, 139–40, 143–4, 190
Whickham 27, 34–5, 37–8, 42–3, 49–50, 61–2,
    93, 102–3
Whitburn 93, 102
Widdifield, Richard 168–70
Widdifield family 60–1, 161–2, 167–70
widowers 53–4, 58–9, 68–9
widow-right 54–5, 76–80
widows 50–63, 68–71, 78–9, 155–6, 186–7
  poor or landless 57–9, 103
  remarriage 54–9
wills 58–60, 103, 149, 151
windows 31–2, 71–2, 103, 173
  curtains 103
wine 3, 103
Witton 59–60, 78–9
wives 50–2, 79–80, 155–6, 178
Wolsingham 93–5, 102–3
Wolviston 1–2, 168–70
wool 1–2, 153, 182–4, 190
  exported 3, 103

yeomen 1–2, 5–8, 30–2, 59–62, 87–8, 101–3,
    139–40, 158–9, 170–1
  rising 1–2, 17–20, 97–8, 103, 144, 180
York 152–3
Yorkshire 27–9, 157, 167–8